Game
Changers

GAME CHANGERS

EDUCATION and INFORMATION TECHNOLOGIES

Edited by **DIANA G. OBLINGER**

EDUCAUSE

FROM THE EDITOR

I would like to thank the many people who made this book possible, particularly Gregory Dobbin for managing the project and Karen Mateer for her research.

—Diana G. Oblinger

EDUCAUSE

EDUCAUSE is a nonprofit association and the foremost community of IT leaders and professionals committed to advancing higher education. EDUCAUSE programs and services are focused on analysis, advocacy, community building, professional development, and knowledge creation because IT plays a transformative role in higher education. EDUCAUSE supports those who lead, manage, and use information technology through a comprehensive range of resources and activities. educause.edu

Game Changers: Education and Information Technologies is published by EDUCAUSE, with generous support from Ellucian.

Cover and interior design by Michael Brady Design (michaelbradydesign.com).

Printed by Allen Press, Inc., Lawrence, KS.

MIX
Paper from
responsible sources
FSC   FSC® C006300
www.fsc.org

Game Changers: Education and Information Technologies

Today's knowledge revolution isn't about how much information is available. It's about how fast knowledge can travel through vast, connected networks of people—and how it can grow exponentially.

Ten years ago we knew that technology would change the face of education, and we were just beginning to imagine the ways. Today, learning can happen anywhere. More people, with increasingly diverse needs, are seeking education, and almost every country is promoting greater access to education. At a time when educational attainment is a global priority, the need to reimagine the education experience has never been greater.

Game Changers: Education and Information Technologies explores the tools and processes that can improve the quality, flexibility, and scalability of postsecondary education. The book takes a hard look at the education landscape today and asks what that landscape might look like tomorrow. It asks important questions and pushes us to open our minds about how technology will shape the universe of possibility for tomorrow's students.

- *How will your institution negotiate the new geography of learning?* Technologies are reshaping how people learn and connect, and people are connecting to a global learning network previously inconceivable.

- *In a world where information is always accessible, how will teaching and learning change?* Learning is no longer bound by classrooms, libraries, or even instructors. Online tools make resources available to learners everywhere. Open-source learning can reach thousands of learners in nontraditional ways.

- *What will constitute an institution of higher education in the future?* More and more, competencies, not credit hours, determine credentials. A degree is no longer the only indicator of success. How we understand and assess learning is changing. Portfolios will augment standard assessment tools.

- *How do we ready our institutions, our students, and ourselves for what higher education can—and must—become?* Many institutions are piloting innovative models for education, and the entire community can benefit from the lessons learned.

These are questions that we at Ellucian ask ourselves every day as we work to help more than 2,300 colleges, universities, state systems, and foundations around the globe thrive in today's dynamic world. We value our collaborative and long-standing relationships with EDUCAUSE and the amazing community that makes it strong. Working together, our collective intelligence will help shape the future of education.

Ellucian is proud to sponsor this book and support ongoing efforts to help higher education meet the challenges of today and those of tomorrow.

John F. Speer III, President and CEO, Ellucian

ellucian.

Contents

Case Studies

Foreword

AMONG THE MANY STRENGTHS OF HIGHER EDUCATION, the ones most frequently mentioned are the roles played by its mission that yield value to society and help create the future. Realistically, our institutions may place more emphasis on one element of higher education's mission—research or teaching or outreach—over another; support different types of students; and serve different geographic areas as well as local, regional, or national constituencies. And some focus on the liberal arts, others on sciences and engineering. The strength of American higher education is found in this rich diversity.

Over time, the diversification within higher education has expanded with the creation of new types of institutions such as land-grant universities and community colleges. In recent years, physical campuses have been increasingly augmented by online offerings. The majority of today's students may be labeled as "nontraditional," with no single definition of what that term indicates. Some are adults who have not graduated from high school. Others seek an education but lack confidence and do not have the required foundational skills in English and/or mathematics. Some have no clear path to or through their education. However, the numbers are clear. No matter how well we do today, we must serve more of all types of students—and serve them more effectively—if we are to reach our national goals for education.

This book helps those in higher education explore important questions through ideas that we might incorporate as we prepare for the next generations of students. While we honor our history—remembering that much of the power of higher education is in its tradition of critical inquiry—we must not shy away from questioning some time-honored practices and previously held assumptions. Let us consider:

- Cognitive science and recent research about the human brain are giving us new insights into how students learn. Can we ensure our educational system is flexible, incorporates new approaches in line with the way we learn, and adapts its organizational structures to the needs of the learner rather than constraining the learner's options?

- What new models currently exist and what models can we create that better serve our students as individual learners as well as society as a whole? And can we celebrate the creation of new models that serve unique needs without having qualms about the differences?

- Today we have tools that were virtually unknown a few years ago. Which of these are most promising in the digital world our institutions helped produce? Given these tools, are there foundational competencies that can be mastered through multiple means?

- What can we learn from disruptive change in other sectors? Do we have the leadership that pushes us to think and act differently to achieve our goals?

- If we were to reset or reinvent higher education for the future, what would we continue, discontinue, or change?

The needs of our society are clear. Quality education, broadly available, is an imperative. It is not enough to open the doors to more learners—we must do more to help them achieve the education and preparation they seek and that today's world demands. Currently, our aspirations are greater than our accomplishments. We must ensure we are not overlooking options from which we have previously turned away or that we failed to explore. Higher education fosters creative insights and innovative questioning, and the contributors to this book offer a range of models and a wealth of examples to help us think outside our comfort zone. These models can serve as a starting point for exploring game changers that will strengthen the learning experience for students and the institutions of higher education that serve them, ultimately enriching our society.

We are justifiably proud of our unique and diverse system of higher education. We must also have the humility to know that it can be even better. The game changer we need may depend on how well we expand access and improve attainment through the intelligent use of information technology to enhance learning. Many are looking to our colleges and universities for the answers; their future is up to us.

Molly Corbett Broad

Game Changers

Introduction

Diana G. Oblinger

THIS BOOK IS DEDICATED TO EDUCATION. We need more education, deeper education, more effective education, more access to education, and more affordable education. While education works well for millions of learners, it doesn't work for everyone. There are millions more whose lives could be transformed by education. For education to do better we cannot just keep doing the same things. This book is also dedicated to finding the game changers that will help us move education to the next level, whether those game changers are information technology, new models, or institutional vision.

Education is complex. Each learner's needs, preparation, personal circumstances, and aspirations are different. Learning is an interaction involving the learner and content, instructors, other learners, systems, and the environment. Learners must play an active, informed role in their education. And their experience is made up of thousands of interactions associated with courses, student services, administrative functions, technology, and people.

Learners encounter roadblocks. Some aren't prepared for college-level work. Many don't have strong study or personal skills. Others have financial challenges. Competing demands from family and work can distract. Some aren't well suited for the major they chose, and many don't know what courses to choose to graduate on time.

Educational institutions have their own roadblocks. Escalating costs. Decreased funding. Rising demand. Increased oversight and regulation. Entrenched practices. Dated models. Constraining policies.

If education is a game changer, what are the game changers for education? This book presents some of those game changers.

How one conceptualizes the educational experience can be a game changer. Institutions such as Western Governors University, Empire State University,

University of Maryland University College, Athabasca University, and University of the People began with unique ideas about how education might be structured, delivered, and assessed.

Information technology is a game changer. It can deliver content instantly, bring distant individuals together, and make administrative processes faster. But IT can be more than a delivery channel. IT can change the educational experience through simulations, games, haptic devices that allow users to "feel," augmented reality, and more.

But to really change the game, IT must be used differently. Because of IT we can collect data on individual interactions and use that information to predict who is at risk of failing, tailoring interventions to their needs. That same data can be used to create recommendation engines, reminiscent of Amazon or Netflix, that help students select the best courses for their skill level and needs or plan a more efficient pathway to their degree. IT allows people from around the world to collaborate, learning from each other and creating more than any one person could individually.

The book begins with some fundamental questions we must ask about education. Beyond describing the challenges of funding, demographics, and the demand for education, educators must ask what we need to do and how we know if we've been successful. Lingenfelter describes many of the challenges of the current environment, including cost, productivity, quality, and how to more seamlessly integrate K–12 and higher education. Humphreys challenges us to first set the priorities for higher education before then looking to technology and other solutions for a means to reach those goals.

A number of game changers are described, including information technology, openness, analytics, assessment, and public-private partnerships. The most important drivers of innovation are the models that harness the power of IT to deliver educational value. Beyond delivering information, IT can power recommendation engines, co-creation, and analytics and enable the unbundling and rebundling of traditional processes. As Wiley and Green illustrate, openness is a philosophy, as well as a model for innovation and business. Through sharing, remixing, and repurposing, value can be created and captured, whether the focus is content or new ideas. Analytics (trend analysis, forecasting, prediction, optimization) allows educators to identify at-risk students and intervene, improving the chances for student success. Analytics is used for course improvement, as well. Baer and Campbell also suggest future directions for analytics. Adult learners bring their own special circumstances, such as the need for recognition of prior learning. Tate and Klein-Collins describe a variety of systems (e.g., prior-learning assessments) that, although designed for adult learners, are broadly applicable. Describing an approach that may allow more institutions to expand into online and specialized programs, Pianko and Jarrett highlight the growth of public-private partnerships. Smith explores potential models that combine the use of IT and alternate models for course completion and credentialing, providing the potential for greatly reduced costs.

There are multiple examples of institutions that have taken alternative approaches: Western Governors University, the University of Phoenix, Empire State College, Athabasca University, and University of the People. Each institution employs unique combinations of IT, openness, analytics, and student engagement to achieve its goals. Using analytics to drive student achievement, course improvement, and cognitive science is exemplified by Carnegie Mellon University's Open Learning Initiative. Cavanagh describes the use of blended learning and research to create a postmodality era—instruction is no longer face-to-face or online, it exists wherever you want it, having moved past traditional modes. Public-private partnerships are allowing institutions such as the University of Southern California to leverage their expertise and grow programs that were designed digital.

The chapters alone cannot illustrate all the innovative approaches using information technology that might change the game for education. In the book's final section, over twenty case studies provide a wealth of examples of how institutions are improving education with information technology. The case studies span the globe and address new learning environments, approaches to sharing open content, recommendation systems that help students improve course success and reduce time to degree, how IT is enhancing "traditional" courses, and alternative credentialing systems. The cases also describe how research and analytics can drive and support change. Multiple themes are highlighted by these case studies.

- **Changing the learning experience:** Time, convenience, and integration of information can change the educational experience. Institutions such as Ball State University, University of Maryland Baltimore County, and Georgetown University are consciously using IT to change the learning experience, making it more immersive. CS50 at Harvard and Penn State's CHANCE program use technology to enhance traditional environments, resulting in motivating and highly effective learning experiences.

- **Guiding and personalizing:** IT allows students to get the information they need to make better decisions, such as about course selections, transfer options, and degree programs. Helping students make better choices are the goals of the University of Hawaii's STAR program and the University of Hong Kong's iCounseling system. IT can recognize patterns and match individuals with the courses and program that best suit them. Austin Peay State University's Degree Compass personal recommendation system represents a new era in personalization, which is particularly important for at-risk students. Valencia College created LifeMap and is now extending the student-support system to other institutions. Central Piedmont Community College's Online Student Profile (OSP) system helps ensure that students are successful and is also being adopted by six other institutions.

- **Learner-centered design:** Many case studies illustrate how the learner is at the center of a program's design, such as the Olin College of Engineering and Penn State's World Campus. Norberg describes a blended model in Norway that was designed to meet the needs of students in rural areas. When Royal Roads University began "rethinking residencies," they created virtual-experience laboratories as an alternative to face-to-face residencies. Recognizing that not all students have the same needs is critical.

- **Research:** Research on students and on what works drives innovation and adoption. Walker and his colleagues describe the research programs that support educational innovation at the University of Minnesota and the University of Central Florida. Dulin, Delquadri, and Melander illustrate the essential role of research with the Achieving the Dream reform network and Yakima Valley Community College's Office of Institutional Effectiveness.

- **Open solutions:** Open educational resources are inherently scalable because they can be reused, remixed, and repurposed. The OpenCourseWare Consortium, the Saylor Foundation's open college courseware, and the Washington State Board for Community and Technical Colleges' Open Course Library are examples. And, Mozilla's Open Badges project, in an effort to leverage open educational resources and find a more flexible model for credentialing, provides an alternative to traditional models.

- **Scaling:** Scaling may hinge on moving beyond a not-invented-here mind-set to one that values sharing, allowing institutions to reach more learners and use resources more efficiently. Indiana University's eTexts program is saving students 40 percent or more on textbook costs by aggregating demand and negotiating reduced costs of electronic resources. The Great Plains Interactive Distance Education Alliance is a virtual faculty consortium that allows institutions to more agilely respond to changing educational needs, offering degrees and certificates.

Colleges and universities are complex adaptive systems where people and technology can work together to create value. The college or university learning experience is more than "the classroom." For institutions to make the best use of technology to address educational needs, they must understand the learner and design the desired experiences, taking into account the many social, technical, and intellectual interactions among students, faculty, and staff; the organization; and the infrastructure.

Institutions must design processes and experiences that will allow students to solve their problems and achieve their goals, as well as create long-term educational value both for students and society. However, multiple models will be required, because student readiness, needs, aspirations, and circumstances vary. If students are unprepared, institutions must ask what services and experiences could better prepare them. If students are fully prepared, institutions can still create new and innovative ways to add even greater value to their educational experience.

Much of the use of information technology to date has focused on content delivery that emphasizes information or course management systems rather than on student support or collaborative, interactive, and immersive learning environments. The educators represented in this book are innovating as individuals, programs, and institutions. They are focused on student needs and are designing alternative models that allow students to achieve more of their potential.

Education is a game changer. We owe it to ourselves, our students, and our society to keep working to change education for the better.

Diana Oblinger *is President and CEO of EDUCAUSE. She is known for launching innovative initiatives, such as the EDUCAUSE Learning Initiative (ELI) and the Next Generation Learning Challenges. Previously, she held positions at the University of North Carolina system, University of Missouri, Michigan State University, IBM, and Microsoft. Oblinger has authored and edited numerous books and publications, including the award-winning* What Business Wants from Higher Education.

1

The Knowledge Economy: Challenges and Opportunities for American Higher Education

Paul E. Lingenfelter

THE LATE PETER DRUCKER apparently first used the phrase "the knowledge economy" in his 1969 book *The Age of Discontinuity.*[1] Thirty-two years later, still going strong, Drucker wrote in the November 2001 edition of *The Economist*:

> The next society will be a knowledge society. Knowledge will be its key resource, and knowledge workers will be the dominant group in its workforce. Its three main characteristics will be:
> - Borderlessness, because knowledge travels even more effortlessly than money.
> - Upward mobility, available to everyone through easily acquired formal education.
> - The potential for failure as well as success. Anyone can acquire the "means of production," i.e., the knowledge required for the job, but not everyone can win.[2]

By the time Drucker wrote those words in 2001, a great deal of evidence had accumulated to confirm his earlier foresight. Four years later, in 2005, Tom Friedman in *The World Is Flat* essentially announced that Drucker's "next society" has arrived. Friedman argued that the following events and innovations have rapidly and dramatically redistributed economic advantage around the globe:

1. Fall of Berlin Wall (November 9, 1989)
2. Netscape—first mainstream web browser goes public (August 8, 1995)
3. Workflow software—standardized applications, PayPal, eBay, et al.
4. Open-sourcing—Adobe Acrobat Readers, Linux
5. Outsourcing—Y2K, spin-off functions to India
6. Offshoring—China in the World Trade Organization (WTO), capital flows to find cheap labor

7. Supply-chaining—Wal-Mart retailer to manufacturers
8. Insourcing—UPS services linked to shipping
9. In-forming—"Google-like" intelligent searches and data mining
10. "The Steroids"—wireless mobile digital communication[3]

As I write, popular uprisings in the Middle East are the latest example of the political and economic implications of these forces. While events (and especially the pace of change) are frequently surprising, it is not difficult to speculate about the future implications of the knowledge economy for higher education. In this chapter I will focus on four issues and discuss their implications for IT professionals. The issues are as follows:

- Higher education must become less of an elite enterprise; a much larger fraction of the world population will need higher education. Everybody will not need or achieve a four-year degree, but many more people must be educated to a higher standard than previously required. Achieving this goal will require both more effective education of disadvantaged groups and social policies to enable them to pay the costs of higher learning. Moreover, people are likely to obtain higher education throughout life, both as an economic necessity and as a "consumer good." Many young people are likely to make the transition from adolescence to adulthood in "brick and mortar" colleges and universities, but this will not be the end of their higher education.

- Higher education in the United States will continue to be a high social and political priority, but the economic stress of an aging population, health-care costs, growing deficits, and resistance to tax increases will require colleges and universities to increase productivity substantially in order to meet national goals. Achieving productivity gains while enhancing quality is the most significant challenge facing higher education. IT is a critically important resource for meeting this challenge.

- The diversity of knowledge providers and delivery systems requires reengineered postsecondary systems to assure quality and promote improvement. More transparent and clear definitions of degree qualifications and new approaches to accreditation and the assessment and certification of learning are needed.

- The growing importance of educational attainment will require more robust relationships between elementary, secondary, and postsecondary education. Stronger, more meaningful P–20 relationships in standards, professional development, and data systems are essential.

The Imperative for "Mass" Higher Education

When discussing the growing demand for postsecondary education I've frequently heard, "Everybody doesn't need to go to college." Charles Murray, in his 2008 book *Real Education*,[4] elaborated this caution at length, but with a fundamentally tautological argument. Murray maintains that a college education is "real" only when it results in the knowledge and skill traditionally achieved by the most intellectually gifted people who also have enjoyed extraordinary opportunities to develop their talents. If "real education" is defined in elitist terms, quite naturally only a few people will attain it.

One doesn't have to believe everybody can become Shakespeare or Einstein to realize that Murray's definition of "real education" is far too narrow for the twenty-first century. All people must have more knowledge and skill in a knowledge economy. Moreover, while wisdom and education are far from perfectly correlated, wisdom *requires* knowledge. Better-educated citizens are essential for the world to cope with the political and environmental issues of our era. Nothing in history or current experience suggests we have exhausted the capacity of human beings to learn or their need to benefit from more learning. H. G. Wells's 1919 summation "Human history becomes more and more a race between education and catastrophe"[5] is even more pertinent today.

The facts in the labor market also contradict Murray. Many who deny the growing need for postsecondary education seem to be recalling the workforce of the 1960s and 1970s. Even though many countries have erased the advantages previously enjoyed by the United States workforce, the educational attainment of U.S. workers has grown dramatically. In 1973 it had a labor force of 91 million. High school dropouts held 32 percent of those jobs, and high school graduates held 40 percent. Workers with no college education accounted for 65.5 million jobs in the 91-million workforce. The other 25.5 million jobs (28 percent of the total) were held by college graduates (16 percent) and people with some college (12 percent). See Figure 1.

In 2009, the United States had a labor force of 155 million employees. Only 14 percent of those jobs were held by high school dropouts, and 31 percent were held by high school graduates. Their share of the workforce dropped from 72 percent to 45 percent in 36 years. Workers with no college held 69.8 million jobs in 2009.

By comparison, the number of jobs held by people with college degrees or some college jumped from 25.5 million in 1973 to 85.3 million in 2009. Postsecondary trained workers now account for 55 percent of employees. *Nearly all the job growth in the past thirty-six years has been in jobs filled by people with some postsecondary education.*[6] Anthony Carnevale and his colleagues project

Figure 1. **Higher Attainment Levels Needed for Future U.S. Jobs**

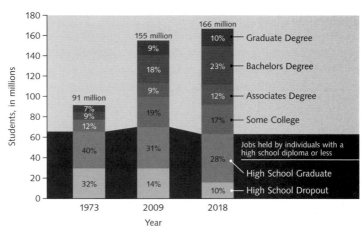

Sources: U.S. Census Bureau, CPS, 1973, 2009; Anthony Carnevale, *Help Wanted* (June 2010): 14.

this trend to continue, resulting in only 63 million jobs for high school graduates or dropouts in 2018, fewer than held by this group in 1973.

College-educated workers are better paid as well as more plentiful. In 2002, a Census Bureau study found that college graduates earned 75 percent more than high school graduates over a lifetime; a 2011 study by the Georgetown University Center on Education and the Workforce indicates that "the premium on college education has grown to 84 percent."[7]

Unsurprisingly, the decreasing value of a high school education has motivated youth to increase their educational aspirations. In an NCES (National Center for Education Statistics) survey of high school sophomores in 2002, 72 percent said they plan to obtain a baccalaureate degree, and 36 percent aspired to a graduate or professional degree. Only 8 percent indicated no plans for postsecondary education.

So *who* must become better educated? Obviously, those who currently are less well educated—the poor, the children of the less well educated, those who for any reason (poverty, race, ethnicity, or recent immigration to the United States) tend not to participate and thrive in postsecondary education. While some seem to think such groups generally have lower academic ability, the facts indicate otherwise.

The college *participation rate* is high for students from high socioeconomic-status (SES) families, regardless of academic ability and preparation. The college participation rate is substantially lower for students from low

Figure 2. **College Participation by Socioeconomic Status (SES)**

		SES Quartile	
		Lowest	Highest
Achievement Quartile	**Highest**	78%	97%
	Lowest	36%	77%

Source: U.S. Department of Education, February 2001.

socioeconomic-status families, even when they are high in academic ability and preparation (see Figure 2).[8]

The college *graduation rate* is even more dramatically influenced by socioeconomic status. Using data from the National Education Longitudinal Study to examine the graduation rate at a BA or higher level, Anthony Carnevale found that lower SES students at every level of academic ability obtain the baccalaureate degree at a substantially lower rate than students with higher SES and comparable SAT scores.[9]

As shown in Figure 3, the most dramatic and worrisome differences are for the large number of average students, those with an SAT score between 1000 and 1100, roughly one standard deviation above the average of 1000. Roughly 65 percent of high SES students in the average-ability group obtain a BA or higher degree. About 40 percent of students in the second quartile of SES with average academic ability obtain a BA or higher, and fewer than 20 percent of average-ability students in the lowest quartile of SES obtain a BA or better.

Completing a postsecondary degree or certificate, however, will be just the beginning. As we've learned in the past quarter century, every worker—and especially every professional worker—must continually acquire new knowledge and skills in order to avoid occupational obsolescence. U.S. Department of Education surveys have found that among adults, better-educated people most frequently acquire further education. Education is a growth industry, without a doubt. The relevant questions are, Who will provide educational opportunities, through what means will they be provided, and how valuable, how productive, will they be?

Implications for IT professionals: While IT professionals are needed to make many contributions to more widespread educational attainment, the

Figure 3. **Degree Attainment by SAT Scores and SES**

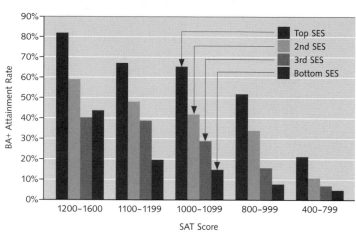

Source: Anthony P. Carnevale, "A Real Analysis of *Real Education*," *Liberal Education* 94, no. 4 (Fall 2008): 58.

most fundamental of these may be the development of more effective *knowledge-providing* data systems to inform educators, policy makers, and the public. The mobilization of public commitment to educational improvement requires reliable information about educational attainment and the effectiveness of instruction; sustaining that commitment requires evidence of continuing progress. Two crucial recent developments serve these purposes: statewide longitudinal data systems to monitor student progress over time and among schools, and the Common Education Data Standards to provide a shared, consistent P–20 vocabulary.[10]

Widely cited educational information (including the above statistics on the relationship between SES status, academic ability, and educational attainment) has been most often available only through survey research using national samples. In *particular places* (schools, cities, and states), educators and the public have lacked reliable, comparative information about educational achievement due to inconsistent data definitions and our inability to examine the progress of groups of individual students as they move among schools, colleges, and universities. It is in *particular places* where human effort is needed to yield improvement. In a country where retailers have detailed information on the buying patterns of customers and lenders can almost instantly qualify or disqualify a person for a loan, we have found it quite difficult to know how many students finish high school or college on time, or how students from particular schools fare in successive steps of the educational journey.

These problems have been politically, not technically, difficult to solve, but we are making progress. IT professionals need to support such efforts. They also need to build public confidence in our abilities to provide and continually improve the privacy safeguards required for education and the many other important areas of life where personal information is stored and analyzed in data systems.

The Demand for Productivity Gains in Education

Some of those who deny the need for mass postsecondary education are surely worried about its cost. And those who affirm the imperative for mass higher education are likely worried that recent trends suggest society won't be willing to pay what is required. A little history may be useful for understanding the situation.

From 1961 to 2000, almost without pause, postsecondary education in the U.S. grew in both enrollments and publicly provided revenues. In those forty years, state funding for operations grew from $1.4 billion to $60.7 billion, increasing dramatically each decade. The fastest growth occurred in the 1960s, but it didn't stop. From 1970 to 2000, enrollments grew from 4.5 to 8.6 million, and state support per FTE (full-time equivalent) student in public institutions generally kept pace with enrollment growth and inflation—falling a bit in recessions, but recovering afterward. Tuition and fee charges generally grew faster than inflation during recessions and then remained at the higher level, even after state support recovered.

By 2000, revenues from state support and tuition reached an all-time high of $11,371 per student (2010 dollars), and 29 percent of the total came from tuition and fees. By comparison, in 1985 total revenues were $9,753 (2010 dollars), and 23 percent came from tuition and fees.

Things have changed in the past ten years, and they changed in ways that may provide a view of the future. Public FTE enrollments grew by 35 percent from 2000 to 2010 (8.6 to 11.6 million), the fastest ten-year growth rate since 1970. But after the recession of 2001, state support stagnated at $70 billion from 2002 to 2004. The growth of state support resumed in 2005, reaching $85 billion in 2008. Then, however, the Great Recession of 2008 effectively ended growth in state funding for the current decade. Federal stimulus funds totaling $7 billion were needed to supplement state revenues and sustain state appropriations for higher education at $85 billion in 2009 and 2010. Due to enrollment growth, constant-dollar state support per student fell to $6,451 by 2010, the lowest level in twenty-five years. Total-per-student revenues fell to

$10,732 (below the 2000 peak, but well above 1985 levels), and 40.3 percent of educational revenue came from tuition and fees.

So while the twenty-first-century economy is demanding ever-higher levels of educational attainment, the United States irrationally seems to be disinvesting in higher education. Some worry these trends signify the abandonment of public education as a priority. I believe that pessimistic view is unwarranted; such trends instead signify the convergence of several factors that are forcing difficult choices and a broad restructuring of public finance and public commitments.

The only group in the U.S. population not expected to grow in the near and intermediate future is that of the prime working years—from ages 25–55. Retirees needing more health care will grow enormously, and students needing education will grow steadily but more modestly. The adverse impact of these demographics is compounded by persistent health-care-cost escalation, inadequately funded pension systems, increased longevity, and tax policies designed for a different economic era.

In 2005, David M. Walker, then comptroller general of the United States appointed by President George W. Bush, projected future federal deficits and spending in 2040. His projections assumed we meet federal obligations for Social Security, Medicare, and Medicaid; sustain current domestic, international, and military spending at the rate of GDP (gross domestic product) growth; and extend all the Bush administration tax reductions now scheduled to expire in 2013. Walker projected that by 2040, interest payments on the federal debt would nearly equal all federal revenues, spending would equal 40 percent of GDP, and revenues would equal less than 20 percent of GDP. In sum, annual spending would equal 200 percent of revenues. This is the problem, no longer avoidable, that now convulses the political process in Washington. Mr. Walker and others have told us it was coming.

The state piece of the resource shortage is driven mostly by four factors: Medicaid, state pension systems, enrollment growth in both higher education and K–12, and the misfit between many state revenue structures and current economic activity. (For example, Internet sales are often not taxed; more spending today is on untaxed services, not taxed goods; and states with high capital gains taxes experience dramatic revenue swings in economic cycles.) Donald Boyd of the Rockefeller Institute, working with The National Center for Higher Education Management Systems (NCHEMS), has analyzed structural deficits in the states for some time; the situation is deteriorating, not improving.[11]

The pressure for increased educational attainment is colliding with the pressures for honoring pension commitments, for providing health care to seniors and the poor, for public safety, for rebuilding the nation's infrastructure, for research and development, for energy autonomy, for avoiding tax increases, and for maintaining the international security and military commitments of the United States.

To make education the lowest priority among all these competing claims on the public purse would be to abandon hope for the future of the United States. Such a public policy decision is inconceivable given the clear personal rewards from education and the human instinct to care for one's progeny. An enduring and growing commitment of state and federal support to education will be needed to meet all of our national goals. But productivity gains in education, both K–12 and higher education, are essential.

The Dilemma of Educational Productivity

Largely because the "price" of higher education (both public and private tuitions) has grown much faster than inflation, the public generally believes that U.S. higher education is generously funded. In those institutions educating the most academically able and high SES students, U.S. colleges and universities *are* generously funded. Our funding is less generous and less adequate for community colleges and other less-selective institutions that educate large numbers of students.

Higher education costs have been explained and justified in many ways. Howard Bowen's revenue theory of spending explained that in pursuit of an infinitely expandable good (knowledge and quality), colleges and universities will spend, justifiably perhaps, all the revenues they can acquire.[12] For decades, educators have argued that productivity gains are infeasible in labor-intensive services such as education, based on the 1966 analysis by William Baumol and William Bowen in *Performing Arts*.[13] More recently, in *Why Does College Cost So Much?*, Robert B. Archibald and David H. Feldman argue that the law of supply and demand (skilled professionals are being paid more), increasing living standards, competition for students, and growing demands for quality enhancements are driving costs inexorably higher.[14] And as noted previously, tuitions increase when states fail to keep up with cost and enrollment increases in public colleges and universities.

The initial public policy response to the rising cost of higher education has been to provide more student aid. In the late twentieth century, state and federal student-need-based aid programs, loan programs and, later, merit scholarships and federal tax credits were established to aid students. During the Bush administration, Pell Grants were increased modestly, and new programs rewarding academic preparation and achievement were established (then later disestablished). The Obama administration set out to make Pell an entitlement and significantly increase the maximum award. While these efforts all aided access, recent growth in enrollments and Pell eligibility have produced skyrocketing, clearly unsustainable budget requirements.

Public policy in 2011 has clearly shifted from financing the cost spiral to fighting it. Congress and the Obama administration are reevaluating federal student-assistance policies. The states are launching initiatives to increase college completions and simultaneously reduce the cost of each degree. A solution to the productivity dilemma must be found in order to meet national goals for educational attainment.

Implications for IT professionals: The idea of computer-assisted instruction as a means of achieving greater efficiency and quality has been around since PLATO (Programmed Logic for Automated Teaching Operations) was conceived in 1960. Although a 1976 book in my office library is entitled *Presidents Confront Reality: From Edifice Complex to University Without Walls*, the rate of progress in developing and implementing computer-assisted learning tools seemed glacial for thirty or forty years. It has now accelerated from a crawl to a gallop. For example, Netscape, the first mainstream browser, did not exist when today's high school seniors were born. Sixteen years later, they and their grandparents check facts on handheld devices in seconds.

At the ACE National Conference on March 6, 2010, William Bowen, coauthor of *Performing Arts,* indicated that, because of the contributions of information technology, he no longer believes productivity gains in education are impossible. Other chapters in this volume will explore that potential, so I will simply observe that information technology can help higher education achieve productivity and quality gains *both* through innovation in instruction and better information for the management of resources. Common data standards and statewide longitudinal student-data systems are also a critical resource for increasing productivity.

More Attainment, *Higher* Quality

The drive for mass educational attainment raises legitimate concerns about quality. Inflated grades or, worse, inflated degrees are no substitute for authentic knowledge and skill. Expanding participation and attainment requires helping average—perhaps even marginally prepared—students succeed at unprecedented rates. State and federal governments have provided incentives and supports for institutions to enroll such students, but the record of student achievement is unsatisfactory. Many accredited institutions (both traditional and "innovative") have poor graduation rates, and graduating students are not always adequately educated. Academic leaders associated with Liberal Education and America's Promise (LEAP), an initiative of the Association of American Colleges and Universities, have clearly called for *higher* levels of student learning, not simply avoiding the compromise of prevailing standards.

We used to solve the quality-assurance problem by looking at inputs, student quality, faculty quality, library books, facilities, and the like. While inputs still matter, the old models no longer work well, especially for online instruction. In distance learning, faculties are usually temporary, not permanent, employees, and students also participate in episodic ways. Although the distance-education community has defined quality standards for program operations,[15] the use of these standards by accreditors and states is not widely visible.

Traditionally, we have measured student and institutional work by seat time rather than learning (time is the constant, learning the variable), obviously a problem for distance-learning programs. A general consensus is emerging that higher education should focus on generating and certifying knowledge and skill, regardless of the means or duration of instruction. But we lack transparent, generally accepted standards and assessments for knowledge and skill (most especially for nonprofessional degrees), and it is difficult to wean ourselves from the financing system that has based student prices and institutional subsidies on the acquisition of student credit hours.

The growing practice of enabling students to more easily gain credit for prior learning is a welcome development as a means of increasing both productivity and attainment. For its potential to be fully recognized we need (a) more widely accepted standards and assessments of course-equivalent or degree-equivalent knowledge and skill, and (b) appropriate prices for certification where there is minimal or no instruction so that students and those providing financial assistance are not inappropriately exploited.

Both explicit academic standards and the pricing problem are formidable challenges, but we are making some progress on the former. The Bologna Process in Europe, the Degree Qualifications Profile in the United States, and "tuning" (the development of clear learning objectives within a discipline) are interinstitutional, policy-level efforts to achieve common definitions of degrees and ease transferability among institutions. LEAP is challenging institutions and students to pursue the learning outcomes people need to be productive, responsible citizens in the twenty-first century. The Presidents' Alliance; the Voluntary System of Accountability (VSA), sponsored by the Association of Public and Land-grant Universities (APLU) and the Association of State Colleges and Universities (AASCU); the Voluntary Framework of Accountability (VFA), developed by the American Association of Community Colleges (AACC) and College Board; and the National Association of Independent Colleges and Universities'

(NAICU) U-CAN framework are all efforts to focus on enhancing learning and student success within institutions. The National Institute for Learning Outcomes Assessment (NILOA) is surveying the evolution of institutional practices and promoting both improvement and greater transparency.

Implications for IT professionals: The use of IT to achieve greater instructional efficiency becomes possible only when faculty collaboratively define explicit learning objectives, develop instructional materials to enable students to achieve them, and create the tools necessary to assess outcomes. Collective faculty work (together and with IT professionals) is essential; productivity gains require overcoming the robust tradition of professor as soloist. Collaboration and creativity are not antithetical, just as standards and well-defined foundational knowledge and skill are not irreconcilable with diverse views, nuance, and legitimate intellectual debate. While it is difficult for me to imagine effective higher education without discussion and argument, it is increasingly evident that information technology can play a useful role in virtually every aspect of the learning process, including online seminars and conversations.

Others are better prepared to cite the best work in the field and elaborate on significant past or potential contributions, but I can share the perspective of an interested, non-specialist bystander. Many groups of faculty have made great progress in developing clear objectives, aligned instructional materials, and useful non-standardized and standardized approaches to assessment. With the help of IT professionals in employing technology, educators are getting much better at the efficient transmission of knowledge.

The next frontier seems to be using information technology for improving the speed and quality of learning for particular individuals. The Open Learning Initiative at Carnegie Mellon, the NEXUS Research and Policy Center, and others are collecting and analyzing data on student interactions with computer-based learning materials as a means of improving their design in order to accelerate and deepen learning. A growing movement to improve remedial/developmental education is employing diagnostic assessments to identify knowledge gaps and close them more efficiently with well-focused teaching strategies. And with support from the William and Flora Hewlett Foundation and the Bill & Melinda Gates Foundation, the Learning Resource Metadata Initiative (http://www.lrmi.net) will specify the properties of learning resources in a way that can help Google, Yahoo!, and Microsoft Bing be more effective tools for teachers and students. Creative Commons and the Association of Educational Publishers are co-leading the project.

These efforts are headed toward a vision of instruction on a massive scale customized to the goals and current characteristics of individual learners. It is hard to know whether the most difficult challenge in such a vision will be assembling a broad, deep, and credible collection of learning materials, or ascertaining the constantly changing needs of individual learners and providing instructional materials tailored to those needs. But the vision is exciting; even if it is only partially realized, these efforts could be extremely valuable.

Stronger Relationships between Elementary, Secondary, and Postsecondary Education

Authentic, widespread postsecondary attainment cannot be built on a shaky foundation of elementary and secondary education. Of course, when criticized for failing to prepare students for postsecondary success, K–12 educators can and do deflect the criticism to the colleges and universities that prepare teachers and school leaders. Obviously, reciprocal finger-pointing is foolish; higher education and K–12 education are utterly interdependent. The sectors share a common mission that can be achieved only through deep and extensive collaboration.

The California Partnership for Achieving Student Success (Cal-PASS), founded in 1998, is an exemplar of such collaboration. It began by collecting and sharing anonymous student transcripts and performance information among K–12 schools, community colleges, and universities. (The resulting database now holds over 430 million records from over 8,200 educational institutions.) In an early use of these data, faculty from the Grossmont-Cuyamaca Community College District in El Cajon, California, met with local high school faculty to explore the reasons so many (67 percent) students who received good grades in high school English required remediation in college.

After developing relationships of mutual respect and trust, the K–12 and postsecondary faculty determined that high school English instruction was not preparing students to critically read, develop, and employ expository texts, the predominate focus in much of college work. A systematic effort to address this issue in a pilot group of high schools has materially increased student performance and reduced students' placement in postsecondary remedial courses. The Cal-PASS project, now managed by the Institute for Evidence-Based Change, also includes K–12/postsecondary collaboration in mathematics. This kind of work—faculty dialogues to improve instruction informed by student performance data—should become commonplace in every state and every sector of education.

The development of Common Core State Standards in mathematics and English language arts by the Council of Chief State School Officers (CCSSO) and National Governors Association (NGA) offers an enormously promising opportunity to improve the effectiveness and productivity of education in the United States. The initiative has aspired (1) to define the knowledge and skills in English and math that, at the completion of high school, would signify that a student is ready for success in college or a career; (2) to define the learning progression through elementary and secondary education needed to achieve college and career readiness; and (3) to provide valid, formative, and summative assessments of student progress toward college and career readiness through each stage of elementary and secondary education.

The guiding principles behind the standards have been "fewer, clearer, higher, evidence based, and internationally benchmarked." Virtually all who have studied the Common Core State Standards agree that the capabilities of U.S. high school graduates will be dramatically higher if these learning objectives are widely achieved. Significant educational progress may be within our grasp if educators in the United States can stay tightly focused on these learning objectives and develop curricula and instructional approaches that will help students achieve them in far greater numbers. The absence of clear, common, and parsimonious learning objectives as well as accepted metrics for assessing achievement surely has contributed to reform movements dominated by contention, rather than the pursuit of common purposes. Well-defined fundamental learning objectives, supported by widely accepted "yardsticks" for assessing student achievement, could become a constructive, enormously powerful tool.

Implications for IT professionals: The Common Core State Standards for mathematics and English language arts and the Common Education Data Standards are creating new opportunities to help U.S. educators meet the challenges of the knowledge economy. Increasingly, information technology can help accelerate educational progress by providing better information about student needs and student performance to instructors, educational leaders, and policy makers.

Explicit learning objectives and assessments and "standard" data on educational achievement are clearly essential in order for information technology to be most useful. They are also essential for achieving widespread educational attainment, but they are not ends in themselves. The "end" of education is not the acquisition of a fixed body of knowledge, but the ability to apply knowledge and skill to the problems of life and to the exploration of new frontiers. These capabilities are the coin of the realm in the knowledge economy.

While the potential of these opportunities is exhilarating, it is sobering to contemplate the scope of human knowledge (and ignorance) and the uncertainties and debates we must navigate as researchers and instructors in order to realize their potential. Real progress will require long, serious conversations about questions of priority, scope, and sequence, but given time and goodwill, real progress is within our grasp.

Notes

1. Peter F. Drucker, *The Age of Discontinuity: Guidelines to Our Changing Society* (New York: Harper and Row, 1969).
2. Peter F. Drucker, "The Next Society," *The Economist* (November 1, 2001), http://www.economist.com/node/770819.
3. Thomas L. Friedman, *The World Is Flat: A Brief History of the Twenty-First Century* (New York: Farrar, Straus & Giroux, 2005).
4. Charles Murray, *Real Education: Four Simple Truths for Bringing America's Schools Back to Reality* (New York: Random House, 2008).
5. H. G. Wells, *The Outline of History Part II* (George Newnes, 1919).
6. Source: Anthony Carnevale, Georgetown University Center on Education and the Workforce's Analysis of Macroeconomic Advisers (MA) Long-Term Economic Outlook, March 2009.
7. Anthony P. Carnevale, *The College Payoff: Education, Occupations, Lifetime Earnings* (Washington, DC: The Georgetown University Center on Education and the Workforce, 2011).
8. Source: U.S. Department of Education, February 2001.
9. Anthony P. Carnevale, "A Real Analysis of *Real Education*," *Liberal Education* 94, no. 4 (Fall 2008): 54–61, http://www.aacu.org/liberaleducation/le-fa08/documents/le-fa08_Carnevale.pdf.
10. More information on the Common Education Data Standards can be found at http://commoneddatastandards.org/ and at http://ceds.ed.gov/.
11. Don Boyd, *State Fiscal Outlooks from 2005 to 2013: Implication for Higher Education* (Boulder, CO: National Center for Higher Education Management Systems, 2005).
12. H. R. Bowen, *The Costs of Higher Education* (San Francisco: Jossey-Bass, 1980).
13. W. J. Baumol and W. G. Bowen, *Performing Arts—the Economic Dilemma* (New York: The Twentieth Century Fund, 1966).
14. Robert B. Archibald and David H. Feldman, *Why Does College Cost So Much?* (New York: Oxford University Press, October 2010).
15. See, by way of comparison, http://net.educause.edu/ir/library/text/CEM9613.txt.

As President of the association of State Higher Education Executive Officers (SHEEO), **Paul E. Lingenfelter** *has focused on increasing successful participation in higher education, improving student learning, finance, and building more effective relationships between K–12 and postsecondary educators. He previously was Vice President of the MacArthur Foundation and Deputy Director of the Illinois Board of Higher Education.*

2

The Questions We Need to Ask *First*: Setting Priorities for Higher Education in Our Technology-Rich World

Debra Humphreys

NEW TECHNOLOGIES—and particularly new information technologies—are dramatically changing higher education institutions and practices. Advances in technology, of course, are also changing many sectors of society other than education, including the news media, culture, music, marketing, philanthropy, community organizing, and politics. All these varied enterprises are roiled by new ways of sharing information and producing cultural products, new ways of organizing workplaces and work functions, and pressures on older business models. Many articles in this book address the myriad ways that technology is changing our enterprise. As those changes proceed, on another track, political leaders are crafting new policies that are setting the stage for a revolution in how colleges are financed and how they are held accountable for meeting increased expectations with fewer resources. College presidents face daunting challenges as they lead their institutions through this volatile period. Below, I suggest a set of "prior" questions that both educational and policy leaders should ask before setting their priorities—including those related to technology.

In a recent guest blog post in the *Washington Post*, L. Randolph Lowry, president of Lipscomb University, made several useful suggestions about how college presidents should be meeting new challenges they are likely to meet in 2012. Among the ten challenges he discussed, he noted that "Technology rules. Changes in technology *define* how we deliver an education. It *defines* what we do, and it *defines* our students even down to how they think and process learning [emphasis mine]."[1] On this particular point, I think Lowry is mistaken. While new technology developments are certainly *changing* how educational institutions operate, technology alone does not—or should not—"define" what we do. Technology is, indeed, having an impact on two things at least. It is changing how students think about learning and their educational

---

© 2012 Debra Humphreys

pathways. It is also, of course, changing how educators do their work. However, leaders and educators on the ground are the ones steering how their institutions invest in and use technology. They are managing the changes being wrought. And priorities and wise decision making are crucial. It isn't technology that "defines" institutional direction. *People* define how technology is deployed, not the technologies that people invent.

The larger aims of education and the practices we use to achieve those aims must be the drivers of our priority setting, not the availability of new technologies in and of itself. Comments from several student speakers at a recent Association of American Colleges and Universities (AAC&U) conference drive this point home. Remarking on what they truly valued in their educational experiences—what was really helping them achieve important learning outcomes—students expressed frustration with *too much* focus on technology usage and new online platforms in their classes. One student noted that, "So far, I haven't found that any one of the technologies added to my humanities seminars has added any value." Another student, commenting on some assignments related to fractals, noted that "I found that when I used the computer and the technology available to me, I didn't *think* any more."[2] Educational leaders and good instructors, of course, know that using new technologies doesn't necessarily improve learning and that *educational* goals rather than just the *availability* of new technological innovations should drive their setting of priorities. But it is helpful to be reminded by students themselves that they, too, understand that, while they may be "digital natives," new technologies are just tools—means rather than ends to educational goals.

Keeping this in mind and especially during times of rapid change, then, it is imperative for leaders to be very clear about their first principles. And, in the educational sector, those principles must, first and foremost, address the quality and learning outcomes of our educational programs. Whatever the profound changes are that we and our students are facing, at a basic level, the larger aims of education are pretty enduring. As college educators, we aim to equip our students with the capacity to function successfully as responsible citizens and productive members of the workforce throughout their lifetimes. Especially in times as troubling as our own, we must also, through our educational choices and practices, enable, equip, and inspire graduates to be agents of change rather than victims of change. We must use technology to educate students who can *create* the next generation of technical tools through which future generations will build new workplaces and institutions of their own.

The Association of American Colleges and Universities published a report in 2007, *College Learning for the New Global Century*,[3] that sketched out a new vision for learning in this rapidly changing twenty-first century. Authored by a national leadership council composed of leaders in business, education, policy, and community action, this report, published as part of AAC&U's Liberal Education and America's Promise (LEAP) initiative, noted that, "In the twenty-first century, the world itself is setting very high expectations for knowledge and skill. This report . . . describes the learning contemporary students need from college, and what it will take to help them achieve it."[4] It further noted the following:

- In an era when knowledge is the key to the future, all students need the scope and depth of learning that will enable them to understand and navigate the dramatic forces—physical, cultural, economic, technological—that directly affect the quality, character, and perils of the world in which they live.
- In an economy where every industry . . . is challenged to innovate or be displaced, all students need the kind of intellectual skills and capacities that enable them to get things done in the world, at a high level of effectiveness.
- In a world of daunting complexity, all students need practice in integrating and applying their learning to challenging questions and real-world problems.
- In a period of relentless change, all students need the kind of education that leads them to ask not just "How do we get this done?" but also "What is most worth doing?"[5]

Technology is, of course, implicated in how we will enable all our students to reach these new levels of achievement and meet all these challenges. And clearly, information technology can help educators develop these capacities in students. But technological innovations alone are not the answer to meeting these raised expectations for learning.

The LEAP report also included a set of learning outcomes that had been developed and deemed essential by leaders and practitioners across a wide array of sectors of the economy, levels of education, and regions of the country (see Figure 1).

These outcomes include many that are shaped by the current technology-rich world of work. They also, however, include several traditional outcomes on which employers say that colleges should be placing more emphasis. Employers, for instance, want more emphasis on oral and written communication, analytic reasoning, quantitative literacy, knowledge of science and society, global knowledge and acumen, intercultural skills, team problem solving, and ethical reasoning and decision making.[6] Some of these outcomes are tried-and-true elements of a quality education and have been for years, but even in

Figure 1. **Essential Learning Outcomes**

The Essential Learning Outcomes

★ ★ ★ ★ ★ ★ ★ ★ ★ ★ ★ ★ ★ ★ ★ ★ ★ ★

Beginning in school, and continuing at successively higher levels across their college studies, students should prepare for twenty-first-century challenges by gaining:

✹ Knowledge of Human Cultures and the Physical and Natural World

- Through study in the sciences and mathematics, social sciences, humanities, histories, languages, and the arts

Focused by engagement with big questions, both contemporary and enduring

---

✹ Intellectual and Practical Skills, including

- Inquiry and analysis
- Critical and creative thinking
- Written and oral communication
- Quantitative literacy
- Information literacy
- Teamwork and problem solving

Practiced extensively, across the curriculum, in the context of progressively more challenging problems, projects, and standards for performance

---

✹ Personal and Social Responsibility, including

- Civic knowledge and engagement—local and global
- Intercultural knowledge and competence
- Ethical reasoning and action
- Foundations and skills for lifelong learning

Anchored through active involvement with diverse communities and real-world challenges

---

✹ Integrative and Applied Learning, including

- Synthesis and advanced accomplishment across general and specialized studies

Demonstrated through the application of knowledge, skills, and responsibilities to new settings and complex problems

---

Note: This listing was developed through a multiyear dialogue with hundreds of colleges and universities about needed goals for student learning; analysis of a long series of recommendations and reports from the business community; and analysis of the accreditation requirements for engineering, business, nursing, and teacher education. The findings are documented in previous publications of the Association of American Colleges and Universities: *Greater Expectations: A New Vision for Learning as a Nation Goes to College* (2002), *Taking Responsibility for the Quality of the Baccalaureate Degree* (2004), and *College Learning for the New Global Century* (2007). For further information, see www.aacu.org/leap.

LEAP

these areas, employers want graduates with *much higher* levels of these skills than even the best students attained in years past.

These learning outcomes—and the larger challenges of navigating our complex world—should guide how we lead our educational institutions, how we develop new public policies to support educational institutions in advancing these outcomes, and how we enact new educational practices on the ground. Many of those practices can and should be steeped in new technologies and can and should make use of information technology. But all of our educational practices and policies must be guided by the need to develop these broad outcomes of a more practical and engaged liberal education for our students. It is only this kind of education that will, indeed, prepare them to be effective change agents and navigators of our technology-rich and knowledge-intensive world.

If we listen carefully, in particular, to what employers tell us about the college graduates they are hiring and those they are seeking, we can learn a great deal about priorities for the uses of technology as we reshape our curricular practices and programs. A recent national survey found that 90 percent of employers say that their employees are now expected to "work harder to coordinate with other departments than in the past." Eighty-eight percent note that the challenges employees face within their companies "are more complex today than they were in the past."[7] As we develop new ways to deploy information technology in education, we must ensure that we are not only finding new ways of delivering content more efficiently, but we must seek ways to use technology to enable students to work together effectively in teams, communicate their ideas clearly both online *and* in face-to-face settings, and solve complex problems that may require cross-disciplinary collaboration.

Others in this volume detail some ways technology is changing the higher education enterprise. I want to suggest that it is in these areas of improving learning outcomes that *more* of our technology energies should be focused. Unfortunately, the current national policy dialogue in higher education—and specifically the dialogue about the role of technology in our sector—is not focused on these *educational* challenges. Much positive educational reform work is happening on the ground, but the larger policy conversation has been distorted by the economic downturn and by myopic thinking on the part of some policy makers and educators. Too much discussion about technology and education is filtered exclusively through the lenses of productivity and efficiency. The questions driving this debate often have little or nothing to do with student *learning*. Instead, they are questions about how many more students our current systems can graduate with the same or fewer financial resources. Instead of charting a new course for higher education institutions—including how they are financed—by addressing the larger question of how technological and other societal shifts are changing what *quality* education means, too many are simply focused on whether technology can produce greater efficiency. For example, the National Governors Association (NGA) project Complete to Compete is a multifaceted national initiative focused primarily on "increasing productivity in higher education . . . [by] building strong accountability systems that move away from the ones primarily in use today, which tend to emphasize inputs over outcomes and the collection and reporting of data as opposed to using the information in decision-making."[8] This initiative responds, in part, to President Obama's call for "America [to] once again have the highest proportion of college graduates in the world."[9] As Washington governor Christine Gregoire put it in a letter introducing an NGA report issued in July of 2011, "The road to economic growth and competitiveness runs through our community and technical colleges and our four-year colleges and universities. We need more of our people to have education beyond high school—certificates and degrees—to meet the needs of our economy, now and in the future."[10] All the various initiatives focused on increasing college-degree attainment and completion levels, then, are rightly responding to the changing knowledge economy that, indeed, is demanding more *numbers* of college-educated workers. However, research commissioned by AAC&U has also shown that this new economy is demanding more *skills and knowledge* as well as just more college-educated people.[11] Complete to Compete and other partner efforts such as Complete College America, however, are focused on "efficiency and effectiveness metrics" and on "using metrics to make and evaluate policy decisions."[12] Unfortunately, the metrics on which they focus don't address what students are learning, but instead address only their general progress in accumulating credits efficiently. The NGA Center for Best Practices urges governors to collect data on questions such as, "How many students at public institutions are graduating relative to total enrollment?" and "What is the return on states' and students' investment in public institutions in terms of completed certificates and degrees?"[13] The policy recommendations the NGA offers to states also focus on changing "financing structures to incentivize improved performance," with performance measured by graduation rates and time to degree alone. In one of the early reports from Complete to Compete, NGA staff members suggest that states focus particularly on serving adult students. They offer four goals related to this effort: "Provide flexible and integrated learning environments, offer comprehensive support services, use cross-institutional data to track performance, and create financing structures to incentivize improved performance."[14] While each of these goals is worthy in and of itself, none addresses the larger issue of how we ensure that all students, including returning adult students, attain the most important learning outcomes—outcomes that will really enable them to compete in a rapidly changing knowledge economy. Information technologies can and should play a role in meeting all these goals, but too little focus is currently being directed toward the *learning* goals and too much is focused on the efficiency goals. For example, in its focus on adult students, the NGA sees a lack of "flexible learning environments" for these students. It notes the role of technology in solving this problem, focusing exclusively on issues of course scheduling and *availability* of asynchronous or online learning opportunities to "enable students to complete classes on their own schedules."[15] While these goals are certainly worthy ones, they miss entirely attention to *how* those online learning environments can and should be designed to advance important learning outcomes. I have written elsewhere that "It should be a national priority to pursue productive approaches that help different groups of students stay in college and graduate on time, but that isn't all we should do. We also must attend simultaneously to the serious quality of learning shortfall that threatens to get even worse if we maintain an exclusive focus on completion and efficiency."[16] There are ways that the NGA and other policy leaders could help advance more-productive and "quality-driven" policy and data-collection changes. For instance, state-level agencies could require colleges and universities to clarify the broad learning outcomes required for the awarding of degrees. They could also collect data not just on credits accumulated, but on how many and which students in an institution or system are participating in high-impact educational practices (e.g., first-year seminars, learning communities, service learning, or undergraduate research programs) delivered in either online or face-to-face settings.

Information technology may indeed produce efficiencies within our sector as it has in other sectors. But if it does so at the expense of our ability to truly prepare students with the capacities they need in our complex world, we will have failed them and our larger mission. Ironically, we also will have squandered the true promise of technology—which is to significantly *improve* educational outcomes; increase the opportunities students have to interact with each other, with scholars around the world, and with faculty; and help a diverse array of students learn in new and more effective ways.

How then can we avoid thinking too narrowly about technology and the ways in which higher education can and must change in our time? To answer this question, we might turn to an unlikely source in another sector. We can extract a valuable lesson by looking to the news media and, in particular, to one influential institution at the center of that sector, the *New York Times*. Like every print news organization in the country, the *Times* has been forced into wrenching changes as it has weathered the recent economic downturn and broader trends in the ways in which people access information and "consume" news. Seth Mnookin described it this way in a recent article in *New York Magazine*. "The paper's financial troubles . . . appeared to have pushed it to the brink of extinction. For well over a decade, the Internet had been relentlessly consuming the paper's business model. . . . In the months after the collapse of the credit market in the fall of 2008, the company was forced to take drastic measures to stay afloat."[17] Mnookin proceeds from this gloomy beginning to tell a story of how the *Times* took drastic measures but ultimately came out in a very strong position by staying true to the company's core principles, doubling down on its reputation for quality while also investing in both information technology and in the fundamentals of good national and international reporting. American higher education institutions could learn something from this company's recent decisions. We can, as a sector or as institutions within the sector, take a strong stand on the quality of education as our touchstone—and all decisions related to technology or anything else will be measured by how much the quality of learning can be improved. As Mnookin notes about the *New York Times*, "The *Times* has taken a do-or-die stand for hard-core, boots-on-the-ground journalism, for earnest civic purpose, for the primacy of content creators over aggregators, and has brought itself back from the precipice."[18] College and university leaders can also take a do-or-die stand for the primacy of high-quality faculty-student interactions, for the commitment to broad learning outcomes for both work and responsible civic engagement, and for the development of high-quality learning experiences that produce in all students sophisticated and lasting competencies. The *New York Times* has poured money into its website, but not in a quest to somehow reduce the costs of creating its "product." Instead, it has used technology to *improve* the quality of the product it provides—it has built on the foundation of its news-gathering operation but added online features to enhance the information it provides to its readers. We should do the same—keeping in mind that "quality" means something different today than it did years ago. Attending to quality isn't just about ensuring that we don't lose ground from the status quo. It means actually increasing the levels of student achievement on a host of important learning outcomes.

How would an analogous strategy work in higher education? Again, it is instructive to turn to the employers of our graduates for perspective. Employers are calling for more focus on requiring students to take courses in wide areas of knowledge and skill, but also on educational practices that require students to do research projects and to apply what they are learning in real-world settings. How can we use the Internet to help students conduct research? How can we use technology to free up faculty to spend more time helping students do applied-learning projects in their communities or in high-tech laboratories rather than just delivering lectures in person or online to passive students? Eighty-four percent of employers believe that requiring students to complete a significant project before graduation that demonstrates their depth of knowledge in their major and their acquisition of analytical, problem-solving, and communication skills would help prepare them for success in the global economy. Eighty-one percent of employers believe that requiring students to complete an internship or community-based field project to connect classroom learning with real-world experiences would also help better prepare students.[19] How can technology help us do this better and for more students?

There are myriad examples of individual institutions and faculty members advancing complex learning goals such as these through new uses of technology. I share only a few here as an illustration of the kinds of technological innovations that deserve more attention from the media, policy makers, and educators. We know that survey after survey suggests that employers want new college graduates to be skilled in working collaboratively in technology-rich environments. Queensborough Community College in New York has developed an interdisciplinary group Wiki project designed specifically to meet six educational objectives, including such things as improving students' abilities to "collaborate across disciplines and departments," "communicate effectively," "use analytic reasoning to identify issues or problems," and "use information-management and technology skills effectively for academic research and lifelong learning," among others. The project partners English, basic educational skills courses, and additional content courses in education, nursing, social sciences, and speech/theater. Students in these linked courses use a shared online work space through which they archive and share their written, visual, and aural compositions with each other. Through this virtual learning community, students share their work, gain feedback on it from their peers as well as from their instructors, and reflect on their achievements.[20] Another example of technological innovation put to use in the service of advancing specific learning outcomes comes from the Center for Global Geography Education (CGGE). Since 2003, CGGE has built a collection of online modules for undergraduate courses in geography and related social and environmental sciences. The modules don't replace faculty members or existing campus-based online or face-to-face classes, but provide to faculty teaching geography courses around the world online materials, case studies, and access to collaborative projects that their students can do with students in different countries. Using a Moodle e-technology platform, students from a wide array of countries work on collaborative projects on such issues as migration, global climate change, water resources, global economic change, and national identity.[21]

Thousands of such examples of advancing twenty-first-century learning outcomes through new uses of information technology exist—and investing in the development and spread of these kinds of educational innovations is one way we in higher education can, like the New York Times, "double down" on quality. I conclude with just one final example of a technological innovation that shows great promise in this area and that might also help in increasing retention and completion rates as well. Many colleges and universities across all sectors have increased their investments in electronic portfolio tools and services.[22] Educators from a variety of institutions and from many disciplines are using these particular tools to deepen learning and facilitate knowledge and skill transfer and to foster students' abilities to make connections between their learning experiences in an assortment of classroom, workplace, and community settings. As e-portfolio experts Helen L. Chen and Tracy Penny Light put it,

> E-portfolios offer a framework within which students can personalize their learning experiences (student ownership of the e-portfolio and its contents leads to greater responsibility for learning); develop multimedia capabilities to support student-created media; and create representations of their learning experiences for different audiences. Moreover, unlike other assessment tools, e-portfolios enable students to represent their own learning as well as their interpretations of what Kathleen Yancey calls the multiple curricula within higher education: the *delivered* curriculum, which is defined by the faculty and described in the syllabus; the *experienced* curriculum, which is represented by what is actually practiced by the student in the classroom; and the *lived* curriculum, which is based on the individual student's cumulative learning to date. At least potentially, e-portfolios provide insight into the curriculum as students have both *lived* and *experienced* it.[23]

Other unpublished research also suggests that this technological innovation—and the exploitation of it for intentional educational purposes—may also produce better results in terms of student retention and graduation rates.[24] We can see, then, that this kind of technological innovation can be developed in ways wholly consistent with the larger aims of education, but also in ways that may advance a more cost-efficient educational institution. First and foremost, however, this tool is being developed to improve the quality of students' learning. As Ross Miller and Wende Morgaine put it, "E-portfolios provide a rich resource for both students and faculty to learn about achievement of important outcomes over time, make connections among disparate parts of the curriculum, gain insights leading to improvement, and develop identities as learners or as facilitators of learning."[25] Given how important it is in today's economy for graduates to have the capacity to continue learning over time, especially in technology-rich environments, investing in this kind of technological innovation is exactly the kind of "bet on quality" we should make.

It is important for our nation to invest in productive and affordable ways to increase the numbers of people who obtain college degrees. But the economy also needs those graduates to be more capable and better educated in many ways. We must ensure that every college graduate is informed and committed to using technology and other tools to build an economy and civil society that is more equitable and just and that includes more effective democratic decision making. Both these goals—increasing the number of college graduates and the number of responsible and engaged citizens—depend on how we deploy technology not only to deliver information more efficiently, but also to help define and assess educational *outcomes* and craft and implement *practices* that build student and societal capacity for constructive change.

Notes

1. L. Randolph Lowry, "Guest Post: 10 Challenges for College Presidents in 2011–12," on Daniel de Vise, *College Inc.* (blog), *Washington Post*, September 9, 2011.
2. Association of American Colleges and Universities (AAC&U), "Giving Voice to the Future: Students Take the Mic," podcast of student panel at AAC&U meeting held November 5, 2011, accessed December 2, 2011, http://www.aacu.org/podcast/feed/159/nov5_studentpanel.mp3.
3. Association of American Colleges and Universities, *College Learning for the New Global Century* (Washington, DC: Association of American Colleges and Universities, 2007): 1.
4. Ibid., 1.
5. Ibid., 13.
6. Hart Research Associates, *Raising the Bar: Employers' Views on College Learning in the Wake of the Economic Downturn* (Washington, DC: Association of American Colleges and Universities, 2010).
7. Ibid., 5.
8. T. Reindl and Ryan Reyna, *From Information to Action: Revamping Higher Education Accountability Systems* (Washington, DC: National Governors Association Center for Best Practices, July 2011): 3.
9. B. H. Obama, "Remarks of President Barack Obama—As Prepared for Delivery; Address to Joint Session of Congress," February 24, 2009, http://www.whitehouse.gov/the_press_office/Remarks-of-President-Barack-Obama-Address-to-Joint-Session-of-Congress.

10. Reindl and Reyna, *From Information to Action.*
11. Hart Research Associates, *Raising the Bar.*
12. Reindl and Reyna, *From Information to Action,* 1.
13. Ibid., 3.
14. L. Hoffman and T. Reindl, *Improving Postsecondary Attainment among Adults* (Washington, DC: National Governors Association Center for Best Practices, February 2011): 5.
15. Ibid., 9.
16. D. Humphreys, "What's Wrong with the Completion Agenda—And What We Can Do About It," *Liberal Education* 98, no. 1 (Washington, DC: Association of American Colleges and Universities, forthcoming).
17. S. Mnookin, "The Kingdom and the Paywall," *New York Magazine,* July 24, 2011, 1.
18. Ibid., 2.
19. Hart Research Associates, *Raising the Bar.*
20. Jean Darcy and Michele Cuomo, "Queensborough's Student Wiki Interdisciplinary Group," http://leap.aacu.org/toolkit/high-impact-practices/2011/queensboroughs -student-wiki-interdisciplinary-group.
21. AAG Center for Global Geography Education, "Internationalizing the Teaching and Learning of Geography" (2010), http://globalgeography.aag.org.
22. K. Green, *Campus Computing 2008: The 19th National Survey of Computing and Information Technology in American Higher Education* (Encino, CA: Campus Computing Project, 2008); D. Schaffhauser, "Here, There, and Everywhere," *Campus Technology* (2009), http://campustechnology.com/Articles/2009/11/01/ePortfolios.aspx?p=1.
23. H. L. Chen and T. P. Light, *Electronic Portfolios and Student Success: Effectiveness, Efficiency, and Learning* (Washington, DC: Association of American Colleges and Universities, 2010): 3.
24. Bret Eynon, "Making Connections: High Impact Practices & the Integrative ePortfolio" (PowerPoint presentation slides), accessed December 6, 2011, http://www.aacu.org/meetings/institute_gened/documents/EynonePandIntegrativeLearningAA-CU2011.06.15.pdf.
25. R. Miller and W. Morgaine, "The Benefits of E-portfolios for Students and Faculty in Their Own Words," *Peer Review* 11, no. 1 (Washington, DC: Association of American Colleges and Universities, 2009): 8–12.

Debra Humphreys, *Vice President for Communications and Public Affairs at the Association of American Colleges and Universities, oversees public affairs programs and outreach and regularly serves as AAC&U's official spokesperson. She leads national advocacy efforts related to student success and the quality of student learning through AAC&U's signature initiatives, Liberal Education and America's Promise and The Quality Collaboratives.*

3

IT as a Game Changer

Diana G. Oblinger

INFORMATION TECHNOLOGY CAN BE A GAME CHANGER in higher education, as it has been in other sectors. IT has brought about much of the economic growth of the past century, accelerating globalization and fostering democracy. Such broad impacts would be impossible if "information technology" were only a set of technologies. As our use of mobile devices, games, and social networks illustrates, IT can create new experiences. But more importantly, IT enables new models. It can disaggregate and decouple products and processes, allowing the creation of new value propositions, value chains, and enterprises. These new models can help higher education serve new groups of students, in greater numbers, and with better learning outcomes.

As important as IT might be, technology does not have impact in isolation—it operates as one element in a complex adaptive system. For example, in order for IT to be a game changer, it requires that we consider learners as well as the experience that the student, faculty, institution, and technology co-create. The system is defined, in part, by faculty workload, courses, credentialing, financial models, and more. To realize changes through information technology, higher education must focus on more than technology.

This chapter explores many ways that information technology can be a game changer. Some are as simple as using IT as a delivery channel for information or services. In other cases, IT creates unique experiences, whether in learning or student support. Perhaps most important for the future are the examples of IT enabling alternative models that improve choice, decision making, and student success.

Convenience

Information technology is a tool of convenience—IT can change the game by making it easier for us to do the things we should. For example, mobiles allow us to stay in touch anywhere. Mobile applications help us find the fastest route to our destination, the best restaurants, and the least-expensive gasoline. Mobile applications allow students to receive grades, register online, anticipate the arrival of the bus, listen to lectures, collect field data, connect to their tutor, look up resources, and more. Even simple, convenient tools such as e-mail have been transformative for students and faculty, providing better communication, instant assignment submission, and exchanges outside of office hours.

Convenience is the primary value students cite for technology in higher education today. It makes accessing resources, administrative tasks (e.g., registering for classes, paying tuition), and academic work faster and easier. Students believe technology makes them more productive. Students own many different kinds of technology, but their preference is for small, mobile devices. A majority of students own a laptop (87 percent), an iPod (62 percent), a smartphone (55 percent), a digital camera (55 percent), and a webcam (55 percent). Communication with technology is convenient. Virtually all students (99 percent) use e-mail, text messaging (93 percent), Facebook (90 percent), and instant messaging (81 percent).[1]

IT serves as a delivery channel for information of all kinds, increasing convenience, access, and flexibility. Millions of books are available online (e.g., Google Books); lectures come in all formats (e.g., podcasts, YouTube, Khan Academy). Beyond information, IT serves as a convenient delivery channel for academic support programs (e.g., Smarthinking) and online courses (e.g., StraighterLine). Access to colleges or universities, whether to their student services, instruction, or the library, can occur anytime and anywhere. Alternative models for cost and pedagogy are possible when information and processes move online, but convenience alone can change the game.

Improving the College Experience

IT's impact goes beyond convenience—it can change the game through the student's experience. The college or university "experience" is more than the classroom, the course, or the campus. The experience is determined by social, technical, and intellectual interactions involving students, faculty, and staff; the organization; and the infrastructure, including technology. Contrast the student experience—before and after IT—of registration, the "card catalog," or receiving grades. The value is not in the tool, per se, but in the streamlined, more user-friendly experience IT can help create.

Experts in service science and service systems are applying the discipline to higher education.[2] Service science asserts that the customer and the service provider co-create value. Value is not in the product (e.g., a course or a degree) but in the experience created by interaction, such as that occurring between faculty and students. For example, the real value of a course may lie in the critical thinking a faculty member encourages in a student, the integration of content with real-world experience, and the motivation to continue learning and solve important problems.

Learners' backgrounds and expectations impact their college experience and what they value. Students bring radically different levels of readiness, goals, and needs to higher education. Some value the on-campus experience; others are more focused on employability. A range of educational options are emerging to accommodate this diversity. These models are increasingly predicated on personalization and support systems that allow students to address their challenges and achieve their goals, whether they are well prepared or unprepared for college. For those students who come fully prepared, higher education can find new and innovative ways to add even greater value to their educational experience.[3]

The "college experience" has many facets. Learning and student support illustrate how IT can change their experience.

Learning

A high-quality learning experience changes the game for students. Unfortunately, our existing structures for teaching are not adequate for our current understanding of learning—which is experiential, socially constructed, and interdisciplinary.[4] If learning is assumed to be confined to the classroom or a lecture, valuable opportunities are lost.

Consider a student's traditional class experience being transformed with augmented reality, which uses mobiles and context-aware technologies to allow participants to interact with digital information, videos, visualizations, and simulations embedded in a physical setting (e.g., see http://ecomobile.gse.harvard.edu).[5] Assessment is another element of the learning experience. Paper and pencil tests cannot measure what students really know. IT enables very different assessments through detailed observations of performances. For example, a simulation can present students with a six-legged frog, asking students for a hypothesis, and letting them choose what to do, as well as how. In the process, they illustrate their ability to

- design a scientific investigation;
- use appropriate tools and techniques to gather, analyze, and interpret data;
- develop prescriptions, explanations, predictions, and models using evidence; and
- think critically and logically.[6]

39

Today, courses may be better thought of as tools to manage time, staff, and resources or as building blocks for the discipline. However, the bounded, self-contained course can no longer be the central unit of analysis of the curriculum because it may no longer be the place where the most significant learning takes place.[7] In the "postcourse era," learning occurs through inquiry and participation, social connections (e.g., blogs, wikis), and reflection.

Features of valuable learning experiences, which may be found inside or outside of courses and enabled by information technology, include:[8]

Pro-am: The apprenticeship model embodies a professional-amateur ("pro-am") approach to learning—also called "cognitive apprenticeship."[9] Learners gain skills and accelerate their development by interacting with others who are more expert. Online communities such as nanoHUB.org (http://nanohub.org) can provide such pro-am opportunities. NanoHUB.org is a collaborative community involving undergraduate and graduate students, faculty, and industry experts. This "pro-am" network shares instruction and simulations, as well as research tools and results.

Hard fun: Learning experiences that are instructionally and intellectually challenging and engaging are "hard fun."[10] Emotional engagement (surprise, puzzlement, awe) increases learner effort and attention, improving learning outcomes. Games are designed to provide "hard fun," as are simulations and other immersive environments.

Real world: Students are motivated by engaging in real-world problems that matter to them. Technology provides new opportunities for "real-world" experiences through simulations, virtual environments, gaming, open-innovation networks, and other approaches. For example, virtual trading rooms allow students to "trade" stocks. Nursing students use mannequins and simulations to practice procedures. Capstone experiences often focus on real-world problems. Such activities have high impact because students discover the relevance of learning through real-world application.[11]

Feed-forward: Along with providing feedback, the learning experience should draw learners into new experiences, engaging them in "wanting to know" and connecting them with how to learn more. Recommendation systems can support "feed-forward" mechanisms, e.g., suggesting the next course or experience.

Structured autonomy: Students can drive their own learning, but not without structure or support. Assistance can be provided by motivating students, providing them with a road map or pathway, and by providing the prompts, guides, and hints that can help learners past obstacles. Carnegie Mellon University's Open Learning Initiative (OLI) provides these types of guides and supports for learners (see Chapter 15). Online communities—formal and informal—can provide support, as well.

Support Services

Information technology can change the college or university experience through its impact on support services. The "experience" of the library is no longer a card catalog (even one online)—it is about portals, learning commons, and integrated support. The "experience" of advising is not limited to course selection—it is a reflective and integrative experience involving e-portfolios, allowing students to organize learning around themselves (aspirations, achievements, and reflections), rather than just around courses or the curriculum.[12] Beyond the many examples of how IT changes student support, the way it shifts models is also important. Three examples illustrate some options.

Peer-to-peer: Academic support can be distributed throughout the community—a peer-to-peer approach—rather than being provided by an "expert." For example, OpenStudy (http://www.openstudy.com) allows students to help each other rather than relying on a faculty member. OpenStudy is a social-learning network where students can give and receive help. Assistance may be in the form of a live chat, a response posted online, or through a drawing board where users help each other solve problems. Grockit (https://grockit.com/) is another example of an online social-studying network, with participants in 170 countries. Few institutions can provide expert help 24/7 within traditional structures. A shift to a peer-to-peer model provides new opportunities.

External service provider: Services are provided by organizations outside of higher education. For example, Parchment (http://www.parchment.com) allows users to request, store, and send educational credentials. Beyond sending transcripts to prospective institutions, students can use their transcript to compare their credentials with what colleges require, receiving recommendations about where to apply. Parchment also allows students to estimate their chances of being admitted to a specific institution and to compare themselves with other applicants.

Informed choice: Other services link education and careers, helping students make better-informed choices. Career Cruising (http://public.careercruising.com/us/en) encourages students to think about their future career goals and the studies required to achieve those goals. For younger ages, an educational game helps students learn more about careers, life planning, and social skills. Other related services are provided as well, such as test preparation (e.g., for ACT and SAT exams), tools to help students manage college applications, and role-playing modules.

Collaboration

IT can change the game through its catalytic role in collaboration. With the Internet, everything and everyone is connected. It provides an architecture for participation and collaboration.[13] Individuals are empowered with information. Teams can form around any topic or problem. IT has created a participatory culture.

Wikipedia is a well-known example of participation and collaboration. The technology provides an infrastructure that allows individuals to contribute what they know to a collective work that becomes better through sharing and use. Individual contributions are not limited by training, title, or employer. Wikipedia illustrates the subtle shift in emphasis from IT as a technology to its value in facilitating a process of collaboration whereby value is created through the interaction of contributors and users.[14] The result is a community product.

IT and collaboration form the basis for crowdsourcing, such as when innovation and problem solving come from the global community, not just an internal R&D unit. At a scale never before possible, collaboration is being harnessed to solve some of higher education and society's most challenging problems. These collaborations are important for higher education because they represent real-world experiences, personal contributions, and opportunities for research, as well.

For example, Innovation Exchange (http://www.innovationexchange.com) allows community members to respond to challenges sponsored by Global 5000 companies and not-for-profit organizations (e.g., minimizing the water used for cleaning and sanitizing, making multilayered packaging more recyclable). The web-based community expands the sponsors' innovation capacity beyond their internal research and development teams. Innovation Exchange uses a pay-for-performance model (e.g., prizes of $50,000). TopCoder (http://www.topcoder.com) brings together a competitive software development community with over 250,000 coders from 200 countries. The individual or individuals who develop the best code receive a prize.

Whether called open innovation, innovation intermediaries, or crowdsourcing, innovation is "outsourced" to the community, tapping into individual expertise, passion, and competitiveness. Because the work is not sourced "in-house," the model, costs, and reach all shift.

Colleges and universities engage in a variety of research and instructional collaborations. For example, a large cancer-research collaboration, caBIG, brings together a virtual network of data, individuals, and organizations to focus on cancer research. The community has redefined how research is conducted by adapting or building its own tools, connecting the community through sharable, interoperable digital infrastructure and a common set of standards (http://cabig.cancer.gov/about/).

Citizen science is another manifestation of collaboration. Cornell University, for example, hosts a citizen-science site on ornithology (http://www.birds.cornell.edu). More than 200,000 people gather data, which allows scientists to determine how birds are affected by habitat loss, pollution, disease, and so forth, resulting in scientific papers (more than sixty since 1997), as well as management guidelines and advocacy material. Participation by "citizen scientists" (e.g., 1,000,000 bird observations reported to eBird on average each month; 15,000 people count birds at their feeders for Project FeederWatch) allows the researchers to extend their reach well beyond the university team.

Collaboration is tapped through a variety of formats, including games. Foldit (http://fold.it/portal) is a computer game enabling users to contribute to research about protein folding. Proteins influence many diseases (e.g., HIV/AIDS, cancer, Alzheimer's); they can also be part of the cure. Protein structure determines how the protein works and how to target it with drugs. Protein folding is complex; current research methods are expensive even with supercomputers. Foldit takes advantage of humans' puzzle-solving intuitions—people play competitively to fold the proteins. Players also can design proteins to help prevent or treat important diseases. Foldit papers have been accepted in scientific journals such as *Nature Biotechnology*, *Nature*, and the *Proceedings of the National Academy of Sciences*.

Shared Infrastructure

IT enables sharing, including the sharing of expensive infrastructures—whether those are information, technology, or people. Because digital resources can be shared and are independent of time and location, it is increasingly possible for resources to be shared among institutions—aggregating supply/demand or use/curation. For example, digital copies of books can be used by multiple parties, even simultaneously. Rather than each institution digitizing copies of the same books, colleges and universities can choose which institution digitizes which volumes and which institution stores the original print version. Such collaborations can reduce costs (digitization, storage, etc.) and stretch resources.

For example, the libraries at Columbia University and Cornell University collaborate on digitizing and sharing library collections in a project named 2CUL (the moniker, pronounced "too cool," is derived the from libraries' acronyms). Although the broader 2CUL initiative encompasses many areas of shared library services, such as collection development, cataloging, and staff expertise, a key focus of the project is developing the technology infrastructure that enables the partners to improve book and digital-document delivery and e-resource management, as well as provide a shared long-term archive of digital materials. Columbia and Cornell believe this shared service will transform the way their library systems provide content and services to their constituencies, realizing that they can achieve more together than they can alone.

HathiTrust provides another example of shared infrastructure. HathiTrust is a large-scale repository of digital materials owned by a collective of over sixty research libraries in the United States and one in Europe. HathiTrust operates on a model of shared governance and financing, collecting, preserving, and making digital materials accessible. Also, HathiTrust is developing discovery and computational tools that enable researchers to search and analyze digital content, including formats other than books and journals. As of late 2011, the trust's repository contains almost 10 million digital volumes, 27 percent of which are public domain titles.

Other types of infrastructure can be shared as well, such as networks, processing capability, and data storage. For example, TeraGrid was a grid computing infrastructure (high-performance computing resources, databases, tools, and experimental facilities) combining the resources of eleven institutions. Learning tools can also be shared. For example, iLabs is a collection of online laboratories that can be accessed through the Internet, allowing students to conduct lab experiments anywhere and at any time. Open-courseware collections could be considered a shared infrastructure. For example, the Saylor Foundation's Saylor.org is an open-access online-learning platform that provides self-paced college-level courseware to the public free of charge.

Informed Decision Making

IT can change the game by enabling better decisions. Colleges and universities strive to improve their decision making, often turning to analytics. Analytics can include trend analysis, regression analysis, forecasting, simulation, prediction, data visualization, and optimization. Analytics can be used to spot trends or make choices. In business, for example, analytics is used to monitor credit cards for fraud, predict product needs, monitor "reputation" on social networks, and optimize workloads.

Higher education uses analytics to inform decisions about admissions, fund raising, learning, student retention, and operational efficiency. In an era of "big data," analytics is more than reporting. There are more data than ever, and the speed of processing allows questions to be asked:

- What happened?
- How often and where?
- What exactly is the problem?
- What actions are needed?
- Why is this happening?
- What if these trends continue?
- What will happen next?
- What's the best that can happen?[15]

Higher education's adoption of analytics is growing in response to demands for accountability and the need for greater efficiency and continuous improvement.

Analytics can track and predict student performance, providing alerts to students when their patterns indicate they are at risk of poor performance. In other cases, faculty or advisors are alerted to potential problems, allowing them to intervene and provide specific types of assistance to students.

Purdue University's Course Signals project uses data from course management systems and other data sources. Algorithms are used to highlight patterns associated with poor performance. Alerts (e.g., e-mails) can be sent to students or faculty flagging those who might be at risk. With Course Signals, grades improved consistently at both the course and departmental level. Students in courses using Course Signals received more Bs and Cs, with fewer Ds and Fs, than those in sections that did not use the tool. For example, in a large undergraduate biology course, there was a 12 percent improvement in B and C grades, with a 14 percent reduction in D and F grades. While withdrawals remained about the same, there was a 14 percent increase in early withdrawals (those done early enough to avoid affecting the student's GPA).[16] In some courses, As and Bs increased as much as 28 percent.[17]

The University of Maryland, Baltimore County, uses analytics so that students can compare their progress with that of their peers through a self-service feedback tool, Check My Activity (CMA). CMA uses data from the university's course management system, allowing students to compare their online course activity against an anonymous group of peers who earned the same, a higher, or a lower grade for any assignment. Peer comparisons improve students' awareness and understanding of the link between their behaviors and performance as they monitor their course progress.[18]

Analytics can provide feedback to faculty and course designers, allowing them to make targeted improvements to course material. Carnegie Mellon's Open Learning Initiative (OLI) uses analytics to gather feedback at multiple levels for continuous improvement, as well as for research. While students are working through the course, data are collected to provide insight to students, faculty, course designers, and learning scientists. In a study of the OLI statistics course, students learned a full semester's worth of material in half the time and performed as well as or better than students using traditional instruction over a full semester. Retention of material was not significantly different when OLI and traditional students were tested more than a semester later.[19] In tests of OLI at community colleges, students learned 33 percent more material in the OLI sections.[20] (See Chapter 15.)

Making good choices about a program of study may be as important as knowing how well a course is progressing. Choosing the best course, sequence of courses, and program of study is a game changer for students and institutions. *Ambient intelligence* is a term used to describe services that personalize recommendations for users, such as recommendations one might receive on Amazon. Ambient intelligence is dependent on information technology to collect fine-grained information about users, compare it with information from millions of others, and return tailored recommendations that are adaptive (e.g., change in response to users), personalized, and anticipatory. Ambient intelligence powers sites such as eHarmony, Netflix, and others.

Many students have difficulty knowing what courses to take—courses that will apply toward their degree as well as courses that suit their learning style or schedule. Applications that compare a student with others who have similar goals and preferences can suggest courses or degree options for students. With hundreds or even thousands of options, students (and advisors) may find the alternatives too overwhelming to make the best-informed choice.

Applications such as SHERPA (Service-Oriented Higher Education Recommendation Personalization Assistant), developed by Saddleback College in Orange County, California, remember students' preferences and make recommendations for courses, scheduling, and open sections. Such recommendation engines can help both students and advisors who are challenged to know all the available and appropriate options—especially if students have work schedules or other personal circumstances to accommodate.[21]

Austin Peay State University's course recommendation system, Degree Compass, provides personal recommendations to students for courses that best suit their program of study and their talents. The recommendations are not based on what students will "like" the most, but on the courses that apply to the students' program of study, course sequencing, and where they are likely to achieve the best outcomes. The system provides information to advisors and department chairs to help them target interventions and adjust course availability, as well. Students benefit through reduced time to graduation. Future enhancements may help students select majors. (See Case Study 3.)

Other recommendation engines are being developed to help guide students through transfer and degree completion, such as the University of Hawaii's STAR program. (See Case Study 7.) The cost and time savings could be significant. One national estimate of the redundant costs to students, institutions (e.g., financial aid), and government (e.g., delayed tax revenue) for students who take too many credits (through inefficient transfer or excess credits) is $30 billion per year. The annual costs for credits that do not help a student move toward a degree are estimated to exceed $7 billion.[22]

Unbundling and Rebundling

Beyond its value as technology, IT is a game changer by enabling new models through its ability to decouple, disaggregate, and dematerialize.[23] Clayton Christensen's theory of "disruptive innovation" highlights IT as the catalyst of new models that may be a result of splitting, substituting, augmenting, excluding, and/or inverting. Such models not only use technology but are based on different business models.

A business model is an organization's blueprint for creating, delivering, and capturing value. All models involve a "customer value proposition," a "value chain," and a revenue formula. Possible models for higher education include:[24]

- Open business models—these models use external as well as internal ideas and resources. For example, an "outside in" model uses external ideas and resources to support the institution (e.g., open educational resources used in courses).

- Unbundled models—in these models, providers of specific products (e.g., student recruitment services or infrastructure services) are integrated into an institution's structure.

- Facilitated network models—these bring together a mixture of products and services from multiple organizations to improve a service.

Information technology allows institutions to unbundle and rebundle many activities that were previously bound to a physical location (e.g., the campus) or assumed to be the role of a single individual (e.g., a faculty member). This ability to mix-and-match in new ways makes it possible for institutions to change traditional models. Institutions such as BYU-Idaho are choosing to not replicate all the elements of a traditional college or university model. In the case of BYU-Idaho, the academic calendar, faculty rewards, intercollegiate athletics, and instructional models are different.[25] They have documented improvements in the quality of the student experience, lowered the relative cost of education, and served more students.[26]

Western Governors University is a well-known institution that has selectively unbundled and rebundled traditional university functions. For example, WGU has separated traditional faculty roles, unbundling curriculum development from course delivery. Faculty identify the best courses but do not write the courses themselves. Mentoring is provided at the course level as well as through the student's program of study; mentors do not develop the curriculum. Credit hours as the unit of measurement have been displaced by competency exams (see Chapter 9). Similarly, the University of Phoenix distributes faculty roles differently from traditional institutions, centralizing course development, for example (see Chapter 10).

Peer 2 Peer University (P2PU) is an open-education project that uses peer learning rather than instructor-led learning, unbundling and rebundling a number of traditional elements. P2PU uses volunteer-facilitated courses, informal study groups, and one-on-one mentorship and community support. Anyone can decide to run a course or create a study group. Open educational resources and online social learning provide the learning experience. P2PU does not certify learning or offer degrees.

Experiments on the certification of learning are being conducted through programs such as Mozilla Badges (see Case Study 6) and OER university (http://wikieducator.org/OER_university/Home). These models decouple learning and certification. OER university, for example, is not intended to be a formal teaching institution. Rather, it is designed as a partnership with accredited institutions that provides credit for open educational resources–based learning.

Although more common in business and industry, many organizations contract for their online services through others (e.g., Target's online site is powered by Amazon). Higher education institutions contract for services with hundreds of firms. Institutions such as the University of Southern California (USC) have outsourced online program development (e.g., to 2tor for the USC Master of Teaching program; see Chapter 17). Other providers, such as Altius Education, provide online program-development services to institutions such as Tiffin University.[27]

The number of organizations providing disaggregated services has grown significantly in the last several years. Smarthinking provides course support. Khan Academy and YouTube provide videos and online lectures. Groups such as GoingOn provide platforms for academic and social engagement through online communities and Facebook-like exchanges. Courses are provided through such avenues as the OpenCourseWare (OCW) initiative, a large-scale, web-based publication of MIT course materials. These organizations make it easier for higher education to assemble the most appropriate mixture of products and services, offered by multiple organizations. These services help institutions achieve greater economies of scale—and economies of scope, by offering the wide array of programs and services desired by students.[28] Colleges and universities can selectively assemble the elements that best serve their needs.

Conclusion

We ask a great deal of higher education: "to prepare leaders, train employees, provide the creative base for scientific and artistic discovery, transmit past culture, create new knowledge, redress the legacies of discrimination, and ensure continuation of democratic principles." No matter how much higher education has achieved, we have greater expectations—for our students, our institutions, and our society. In an age reshaped by technology, we have great expectations that IT can help higher education achieve even more.

A large number of educational practitioners are using IT to reshape education. The hope is that even more individuals and institutions will do so. Our greatest challenge will not be IT but our ability to *un*learn our experience of higher education. Our assumptions, beliefs, and behaviors may be unconscious.[29] What kind of higher education enterprise would we create if we treated all beliefs as hypotheses rather than rigid legacies?[30] Information technology can be a game changer in the complex adaptive system that is higher education. Consider the technologies that have changed the game and changed our models—the Internet, e-mail, Facebook, Twitter, instant messaging, Wikipedia, and more.

Higher education must move beyond the fear of what we have to lose with IT and new models. Different models serve different needs. For higher education to achieve its mission, we owe it to ourselves and society to use IT well and wisely. It can be a game changer.

Notes

1. Eden Dahlstrom, Tom de Boor, Peter Grunwald, and Martha Vockley, *ECAR National Study of Undergraduate Students and Information Technology, 2011 Report*, with

foreword by Diana Oblinger (Boulder, CO: EDUCAUSE Center for Applied Research, October 2011).

2. Amy L. Ostrom, Mary Jo Bitner, and Kevin A. Burkhard, "Leveraging Service Blueprinting to Rethink Higher Education," October 2011: 9, http://www.americanprogress.org/issues/2011/10/pdf/service_blueprinting.pdf.

3. Ibid.

4. Randy Bass, "Disrupting Ourselves: Cherished Assumptions, New Designs, and the Problem of Learning in Higher Ed" (keynote at EDUCAUSE Mid-Atlantic Regional Conference 2012, Baltimore, Maryland, January 11, 2012).

5. Chris Dede, "Transforming Higher Education with Emerging Technologies" (speech at *EDUCAUSE Learning Initiative Annual Meeting*, Austin, Texas, February 14, 2012).

6. Ibid.

7. Bass, "Disrupting Ourselves."

8. Diana Rhoten, Laurie Racine, and Phoenix Wang, "Designing for Learning in the 21st Century" (working paper), http://startl.org/wp-content/uploads/2009/11/21stCenturyLearning1.pdf

9. J. S. Brown, A. Collins, and S. Duguid, "Situated Cognition and the Culture of Learning," *Educational Researcher* 18, no. 1 (1989): 32–42.

10. Seymour Papert, "Hard Fun," http://www.papert.org/articles/HardFun.html; Seymour Papert, "Does Easy Do It? Children, Games, and Learning," http://www.papert.org/articles/Doeseasydoit.html.

11. Bass, "Disrupting Ourselves."

12. Ibid.

13. "EDUCAUSE Values: Collaboration," *EDUCAUSE Review* 47, no. 2 (March/April 2012).

14. Henry Jenkins, "What Wikipedia Can Teach Us About the New Media Literacies," ELI Annual Meeting, January 28, 2008, San Antonio, TX.

15. SAS.com Magazine, "Eight Levels of Analytics," http://www.sas.com/news/sascom/2008q4/column_8levels.html; George Siemens, "Leaping the Chasm: Moving from Buzzwords to Implementation of Learning Analytics" (speaker at EDUCAUSE Live! webinar, February 1, 2012).

16. Kimberly Arnold, "Signals: Applying Academic Analytics," *EDUCAUSE Quarterly* 33, no. 1, (2010).

17. John P. Campbell and Kimberly Arnold, *Course Signals: The Past, Current, and Future Application of Analytics* (report from 2011 EDUCAUSE Annual Conference, Philadelphia and Online, October 18–21, 2011), http://www.educause.edu/sites/default/files/library/presentations/E11/SESS031/CS%2BED2011.pdf

18. See http://www.educause.edu/EDUCAUSE+Quarterly/EDUCAUSEQuarterlyMagazine Volum/VideoDemoofUMBCsCheckMyActivit/219113 and http://www.slideshare.net/BCcampus/learning-analytics-fritz.

19. Ross Strader and Candace Thille, "The Open Learning Initiative: Enacting Instruction Online," in *Game Changers: Education and Information Technologies*, ed. Diana Oblinger (Washington, DC: EDUCAUSE, 2012), citing M. Lovett, O. Meyer, and C.

Thille, "The Open Learning Initiative: Measuring the Effectiveness of the OLI Statistics Course in Accelerating Student Learning," *Journal of Interactive Media in Education* (2008), retrieved from http://jime.open.ac.uk/2008/14/.

20. Strader and Thille, "The Open Learning Initiative," citing C. D. Schunn and M. Patchan, *An Evaluation of Accelerated Learning in the CMU Open Learning Initiative Course Logic & Proofs* (technical report by Learning Research and Development Center, University of Pittsburgh, Pittsburgh, PA, 2009).

21. See http://www.ocregister.com/news/sherpa-268815-college-students.html.

22. See http://www.academyone.com/Portals/1/Collateral/Clear%20Roadblocks%20for%20College%20Transfer%20Students_AEI_May_2010.pdf.

23. Gary Hamel, "Reinventing Management for a Networked World" (presented at EDUCAUSE Annual Conference 2010, Anaheim, California: October 12–15, 2010).

24. Robert Sheets and Stephen Crawford, "Harnessing the Power of Information Technology: Open Business Models in Higher Education," *EDUCAUSE Review* 47, no. 2 (March/April 2012).

25. Clayton M. Christensen and Henry J. Eyring, *The Innovative University: Changing the DNA of Higher Education from the Inside Out* (San Francisco: Jossey-Bass, 2011).

26. Clayton Christensen, "How to Manage the Disruption of Higher Education" (in *Forum Futures 2010*, a compilation of summaries of the papers presented and discussed at the Forum for the Future of Higher Education's 2009 Aspen Symposium).

27. See http://chronicle.com/article/Investor-Groups-May-Be-Nonp/63876/.

28. Sheets and Crawford, "Harnessing the Power of Information Technology."

29. Ibid.

30. Hamel, "Reinventing Management."

Diana Oblinger is President and CEO of EDUCAUSE. She is known for launching innovative initiatives, such as the EDUCAUSE Learning Initiative (ELI) and the Next Generation Learning Challenges. Previously, she held positions at the University of North Carolina system, University of Missouri, Michigan State University, IBM, and Microsoft. Oblinger has authored and edited numerous books and publications, including the award-winning What Business Wants from Higher Education.

4

From Metrics to Analytics, Reporting to Action: Analytics' Role in Changing the Learning Environment

Linda Baer and John Campbell

WHAT WILL THE GAME-CHANGING TOOL KIT LOOK LIKE for next-generation learning? How can institutions prepare to meet the increasing demands? Institutions will be required to transition from metrics to analytics and from reporting to actionable interventions. In this next generation of the learning environment, analytics will play a role in higher education. But leading the institution from metrics to analytics and reporting to action will require a significant institutional shift.

Setting the Context

A renewed sense of urgency for improving higher education's accountability, transparency, and performance is in place—the result of a perfect storm of state budget challenges, the ongoing transition from a manufacturing to a knowledge economy, and the inability of the value of higher education to be appropriately articulated. Students, parents, accreditation agencies, and other external constituencies are demanding more from higher education, searching for an overall return on this investment from the student, state, and federal perspective. Issues requiring attention include increasing degree completion and decreasing the achievement gap, as well as changing the focus from access to success and from seat time to competencies. As with all aspects of learning, these challenges cannot be met with simple changes. Institutions must strive to develop analytics or "actionabl e intelligence" in all institutional areas—particularly in learning.

Higher education has access to more data than ever before. Technological tools and resources are strengthening the institutional capacity to access data to improve decision making. Smarter tools that are leading to adaptive learning and personalized opportunities will soon be a reality. In fact, analytics on institutional data will prove key to transforming student retention, graduation, and success.

Performance metrics on student learning, progression, and completion are becoming more prevalent across the country, driven by efforts from the White House, statehouses, accrediting agencies, and local communities.

- The American Graduation Initiative, proposed by the Obama administration (but not passed), called for states and colleges to "establish quantifiable targets for improving graduation rates" in order to access available federal funds.[1]

- The Obama administration seeks to increase the number of college graduates by 5 million by 2020. The administration believes this is necessary to rebuild the capacity and competitiveness of America's workforce.[2]

- Twenty-nine states have joined the Complete College America Alliance of States to develop specific plans to improve college completion rates.[3]

- The National Governors Association targeted the Complete to Compete initiative, which focuses on increasing the number of students in the United States who complete college degrees and certificates.

According to Complete College America, nearly one in two students pursuing a bachelor's degree will not obtain that credential within six years, and fewer than one in three will complete a two-year college degree in three years. Sixty-two percent of jobs will require college education by 2018, and more than half of those will require at least a bachelor's degree.[4]

In *Education Pays,* Baum and Payea describe the value of a college education. Higher education continues to help people attain success both socially and economically. In addition, college graduates experience a host of other benefits from a college education, such as increased earnings, increased voting behavior, lower rates of incarceration, and higher rates of good health and charitable activity.[5]

A college degree nearly doubles annual earnings. The report entitled *The Big Payoff*[6] reveals that over the course of an adult's working life, high school graduates can expect, on average, to earn $1.2 million; those with a bachelor's degree, $2.1 million; and people with a master's degree, $2.5 million. Persons with doctoral degrees earn an average of $3.4 million during their working life, while those with professional degrees earn the most, at $4.4 million. This additional income will fuel the national economy and raise the standard of living.[7]

Yet, results from a recent report by Complete College America entitled *Time Is the Enemy*[8] indicate that

- 75 percent of today's students are juggling family, jobs, and college while commuting;
- part-time students rarely graduate;
- poor students and students of color struggle the most to graduate;
- students are taking too many credits and too much time to complete; and
- remediation is broken, producing few students who ultimately graduate.

With the national, state, and local calls for more accountability comes the need for institutions to develop more data capacity and to optimize student retention and completion. According to Bailey et al. in *Unleashing the Potential of Technology in Education,* "We are at the dawn of an era in which educators have the potential to harness technology to produce a step change in student achievement. Although visionaries have been promising for years that technology would transform primary and secondary education—and despite the billions of dollars spent on networking schools and equipping them with computers and other devices—the actual impact on student outcomes to date has been disappointing. Yet when technology is strategically introduced into every step of the educational value chain, it does, in fact, have the potential to enhance every aspect of instruction and learning." In order to dramatically improve student outcomes, technology must be fully aligned with educational objectives, standards, curricula, assessments, interventions, and professional development.[9]

Emergence of Analytics: An Evolution of Enterprise and Instructional Systems

The interest among higher education institutions in analytics has grown since early projects impacting student success were highlighted by Campbell, DuBlois, and Oblinger. In their 2007 article "Academic Analytics," the authors cite that institutions' response to internal and external pressures for accountability in higher education, especially in the areas of improved learning outcomes and student success, will require IT leaders to step up and become critical partners with academics and student affairs. They argue that IT can help answer this call for accountability through academic analytics, which was emerging as a critical component of the next-generation learning environment.[10]

As the interest in academic analytics in higher education has grown, so have the escalating accountability demands that are driving performance measurement and improvement in interventions. Improving performance will require coordinated measurement, intervention, and action across the entire education/workforce spectrum—from "cradle to career."[11]

There is a wide continuum of activities within the ecosystem of analytics. As Phil Long and George Siemens relate: "Analytics spans the full scope and range of activity in higher education, affecting administration, research, teaching and learning, and support resources. The college/university thus must become a more intentional, intelligent organization, with data, evidence, and analytics playing the central role in this transition."[12]

The emergence of analytics is the result of the evolution of enterprise and instructional systems,[13] which began in the 1990s when administrative systems were stand-alone, legacy systems. Hardware decisions pit mainframes against minicomputers. Business operations and information were siloed. Pre-1995 teaching and learning systems were fragmented. By the late 1990s, enterprise systems were becoming better integrated, resulting in data being more easily integrated. Over time, technology advances enabled more "fully integrated systems"[14] allowing for greater transactional efficiency, information integration, reporting and business analytics, business intelligence, as well as recruiting and retention improvements.

Academic systems were slower to develop, but eventually course information systems (CIS), course management systems (CMS), and learning management systems (LMS) were developed. Later, Internet and web-based products and services began to emerge. This allowed for the convergence of administrative and academic systems at the enterprise level. Institutions began to address enterprise-wide systems including LMS and student information systems. Enterprise portals continued the evolution with the ability to access and integrate ERPs, LMS, and knowledge assets, creating a self-service foundation for students, faculty, and staff.

By 2004, the technology infrastructure fused networking, integrated software (e.g., ERP), security, and vast digital resources. Open source application software grew steadily, with technology focusing on security, open sources, web services, and network services.

For the past fifteen years, the emphasis of IT has been on the development of technology infrastructure. Today the emphasis goes beyond the infrastructure and includes business processes and strategic alignments. Calls for enhanced performance and demonstrated value have moved to the development of open-source/open-architecture developments and the ability to leverage the stack and the cloud. Today we are seeing the first generation of student/institutional portfolios, executive dashboards, and assessment/performance management systems within an open architecture environment.[15] In addition, in the LMS 2.0, consolidations of campus LMS options were available. Database infrastructures including data warehouses began to be developed.

Analytics will be an essential future part of higher education. Institutions' previous efforts of capturing data, providing availability in data warehouses, and initial data mining efforts are foundational to the next generation of activities. Higher education is benefiting from the extensive business intelligence efforts found in the corporate world and will develop new integrated solutions within the learning environment as one takes advantage of the LMS, SIS, and other emerging tools.

Building Analytics Capacity

Academic analytics relies on the extraction of data from one or more systems, such as the CMS or a student information system. The data, which may be stored in a data warehouse for ongoing use, is analyzed using statistical software, and a mathematical model is generated. Based on the model and predetermined values, a particular action may be triggered, such as sending the student an electronic notification or initiating a personal intervention by college/university staff.

For example, data extracted from a student information system provides baseline student demographic, academic performance, and aptitude information. The CMS provides a snapshot of the student's course-related efforts by providing real-time interaction information that allows for comparison with peers. The two sources of data are combined to predict the probability of student success. Using this probability, the institution can decide whether to take certain actions such as inviting a student to a help session via e-mail or calling a student with an invitation to meet with an advisor.

Beyond the data, technology, and statistical requirements, academic analytics projects require skill and leadership. Three characteristics of successful academic analytics projects include:

- leaders who are committed to evidence-based decision making
- staff who are skilled at data analysis
- a flexible technology platform that is available to collect, mine, and analyze data.

Any academic analytics effort begins with leaders who are committed to decision making based on institutional data. Analytics can be used to examine key institutional issues, such as enrollment or retention, which by their nature are complex and often sensitive, but the decision to move forward with analytics depends on knowledgeable champions among senior administrators.

The second critical component to building an academic analytics initiative is staffing. Staff members involved in analytics efforts often include database administrators, institutional researchers, educational researchers, programmers, and domain specialists (e.g., student services, retention, development/ advancement). Academic computing staff may be needed to collect information from various academic systems such as the CMS. The team must have the skill to build predictive models based on institutional data guided by educational research. Other staff may be needed to focus on policy development and clarify who has access to the data, how the data can be used, and which data-security models are required.

Since analytics requires data analysis, institutions will need to invest in effective training to produce skilled analytics staff. Obtaining or developing skilled staff may present the largest barrier and the greatest cost to any academic analytics initiative. Whether such staff are added to existing institutional research units or are cultivated in the IT organization, student-affairs divisions, or academic units will depend on the organizational culture and the locus of resources.

The third element in any academic analytics project is technology. A data warehouse is the key component of the technology infrastructure, housing information from a variety of sources in a common structure that enables data analysis. To populate the data warehouse, the institution will need to build a "bridge" between the application and the warehouse. For some applications, standard interfaces facilitate the transfer of data. For other applications, interface development requires significant programming effort.

Piecing together a coherent academic analytics effort can be difficult, requiring support from many units: enrollment management, institutional research, IT, the registrar's office, academic divisions, student affairs, and more. Standards must be agreed upon for the data (e.g., is enrollment based on head count on day seven after the start of the semester or on day ten?). Extracting information from academic systems requires careful analysis and programming effort. Building the appropriate models requires staff with statistics and educational research backgrounds. Creating interventions requires domain knowledge (e.g., advising, retention) and advising/counseling skills. For institutions to be successful in academic analytics projects, IT leaders must build a coalition of people.

Leading Change

The role that analytics can play within the learning environment will largely depend on the institution's vision of the next-generation learning environment. Part of that vision can be "actionable intelligence" where tools and data reduce risk of student failure and maximize the odds of student success.

The initial wave of learning analytics tools are emerging. They seek to improve the understanding of the ways students, faculty, and advisors can improve student retention and success. Much as various course management systems emerged in the 1990s, higher education is seeing the first generation of predictive modeling, adaptive learning tools, early warning tools, and new data visualization tools to enable decision makers to access and use data in a timely manner. As with early course management systems, institutions should also anticipate a significant evolution in tools and capabilities.

Leaders need to create an institutional culture to use analytics tools to maximize the potential for improved student access, student learning, progression, and success.

An institution should consider several key steps to the adoption of analytics:[16]

- Identify thought leaders for using data to solve instructional challenges.
- Build the existing predictive modeling capacity and expand across the programs.
- Identify what data are important and the metrics used to measure them.
- Identify best-in-class analytical and predictive modeling tools, applications, and processes.
- Embed changes in analytics in institutional processes.
- Aggressively develop organizational capacity for using analytics.
- Create a communication plan.

Identify thought leaders for using data to solve instructional challenges: As previously indicated, the three characteristics for a successful academic analytics effort are leaders, staff, and technology. It is the people at the institutions that are the most critical component to leading a successful change. One should begin by identifying individuals who are looking to make data-based decisions, which might include a mix of faculty, advisors, student services, and technology staff. Identifying a mix of people that includes those who are already making small decisions based on data with those looking to address larger institutional goals will be essential to success.

Build the existing predictive modeling capacity and expand across the programs: What programs and departments are already utilizing predictive modeling at institutions? Take a proactive approach and open the discussions with the campus community. A number of smaller models might already exist. For example, a department might have already connected attendance at orientation sessions for returning adult students with likely success in the programs. Institutions can also begin by examining their admissions process—what are the key factors to being admitted to the institution? Based on the existing models and those perceived models, how might they be combined to provide a more holistic view?

Identify what data are important and the metrics used to measure them and the alignment to institutional goals: Based on the key institutional goals, what data would help inform the potential solutions? For example, if the institution is focused on retention, what data might help inform staff on the potential for an individual student to remain at the institution? One might consider academic preparation (application data, placement tests, etc.), effort (learning management system, attendance, etc.), integration into the campus community (participation in learning communities, student activities, etc.), and willingness to seek help (visiting advisors, help centers, etc.). Each of the data sources could provide insight to the overall problem. The key element for success is identifying a starting point and continually adding new data to develop additional insights.

Identify best-in-class analytical and predictive modeling tools, applications, and processes: Many tools and resources are available to better serve students across their educational pathway. The field is seeing the increase in adaptive learning tools, early warning tools, use of social data to better understand student engagement and integration to campus, and new data visualization tools to enable decision makers to access and use data in a timely manner. What tools are institutions most interested in learning more about to improve student success? Leaders need to better understand how to select and use analytics tools for changing the learning equation to improve student access, progression, and success. They need to draw on data-supported evidence, which is now even more powerful with the expanded capabilities of learning analytics, predictive modeling, and tools that map to interventions that assist students. Leaders also need to understand the importance of building learning environments that support evidence and inquiry across the institution. Analytical packages should be considered as the first generation; be prepared to actively engage providers/consortia on new functionalities or even to migrate to new solutions.

Embed changes in analytics in institutional processes: Institutions should consider how to embed small analytics projects within existing programs, leveraging existing data and integrating into current student-success efforts. For example, if the biology department is seeking to increase retention of majors, what data might indicate a likelihood of students staying within the major? Leaders need to consider methods of going beyond reporting and find new ways to proactively assist students. In addition to a programmatic approach, the institution should identify mechanisms in which data is available for all areas that it can utilize.

Aggressively develop organizational capacity for using analytics: Analytics is a new tool for the next generation of learning. As such, the skills must be developed. While the need for the technical skills of data mining and statistical analysis is obvious, such skills as process analysis, assessment, and instructional design are also essential to the process. The goal for analytics must remain "actionable intelligence," and as such, the capacity for analytics must go beyond data and statistics and focus on how the information must be utilized.

Create a communication plan: In order to sustain and scale the development of an analytics agenda, it is imperative that leaders regularly communicate with stakeholders about the process and the outcomes. Focus and attention on how the analytics strategies affect performance, productivity, and value will form the foundation for the next-generation learning model. The organization use visualization tools to maximize the message while customizing reports for the right stakeholders. Regular communication will increase the trust and overall use of the analytics, which can build the culture of evidence and inquiry required to sustain the efforts.

The Future

Innovation has been characterized as new creative products, ideas, activities, or interventions that produce an improved result. The future of analytics promises to be both a sustaining and disruptive innovation for education. Analytics as a sustaining innovation refers to the normal upgrading and integration of analytics into current teaching and learning tools. Today, institutions can implement a variety of analytics solutions as part of the course management and student information systems. Analytics as a sustaining innovation will serve higher education by providing incremental improvements in the existing system, while not widely disrupting the institutional processes. An example of a sustaining innovation is using predictive analytics to identify at-risk students early so institutions can intervene in a timely manner to increase the likelihood of success. Research in the report *Time is the Enemy* by Complete College America references several ways to improve success for full-time and part-time students, including simplifying the registration process; accelerating the time to degree completion; blocking schedules with fixed, predictable classroom meeting times; forming peer support and learning networks; embedding remediation into the regular curriculum; and reducing time in the classroom through the use of online technologies.[17]

Analytics as a disruptive innovation refers to new products, ideas, activities, or interventions that require changing behavior/processes or modifying other products/services. Analytics in this form breaks with current practice to serve the student, faculty, and administrative users in radically different ways; it serves new populations (or serves an existing population in radically different ways) and, in so doing, creates entirely new systems to accomplish this.[18] As the organization maps analytics strategies, both sustaining and disruptive innovations are possible

We can anticipate several new disruptive innovations from analytics:

- Utilizing "social" data to better understand student integration into campus. Research has found that environmental factors are equally as important as academic factors in student retention. How a student integrates into the social fabric, the formation of friendships and support groups, the adjustment into student housing, and similar factors all play an important role in student success. As the use of social media continues to increase, one could imagine mapping social connections to determine which students are having difficulty with connecting to the institution. Collecting, analyzing, and acting upon such data could potentially bring new groups together, ranging from housing, advising, and student groups.

- The growth of CRM as a collection point. Traditionally the "customer relationship management" (CRM) system has been focused on the admissions process. One could imagine future analytical tools coming together in a "learning relationship management" (LRM) system that would be open to faculty and advisors. The system would not only provide a central point for analytics data, but would also provide a way of tracking interventions and related results. The LRM system would provide a comprehensive foundation for end-to-end student support.

- Emergence of adaptive learning. If efforts to use analytics to predict success proved fruitful, the next significant step would be to use analytics to power adaptive systems that adapt to the learner's needs based on behaviors of the individual as well as of past students' patterns.

- Disaggregation of the data sources and the emergence of new analytics techniques. Analytics has focused primarily on integrating techniques into the course management and student information systems. When data from many different sources can be integrated, including audience response systems, publisher content, social media, and other data, new innovations will be possible.

- Mapping to interventions. Analytics can link suggested interventions to the use and impact of the interventions. If the intervention suggested utilizing the "math help desk," did the student use the resource? If so, for how long and while doing what activities? To enable such mapping, new systems must be established to share data between organizations to ensure privacy, while still allowing for impact.

Conclusion

If educational completion is one of the most important achievements for every American student, we need to leverage the technologies and analytical tools that will eradicate the most common educational mistakes (taking wrong turns, running out of academic gas, miscalculating the distance, underestimating the costs, and not having a "norm" to compare a personalized educational journey against). What might a futuristic analytics tool set look like? One that was personalized, adaptive to the individual learner needs, and that provided pathways and routes to maximize student success.

The world has become accustomed to using the Global Positioning System (GPS); now it needs an Educational Positioning System (EPS). All students would be furnished with this EPS, enabling them to navigate their educational journey in the same relatively simple manner they used their GPS system for locating their campus for the first time. Technologies currently exist that would allow students to map their educational starting point and destiny, determine how many educational units per dollar they are getting with their funding and how much time is left on their educational journey, interpret the academic gas tank indicators, and compare how they are stacking up against the educational norm during all points of their journey.[19]

Leaders can use these next generation of game-changing tools to develop actionable strategies and interventions to optimize institutional and student performance. And with these tools, institutions can focus on learner relationships, customization, and personalization and on interventions that meet learners where they are and help them get where they need to go. We need to embrace changes that optimize lifelong learning.

"The best way to predict the future is to invent it."[20] Higher education has both a great responsibility and a great opportunity to improve student success.

Today, the demand for better metrics and improved productivity, accountability, and performance has brought an important tool to higher education in the form of analytics. The future holds much promise.

Notes

1. American Graduation Initiative (American Association of Community Colleges), http://www.aacc.nche.edu/Advocacy/aginitiative/Pages/default.aspx.
2. July 14, 2009, http://www.whitehouse.gov/the_press_office/Excerpts-of-the-Presidents-remarks-in-Warren-Michigan-and-fact-sheet-on-the-American-Graduation-Initiative/.
3. The Alliance of States, http://www.completecollege.org/alliance_of_states/.
4. Complete College America, http://www.completecollege.org.
5. Sandy Baum and Kathleen Payea, *Education Pays: The Benefits of Higher Education for Individuals and Society 2004* (Washington, DC: College Board, 2005).
6. U.S. Census Bureau, *The Big Payoff: Educational Attainment and Synthetic Estimates of Work-Life Earnings* (report, July 2002).
7. Robert Longley, "Lifetime Earnings Soar with Education," About.com, August 24, 2011, http://usgovinfo.about.com/od/moneymatters/a/edandearnings.htm.
8. Complete College America, *Time Is the Enemy* (report, September 2011), http://www.completecollege.org/docs/Time_Is_the_Enemy_Summary.pdf.
9. Alison Bailey, Tyce Henry, Lane McBride, and J. Puckett, *Unleashing the Potential of Technology in Education* (The Boston Consulting Group, 2011).
10. John Campbell, Peter DeBlois, and Diana Oblinger, "Academic Analytics: A New Tool for a New Era," *EDUCAUSE Review* 42, no. 4 (July/August 2007): 40–57.
11. Donald Norris, Linda Baer, Joan Leonard, Louis Pugliese, and Paul Lefrere, "Action Analytics: Measuring an Improving Performance That Matters in Higher Education," *EDUCAUSE Review* (January/February 2008): 43–67.
12. Phil Long and George Siemens, "Penetrating the Fog: Analytics in Learning and Education," *EDUCAUSE Review* (September/October 2011): 31–40.
13. Donald Norris, "Technology, Analytics and Lifting Out of Recession" (unpublished paper, July 2009).
14. Ibid., 9–13.
15. Ibid.
16. Adapted from Donald Norris, "Creating a Culture of Performance Measurement and Improvement" (presentation at the iStrategy User Conference, September 24, 2008), and *Making the Numbers Add Up: A Guide for Using Data in College Access and Success Programs* (report, Lumina Foundation, October 2009).
17. Complete College America, *Time Is the Enemy*.
18. Adapted from Geoffrey A. Moore, *Crossing the Chasm: Marketing and Selling Disruptive Products to Mainstream Customers* (New York: Collins Business, 2002).

19. Michael Mathews, "What If Steve Jobs Had Been an Educator?," from Bill Grave's *The Learning Cloud* blog, http://institutionalperformance.typepad.com/.
20. Alan Kay, *The Quotations Page*, http://www.quotationspage.com/quote/1423.html.

Linda Baer *has served in numerous executive-level positions in higher education including Senior Program Officer in Postsecondary Success for the Bill & Melinda Gates Foundation, Senior Vice Chancellor for Academic and Student Affairs in the Minnesota State College and University System, and Senior Vice President and Interim President at Bemidji State University. Currently, she works to inspire leaders to improve student success and transform institutions for the future.* **John Campbell** *is the Associate Vice President of Academic Technologies at Purdue University. During the past 10 years, Campbell has examined methods to use academic analytics to identify students at risk within courses. He was the founder of the Signals project, which has been featured on NBC and in the* Chronicle of Higher Education.

5

IT Innovations and the Nontraditional Learner

Pamela Tate and Rebecca Klein-Collins

Introduction

IN 1998, THE COUNCIL FOR ADULT AND EXPERIENTIAL LEARNING (CAEL), a national nonprofit organization dedicated to the adult learner, hired the American Productivity & Quality Center (APQC) to conduct a benchmarking study of adult-learning-focused colleges and universities. We wanted to answer the question "What are the postsecondary services and programs that best serve adults—especially those who are working full time—and their special needs and challenges?"

Among best-practice principles was the belief that the use of technology to enhance the learning experience of adults was of critical importance.[1] In 1998, this was not tremendously surprising. E-mail and the Internet were already fairly well established in offices as well as in many homes. Students used computer databases to organize and access information. However, we were a long way from where we are now. Then, online learning was a fledgling offering by just a few institutions and providers. Most homes had only dial-up access to the Internet, rather than today's high-speed broadband. And college applications were still mostly paper-based rather than online forms.

The subsequent speed with which online learning went from a niche offering to one that is a common option within academia has been striking. The National Center for Education Statistics (NCES) reports that in 1999–2000, only 8 percent of undergraduates took at least one distance-education (including online) course during the survey year, but by 2007–2008, more than 20 percent of undergraduates had done so. This more than doubling of participation in distance/online learning in eight years is even more remarkable given that in 1995–1996, NCES surveys did not even include the question about distance education.[2]

Since that APQC benchmarking study, we have seen the kind of technological progress that many of us could not have imagined, including technology's applications in postsecondary learning and degree completion. This book is highlighting how these advances have changed the college experience and its outcomes; this chapter focuses on some of the game changers that CAEL and other organizations have worked to develop for the *nontraditional student*. One of these game changers is the use of online learning and degree programs specifically tied to career pathways, another is the use of online portals that recognize and document college-level learning from various sources, and a third is the development of online tools that help students understand the connections between and among current skills, degree programs, and possible occupations.

These innovations are helping to highlight learning outcomes rather than inputs, and they are helping nontraditional learners access degree programs that employers value and that accommodate the schedule of the working world.

The Nontraditional Learner and Postsecondary Learning

CAEL's focus has always been the "adult learner," but these days, we are more likely to use the term "nontraditional learner" in recognition of the fact that a broader group of people attending college today share many of the same characteristics and barriers of the 25-and-older crowd. Even younger individuals can have life experiences and labor-force participation that create barriers to postsecondary success.

The NCES defines the nontraditional learner as a student with one or more of the following characteristics:

- has delayed enrollment in postsecondary education beyond the first year after high school graduation
- attends part time
- is financially independent from parents
- works full time
- has dependents other than a spouse
- is a single parent
- has no high school diploma or GED[3]

NCES found that in 2002, 73 percent of all enrolled students had at least one of the above characteristics, and 56 percent had two or more characteristics.[4] While these students may be considered nontraditional, they are no longer uncommon.

Some postsecondary institutions have recognized this emergence of nontraditional learners in higher education and have been proactive in addressing their needs and barriers.

The barrier of time and place: One significant barrier for the nontraditional learner is the lack of time to take classes while also working full time. In the past, institutions would try to lower this barrier by offering classes in the evenings or on weekends. Today, institutions serving nontraditional learners might be just as likely to offer courses that are compressed into a shorter time frame, in addition to online learning options.

The need for relevance: Younger students right out of high school may not have a good sense of what a college education should provide, but students who have spent some time in the workplace and who choose to go to college do so because they want to improve their work or career situation. They therefore have expectations that college will teach them things that they can use in the workplace or that will help them advance in their careers. Programs that are designed for adults are therefore often contextualized in that the instruction draws upon real examples from meaningful academic, real-life, and occupational contexts.[5]

The frustration of college-level learning that isn't recognized: While we are no longer defining the nontraditional learners merely by age, almost one-third of all undergraduate students are, in fact, older than the traditional 18- to 24-year-old student.[6] Nontraditional learners may have dropped out of an earlier try at college, or they may have chosen not to continue education after graduating from high school. In either case, they have been in the workplace, in the military, and in their communities, and they have been gaining new skills and knowledge in these environments. When they do return to learning, they often find themselves in courses that cover material that they already know. Therefore, another best practice for serving these learners is to offer options for evaluating that prior learning so that they can gain advanced standing in a degree program or earn college credits for the college-level learning they already have. Prior learning assessment, or PLA, is the term that CAEL has used for more than thirty years to describe the range of evaluation methods used for this purpose, including standardized exams (e.g., advanced placement [AP] and College Level Examination Program [CLEP]), challenge exams, and portfolio evaluation.

The challenge of navigating a complex labor market and higher education system: Workers without postsecondary credentials often know that they need more education to be more employable, to advance in their careers, or to hold on to a job in a tight labor market. However, today there is a wide variety of possible occupations and career paths, many of which may not even be known to the average worker. It is also not immediately apparent which occupations have staying power in this ever-changing, knowledge-based economy. And finally, even if the career pathway may be clear to the worker, determining what to study or what institution to attend is nearly as difficult.

None of the above challenges and frustrations facing adults is easy to solve, and yet technological solutions have made significant progress in innovative ways. Online learning programs have been developed in collaboration with business and industry, so that the programs are not only accessible to persons working full time, but they are also leading to credentials that are relevant to their work and valued by the employers. Online service providers have emerged to help individuals with extensive skills and knowledge gained outside the traditional classroom, or who have earned credits from multiple institutions. These sites provide the student with a way to have that knowledge evaluated, documented, and translated for use in postsecondary institutions. Finally, web-based tools and databases are available to provide guidance to various target populations on the career options and related educational programs that build on the students' previous experiences.

These innovations may not be well known in the average American household, but in our view, they are important developments, made possible only through technology, for helping the adult or nontraditional learner.

Online Learning Tied to Career Pathways

The field of workforce development had for many years been primarily the purview of employers, corporate trainers, and public-sector job-training operations. Employers and corporate trainers addressed job-related training of the incumbent workforce, and public-sector agencies provided training to the unemployed to become more viable in the labor market. Community colleges offered some vocational training, but for the most part, postsecondary institutions were not closely attuned with the realities and skill requirements of the workplace.

As the economy changed, or rather, as the United States migrated to more of a knowledge-based economy, colleges and universities have become much more aware of the connection of learning to the workplace, and of learning to long-term employability in a wide range of industries. As a result, industry-specific degree-program offerings have expanded, and there has been a growing focus within both workforce development and postsecondary education on the concept of career pathways.

Programs designed for career pathways are not focused on preparing someone for a single job, but rather for entry into an industry position with long-term employment and advancement potential. The entry step on a pathway may or may not require high skill levels, but as the worker gains new skills on the job and through additional postsecondary studies, the worker can access higher-level, higher-paying positions along a pathway. The pathway may not be linear, and it may at times resemble more of a lattice or spiderweb, but there is an explicit understanding that incremental gains in skill and knowledge make the pathways accessible.

One example of a career pathway is provided on the website of the Advanced Manufacturing Career Collaborative, a partnership of education and workforce organizations, industry associations, and local industry in southwest Pennsylvania. Figure 1 is a career pathway in manufacturing, which shows how additional education and training leads to higher-level positions along a pathway.

One thing that technology has brought to these career-pathway initiatives is greater accessibility to the training that leads to higher-level positions. Before the easy access to online learning, a worker in a lower-level job might find attending classes after a full day's work nearly impossible. It might have been geographically unmanageable to get to school on time after work, or family responsibilities might have posed a different set of challenges. The flexibility of online learning made postsecondary learning far more accessible to working adults. The ability to remove time and place barriers also allowed, in some cases, for greater involvement of business and industry in career-pathway initiatives.

To illustrate this point, it may be helpful to again revisit the 1990s, a time when it was becoming clear that the United States was shifting to a knowledge-based economy, and that the success of business and industry depended upon a workforce that was able to learn and adapt to constantly changing market conditions.

Large employers were able to build extensive employee-training departments to address this need, but smaller employers typically did not have the resources to follow suit. CAEL worked with many small manufacturers in the 1990s and, in some cases, proposed the development of what we called "employer learning consortia." A learning consortia was an alliance of employers in the same industry that would pool their training dollars in order to offer courses for employees throughout the industry, but primarily for the incumbent workers of the consortia companies. In this way, the companies could create some economies of scale to meet their employee learning and development needs.

The limitation of this approach was geography. In order to be able to offer a course that could be attended by employees from different companies, those

Figure 1

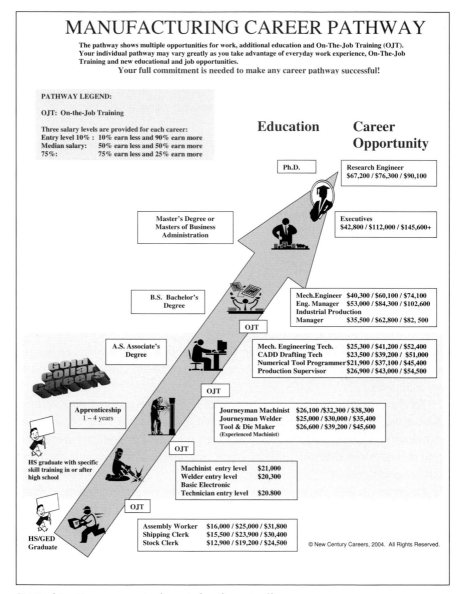

MANUFACTURING CAREER PATHWAY

The pathway shows multiple opportunities for work, additional education and On-The-Job Training (OJT). Your individual pathway may vary greatly as you take advantage of everyday work experience, On-The-Job Training and new educational and job opportunities.

Your full commitment is needed to make any career pathway successful!

PATHWAY LEGEND:

OJT: On-the-Job Training

Three salary levels are provided for each career:
Entry level 10% : 10% earn less and 90% earn more
Median salary: 50% earn less and 50% earn more
75%:   75% earn less and 25% earn more

Education

Career Opportunity

Ph.D.

Research Engineer
$67,200 / $76,300 / $90,100

Master's Degree or Masters of Business Administration

Executives
$42,800 / $112,000 / $145,600+

B.S. Bachelor's Degree

Mech.Engineer	$40,300 / $60,100 / $74,100
Eng. Manager	$53,000 / $84,300 / $102,600
Industrial Production Manager	$35,500 / $62,800 / $82,500

OJT

A.S. Associate's Degree

Mech. Engineering Tech.	$25,300 / $41,200 / $52,400
CADD Drafting Tech	$23,500 / $39,200 / $51,000
Numerical Tool Programmer	$21,900 / $37,100 / $45,400
Production Supervisor	$26,900 / $43,000 / $54,500

OJT

Apprenticeship 1 – 4 years

Journeyman Machinist	$26,100 /$32,300 / $38,300
Journeyman Welder	$25,000 / $30,000 / $35,400
Tool & Die Maker (Experienced Machinist)	$26,600 / $39,200 / $45,600

OJT

HS graduate with specific skill training in or after high school

Machinist entry level	$21,000
Welder entry level	$20,300
Basic Electronic Technician entry level	$20.800

OJT

HS/GED Graduate

Assembly Worker	$16,000 / $25,000 / $31,800
Shipping Clerk	$15,500 / $23,900 / $30,400
Stock Clerk	$12,900 / $19,200 / $24,500

Gold Collar Careers

© New Century Careers, 2004. All Rights Reserved.

Source: http://www.amcsquared.com/mfgpathways2.pdf.

72

companies all needed to be in the same geographic area. As a result, CAEL's work with consortia was primarily in industries where smaller suppliers tended to be in close proximity to the prime companies. For several years, for example, CAEL supported the development of a supplier learning consortium for the steel industry in Indiana, which at that time had a number of such suppliers.

With the emergence of the Internet, that geographic limitation has all but disappeared. In 1997, with initial funding from the Alfred P. Sloan Foundation, CAEL began developing a new kind of learning consortium that we called an online industry alliance. This new approach could be national, could include large and small employers in an industry, and could include the involvement of employer associations and labor unions.

CAEL established the Energy Providers Coalition for Education (EPCE), an online industry alliance for the energy industry, and the National Coalition for Telecommunications Education and Learning (NACTEL), an alliance for the telecommunications industry, both of which have continued to grow and thrive. Each of these initiatives

- targets both incumbent workers and those new to the industry;
- partners with carefully selected high-performing online education and training providers;
- is led by a broad-based industry coalition;
- provides curriculum content codeveloped by industry and educational experts; and
- reaches participants nationally and internationally.

The EPCE industry coalition currently represents approximately 65 percent of the electric utilities industry. The initiative offers associate's degrees and certificate training through Bismarck State College, and program enrollments currently average 1,500 a year. Additional degree and certificate programs have been developed with Bismarck State College for the nation's nuclear power plants. Now, EPCE is working on a partnership with Clemson University to offer an online electrical engineering degree, with prerequisite courses provided by Colorado Community College Online.

The most recent expansion has been the Light Up Your Future program, which is a partnership with a utility employer, Virtual High School (VHS), Bismarck State College, and local high schools. This model now complements the college-level online learning through EPCE's practice of connecting high school students to a potential future with their local energy employer.

The NACTEL program partners represent nearly 2 million telecommunication workers. The curriculum is offered through Pace University, and since its start in 1999, the programs have continually grown to reflect the evolving telecom industry. The curriculum includes an associate's degree program in applied information technology, a bachelor of science in telecommunications degree program, and an advanced certificate in emerging telecommunications technologies.

Today, NACTEL is the premier source for industry-based telecommunications education. The Pace University programs are now beginning their thirteenth year, with more than 550 students taking an average of 2,500 courses each year.

Online Portals That Recognize and Document Previous Learning

As noted earlier, many nontraditional learners are students who are coming to postsecondary education several years after graduating from high school. During this time, they may have taken courses from one or more postsecondary institutions in previous attempts at a degree. In addition, they may have gained college-level skills and knowledge from their life experiences. Such skills and knowledge can often be acquired from experiences such as serving in the military, working, volunteering in the community, self-study, or a combination of these activities.

Nontraditional learners therefore may have college credits from various sources in addition to possessing knowledge and skills gained outside of the classroom that may be at the college level. The challenge for the learners is that often this prior learning is not recognized for their degrees. Colleges and universities have widely varying policies concerning how many credits and what kind of credits can be accepted in transfer, as well as the evaluation of prior learning for credit.

Advances in information technology are helping to address some of these challenges. Today, there are online services that help students find ways to maximize their prior learning. These services include online credit-transfer support services and online prior-learning assessment services.

Online credit-transfer support services: Today there are more than 43 million Americans age 25 and older who have some college credit but no degree.[7] When these individuals make the decision to return to school to complete a degree, they do not always return to the same institution they attended before. Often they are surprised to learn that some or all of the credits they earned previously will not be accepted in transfer or will not count toward their degree at the new institution.

Some students faced with this challenge search out an institution that will accept their previous credit. Unfortunately, this is akin to taking a shot in the dark. Students may need to contact a number of different institutions to determine which colleges or universities will accept the most credits in transfer, and not everyone is willing or able to do this kind of legwork. It is no wonder, then, that the average community college student will earn a total of 140 credits while pursuing a bachelor's degree even though typically only 120 credits are necessary.[8]

In recent years, the Internet has provided better ways for the nontraditional learner to search for transfer-friendly institutions, as there are now web-based credit-transfer support services that provide information about articulation and transfer policies in various states and for specific institutions.

Some states, for example, offer web-based services with information on credit-transfer policies that help students plan for future transfers. The Alabama Statewide Transfer and Articulation Reporting System, or STARS, is an articulation website and database developed by a state mandate in 1995 in response to the large number of community college students losing credits after transferring to a four-year institution. Officially implemented in 1998, STARS provides Alabama students with information that can guide them through their first two years of coursework and prevent them from losing credit hours when they transfer to public four-year universities in the state.

A representative of the system reported last year that over 625,000 transfer guides had been viewed or printed through the state's articulation website since 1998, and over 86,000 transfer students, academic advisors, faculty members, and college administrators obtained or viewed transfer guides online using STARS in the 2008–2009 academic year alone.[9]

Students clearly benefit from having access to this kind of system, since it will save them from wasting time and money on courses that do not transfer. The system is also helping the state's two-year colleges provide better advice to students while streamlining their courses to be a better match for transfer requirements.[10]

Nationally, there are web-based credit-transfer support options as well. Academy One is one organization that provides students with national information on institutional credit-transfer policies, while also providing unique tools to help students document their previous academic histories and other learning experiences.

One such tool is a student "passport," which is a web-based platform for consolidating a student's academic history in a single online location. Academy One then provides students with information on which institution's degree programs and course offerings are the best fit for the student's prior learning (both college credits earned as well as prior learning that has not yet been evaluated for credit).[11]

Online evaluation and transcription of prior learning: Nontraditional learners often have had extensive life experiences from which they have learned, and often this learning is comparable to what is taught in college-level courses.

Prior learning assessments (PLA) measure what a student has learned outside of a college course. Through a variety of different assessment methods, institutions can determine what the student knows, and then evaluate whether that learning is college level and how many college credits are equivalent to that learning.

PLA includes the following methods:

- **National standardized exams** in specified disciplines, e.g., Advanced Placement (AP) exams, College Level Examination Program (CLEP) tests, *Excelsior College Examinations* (*ECE*), DANTES Subject Standardized Texts (DSST)
- **Customized exams,** also called "challenge exams," which are offered by some colleges to verify learning—these may be current course final exams or other tests developed at the department level for assessing general disciplinary knowledge and skill
- **Evaluation of noncollege programs,** e.g., American Council on Education (ACE) evaluations of corporate training and military training
- **Individualized assessments,** particularly portfolio-based assessments

Students who earn credits through PLA often save time by not having to take courses in subjects they have already mastered. They also may save money, since PLA assessments typically cost less than the tuition and fees for courses that student might otherwise need to take. Further, a recent CAEL study found that PLA may serve as a motivator to adult learners: in examining the academic records of more than 62,000 students from 48 institutions, CAEL found that more than half (56 percent) of adult PLA students earned a postsecondary degree within seven years, while only 21 percent of non-PLA students did so.[12]

Despite the benefits to students from PLA, credit for prior learning is not universally available in higher education. Many postsecondary institutions recognize AP and CLEP credit, but offering a formal program for helping students develop portfolios and then formally evaluating those portfolios for credit requires an investment of staff and ongoing training of faculty evaluators. Many institutions do not make that investment.

Challenging this reality has been possible through advances in information technology. This past year, CAEL collaborated with the ACE and the College Board to develop an online PLA service called LearningCounts.org, which makes PLA more widely available to students nationally. Through

LearningCounts.org, CAEL offers portfolio courses and faculty evaluations of student portfolios and refers students to the College Board for standardized exam services and to ACE for credit recommendations for the student's military or corporate training.

During its initial pilot stage, LearningCounts.org is working with a group of more than one hundred postsecondary institutions to serve students on a referral basis. The vision is for LearningCounts.org to eventually serve thousands of students per year, including students not yet affiliated with a specific institution.

The online model allows for easy access to PLA for all adult learners, it increases the number of colleges that are able to grant credit for prior learning, and it will build awareness of PLA among currently enrolled adults as well as those adults considering college.

Tools for Understanding Career and Education Options

Technology has allowed workers to access industry-based degree programs, and it is also revolutionizing the way adults gain recognition for their previous learning experiences. But before any of that can happen, these adults need to determine what their career goals are and how to reach those goals through education.

Such important decision making is made more difficult by the fact that in this global economy, industries and jobs are rapidly changing. Jobs that once allowed someone to support a family without a college degree have all but disappeared (e.g., manufacturing), and many other jobs that once provided entry to various industries are vanishing as well (e.g., meter readers in the utilities industry and customer-service jobs that have moved to other countries). Pre-1980, the high-growth companies were the large Fortune 500 companies, whereas today most of the job growth is in companies with fewer than 500 employees.[13] The challenge for individual job seekers is that career opportunities and pathways in these smaller and emerging companies are much more difficult to identify and often result in a number of detours or wrong turns along the way.

Meanwhile, the world of higher education is also dramatically different than it was in years past. At community colleges, for example, current offerings are much more varied than earlier generations would have experienced, ranging from vocational programs to liberal arts, and from professional certifications to online degree programs. There are also many more for-profit offerings and distance-learning opportunities. Some colleges cater to the adult learner, while other institutions have made few accommodations for nontraditional learners.

When adults are motivated to pursue postsecondary education, they are faced with a dizzying array of options in terms of both career pathways and educational programs. Navigating these choices is nearly impossible without some guidance. A lucky few have access to professional advisors through work, and other individuals who understand the need for advice and who have the personal resources to pay for it might seek out such assistance independently.

Information technology has opened up a third option: technology-based tools for helping prospective students make better-informed decisions about where to enroll and what to study. There are numerous web resources that provide information about the different kinds of postsecondary institutions, what kinds of degree programs they offer, how much they cost, and so on. There are also other online resources that take it several steps further by helping to match the student to career pathways and educational programs that build on the student's existing skills and knowledge.

One example of this kind of online resource is offered by the Minnesota State Colleges and Universities System (MnSCU) for veterans who are considering postsecondary education. The site is called GPS LifePlan, with pages of links to online resources and tools for career and education planning, decision making, financial assistance, and personal goal setting. One of the resources is Veterans Education Transfer System (VETS), an online application that helps past, present, and future servicemen and servicewomen determine how their military training can count for credit at Minnesota State Colleges and Universities institutions.

Through the VETS site, the veteran enters information about his or her past military occupation and training, as well as the career that the veteran is considering. The website then provides a link to labor-market information about that career as well as a list of degree and certificate programs for that career offered by various state colleges and universities. If a particular education program is of interest to the veteran, the site provides a direct link to an application for a "request for transfer evaluation." An evaluator for MnSCU then examines the skills and knowledge required for that veteran's previous military occupation and makes a recommendation for awarding credit to that individual for the desired degree program. As more veterans use this system and request transfer evaluations, the transfer-evaluation process will become more automatic.

What makes the VETS tool a game changer is its ability to connect military occupations to civilian jobs and degree programs, while also recognizing the college-level skills and knowledge that service members demonstrate through their military occupations. Information technology makes this service accessible to veterans at any stage of their decision-making process, and it also automates the navigation through a complex labor market and an offerings-rich educational system.

Conclusion

As game changing as the innovations just discussed are, we have probably only just scratched the surface of what might be possible to make higher education more accessible to nontraditional students and to help those students reach their postsecondary goals.

We can envision, for example, even greater innovations in career and education advising. This chapter has noted the challenges students have in understanding what their career options are and in navigating their educational options. It would be a tremendous benefit to have more advanced tools to help with these challenges. These tools would help students avoid spending their limited time and money on educational pursuits that turn out to be a bad fit or that lead to career paths with limited opportunities. The tools that are emerging on various websites are a promising start, but we can imagine a world where algorithms are developed to assist decision making in a much more sophisticated way.

These and other advances would be helped by institutional, state, and federal policies that are more in step with the needs of the nontraditional learner. The recognition of prior learning for credit, for example, is challenging when public policy and accrediting bodies define the credit hour—the primary unit used to measure learning—in terms of time spent in learning activities rather than in terms of learning outcomes. There is a greater focus on learning outcomes today than in previous eras, but there is nevertheless a reluctance to move too far from the "seat time" approach, and so we remain on the cusp of real change.

Further, IT innovations can only change the game for nontraditional learners if people have access to that technology. The United States is behind other developed nations, ranking only fourteenth in the world in its broadband penetration rate.[14] Policies that expand this access will help put new tools into the hands of nontraditional learners that will facilitate good educational choices, ensure the recognition of their previous learning, and enable them to be successful in meeting their postsecondary goals.

IT innovations have indeed helped nontraditional learners have greater access to learning opportunities. It is with great anticipation that we look to the future and what may still be possible.

Notes

1. Thomas A Flint & Associates, *Best Practices in Adult Learning: A CAEL/APQC Benchmarking Study* (Council for Adult and Experiential Learning, 1999).
2. U.S. Department of Education, *Profile of Undergraduate Students: Trends from Selected Years, 1995–1996 to 2007–2008* (National Center for Education Statistics, 2010): 220.
3. Susan Choy, *Nontraditional Undergraduates* (Washington, DC: U.S. Department of Education, National Center for Education Statistics, 2002).
4. Ibid.
5. Richard Kazis, Abigail Callahan, Chris Davidson, Annie McLeod, Brian Bosworth, Victoria Choitz, and John Hoops, *Adult Learners in Higher Education: Barriers to Success and Strategies to Improve Results* (a report by Jobs for the Future and Eduventures for U.S. Department of Labor, Employment and Training Administration Occasional Paper 2007–003, March 2007).
6. National Center for Education Statistics, 2009.
7. American Community Survey, 2009.
8. Josipa Roksa and Bruce Keith, "Credits, Time, and Attainment: Articulation Policies and Success after Transfer," *Educational Evaluation and Policy Analysis* 30: 236–54. Cited in Sara Goldrick-Rab and Josipa Roksa, *A Federal Agenda for Promoting Student Success and Degree Completion* (Washington, DC: Center for American Progress, 2008).
9. Rebecca Klein-Collins, Amy Sherman, and Louis Soares, *Degree Completion beyond Institutional Borders: Responding to the New Reality of Mobile and Nontraditional Learners* (Center for American Progress and Council for Adult and Experiential Learning, 2010).
10. See additional information at the STARS website: http://stars.troy.edu/stars/stars.htm.
11. See additional information at http://www.academyone.com.
12. Rebecca Klein-Collins, *Fueling the Race to Postsecondary Success: A 48-Institution Study of Prior Learning Assessment and Adult Student Outcomes* (Chicago: CAEL, 2010).
13. Zoltan Acs, William Parsons, and Tracy Spenser, *High Impact Firms: Gazelles Revisited* (Washington, DC: Office of Advocacy, U.S. Small Business Administration, 2008).
14. Organization for Economic Cooperation and Development, *OECD Broadband Portal*, http://www.OECD.org (Table 1 [1d]).

Pamela Tate *is nationally and internationally recognized for her work in facilitating workforce education and training programs among educational institutions, business, labor, government, and economic development agencies, and for her efforts in assisting colleges and universities to develop systems of Prior Learning Assessment and quality assurance in adult learning programs.* **Rebecca Klein-Collins** *is the Director of Research for the Council for Adult and Experiential Learning (CAEL), overseeing the organization's research in topics related to workforce development policy and practice, lifelong learning, and prior learning assessment.*

6

Why Openness in Education?

David Wiley and Cable Green

IN THIS CHAPTER, we explore a number of ways openness affects the practices of teaching and learning and the motivations behind supporters of these emergent practices. We discuss the three principal influences of openness on education: open educational resources, open access, and open teaching.

Open Educational Resources

"Open educational resources" (or OER) have become a widely discussed topic in recent years. Open educational resources are educational materials (e.g., course textbooks, research articles, videos, assessments, simulations, etc.) that are either (a) licensed under an open copyright license (e.g., Creative Commons[1]) or (b) in the public domain. In both cases, every person in the world enjoys free (no cost) access to the OER *and* free (no cost) permission to engage in the "4R" activities when using the OER:

- *Revise*—adapt and improve the OER so it better meets your needs.
- *Remix*—combine or "mash up" the OER with other OER to produce new materials.
- *Reuse*—use the original or your new version of the OER in a wide range of contexts.
- *Redistribute*—make copies and share the original OER or your new version with others.

Many struggle to understand why there are those who would take the time and effort to craft educational materials only to give them away without capturing any monetary value from their work. There are several lines of thought that motivate participants in the open educational resources community. Some of these motivations are listed below.

Education Is Sharing

Education is, first and foremost, an enterprise of sharing. In fact, sharing is the sole means by which education is effected. If an instructor is not sharing what he or she knows with students, there is no education happening.

Those educators who share the most thoroughly of themselves with the greatest proportion of their students are the ones we deem most successful. Do students come away from a course in possession of the knowledge and skills the instructor tried to share? (In other words, is the instructor a successful sharer?) If so, we call the instructor a successful educator. If an instructor's attempts at sharing fail, we call that instructor a poor educator. *Education is a matter of sharing, and the open educational resources approach is designed specifically to enable extremely efficient and affordable sharing.*

Leveraging the Internet: The Internet has frequently been compared to the printing press, which was in turn frequently compared to the process of writing books by hand. Today, the cost of having a 250-page book transcribed by hand is about $250. The cost of printing that same book with a print-on-demand service is about $5. The cost of copying an online version of that same book (e.g., an ePub file) is about $0.0008. The cost of shipping either the handwritten or printed book is about $5. The cost of distributing an electronic copy of the book over the Internet is approximately $0.0007.

Clearly, the Internet has empowered us to copy and share with an efficiency never before known or imagined. However, long before the Internet was invented, copyright law began regulating the very activities the Internet makes essentially free (copying and distributing). Consequently, the Internet was born at a severe disadvantage, as preexisting laws discouraged people from realizing the full potential of the network.

Since the invention of the Internet, copyright law has been "strengthened" to further restrict the Internet's copying and sharing capabilities. While existing laws, business models, and educational practices make it difficult for instructors and learners to leverage the full power of the Internet to access high-quality, affordable learning materials, open educational resources can be freely copied and shared (and revised and remixed) without breaking the law. *Open educational resources allow the full technical power of the Internet to be brought to bear on education. OER allow exactly what the Internet enables: free sharing of educational resources with the world.*

The $5 textbook: According to U.S. PIRG,[2] college textbook prices have increased at nearly four times the rate of inflation for all finished goods since 1994. College students spend an average of $900 per year on textbooks—26 percent of the cost of tuition at a public, four-year university. And this has occurred at the same time tuition and fees at universities have blossomed 130% over the same period, while middle-class incomes have stagnated.[3] The cost of textbooks is a significant factor in the cost of higher education, growing beyond the reach of more individuals each year. OER have considerable potential to be a part of the solution to this problem.

Faculty, governments, and foundations are building and/or commissioning and sharing high-quality, openly licensed textbooks with the world. Many open textbook projects allow the textbooks to be used free online and provide a method for purchasing a printed copy for those who prefer printed books. Examples of open textbook providers include Flat World Knowledge (http://www.flatworldknowledge.com) in the postsecondary space and CK–12 (http://ck12.org) in the K–12 space. Utah recently demonstrated that high school science textbooks starting from CK–12's open textbooks can be aggregated, printed, and delivered to thousands of students for less than $5 per book. The Open Education Group at Brigham Young University also found there was no difference in learning outcomes between students who used open textbooks and students who used traditional, proprietary textbooks.[4] In an era of stagnant or shrinking education budgets, open textbooks seem to be a simple solution to an expensive problem. *Open educational resources provide an immediate, proven way to make education significantly more affordable and accessible for students.*

Continuous quality improvement: For as long as we can remember, instructors have been "supplementing around" problems with textbooks. When we can't find a single textbook that meets our needs, it is not uncommon for us to assign two or more textbooks, intending only to use parts of each. Because printed, copyright-protected learning materials are not easily (or legally) revised and remixed, it is unthinkable that we might simply start taking books apart in order to assemble exactly what we want and exactly what our students need. Instructors and students are constantly "making do" with suboptimal materials—and spending more than necessary as they do so.

Under the current copyright laws, instructors are essentially powerless to legally improve the materials they use in their classes. *OER provide instructors with free and legal permissions to engage in continuous quality-improvement processes such as incremental adaptation and revision, empowering instructors to take ownership and control over their courses and textbooks in a manner not previously possible.*

Buy one, get one: The "buy one, get one" sale has become a fixture in American advertising. Implied in the special offer is the promise that when you buy one item, like a pizza or T-shirt, you'll get a second one free. However, there is a more literal way of interpreting the phrase: when you buy something, you should actually get the thing you paid for. Imagine paying in advance for a week's vacation in a cabin by a beautiful lake, only to be charged a second time when you arrive and check in. You would never stand for such a thing, because everyone understands that when you buy one, you should get one.

State and federal governments frequently fund the development of education and research resources through grants made by the National Science Foundation, the Departments of Labor, Education, Energy, and other entities. Through these grants, state or federal governments commission the creation of these resources using taxpayer dollars. In other words, when the National Science Foundation gives a grant to a university to produce a pre-engineering curriculum, you and I have already paid for it. However, it is almost always the case that these products are commercialized in such a way that access is restricted to those who are willing to pay for them a second time. Why should we be required to pay a second time for the thing we've already paid for? Or worse—if every school district in your state pays to license the curriculum, you've now paid for it 250 times.[5]

Governments and other funding entities that wish to maximize the impacts of their education and research investments are moving toward open policies. National/state/provincial governments and education systems all play a critical role in setting policies that drive education investments and have an interest in ensuring that public funding of education makes a meaningful, cost-effective contribution to socioeconomic development.[6] Given this role, these policy-making entities are ideally positioned to encourage or require recipients of public funding to produce educational resources under an open license. Open policies typically embrace the concept that all publicly funded education and research resources should be openly licensed resources.

Because the bulk of education and research funding comes from taxpayer dollars, it is essential that OER and open access have open policies. As governments move to require open policies, hundreds of billions of dollars of educational and research resources will be freely and legally available to the public that paid for them. *Every taxpayer has a reasonable expectation of access to educational materials and research products whose creation tax dollars supported.*

Early collections of open educational resources include Rice University's Connexions project (http://cnx.org) and MIT's OpenCourseWare (http://

ocw.mit.edu). More recent examples include the state of Washington's Open Course Library (http://www.opencourselibrary.org).

Open educational resources represent multiple opportunities to innovate in the teaching and learning context, including the ability to dramatically improve the affordability of education and enable better personalization of instruction.

Open Access

"Open access" refers to research articles that are freely and openly available to the public for reading, reviewing, and building upon. From one perspective it can be seen as a special case of the "buy one, get one" example just described. But there are other reasons why many support the open access model. A brief parable illustrates the point:

> Once upon a time there was a brilliant inventor who one day had a "eureka!" moment. She sketched out the design of her breakthrough product and worked and reworked the design. When she was satisfied that the design was ready to take to production, she began contacting potential funders. After a long process, she acquired the funding needed to put her ideas to work.
>
> Money in hand, she began searching for employees—production specialists, designers, marketing experts, and others. They all set to work. They persevered through false starts and breakthroughs, and finally the day arrived when they had a product ready to ship! Relieved, the inventor began contacting shipping companies. To her disbelief, the shipping companies would only deliver her goods under the following conditions:
>
> - The inventor had to agree to ship her product via the one shipping company exclusively.
> - This exclusive shipping deal had to be a perpetual deal, never subject to review or cancelation.
> - The inventor had to sign over to the shipping company all of the legal rights to her product.
> - The shipping company would be the seller of her product to the public, and it would retain all the profits from these sales.

The parable is, of course, analogous to a researcher and her interactions with the academic-journal publishing industry. Under the traditional system, journal publishers hold the legal rights to reproduce and distribute the research results published in their journals. A comparison of the relative effort and intellectual contribution invested by the researchers and the publishers, however, suggests an imbalance.

In terms of effort of contribution, the researcher is responsible for

- generating original, significant ideas for new research,
- competing for and winning grant funding for the research,
- identifying and hiring highly qualified students and other professionals to conduct the research,
- rigorously and responsibly carrying out the program of research, and
- writing up the results of the research in a communicative manner.

In terms of effort of contribution, the publisher is responsible for

- coordinating volunteers who review the merits of the research results (these volunteers are other researchers who review at no cost to the publisher),
- making a publication decision about the research results,
- copyediting and formatting the final version of the research results, and
- publishing and distributing the results.

The researcher is responsible for the overwhelming majority of the effort that goes into conceiving, conducting, and reporting the research. The publisher is responsible for only the portion of effort that goes into publication. The publisher makes a much less significant intellectual contribution to the papers it publishes (note again that the publisher itself does not review the written results for intellectual rigor and quality; rather, it coordinates the review efforts of other researchers who volunteer to perform the reviews). At the end of the lengthy research process in which the publisher mainly makes coordinating and editorial contributions, the publisher then requires exclusive legal rights to control the reproduction and distribution of the researcher's work's results. And, publishers often also charge the original researcher for copies of his or her work. Many feel that this represents a scholarly publishing status quo that is completely out of balance and that the researcher should control the reproduction and distribution rights to his or her work.

We can conduct a similar analysis from a financial perspective. The average annual dollar value of a National Institutes of Health (NIH) grant is between $210,769[7] and $239,826.[8] The scholarly published output of the average NIH grant is approximately 1.6 research articles per year.[9] This puts the average financial cost of generating a research article somewhere between $105,385 and $119,913 per article. By contrast, the average cost for a traditional, high-quality journal to publish an article, including administrative and other costs, is $2,750.[10]

In terms of average financial investment per article, the publisher is responsible for 2–3 percent of the overall investment. Because of this imbalance, and the desire and right of individual researchers to control the reproduction and distribution rights of their own work, thousands of open journals (7,459 listed in the Directory of Open Access Journals, http://www.doaj.org, as of February 2012) have emerged to host openly licensed research articles. Faculty are also responding by voting to support "open access policies" at their universities (see http://roarmap.eprints.org), which typically grant the university the rights necessary to archive and make articles written by faculty freely and openly available on the Internet.

Open Teaching

"Open teaching" began as a practice of using technology to open formal university courses for free, informal participation by individuals not officially enrolled in the course. In the university context, open teaching involves devising ways to expose the in-class experiences to those who are not in the class so that they can participate as fully as possible. Some popular strategies include

- posting syllabi in publicly viewable blogs or wikis, where everyone can view them;
- assigning readings that are freely and openly available, so that everyone can access and read them;
- asking students to post homework assignments and other course artifacts on publicly viewable blogs or wikis, so they can catalyze further discussion of relevant topics; and
- using a wide range of traditional and social media, including e-mail, microblogging, and blog comments, to carry on the course discussion.

Early examples of open teaching include Utah State University's Introduction to Open Education course (http://opencontent.org/wiki/index.php?title=Intro_Open_Ed_Syllabus); recent examples include Stanford's Introduction to Artificial Intelligence (AI) course (https://www.ai-class.com).

Some open teaching courses have provided alternative credentials to participants as well. Informal participants in both the Introduction to Open Education course and the Stanford AI course who successfully completed the assigned work could receive certificates of completion from the faculty. It is critical to note here that the certificates are not issued by the faculty member's university and do not bear any credit toward graduation or anything else. They are simply statements of achievement signed by the faculty members.

The open teaching model has also been applied to structured learning experiences that did not begin as university courses. These tend to be gathered under the moniker "Massive Open Online Course," or MOOC. An example of a MOOC is Welcome to Change: Education, Learning, and Technology (http://change.mooc.ca). MOOCs are typically based on a "connectivist" philosophy that eschews educator-specified learning goals and supports each person in learning something different. One way of understanding the MOOC design is to say that it applies the "open" ethos to course outcomes. In other words, students are empowered to learn what they need/want to learn, and the journey of learning is often more important than any predefined learning outcomes.

Additional teaching and learning models such as Peer 2 Peer University (http://p2pu.org), OER university (http://wikieducator.org/OER_university/Home), and University of the People (http://www.uopeople.org) are emerging, and they synthesize OER, open textbooks, open access, Open Badges (https://wiki.mozilla.org/Badges), open tutoring, and open teaching. It is an exciting time for education. *Open teaching provides individuals who might otherwise never have the opportunity to experience postsecondary learning a free and open chance to participate.*

Conclusion

Openness is impacting many areas of education—teaching, curriculum, textbooks, research, policy, and others. How will these individual impacts synergize to transform education? Will new and traditional education entities leverage the Internet, the affordances of digital content (almost cost-free storage, replication, and distribution), and open licensing to share their education and research resources? If they do, will more people be able to access an education and, if so, what will that mean for individuals, families, countries, and economies? If scientists and researchers have open access to the world's academic journal articles and data, will diseases be cured more quickly? Will governments require that publicly funded resources be open and free to the public that paid for them? Or will openness go down in the history books as just another fad that couldn't live up to its press? Only time will tell.

Notes

1. Creative Commons licenses are typically used to openly license educational and re-search resources. For more information, go to http://creativecommons.org/licenses.
2. U.S. PIRG, "New Report Shows College Textbook Costs Increasing Sharply Ahead of Inflation: Publishers Engage in Practices That Needlessly Drive Up Textbook Costs for Students" (2005), http://studentpirgs.org/news/new-report-shows-college-textbook-costs-increasing-sharply-ahead-inflation.
3. Annalyn Censky, "Surging College Costs Price Out Middle Class," CNN Money (June 13, 2011), http://money.cnn.com/2011/06/13/news/economy/college_tuition_middle_class/index.htm.
4. David Wiley, John Hilton, Shelley Ellington, and Tiffany Hall, "A Preliminary Exam-ination of the Cost Savings and Learning Impacts of Using Open," International Review of Research in Open and Distance Learning (forthcoming).
5. U.S. Census Bureau, Population Division, "Number of School Districts and Distri-bution of the School-Age Population by the Total School District Population: 1990 and 2000," (Table 10, June 3, 2004), http://www.census.gov/population/www/documentation/twps0074/tab10.pdf.
6. Commonwealth of Learning and UNESCO, "Guidelines for Open Educational Resources (OER) in Higher Education" (November 2011), http://www.col.org/resources/publications/Pages/detail.aspx?PID=364.
7. A. Gass, "Paying to Free Science: Costs of Publication as Costs of Research," Serials Review 31, no. 2 (June 2005): 103–6, available for purchase online at http://www.sciencedirect.com/science/article/pii/S0098791305000432.
8. B. G. Druss and S. C. Marcus, "Tracking Publication Outcomes of National Institutes of Health Grants," The American Journal of Medicine 118, no. 6 (June 2005): 658–63, http://www.amjmed.com/article/S0002-9343%2805%2900101-4/abstract.
9. Ibid.
10. Wellcome Trust, "Costs and Business Models in Scientific Research Publishing" (September 2003), http://www.wellcome.ac.uk/About-us/Publications/Reports/Biomedical-science/WTD003185.htm.

David Wiley is Associate Professor of Instructional Psychology and Technology in the David O. McKay School of Education at Brigham Young University. Wiley also serves as Associate Director of the Center for the Improvement of Teacher Education and Schooling with responsibility for the research unit, where he directs the Open Education Group. **Cable Green** is the Director of Global Learning for Creative Commons. Green works with the global open community to leverage open licensing, open content, and open policies to significantly improve access to high-quality, affordable education and research resources so everyone in the world can attain all the education they desire.

7

Early Days of a Growing Trend: Nonprofit/For-Profit Academic Partnerships in Higher Education

Daniel Pianko and Josh Jarrett

HIGHER EDUCATION PRESIDENTS have lamented that the sector is caught in an "iron triangle," where access, quality outcomes, and costs are so tightly linked that institutions cannot improve one without negatively affecting the other two.[1] However, enterprising college and university leaders are increasingly exploring a little-used strategy of nonprofit/for-profit academic partnerships to break this iron triangle. The best of these partnerships appear to be simultaneously expanding access, improving quality, and delivering financial sustainability. The worst of these partnerships trigger controversies with faculty, debate over mission alignment, bickering over resources, and unrealized benefits. Partnerships successfully break the iron triangle when each partner delivers specific value to a thoughtfully designed relationship with mission alignment and when carefully structured.

Does this herald a new era of collaboration and acceptance between the nonprofit and for-profit sectors, which have traditionally been at loggerheads, or is this a passing fad? This chapter argues that this is a trend that is here to stay and that we are in the early stage of rapid growth in these partnerships. We will provide a brief history of nonprofit/for-profit academic partnerships, explore the forces driving the growth in these partnerships, present lessons from successful partnerships, and asks questions for the future.

A Long, Quiet History of University Partnerships

The tradition of sharing best practices, learning, and resources is almost as old as the university itself. The first networks of universities have shared their library volumes—the heart of the research function—almost since their inception. Modern universities have increasingly outsourced core functional roles such as residence halls, food service, back-office processing, and academic-related areas such as book publishing or course design. As the market for education has become increasingly competitive, some universities have explored nonprofit/for-profit academic partnerships to bring needed capital and expertise to their institutions.

The modern nonprofit/for-profit partnership began in an unlikely place. One of the first such partnerships began in 1972, when Antioch College partnered with a for-profit group to create an adult-education center to reach African American students. That partnership eventually grew into what is now the nonprofit, historically black Sojourner-Douglass College. The Apollo Group, best known for the University of Phoenix, later started the Institute for Professional Development (IPD) to help nonprofit institutions build and manage their accelerated degree programs. However, some nonprofits viewed University of Phoenix as a threat or as a low-quality provider, and IPD's impact plateaued after some initial success. Nonprofit Regis University, a former IPD client, decided to build a nonprofit organization to provide such services at scale. Regis's New Ventures group grew quickly to over 10,000 students in only a few years. Together, Regis, Apollo Group, and a few other organizations represent the first generation of partner-led provision of core academic operations and functions to higher education institutions.

While the focus of this chapter is on nonprofit/for-profit partnerships, tax status is actually less relevant than provision of capital and skills. The Regis example proves that tax status is not a determinant of success or capability. One recent incarnation of a partnership structure—without the partner—is the University of Southern New Hampshire's online program, which has grown to over 7,000 students in just a few years through the separation of the capital and skill set required to build online to scale in a separate organization.[2]

Why Turn to Third Parties?

At their core and from the start, traditional colleges and universities are built to service 18- to 25-year-old students in a full-time residential setting. The traditional academic environment, ranging from summers off to baseball fields, is not designed to teach working adults whose jobs do not include breaks of more than three months or time for collegiate athletics. As nontraditional learners have driven the bulk of enrollment growth in higher education over the past two decades, attempts to support them have engendered nonprofit/ for-profit academic partnerships.

Many institutions have discovered that moving outside their core expertise is extraordinarily difficult. Faculty, alumni, and other constituents sometimes object to perceived damage to the brand or to a potential adverse impact on their traditional operations. However, it has become clear that programs ranging from adult education to online learning require a radically different "product" to be successful.

Adults, for example, prefer an evening schedule and an *andragogy*-based approach to learning. The accelerated learning environment is typically located in a commercial real estate setting with instruction from practitioners rather than researchers. Nontraditional students generally consider their higher education options through direct marketing—a skill set unfamiliar to most admissions officers. From instruction by practitioners to the need for large call centers, few traditional institutions have the skills and personnel necessary to target this market.

Beyond the skill sets required and ambivalence from constituents, nontraditional learning environments require significant up-front capital investments and ongoing expenditures. Traditional institutions may have trouble allocating scarce capital resources toward renting new office space off-campus or spending the more than $1 million annually on advertising campaigns often necessary for reaching the nontraditional audience.

Partnership structures have evolved out of the long history of partnerships by and between colleges and universities. At times, universities have a specific need (e.g., how do we provide adequate remedial instruction?) or want to develop a new programmatic approach to further their mission. These partnerships can be divided into four primary areas (see Table 1).

Why the Renewed Focus on Partnerships?

There are approximately two hundred nonprofit/for-profit academic partnerships serving upwards of 400,000 students.[3] Virtually all of these partnerships are the Contract—New or Contract—Replica relationships described in Table 1.

1. Contract—New: IPD alone has more than twenty partnerships with other providers, including Deltak. Regis partnered with another twenty institutions combined.

2. Contract—Replica: The largest provider is EmbanetCompass, with approximately fifty relationships. Bisk Education is likely the second largest, with more than ten relationships.

Table 1. **Examples of Partnership Structures**

Type	Description	Examples
Support	Outsource a single function or process for a university	California Community Colleges/ Kaplan (high-demand course-capacity expansion)
		Arizona State University/Pearson (enrollment management and remedial math)
Contract– Replica	Third party re-creates an existing program in a new format (e.g., online)	USC/2tor (2tor developed and manages a replica of USC's MAT degree online)
Contract– New	Third-party vendor leverages a university program or brand to create a new program, generally in a new format	Villanova/Bisk Education (Bisk developed courses that were not resident in the same form at Villanova)
		Indiana Wesleyan and various other partners/Institute for Professional Development (IPD) (helps develop and operate adult accelerated-degree programs for small liberal arts colleges)
Joint Venture Model	College/university and third party create a joint venture to build a new program with expectation of creation of new institution	Antioch College/Sojourner Douglass (Sojourner Douglass created as a branch campus of Antioch)
		Sojourner Douglass/Latimer Education (Latimer creating a branch campus from Sojourner Douglass)
		Tiffin University/Altius Education (Altius created Ivy Bridge College as a branch campus of Tiffin)

Virtually all these relationships are low profile, though some, such as Indiana Wesleyan, have over 10,000 students in their IPD partnership. Several recent high-profile partnerships—both successful and unsuccessful—suggest that this is a growing trend. These partnerships are not trivial, requiring the alignment of mission and financial expectations, the garnering of stakeholder buy-in, and the execution of complex legal and operating agreements. Powerful trends must be at work if they plan to continue expanding. Indeed, a combination of forces is simultaneously bringing nonprofit and for-profit institutions closer to each other.

Trends Bringing Nonprofits to the Table

Nonprofit institutions—both public and private—must constantly assess how well they are meeting their missions and what, if anything, they can do to increase their impact in the face of external constraints. Increasingly, nonprofits are willing to explore partnerships with for-profits to help them meet their objectives. There are several trends driving this willingness.

The first trend is the recognition that postsecondary students are increasingly "nontraditional" and need different delivery models to serve them well. Today, up to 75 percent of students currently attending college are "nontraditional" based on Department of Education definitions.[4]

These students, initially older working adults but increasingly traditional-age students, are now flocking to online learning environments for their flexibility, convenience, and cost. A recent U.S. Department of Education meta-study cited evidence that online learning is as good as or better than traditional, in-person higher education.[5] Today, over one in three college students takes at least one online course.[6] See Figure 1.

Figure 1. **Total Undergraduate Enrollments in the United States by Modality**

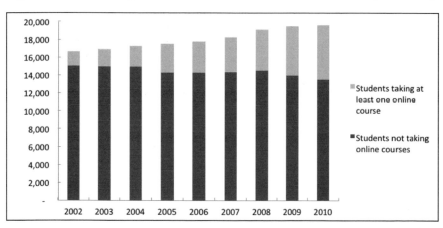

The second trend is that accrediting bodies, state legislators, Congress, students, and parents are increasingly focused on measurable outcomes. The study *Academically Adrift* found that 45 percent of college students make no measurable progress on key skills in their first two years of college.[7] There are few systems in place at traditional colleges to measure student outcomes, even when colleges institute compliant self-studies for their accrediting bodies. Due to the increased regulatory scrutiny of for-profit operators, however, such universities focus substantial resources measuring what they can measure—from employment outcomes to passing third-party exams (e.g., the National Council Licensure Examination for Registered Nurses, NCLEX). Across other disciplines, there are few nonprofit institutions that have scale, whereas for-profit operations have become extremely adept at quality control across multiple locations in complex service-delivery modules.

The third trend is declining resources and constrained capacity, driven largely by the great recession of 2008/2009 and continued fiscal pressures at the state level. Nearly half of the states have had spending cut more than 10% in the last year alone, and the cumulative impact of these reductions is severe. For example, current cuts in Arizona's state support for public universities, combined with previous cuts, reduces per-student funding 50% compared to pre-recession levels.[8] Total revenues of U.S. higher education institutions declined 14 percent from 2007 to 2009, from $481 billion to $405 billion. During this same period, enrollment increased from 18.3 million to 20.4 million.[9] This only compounded the problem. Tuition has risen 439 percent since 1982—almost twice the increase in health care and four times the rate of inflation.[10] Students and their families are beginning to rebel against high costs, and universities can no longer expect tuition to cover a cost structure that is growing at such a dramatic rate.

Institutions simply have not been able to keep up with student demand with their existing funding models. A recent Pearson Foundation/Harris Interactive survey found that 32 percent of community college students were unable to enroll in one or more courses because they were full. This figure was 55 percent for Hispanics, 47 percent in California, and 45 percent among 20- to 21-year-olds.[11] Worse yet, the California Community Colleges System was expecting to turn away up to 400,000 students from its institutions in the 2011–2012 academic year.[12]

The fourth and final trend is the absence of capital to finance growth and innovation. It cost the state of California almost $1 billion and took twenty years to build its latest campus, the University of California, Merced. Virtually no new medical schools have been built in the United States in the past twenty years because the average price tag for a medical school exceeds $100 million. In a time of severe budgetary constraints, it is virtually impossible to imagine statehouses allocating capital to expand capacity or programmatic reach.

At the same time, endowment returns and donations to nonprofit institutions have shrunk significantly in the great recession, with the bulk of funds raised at a limited number of elite institutions. Therefore, nonprofits that serve vast numbers of students will be forced to find expansion capital through other means.

Figure 2. **Enrollment Rises at For-Profit Schools**

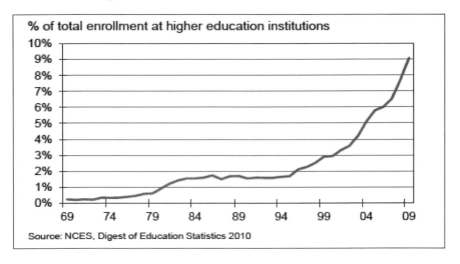

% of total enrollment at higher education institutions

Source: NCES, Digest of Education Statistics 2010

Without their traditional sources of capital, universities will find it increasingly difficult to expand programs, add new sites, or grow online offerings without partnering with the private sector. Such partnerships are already happening in research areas and are rapidly expanding into programmatic areas.

Private sector capital appears willing and even eager to invest in education programs, assuming they can expect a reasonable return on their investment.

Trends Bringing For-Profits to the Table

For-profit investors, and perhaps the existing for-profits themselves, have their own incentives to pursue academic partnerships with nonprofits. Again, there are multiple factors driving this trend.

The first trend is that private-sector investors have experience in actively embracing the market serving nontraditional students—in particular, expanding the use of online learning and developing close employer partnerships. For-profits have experienced rapid growth, accounting for approximately 3 percent of the total market to approximately 9 percent from 1999 to 2009 (see Figure 2).

The second trend is the growing regulatory pressure on for-profits. The U.S. Department of Education has created a series of rules and regulations that primarily target for-profit institutions. These regulations require that the repayment rates of student loans among graduates must meet certain thresholds, and they also require that institutions seek regulatory approval for any new programs to be eligible for federal financial aid. (At the time of this writing, some of these regulations are under review.) These new regulations are on top of previously established rules, including a requirement that at least 10 percent of revenue must come from nongovernmental sources, as well as existing restrictions on competency-based awarding of credit for certain programs. Hybrid structures, in general, allow classification under the nonprofit rules.

The combination of growing regulatory pressure and increasing competition for new enrollment has seen year-over-year growth in new starts at for-profits decline sharply from +19% in 2009–2010 to –17% just a year later in 2010–2011.[13]

The third trend is the need to satisfy accrediting bodies. For much of the early 2000s, for-profits employed a strategy of converting a financially failing nonprofit college into a for-profit and recapitalizing the institution for rapid growth. However, several recent rejections of change of control have put the viability of that strategy into question. In 2010, the Higher Learning Commission denied Dana College's change of control, and other pending deals have dragged out for many months. As a result, for-profit institutions are increasingly looking to partner with nonprofits, as opposed to taking over and starting anew.

While it is still early in the widespread growth of hybrid structures, the accrediting bodies and Department of Education seem to be favorably inclined to approve—if not encourage—such operations. The key issue for accrediting institutions is that the entity that they accredit is the entity that retains academic control. So long as this key tenet remains in place, the accrediting body has limited authority to curtail the activity.

In addition, thousands of partnerships and relationships exist between institutions and vendors. These relationships can be deep-seated. It would be extremely difficult to define acceptable vs. unacceptable behavior. For example, how does an accrediting body draw the line between a college hiring a marketing firm and a call center operator but not a company that combines both? Instead, the accrediting bodies have stuck to their existing governance mechanisms to ensure the primacy of the accredited institution in all academic matters.

Putting Two and Two Together

So where does the value derive from putting nonprofit/for-profit academic partnerships together? There are two key answers: (1) specialization and (2) scale. Nonprofits have lower costs of student acquisition, more established brands, and deep faculty/academic expertise. For-profits have business-process expertise, experience with non-traditional students, access to investment capital, and scale economies. When the skills of each group are brought together, the combined offering can be stronger than either of the partners operating independently. This combination may be the difference between success and failure in an increasingly crowded and competitive marketplace.

Clay Christensen and the Center for American Progress have argued that higher education is undergoing a typical disruptive pattern.[14] First, new technologies such as online learning enter the market. New entrants emerge and slowly gain scale before overtaking their more traditional counterparts. These new entrants create new business models that radically transform the operations of an organization.

At first, the new technology is inferior to traditional methods. For example, the first mobile phones weighed more than 15 pounds and were virtually useless but today's incarnations are an integral part of our lives and in many cases have replaced land-line phones. As new entrants become superior, most midsized players go out of business. Industries are shaped by a small number of large, dominant players that have access to capital and that continue technological innovation, while numerous niche organizations continue to provide some diversity.

Industries from cars to computers to department stores have undergone these dramatic transformations, as innovations in technology eventually lead to massive consolidation. Even in "services businesses," technology breeds a scale that was unthinkable before the disruptive innovation, e.g., there are now only four national banks, and nationwide names such as Wal-Mart and Target dominate the retail landscape.

Education may likely follow a similar path. University of Phoenix is the largest university in the United States. This scale has allowed for massive investment in the educational process. For example, Phoenix recently released a new cutting-edge learning m anagement system and acquired a leading computer-based math learning software.[15] Currently, a University of Phoenix degree is generally regarded by many as low quality—the 15 pound cell phone—but it has been reported that Phoenix invests $200 million per year, or just 4 percent of its revenue, on improvements in its teaching and learning.[16] This annual budget dwarfs the total spending of many individual colleges. The likely result is that over time, Phoenix will have the means to improve its quality on a scale the likes of which most institutions can only dream about.

So how can traditional institutions compete? Think of another analogy: how credit unions have successfully held market share relative to the national banks. Credit unions—virtually all nonprofits—have created partnerships with for-profit organizations in order to provide much-needed technology investment in strong, local brands. A credit union can use one company to process its credit cards while leveraging another service to provide online banking to its customers. Credit unions at this point can partner with for-profits to run virtually every part of their business. Virtually no credit unions attempt to match the capital investments of the big banks, but by working with a small number of for-profit providers, they have achieved scale necessary to compete effectively.

Key Partnership Design and Implementation Issues to Consider

Aligning key incentives between the partners is critical to the success of partnerships. Each partnership structure represents a unique set of issues to consider. Intellectual honesty for both the accredited institution and the for-profit organization is crucial. There are two key issues that tend to underlie successful contractual relationships:

1. **Financial:** Virtually every partnership is driven by a mutual profit motive. The nonprofit envisions using the profits to create incremental resources to support traditional operations, while the for-profit will distribute profits to its investors.
2. **Mission:** Colleges and universities are mission-driven and often seek to expand their reach, service, and impact. Working with a partner that identifies with the accredited institution's mission allows for a more constructive dialogue around the noneconomic issues that inevitably develop in a complex partnership.

A term sheet or a few sentences can define the economic relationship and mission alignment, but successful partnerships require deep thinking to drive through the myriad operational and legal complexities of such arrangements. To ensure a common understanding, the partnerships are structured through long, highly detailed legal contracts that lay out the specific roles and responsibilities of each party. Some of the key issues are as follows:

Accredited status: It is absolutely critical that the accredited institution retain the right to control all academic functions for any degree-granting program. This includes the ultimate approval rights over curriculum design, delivery, academic standards, and so forth. This control must be broad and absolute. However loath an institution is to pull the plug on a program, no accrediting body will accept a transaction whereby the governance of the degree-awarding authority does not continue to reside firmly with the accredited institution.

Key learning: The accredited institution must keep broadly worded control over any academic-program integrity issues. This responsibility must flow throughout the division of responsibility, with the accredited institution retaining specific control over a range of functions such as faculty, admissions requirements, and graduation standards. Best practice is to state the broad right of the accredited institution to oversee the program and then to point to specific standards that must be met. For example, all faculty must have certain types of degrees and the institution must approve all faculty hired, but the service partner can decide which faculty to hire and how much to pay them.

Specific direction for areas of control: Each contractual relationship should specify in specific detail the roles and responsibilities of each party. Documentation should break down the entire student life cycle into its component parts and then allocate responsibilities accordingly. Each party should be responsible for areas of its respective strengths or responsibilities—for example, the accredited institution would set admissions standards and review all applications, whereas the partner is responsible for all marketing and admissions activity.

Key learning: To the extent possible, the respective partners should set up definable rules for decision making ahead of time. For example, if the for-profit partner is responsible for admissions, then the accredited institution should define all admissions standards, including GPA, writing sample, official documents required, etc. It is virtually impossible to try to co-manage roles—and, in fact, generally better for the accredited institution to minimize involvement in decisions that are not core to its functionality. The accredited institution should consciously avoid input into as many tactical areas as possible because the needs of the new academic program will have myriad differences to their core operation. For example, many institutions have salary caps of some kind, but partners may be developing academic programs in areas whereby faculty are paid dramatically more than in a home institution (e.g., nursing faculty). By creating full separation between the institution's salary levels, the partner has the flexibility to hire faculty with specific skills at rates substantially above the levels at the home institution without creating issues at the next faculty senate meeting.

Performance management: Defining quality outcomes is difficult in any academic setting, but partnerships tend to optimize respective talents when each side agrees to the specific measurements of success. The objectives may be highly specific (e.g., pass-rate percentage on a licensing exam) or more qualitative (e.g., similar ratings in clinical placements).

Key learning: To the extent possible, performance metrics should be limited to key outcomes that drive the success of a program. It is difficult for a partnership to structure in advance program-development initiatives, but the partnership could define success as achieving a specific licensure from a specialized accrediting body, for example. If such specific licensure or related metrics are not available, others such as cohort default rate are broadly available and can be included as metrics of quality.

Financial considerations: There is a wide array of financial arrangements for partnerships, depending on the range of services provided by each party and the capital investment. While there are too many potential forms of economic consideration to list here, generally there is either a flat fee (or regulation-compliant per-student fee) or profits interest. The greatest alignment of interests generally comes from equity ownership, but allocating revenues can also allow each party to clearly define expenses related to revenue. In general, "revenue splits" would be something like 50/50 (50 percent to the marketing/financial partner and 50 percent to the accredited institution). For "equity" deals, the accredited institution will generally retain approximately 20 percent of the equity in joint venture agreements, although the market for such relationships is highly fluid, with few publicly available benchmarks.

Key learning: While there are numerous structures, there must be transparent reporting of financial information to all parties. Any partnership should have a third-party audit and frequent communication to ensure both sides understand respective revenues and costs. Long-term relationships work when both parties understand their respective economics, value the skills brought by each organization, and clearly define who gets what when.

Stakeholder involvement: Each institution has a complex web of stakeholders. It is imperative that the key decision makers on any partnership are fully aligned and have fully vetted the project. Generally this will include a board of trustees (or board committee) vote after careful consideration by key faculty and staff. One other note here is that many accrediting bodies know they need to evolve their understanding of such partnerships, but each accrediting body has slightly different rules, and these rules will evolve.

Key learning: Some of the most public failures of the partnership model occur when all stakeholders are not engaged. The most notable are those where the faculty vigorously protest a partnership based on quality concerns.

A View Forward—One Million Students Served Per Year by 2020

In this chapter, we have identified where nonprofit/for-profit academic partnerships have emerged, highlighted trends that are likely to accelerate development of these partnerships, and offered lessons learned to help future partners navigate their relationship. So where will this all lead?

Our back-of-the-envelope estimate is that 1 million students or more will be served by nonprofit/for-profit academic partnerships by 2020. As mentioned earlier, there are approximately 200 partnerships today serving nearly 400,000 students. Because of the trends previously described, we expect both the number and size of partnerships to grow. In recent years, these partnerships have been growing about 20% annually. Extrapolating that growth rate through 2020 would produce an estimate of 2,000,000 students enrolled in partnership programs. Using more-conservative estimates of 10% (the projected growth rate for online education) or 7% (the projected growth rate for the for-profit sector), by 2020 partnerships would reach approximately 900,000 students or 700,000 students, respectively.[17] Despite the range of these estimates (a high of 2,000,000 and a low of 700,000), it is not unreasonable to believe that partnerships will serve 1,000,000 students or more by 2020. Assuming roughly 20 million total higher education enrollments, these partnerships would represent 5 percent of all enrollments.

The growth of nonprofit/for-profit partnerships will likely be steady but uneven over the next decade. There will be many quiet successes and a few public failures, à la the attempted Kaplan/California Community Colleges partnership, which was ended in the face of strong faculty resistance. It appears partnerships will find increasing acceptance among institutions, accreditors, policy makers, faculty, and students.

We will slowly develop a better understanding of what drives success. Many questions remain to be answered; this chapter simply begins the exploration of the issues in hopes that others will look at them more thoroughly over time. Undoubtedly, there will be many important lessons for all in higher education about how to potentially break the "iron triangle" of access, quality outcomes, and costs.

Notes

1. John Immerwahr, Jean Johnson, and Paul Gasbarra, *The Iron Triangle: College Presidents Talk about Costs, Access, and Quality* (The National Center for Public Policy and Higher Education and Public Agenda, October 2008).
2. Marc Parry, "Online Venture Energizes Vulnerable College," *Chronicle of Higher Education*, August 28, 2011.
3. Based on forthcoming research from Innosight Institute, Harvard Business School, and The Parthenon Group.
4. Paul Attewell, "The Other 75%: Government Policy & Mass Higher Education" (unpublished paper, 2008).
5. Barbara Means, Yukie Toyama, Robert Murphy, Marianne Bakia, and Karla Jones, "Evaluation of Evidence-Based Practices in Online Learning: A Meta-Analysis and

Review of Online Learning Studies" (U.S. Department of Education, September 2010).

6. I. Elaine Allen and Jeff Seaman, "Going the Distance: Online Education in the United States, 2011" (Babson Survey Research Group, 2011).

7. Richard Arum and Josipa Roksa, *Academically Adrift: Limited Learning on College Campuses* (Chicago: University of Chicago Press, 2011).

8. See http://www.cbpp.org/cms/index.cfm?fa=view&id=3550.

9. National Center for Education Statistics, *Digest of Education Statistics 2010 (IPEDS)* (46th in a series of publications, April 5, 2011).

10. "Soaring College Tuitions," *New York Times,* December 3, 2008.

11. Harris Interactive, *Pearson Foundation Community College Student Survey* (conducted September 27 through November 4, 2010).

12. Nanette Asimov, "Community Colleges Could Turn Away 400,000," *San Francisco Chronicle*, March 31, 2012.

13. JP Morgan analysis based on start growth at eight industry leading for-profit institutions.

14. Clayton M. Christensen, Michael B. Horn, Louis Soares, and Louis Caldera, "Disrupting College: How Disruptive Innovation Can Deliver Quality and Affordability to Postsecondary Education" (Center for American Progress: February 8, 2011).

15. Courtney Boyd Myers, "Clayton Christensen: Why Online Education Is Ready For Disruption Now" (blog post at http://thenextweb.com/insider/2011/11/13/clayton-christensen-why-online-education-is-ready-for-disruption-now/, November 13, 2011).

16. Christensen et al., "Disrupting College."

17. Based on forthcoming research from Innosight Institute, Harvard Business School, and The Parthenon Group. Future enrollment forecast from Eduventures.

Daniel Pianko *is a partner at University Ventures Fund. By partnering with top-tier universities and colleges and then strategically directing private capital to develop programs of exceptional quality that address major economic and social needs, UV expects to set new standards for student outcomes and advance the development of the next generation of colleges and universities on a global scale.* **Josh Jarrett** *is Deputy Director for Postsecondary Success in the U.S. Program at the Bill & Melinda Gates Foundation. He leads the Next Generation Models portfolio, which supports learning innovations and technologies with the potential to dramatically increase low-income student success and improve affordability. Jarrett has previously served as an entrepreneur and as a consultant for McKinsey & Company and the National Park Service.*

8

Scaling Up: Four Ideas to Increase College Completion

Vernon C. Smith

Introduction

LOW PERSISTENCE AND GRADUATION RATES, especially among low-income young adults and minorities, are ongoing problems that U.S. higher education faces. The College Board's *College Completion Agenda Report*[1] in 2010 tracked how the United States is losing ground in awarding postsecondary degrees in comparison to other industrialized nations. In response, a number of national initiatives have emerged, including President Obama's American Graduation Initiative,[2] Completion by Design,[3] and the Next Generation Learning Challenges,[4] in the hope of increasing the attainment of postsecondary degrees. Research from the Georgetown University Center on Education and the Workforce reports that by 2018, 68 percent of jobs will require postsecondary education, which is a 40 percent increase over the current level.[5]

In spite of the need for education, the uneven distribution of alternatives or the lack of capacity to meet those needs remains a barrier. Recent estimates show that in California, 670,000 potential students are unable to enter the higher education system because of the massive funding cuts that limit institutional capacity to enroll students.[6] In essence, the California system, like other state systems, is oversubscribed. This compounds the completion-productivity equation. As Complete College America reports, "Time is the enemy of college completion."[7] Students stop out and drop out or turn to other expensive options that require taking on greater debt. Sticker shock at the high cost of college is a great deterrent and hurts the national completion agenda.

To increase the number of graduates produced, the nation will need high-quality solutions that leverage technology to achieve impact at scale. This chapter describes some ideas that might allow us to meet our college completion goals.

Ideas for Incubation

Ideas have the potential to alter fundamental assumptions and reveal solutions. While ideas often take a long time to mature, technology can enable those ideas, catalyzing shared reconceptualization that alters the landscape.

At two recent convenings held at Rio Salado College (a Maricopa Community College in Tempe, Arizona) in February and April 2011, thought leaders and other representatives from twelve high-quality, highly scalable online and hybrid colleges and universities came together to identify and incubate ideas surrounding access, retention, and completion in higher education.[8] These ideas have the potential, if given time to incubate, and if enabled by information technology, to change higher education.

Participants considered four ideas to have the most potential for increasing access, retention, and completion in U.S. higher education, and thus the most potential for helping the nation increase to 60 percent the number of college graduates produced by 2020. To be considered, each concept would need to improve student success for more than 100,000 students. These four themes are

- partnerships to serve oversubscribed institutions;
- course and credit exchange in an SOC-like (Servicemembers Opportunity Colleges) network;
- research, analytics, and metrics for student loss and momentum; and
- competency-based design of courses, programs, and degrees.

While the ideas are at different stages of evolution and may not be "ready for prime time," each is catalyzed by IT and has the possibility to alter the landscape of higher education. These ideas are offered as examples of how higher education might be designed in the digital age.

Partnerships to Serve Oversubscribed Student-Serving Institutions

Throw out a statistic such as "670,000 underserved and unserved students in California," and the need for educational options and the dire circumstances of current institutions and students become obvious. And this is just California—the number does not include students in rural areas throughout the country or busy working adults in other states seeking more convenient access to a college degree. A recent Pearson Foundation study indicates that 32 percent of college students nationwide were unsuccessful in enrolling in their desired college course.[9]

Online and hybrid courses can provide the flexibility to cover these supply gaps. Rio Salado College, a Maricopa Community College, is an example of how online courses help students get the classes they want without having to wait for the next semester. At Rio Salado College, online courses never get canceled. If one of over 600 courses is listed in the online schedule, it will be open to students to register. Moreover, online courses are available for forty-eight start dates a year—practically every Monday an online course is available. Technology is key to not only delivering but also to managing online courses and student services in order to rapidly expand capacity. But having technology infrastructure and capacity is not enough. Institutions must address political and policy barriers as well.

Private, for-profit institutions are moving quickly into this online/hybrid course market space. However, their tuition rates tend to be much higher, and even with the help of private providers, it will take an "all-hands-on-deck" approach to ensure students have sufficient access to courses and programs to keep them from stopping and dropping out before reaching their graduation goals. Public nonprofits face their own state-funding crises, and most have underdeveloped capacity or limited access to the capital needed to scale up to meet online/hybrid learning demand. On top of this situation is the recent U.S. Department of Education ruling that requires state authorization of distance learning programs to ensure institutional eligibility to offer students access to federal student financial aid. This policy shift in an environment of shrinking state budgets has triggered caution on the part of online colleges and universities that could serve in overenrolled states as they struggle to understand and manage the additional bureaucratic red tape of over 50 unique state authorization processes. And do not forget that some of those processes reflect the natural turf protection that goes on in any sector, including higher education. Additionally, institutional approval to operate in a state is not the same as having authorization to run a specific program such as teacher preparation, dental hygiene, and nursing—these require additional application processes to obtain approvals.

Even an institution experienced with online programs, such as Coastline Community College in California, cannot serve as many students as it would like. State funding limitations have basically capped its ability to expand its offerings. It has the institutional will, knowledge, and experience to serve more students, but it lacks the resources to capitalize on those strengths and meet the available demand.

Imagine a scenario whereby institutions with a high capacity to deliver online and hybrid courses could partner with oversubscribed or underdeveloped institutions. A partnership or consortium model could remove the barriers to operate and leverage alternative funding mechanisms that already exist. The model found in the Southern Regional Education Board's Electronic Campus, for example, could serve as a starting point for a national model.[10] In the southern region, colleges and universities entered into a consortial agreement that allows online providers preferred access across state lines in an open marketplace. The creation of such a consortium on an even broader scale would benefit students who have been shut out. Moreover, partnership arrangements with other institutions that have already developed capacity would help build a transitional bridge until policies and other political limitations are resolved. A model that would work for institutions in California would most likely also work well for colleges and universities in other states. The technologies and business processes currently exist to address this critical need for flexible and reliable access to higher education, but it will take a higher level of innovation and collaboration to overcome the barriers.

Course and Credit Exchange in an SOC-like Network

The SOC (Servicemembers Opportunity Colleges) network of over 1,900 colleges and universities opens educational opportunities for military service members and their families. Institutions with large online programs such as the University of Maryland University College (UMUC) provide the bulk of instruction.

Service-member students can take advantage of the new GI Bill, as well as the U.S. Department of Defense's tuition-assistance program, which provides $250 per credit hour. They can access information through the GoArmyEd portal and other information sources available through the military. They can also take advantage of the special articulation agreements in the SOC network. Once service-member students are registered, they can take courses at any SOC institution and have the assurance that those courses and credits will seamlessly transfer back to their home institution.

Inspired by the SOC model, some higher education institutions and thought leaders have begun to envision a new course and credit exchange. Such an exchange would follow the SOC network principles but be available to civilians through a new type of consortium. Imagine a scenario in which public and nonprofit institutions with quality, capacity, and scalability come together in a course- and credit-exchange network to serve students who have been shut out of higher education. By combining the lower tuition costs of community colleges and the efficiencies of online universities, this network could significantly drive down the overall costs for students. Seamless and universal transfer of credits in the network would minimize course and credit loss while shortening the time to degree completion. Once the network was established through seed money—both from private foundations and governments—it could help participating institutions achieve scale through a perpetual education funding model. This type of funding mechanism would provide incentives to deliver online and hybrid courses and programs for completion that, in turn, would increase the supply of courses and programs for other institutions. The end result would be new options and pathways that facilitate the easy transfer of credit, lower costs, and acceleration of degree completion. While some states have made great strides in articulating and transferring credit, this new relationship would clarify pathways and reduce risks for students on a national basis, in that access to high-quality institutions online would remove geography as a limiting factor. The utilization of electronic portfolios and other IT supports will be critical to implementing this type of course- and credit-exchange network.

Research, Analytics, and Metrics for Student Loss and Momentum

Colleges and universities collect mountains of data in their student information, learning management, and other systems. At the same time, students come and go—often at predictable "loss points" such as the transition from high school to college, during remedial education, and so on.

In one scenario, higher education would use the power of information technology to mine student information and data on a massive scale across multiple institutions. This would involve aggregating, mining, and identifying the key momentum and loss variables, and then scaling up solutions that effectively address those factors. The idea would be to then create predictive models through the use of advanced statistical modeling that would identify possible stumbling blocks and help drive early interventions for students, especially low-income young adults and minorities. A growing body of best practices and interventions that remove barriers to student progress and success exists, but those interventions would be better informed if they were based on what the research and actual behaviors indicate, rather than on anecdotal notions or experience alone.

An example of this idea that has moved to a "proof of concept" stage is the Predictive Analytics Reporting (PAR) Framework coordinated by the Western Interstate Commission for Higher Education's (WICHE) Cooperative for Educational Technologies (WCET for short), with support from the Bill & Melinda Gates Foundation. In an impressive pilot phase, the PAR Framework project is deconstructing the problems of retention, progress, and completion to find solutions for decreasing loss and increasing momentum and success. Six

PAR partner institutions (American Public University System, Colorado Community College System, Rio Salado College, University of Hawaii System, University of Illinois–Springfield, and the University of Phoenix) are federating and aggregating more than 600,000 de-identified online student records and will apply descriptive, inferential, and predictive analytical tests to the single pool of records to look for variables that seem to have an effect on student achievement. Currently, researchers are focusing early efforts on identifying and exploring the patterns between and among more than thirty variables that are common across participating institutions. This process has accelerated the capture and collection of key student data from multiple student information systems. This identification and harmonization of variables will provide the basis for the inclusion of many more institutions, which will help provide a deeper and more robust view of the factors that decrease loss and increase momentum, and vice versa.

Competency-Based Design of Courses, Programs, and Degrees

Customization and personalization of the student learning experience will increase the number of students who successfully complete their studies in higher education. The ability to implement this online has great potential because of the emergence of adaptive technologies. Students come to college with different experiences and levels of mastery. Students also absorb and apply their knowledge at different rates. While these conditions are self-evident, technology now has a fundamental role to play in the national completion agenda by enabling personalized instruction and learning.

Consider how music for years was packaged and sold in albums to the music-buying public as a metaphor for how learning is designed and delivered in higher education. Anyone who has ever bought an album knows that you must pay for the entire album, even if you only really want one or two songs. But music consumers wanted the choice of purchasing individual songs instead of the whole package (album) and then creating (and re-creating) their own sequence of songs. The advent of digital reproduction and distribution technologies enabled customers to pick and choose only the songs they want without having to buy the entire album. The customer, not the music label, now controls the buying and listening experience.

Packaging music by the album is much like what higher education has traditionally done in packaging learning. For the most part, students have had to buy the entire album in the form of the course. The reality is, for learning to be most efficient and streamlined, students may not, and often do not, need the entire course. Instead they may need only certain aspects of the course to round out their learning. Packaging learning differently could be a game changer in higher education.

Imagine a scenario in which courses were unbundled and disaggregated into competencies that were mapped throughout the course, similar to what the Khan Academy has done in the open educational resource setting.[11] Imagine a scenario whereby students master those competencies through granular modules. As the student progresses, new modules are presented based on previous performance and predictive models that indicate the needed remediation as well as the next steps necessary to progress through the course. Students would spend time on modules where they have gaps in knowledge instead of time on modules where they have demonstrated mastery. Demonstrated mastery of the competency could serve as a new unit of learning for the digital age instead of "seat time," based on industrial-era Carnegie units.

Competency-based assessment in all or part of a course would change the way progress toward college completion is documented, with far-reaching implications. It would facilitate recognition of prior learning for credit if students could demonstrate their mastery of course competencies by a recognized assessment process, which in turn would accelerate time to degree. It would improve the quality of assessment tools and foster their use at a more granular level while at the same time promoting the creation of higher-quality online lesson content. Additionally, course and program competencies could be aligned with business and industry competencies to ensure a highly trained workforce that possesses relevant mastery of the knowledge needed to succeed and compete in a global economy.

For Western Governors University (WGU), this is business as usual. WGU has made tremendous strides in the development of competency-based curricula. The transfer of credits from WGU to another institution remains a struggle, though, as credits have to be translated into traditional units when transferred to another institution (thus making it preferable that students simply graduate from WGU). Recognition of competency-based credits across institutions would change the nature of how higher education packages learning. Instead of committing to the entire curriculum (album), students could select the content (individual songs) that aligns with the competencies they lack.

Acceleration of completion through a competency-based model is challenging. It requires commonly accepted definitions of learning outcomes across courses and programs, many of which will not have defined student success in competency terms. Relevant regulations, such as those governing federal financial aid, are attempting to address alternative models of student work and attainment. However, they are still deeply rooted in the credit hour, requiring institutions to translate newer, more adaptable competency schemas back to the older "full album" model of learning units.[12]

The spirit of innovation in the United States, and the need to increase the knowledge capital and intellectual capacity of its citizenry, calls for different approaches. At minimum, there should be ongoing pilots and evaluations of competency-based approaches with targeted outcomes. Regional accrediting bodies and other policy makers should support forward-thinking institutions in building innovative methods to both recognize and facilitate the seamless transfer of competency-based credits that are not based on seat time. Just as the music industry was forced to reexamine its model of packaging music, higher education needs to reexamine the merits of competency-based courses, programs, and degrees.

Conclusion

Author William Gibson is attributed with saying, "The future is already here—it's just not very evenly distributed." The ideas that have been outlined here are not new. The best practices can be found in pockets across higher education. However, these ideas need to be highlighted, explored, and implemented. It will take additional thinking, awareness building, and promotion of these ideas in order for them to achieve the scale necessary to meaningfully change the landscape of higher education.

Notes

1. The College Board, *College Completion Agenda, 2010 Progress Report,* http://completionagenda.collegeboard.org/reports.
2. The American Graduation Initiative, http://www.whitehouse.gov/blog/Investing-in-Education-The-American-Graduation-Initiative/.
3. Completion by Design, http://completionbydesign.org/.
4. Next Generation Learning Challenges, http://nextgenlearning.org/.
5. Georgetown University Center on Education and the Workforce, http://www9.georgetown.edu/grad/gppi/hpi/cew/pdfs/FullReport.pdf.
6. Steven E. F. Brown, "California's Community Colleges Say 670,000 May Be Turned Away," *San Francisco Business Times,* August 24, 2011, http://www.bizjournals.com/sanfrancisco/news/2011/08/24/california-community-colleges-turn-away.html.
7. Complete College America, *Time Is the Enemy,* http://www.completecollege.org/docs/Time_Is_the_Enemy.pdf.

8. These convenings were made possible through the support of the Bill & Melinda Gates Foundation.

9. *Pearson Foundation Community College Survey,* http://www.pearsonfoundation. org/education-leadership/research/community-college-survey.html.

10. Southern Regional Education Board's Electronic Campus, http://www.electroniccam pus.org/.

11. Khan Academy, http://www.khanacademy.org/about.

12. *Information for Financial Aid Professionals* (IFAP), Federal Student Aid, March 18, 2011, http://ifap.ed.gov/dpcletters/GEN1106.html.

Vernon C. Smith *is Chief Academic Officer and Provost at MyCollege Foundation, dedicated to helping low-income youth gain quality college credentials more affordably. Previously, he served as Faculty Chair, Dean, and Vice President of Academic Affairs at Rio Salado College. Smith serves on the Board of Directors of EDUCAUSE.*

9

Western Governors University

Robert W. Mendenhall

Background

THE INITIAL CONCEPT for Western Governors University (WGU) was developed at a Western Governors Association meeting in 1995. At that time, the governors knew that higher education was at a tipping point and that a nonprofit, flexible, and scalable solution was required to meet the needs of the states. The governors recognized that many college graduates had skills that were unreliable and insufficient to meet the future needs for a highly skilled workforce. Traditionally, underserved students who are minority, rural, low income, or the first generation in their family to attend college struggle to navigate complex higher education and financial aid systems. Access, retention, and graduation rates are a concern for students from these populations, as the traditional higher education system tends to overlook their unique needs.

The governors also felt that the credit hour was not sufficiently measuring what graduates know and can do, and that their new university would have to be competency-based to measure those skills. WGU would also need to increase access for students by being accessible regardless of geographic location and by providing more value at a lower cost than public universities.

- The governors particularly had in mind students in the rural West who were not within driving distance of a college or university and working adults whose schedules did not fit in with classes offered at traditional institutions.

- The lower cost would not only benefit students but also states, as universities rely heavily upon state appropriations to fund higher education.

- The university would also take advantage of the Internet and new technologies to serve large numbers of students from a distance and at a low cost.

The concept for WGU was championed by Republican Utah governor Michael Leavitt and Democratic Colorado governor Roy Romer—a collaboration that reached across party lines. It officially launched in 1997 and was founded by the nineteen governors whose respective states contributed $100,000 each to fund the start-up university. WGU was a public-private partnership; in addition to state contributions, the federal government and corporate partners supported its creation. The result was that for the cost of one new building on a single campus, the states now shared a new university accessible to students across the nation.

The founding governors created WGU as a resource for the states, and as such, the university offers bachelors' and masters' degrees in such key workforce areas as teacher education, information technology, business, and the health professions (including nursing). The university fills an important niche in higher education today by serving a nontraditional student population. The average age of its students is thirty-six, most work full time, and approximately 75 percent fall within an underserved demographic (e.g., low income, minority status, first generation in family to attend college, and students from rural areas). Over 90 percent of students enter with transfer credits—many come to WGU having not been successful at another institution yet still wanting to pursue their dream of a college degree.

Since receiving regional accreditation in early 2003, the university has grown from 500 students to over 30,000, and continues to grow at 30 percent annually. WGU is the only regionally and nationally accredited nonprofit university in the country granting online, competency-based degrees to students in all fifty states. The university is particularly attractive to working adults who already have some competencies, either from prior education or work experience, and who don't have the time to attend class at traditional times in a brick-and-mortar institution.

Although created by governors, WGU does not receive state funding but operates as a private nonprofit university that sustains itself on per-student tuition of approximately $6,000 for a twelve-month year. Its tuition last increased in 2008 by $100 per six-month term, which is especially remarkable considering public state institutions have increased tuition by an average of 5.6 percent per year from 2000 through 2010. The average time to graduate for a student is thirty months for a bachelor's degree, compared to a sixty-month average for other institutions. This time-to-graduate result is not achieved by compromising education standards—students must receive the equivalent of a B grade in each assessment in order to graduate (rather than by achieving an average measure).

A University Designed with Technology in Mind

Western Governors University was designed using technology to provide education that is accessible, flexible, and affordable without compromising quality. The founding governors knew that technology must take a transformational role in education in order to change the way we measure learning, expand the notion of how learning happens, and make possible learning that can take place anytime, anywhere.

Technology has changed the productivity of every industry except education. In fact, in education today technology is most often an add-on cost and not used to change or improve teaching and learning. Even with the improvements in online-learning platforms and resources, the majority of online education is classroom education delivered over a wire at a distance. There is still a professor who teaches a class of 20–30 students and uses a syllabus and textbooks to deliver information, and every course requires a certain number of hours for a predetermined length of time (a term or semester). In this model, technology is not being used to improve the student experience or to innovate beyond the traditional model of classroom education. A recent aggregate Department of Education study of online learning vs. classroom learning found that online was just as "good" as classroom education—because in most cases, they are still the same thing.[1] Whereas technology has improved every other industry, in education it has been used to make things "just as good as" education prior to technological advancements.

WGU utilizes technology to transform the way we educate—to improve the quality of education, drive the cost down, and allow for asynchronous learning. With past technologies, there were not efficient ways to increase productivity while effectively delivering education and measuring learning outcomes. With its creation, the governors saw an opportunity to utilize new technologies to bring this new education model to life—and they recognized that the only way to individualize instruction is through the use of technology so that content is available when students need it and they are able to make progress independent of a set time and place, thus truly enabling competency-based learning. The result is that the university is cost efficient (costing about $6,000 per 12-month-year in tuition, at no cost to the states) and, since the university is competency-based, productivity is increased as a result of technology enabling the measurement of learning rather than time.

Technology at WGU is used to teach students in an independent learning environment, using third-party courseware and learning materials. Technology allows the university to shift the use of labor by having the technology deliver instruction, changing the faculty role to that of a mentor who guides the student rather than delivering content. Faculty use technology to support learning communities, facilitate discussions, work with students one-on-one, and determine where time is best spent in group chats and outreach. The shift provides each student with individualized help and support.

The university does not develop or teach any of its own courses; instead, faculty identify the best existing resources, and WGU acquires the right to use them with its students. These courses include self-diagnostic tools to determine areas of competency, readings, videos, guided tutorials, interactive exercises, and other optional learning tools. Self-diagnostic tools, or "preassessments," are used at the beginning of each course for students to measure their knowledge. The preassessment then identifies areas of strength and weakness for the student, and from there an individualized study plan is developed for the student to fulfill all competencies before taking the assessment.

Online learning resources that can be accessed anytime and anywhere aid students in learning new material. They can engage specific coursework as needed based upon competency, then take the assessment when they have gained the required knowledge and skills for the course. Following completion of self-paced learning modules, students demonstrate mastery of the material by taking assessments. These may be computer-based objective exams, essays, portfolios, or other projects that measure learning outcomes. Tests are administered at a distance through monitored online exams.

Technology further improves internal productivity by automating processes where possible and speeding up the response time on everything from e-mail communication to grading assessments. Technology enables WGU to produce a report every month on every student that monitors progress through each course, measuring satisfactory academic progress and whether or not the student is on track to graduate on time. Student mentors and course mentors use these reports to evaluate student progress and guide their coaching for the student. Course mentors are also able to see where students are commonly struggling with a concept in a course. Faculty can measure the engagement and effectiveness of learning tools and materials, constantly responding to student needs. Technology also helps the university's Office of Institutional Research to track and evaluate its programs, faculty, courses, and new initiatives on an ongoing basis. WGU uses Business Intelligence software to run analytics to determine what is working well within the model and what practices need to be adjusted to better serve students.

Technology brings new ways to measure and credential learning and shifts the emphasis to learner-centric education over the previous faculty-centric model. Learning now happens in a variety of different ways, with information at our fingertips. The objectives for educators now become facilitating learning, creating a supportive environment for the learner, and credentialing what has been learned. WGU uses assessments to measure progress and student knowledge required for each competency.

A New Model for Higher Education

Competency-Based Education

Traditional higher education bases student learning on how many hours have been spent in the classroom (reinforced by

> **See NBC Nightly News Video:**
> http://www.wgu.edu/wgu/nbc_news

federal financial aid regulations), not necessarily on how much a student has learned. Students can pass some classes with a D or a C in a subject, hardly indicative of mastery. It doesn't matter whether or not a student already knows the material; he or she must still sit through class with everyone else. Additionally, the model doesn't account for the struggling student who can't keep up with the rest of the class and who may need more time to learn and master specific concepts. Moreover, the variability of each course within the same department at the same institution means that two graduates from the same program will not have equal levels of knowledge or competence. An employer hiring the two graduates may find that the level of competency is significantly different due to the different experiences of the students.

Competency-based education is a relatively new approach to higher education and challenges the notion that time spent in a classroom equates to learning. Competency-based education is predicated on two things known about adult learners:

- Students come to higher education knowing different things as a result of their different backgrounds and life experiences.
- They learn at different rates—in fact, each individual learns different subjects at different rates.

At WGU, students demonstrate that they have all of the competencies required for their degree by passing a series of assessments that have been carefully developed to measure competency in each area. The university does not award grades but rather a "Pass" on each assessment once competency has been shown. A "Pass" score is equivalent to or better than a B grade. Additionally, students can take their assessments at any time they are confident they can demonstrate the level of knowledge and skills required. With this model, students advance by demonstrating mastery of competencies instead of earning credit hours, which allows them to move quickly through material they already know and focus on new learning—ideal for adult learners with competencies, as many have family and work responsibilities (seventy percent of WGU students work full time). If a student doesn't have prior knowledge, he or she is provided with learning resources, mentors, and learning communities to support learning new material. Learning communities are a virtual community wherein students can interact with course mentors and peers to discuss content and post questions.

The competencies at WGU are defined by a council in each college that is made up of industry professionals and leaders in the field. Councils define competencies based upon what graduates are expected to know in the workplace and as professionals in the chosen career. This ensures that students are receiving degrees that are relevant to workforce needs and industry requirements. In addition to degree-specific competencies, students are expected to demonstrate competency in the liberal arts, including critical thinking, writing and communications, and basic math skills, depending on their degree programs.

Changing the Faculty Role

One of the greatest costs at traditional institutions is funding for the research conducted by university faculty. WGU is a student-centric university, not a research institution, and thus it places the focus on student learning and success. The university's model works well for the students as well as for the faculty. WGU employs full-time faculty as mentors and content experts who work with students one-on-one to offer advising, guidance, motivation, and subject-specific help. Additionally, the faculty role is disaggregated, so different people perform different roles: advising, content help (professor), grading, and course development.

Because the technology primarily delivers instruction to students, the role of the instructor at WGU is unique—faculty time is freed up to help where it is needed (e.g., office hours) instead of being used to deliver content. This model is effective and scalable to many students because of the breakout of educator responsibilities outlined in Table 1.

The disaggregation of the faculty role enables the university to serve a much larger number of students at a lower cost. For example, a writing course

Table 1. **Educator Responsibilities at WGU**

Faculty Role	Alternative Approach at WGU
Delivery of instruction	Technology delivers instruction.
Course design	WGU does not create its own courses or content but rather uses third-party curriculum.
Selecting learning materials	Specialized role where faculty search and select the best online learning resources for each assessment.
Assessment design	WGU's Assessment Department meets with councils in each college to determine competencies, then designs assessments to measure each competency.
Content help or office hours	Subject-specific mentors (called course mentors) are available for one-on-one and one-to-many sessions reviewing content with which students need more help than can be had through independent learning.
Mentoring	Student mentors communicate regularly with students to counsel, advise, coach, organize, and motivate remotely.
Grading	Part-time faculty are hired only to grade student assessments and are trained to grade based upon a specific rubric.

at a public university may cap at one hundred students, at which point another professor is hired. This professor then creates his or her own version of the course—duplicating work—and then serves his or her one hundred students. Perhaps there is the assistance of a graduate student or two to help in grading papers, but otherwise growth is limited to the capacity of what one individual can do. At WGU, the best learning resources are selected and used across the course to deliver the content, the course is designed once, assessments are designed once, and all students have a consistent experience in each assessment. Work is not duplicated in this model. Grading is done from an objective point of view and follows a rubric; passes are awarded to work that is at least a B level. One course mentor can help many students as they progress through an assessment, and all of this person's time is dedicated to personal help with students rather than administrative work or lectures.

Another advantage to disaggregating faculty roles is that each specialist is the best at what he or she does. This means that students aren't getting an instructor who is a great lecturer, average at designing tests, and never available for office hours. Rather, the student is getting a dedicated expert in each area of faculty responsibilities. This separation of roles creates a consistent environment in which objectivity is key; grades are not influenced by student lobbying, mentors/teachers inflating grades, favoritism, or teacher evaluations. Objectivity, learning objectives, competency, consistency, and quality are central to the success of each specialized faculty role.

A unique faculty role that supports the success of its students is mentoring—student mentors and course mentors.

- Student mentors generally hold a master's degree, often in the subject area they advise, and communicate regularly with students. Student mentors help students determine the appropriate place to begin and the appropriate path on which to proceed with their learning while providing support for each student's unique learning needs, following an appropriate, individualized pace, whether fast or slow. The student mentors start with a student the day he or she begins a program and stays with him/her through graduation.

- Course mentors typically have a doctorate degree in their subject area and are available to students for content-specific help and outreach as needed. Students work with different course mentors for each subject area.

The mentoring model is very important to WGU's student-retention rates, as the university currently has a one-year retention rate of 76 percent.

This connection with the mentor can help students avoid feeling as though they are not engaged or as involved in their education as they would be at a traditional institution. As mentors and students work through challenges and celebrate successes together, deep friendships are often formed. The National Study of Student Engagement (NSSE) polls students at traditional and online universities nationwide to gauge student involvement and gather student opinions of the support provided by their institutions. WGU scores compare well to peers and all other universities for questions about support and mentor interaction (see Table 2).

Third-Party Courses

WGU does not create its own learning content and instead looks to third-party resources that utilize technology to deliver quality instruction. The learning resources are chosen by faculty based upon content, ease of use, alignment of competencies, and quality of delivery. The university's courses utilize open-education resources, materials from publishers, and materials

Table 2. **Measures of Support and Mentor Interaction**

Measure	Component	WGU	Private Nonprofit Universities	NSSE 2011
Student–Faculty Interaction	First Year	39.3%	34.4%	34.8%
	Senior	37.7%	41.8%	42.8%
Supportive Campus Environment	First Year	71.2%	63.4%	63.8%
	Senior	67.6%	60.0%+	60.1%
Quality of Academic Advising*	First Year	3.64	3.11	3.13
	Senior	3.64	2.96	2.98
Rating of Entire Educational Experience*	First Year	3.62	3.25	3.28
	Senior	3.58	3.23	3.27

*Mean scores on a four-point scale.

from other colleges and universities, which can sometimes pose a challenge, as many publishers, textbook companies, and the market in general can be behind the curve of online learning. However, recent partnerships have proven to be effective and promising. Ultimately, the goal is to have just one learning resource for each course that can be a diagnostic tool for competency and guide students through areas where they lack competency, and that is interactive, engaging, and can be used on multiple devices.

By employing the best third-party resources on the market, WGU is not using internal resources to create its own content for each course. Experts have developed excellent learning resources at other institutions, and learning providers have developed self-paced learning modules that the university utilizes. This ensures consistency for students across the course and across the university, and faculty time is consequently spent in direct contact with students. Faculty are, to an extent, managing the student experience in each course by determining the learning resources and texts to be used to gain competency.

Another recent improvement at WGU has been its decision to offer all textbooks as e-books free of charge to its students. In doing this, the university hopes to further assist students in effectively managing their time and saving money. If students can immediately access e-books for free, they are able to quickly engage with material in each course rather than waiting for financial aid funds to be disbursed and books to arrive.

Delivery and Grading of Assessments

WGU uses exams, papers, portfolios, projects, and performance assessments to determine a student's competency. A student must demonstrate mastery of all competencies through a series of assessments. Performance assessments require written work or a project and are described within a website that each student accesses to receive assessment directions and the grading rubric, and then creates, edits, and submits the work to receive grading feedback. The student officially submits the performance assessment for grading, it goes into a queue, and the next available grader picks up the assessment to evaluate based upon the rubric.

Graders have at least a master's degree and expertise in the area they are grading and also undergo rigorous training and ongoing quality-assurance checks on their work to ensure that students are being graded fairly and consistently based upon the rubrics. Grading usually takes three or four days; once the assessment has been released to students, they are able to see their scores. At that time, they can see if they have passed the assessment based upon the rubric, or if they need to revisit some areas to gain competency and then be reassessed. Students also typically meet with a course mentor at this time to discuss their weaknesses and where they need to spend more time on the material.

Objective assessments are proctored exams, which are taken after students have either passed a low-stakes preassessment to determine their level of competency or have worked their way through the learning resources to gain competency. The delivery of exams at WGU has evolved over the years. In the past, students took proctored exams at approved testing sites such as a library or nearby college-testing center, and the university covered the testing fees. With high-speed Internet accessible across the country, WGU now administers the majority of exams through web-based proctoring provided by a third-party company. Upon matriculation, students are sent a free webcam that they will use to take their exams. Exams can be taken at home, but must take place in a room where no one else is present and where there are no interruptions. Facial recognition software ensures that the correct student is taking the exam, and the proctoring service monitors the test taker and immediately stops the exam if there is a disturbance or it appears the student is not following test-taking guidelines.

Finally, WGU uses industry-specific performance assessments to ensure quality. In the Teachers College, students are required to complete observations and student teaching for a set period of time. During the student teaching experience, students are observed by a clinical supervisor, principal, and host teacher and complete a series of hands-on assessments to gain competencies needed to teach in the classroom. WGU nursing students are required to demonstrate competency through simulations and clinical hours. Information technology students graduate not only with a bachelor's degree from WGU, but also with 6–7 industry certifications they've earned as part of their degree program.

WGU Results

Access

WGU's model is scalable and can handle rapid growth, as has been shown by continuous

> See WGU Overview video:
> http://www.wgu.edu/wgu/achieve_more_video

growth of over 30 percent in the past several years. Additionally, its programs in high-need areas such as teaching and nursing afford opportunities to qualified candidates who may not have been able to get placed in a certain class due to enrollment caps. Technology expands access to higher education for students who otherwise would not have an option to earn a degree (rural and/ or low-income students or working adults, for instance). Because the university is completely online (except for clinical hours and student teaching), students are able to access it anytime, anywhere. With technology able to deliver content whenever and wherever students need it, access is expanded to include everyone, and the focus shifts to learning rather than trying to figure out how to fit classes into everyday life.

Affordability

WGU has always had a focus on affordability and costs approximately $6,000 per year for most programs. WGU's model is affordable to the student and operates at no cost to the state. As it grows, the institution reinvests funds into updating degree programs and improving the student experience. And as it offers more services to its students, such as free counseling or e-books (both added in 2010), leadership works hard to ensure that the cost is not passed on to the students. The university also makes a point of not increasing its tuition as part of business as usual each year.

WGU's emphasis on affordability is particularly important because tuition costs have been rising steadily for the past two decades and have outpaced even the price of gas and health care in the United States. A 2008 College Board study reports that the average cost of attending a public school increased 47 percent between 2000 and 2007. Students affected by sticker shock tend to delay, stop out, or give up college-degree aspirations, and working adult students find it difficult to dedicate time and money to their degrees in addition to personal commitments. WGU's affordable model is another option for students who have been priced out of the public system, and it also increases accessibility to low-income students who may not otherwise be able to attend college. Further, the university offers federal financial aid to eligible students; in some states, students are able to access state financial-aid funds as well.

As one WGU graduate said in his speech, "We [students] shouldn't have to mortgage our futures to pay for the educational opportunities of today." Because of rising tuition costs, the middle class today is being priced out of higher education, which is especially troubling because more jobs require postsecondary education. In fact, a 2010 report projects that 63 percent of all jobs in 2018 will require some postsecondary education, and that at the current rate of graduate output, the nation will fall 3 million workers short of this need.[2]

Productivity for the Student and University

The competency-based model of WGU enables students to be more productive with the time they have set aside for earning a degree. And, because time is money to many students, the university's competency-based model also has an advantage financially. Students are charged a one-time fee per six-month term (approximately $3,000) for all the education a student wishes to take during that time. Students aren't charged for three credits to pass an assessment; rather, they are charged for a six-month term. Whatever the student can complete beyond the full-time student load is still the same cost. It is to students' advantage to accelerate their degree program as their learning pace and level of competency allow. As a result of its flexible model, the average time to graduate with a bachelor's degree is thirty months, or about two and a half years. Some students will graduate relatively quickly, while others will take more time.

WGU uses technology not just to increase productivity for student learning, but also to automate functions within the university to make it more productive. The university has automated financial aid services, scheduling tools for assessments, and scheduling for course-mentor appointments. Every operation that can be automated allows faculty and student-support services to spend more time directly working with students. Streamlined processes allowed by technology free up students to spend more time on their studies.

Student Metrics

WGU's Office of Institutional Research tracks and evaluates student metrics throughout a student's degree program. These institutional measures of student success are used to help students graduate, as well as to get their degree in a timely manner. Key performance indicators include whether or not students are on track for on-time graduation (completing at least twelve competency units per term for undergraduates and eight competency units for graduates), student satisfaction, student retention, and graduation. These key performance indicators help the university's leadership and faculty determine what program areas need improvement, which students need more support, and where its services can be improved to better serve student needs. Each month a report is generated for every student regarding his or her progress, and student and course mentors also receive the list with information on their students. These reports are used by mentors to keep students on track, identify learning challenges, and track engagement. Additionally, learner analytics are used to monitor whether students are using the learning materials, for how long, and to check for understanding after engagement. Faculty use this information to evaluate the quality and effectiveness of the university's third-party resources, as well as alignment with its competencies.

In addition to tracking key performance indicators, WGU also tracks student pass and completion rates for assessments; student feedback on learning resources; and trends in enrollment, retention, and attrition. It also works with third-party vendors to conduct external surveys. The university is able to quickly identify areas needing improvement because of its metrics and focus on student success. It can also track the effectiveness of changes made and make decisions based upon a performance record rather than just a qualitative analysis.

Quality

A significant part of the university's mission is to increase access and success for students who may not otherwise be able to earn their college degree due to financial or time constraints or geographic location. However, access and success matter only if students are also receiving a high-quality education that has value in the marketplace. The quality of a WGU degree has been a priority since the university's inception. Its model of defining competencies, designing and administering assessments, and selecting learning resources ensures that students receive a rigorous, high-quality education with relevant marketplace skills and knowledge in their degree area.

The university's accreditation status is indicative of the quality of a WGU degree. Western Governors University is nationally accredited by the Distance Education and Training Council (DETC) and regionally accredited by the Northwest Commission on Colleges and Universities (NWCCU). Additionally, the university's Teachers College is the first exclusively online university to receive accreditation for its degree programs that lead to teacher licensure from the National Council for the Accreditation of Teacher Education (NCATE). The university's nursing degree programs are accredited by the Commission for Collegiate Nursing Education (CCNE), and the Health Informatics program is accredited by the Commission on Accreditation for Health Informatics and Information Management Education (CAHIIM). Finally, the university's Information Security and Assurance program has been certified by the National Security Agency's Information Assurance Courseware Evaluation (IACE) program.

Of course, success is measured not only by the number of students attending WGU, earning their degree, and graduating, but by being successful in a job after graduation. To further measure the satisfaction of its graduates and employers, the university received a grant from Lumina Foundation in 2009 to conduct external surveys of graduates and employers of WGU graduates. Key findings are as follows:

Graduates

- WGU alumni across all degree areas are significantly more likely (78 percent said very or extremely likely) than other graduates (60 percent) to attend their alma mater again if given the chance. Additionally, 80 percent overall would be very likely (56 percent extremely likely) to recommend WGU to others; this compares to 62 percent and 31 percent, respectively, from the nationwide sample.

- Seventy percent of WGU graduates rated as excellent or very good their preparation for their chosen field, versus 57 percent of the other alumni.

- Sixty-six percent received a raise, promotion, new position, or new job responsibility as a result of their WGU education. Those who received pay increases reported an average increase of 63 percent, with a median increase of 25 percent.

- Ninety percent of WGU alumni provide positive responses as to how their WGU experience has impacted their success, compared to 75 percent of other alumni.

- Nearly half of WGU alumni say they were more prepared than other graduates for work and rate their alma mater higher than the other graduates do in preparing them.

- Graduates of WGU undergraduate programs are significantly more inclined to continue their education than graduates of other institutions. Nearly half of all WGU graduates are extremely or very likely to pursue education in the future.

Employers

- Most of the employers of WGU graduates interviewed say their personal positive experiences with graduates have impacted their perceptions of WGU for the better; all agreed that they are very satisfied with performance of WGU graduates.
- Two-thirds of those interviewed feel half or more of the skills employees have could be attributed to their WGU education.
- WGU graduates have the skills employers deem most important to their field; one of the most frequently mentioned skills is "communication."
- Ninety-eight percent agree that WGU graduates have equal or superior "soft skills" compared to graduates of other colleges and universities.
- Of the employers interviewed, 90 percent said they are likely or extremely likely to hire another WGU graduate, and 84 percent would be very likely to recommend another to hire a WGU grad.
- Wide majorities of employers say that WGU's preparation for students (93 percent), academic excellence (88 percent), and contribution to the workforce (88 percent) are equal to or better than that of other colleges and universities.

Creating State Models

WGU was originally created by governors to be a resource to the states. Workforce needs require more and more citizens to earn a postsecondary degree, and access and opportunities need to be expanded. The first state to partner with WGU to create a state-branded WGU was Indiana in June 2010, supported by the leadership of Governor Mitch Daniels, who was dedicated to the creation and promotion of WGU Indiana to serve Indiana citizens. The new model of chartering a separate state-branded WGU was created with the expectation that it would expand higher education access in the state beyond what WGU would do without the new subsidiary institution, and it has. WGU Indiana has been so successful that is has been held up as an example to other states of what can be accomplished by promoting WGU within the state and particularly by creating a state-branded WGU.

WGU Indiana

See WGU Indiana video:
http://indiana.wgu.edu/about_WGU_indiana/video

Indiana's comparatively low college-attainment level was the primary motivation behind Indiana policy leaders creating WGU Indiana and for WGU to create the first state-branded university in Indiana. The state of Indiana ranks 42nd in the nation in the percentage of adults 25–64 years old who hold a bachelor's degree or higher; the state has over 700,000 residents with some college but no degree. Historically, Indiana's economy was dependent on a strong industrial and manufacturing base that provided good jobs for high school graduates. As the state has transitioned from an industrial to a knowledge-based economy, increasing educational attainment is essential for the state to ensure a competitive workforce.

Creating a state-branded university offers an opportunity to increase awareness and credibility of a new model of postsecondary education that is more effective and efficient for nontraditional students. WGU Indiana was created as a wholly owned subsidiary of WGU through a partnership between WGU and the state of Indiana via an executive order by Governor Daniels and an addendum to the original *memorandum of understanding (MOU)* creating Western Governors University. WGU Indiana was also supported by funding from the Bill & Melinda Gates Foundation, the Lumina Foundation, and the Lilly Endowment.

The state endorsement of WGU (and in Indiana's case, the governor's endorsement) lends further credibility to it in the eyes of the students. Further, the new university is not meant to compete with existing state universities because it serves a different student population not being served by the state's current higher education offerings.

The state model has already proven successful in Indiana by increasing state enrollment in WGU for Indiana-based students by 400 percent in the first year. When WGU Indiana was first launched, Indiana students made up 1 percent of WGU's total population; after the creation of WGU Indiana, Indiana students represented 10 percent of all new enrollments for WGU. After just twelve months, the 2011 WGU Indiana graduates accounted for 10 percent of the overall growth (from 2010) in new bachelor's degrees produced by public universities in Indiana. If the number of WGU Indiana graduates grows at its current rate, it will account for over half the growth in new bachelor's degrees in three years without any direct funding from the state.

WGU Indiana has had great reach across the state and now has students enrolled from ninety out of the ninety-two counties. At the August

2011 graduation ceremony, 63 percent of the WGU Indiana graduates were first-generation college students. WGU Indiana is clearly fulfilling a need in the state and providing education to those who would otherwise not have access to higher education opportunities.

WGU Washington

In early 2011, Senator Jim Kastama of Washington State introduced a bill to the legislature that would create WGU Washington. The senator recognized the success of WGU Indiana and he saw that it would fill a unique niche in the family of educational opportunities offered by Washington. Washington's state university system was already reaching capacity for community college graduates transferring to bachelor's degree programs, which often delays community college graduates from beginning their bachelor's programs. Many other community college graduates cannot attend state universities because they work full time and are unable to arrange their schedules to attend classes. The university also fits perfectly with Washington's community college system by allowing students to seamlessly transfer associate's degrees earned at a community college to a bachelor's degree program at WGU.

In April 2011, HB 1822 created WGU Washington and recognized it as part of the state system of higher education. Instead of being created by a governor's executive order as Indiana had done, WGU Washington was created by the legislature, and the bill was signed by Governor Christine Gregoire. The Higher Education Coordinating Board in Washington also played a key role in supporting the creation of WGU Washington and expressing the need for another higher education option in the state, particularly for community college transfer students. WGU Washington enrolled its first cohort of students in July 2011, and the response in the state has been positive thus far.

WGU Texas

Not long after the establishment of WGU Washington, WGU Texas was announced in August 2011 by Governor Rick Perry. WGU Texas was created through an executive order by Governor Perry and an addendum to the original MOU creating WGU Texas (which had been signed by then Governor George W. Bush). WGU Texas will offer a flexible and affordable higher education option for the citizens of Texas, particularly for low-income and minority students in the state. WGU Texas officially launched in fall 2011.

Conclusion

Western Governors University was implemented with the mission to utilize technology to develop a new competency-based model in higher education, to make higher education more affordable while improving educational quality, and to expand access to populations that are traditionally underserved by higher education. WGU's model—unique because of its competency-based model, disaggregated faculty roles, the student-centric culture that adapts quickly to emerging student and industry needs, and the fact that it does not develop its own courses—increases accessibility to students through its flexibility and affordable cost, and the mentoring model tailors academic support to each student. In this way, it serves as a valuable resource to students as well as to states in need of an educated workforce equipped with those skills deemed essential in the twenty-first century.

Notes

1. M. Shachar and Y. Neumann, "Twenty Years of Research on the Academic Performance Differences between Traditional and Distance Learning: Summative Meta-Analysis and Trend Examination," MERLOT *Journal of Online Learning and Teaching* 6, no. 2 (2010): 318–34.
2. A. P. Carnevale, N. Smith, and J. Strohl, *Help Wanted: Projections of Jobs and Education Requirements through 2018* (The Georgetown University Center on Education and the Workforce, 2010), retrieved from http://cew.georgetown.edu/jobs2018/.

Robert W. Mendenhall *is President of Western Governors University (WGU). Prior to joining WGU, he was general manager of IBM's K–12 education division, a $500 million worldwide business. From 1980 to 1992, he was president of Wicat Systems, Inc., a public company providing computer-based K–12 education and corporate training.*

10

University of Phoenix

William (Bill) Pepicello

Introduction

THE UNIVERSITY OF PHOENIX WAS FOUNDED IN 1976 on the principle that a large number of people wished to earn a degree but that full-time attendance during the day was impossible for them. The founder, Dr. John Sperling, from San Jose State University, understood that the coming years would bring revolutionary changes to the economic landscape. He was also a strong advocate of lifelong learning and understood that to remain competitive, the United States would have to embrace lifelong learning, as well.

Thirty-five years later, what was initially considered unorthodox is now the norm. Today's college students do not look like the typical student of the '70s—73 percent of college students fall into a nontraditional category. They must work at least part time, cannot rely on parental support or have dependents, and do not stop their lives to continue their learning. These are the people who must be educated to stay competitive in the job market, and they are the people who will help the United States remain globally competitive.

With more Americans wanting and needing quality education—and with American prosperity riding on it—higher education must find a way of accommodating growing numbers of students while ensuring a quality education. Academic quality includes a measure of integrity in which key indicators that tie academic outcomes to student success are part of a system of continuous improvement. The second quality is student achievement.

The University of Phoenix has sought to improve the quality of its educational offerings by focusing on the essential elements of the student academic experience, identifying those elements that must be addressed through an internal system of continuous improvement and elements tied to external benchmarks to ensure that students are being better served.

Through this process we have identified curriculum, assessment of student-learning outcomes, and faculty preparation as basic to our enterprise. These elements must be continually improved as part of the internal integrity process that defines academic quality at the university and that results in student achievement that can be compared externally. This is a three-step process: (1) build quality, (2) measure quality, and (3) deliver quality. The university began this process with the release in 2008 of the *Academic Annual Report* and has continued to do so each year since then. Through the *Academic Annual Report*, the university reports on student outcomes as compared to those of their peers at other institutions, as well as on internal indicators of institutional effectiveness.

The evolution of the University of Phoenix has been inextricably linked with advances in technology. Computers and laptops have given way to smartphones and computer touchpads with previously unimagined capacities and capabilities. Dr. Mark Weiser, chief technology officer at Xerox Palo Alto Research Center (PARC), understood this when in 1991 he said, "The most profound technologies are those that disappear. They weave themselves into the fabric of everyday life until they are indistinguishable from it. Say goodbye to your computer—it's about to disappear. That is, it will be so much a part of your life that you won't even know it's there."[1] Dr. Weiser's vision is close to reality in almost every aspect of life today, with one notable exception—higher education.

Education Responsive to Learner Needs

Today's students have changed; their lives have changed. The way they are expected to learn has not.

The skills required for today's workplace are far different than they were in the manufacturing age. Students must have global awareness and financial and entrepreneurial literacy, as well as information and media literacy. Along with these skills, employers seek workers who are innovative and creative and who have honed their abilities in critical thinking and problem solving, self-direction, and adaptability and accountability.[2] Institutions must be able to make adjustments quickly to respond to student needs and to the marketplace.

If higher education is to change, traditional beliefs and roles will have to be challenged. Consider the role of faculty. Many faculty view their role as being the locus of all knowledge transfer through teaching. Many believe the lecture/midterm/final paradigm is tried-and-true. However, this model does not fit all students, particularly those who have grown up in a world of immediate information, immediate feedback, and immediate results. It is critical to move from a teaching focus to a learning focus.

University of Phoenix Adaptations

Students should have an engaged learning experience, resources that support students' success, and interaction with faculty and classmates. From the outset, the University of Phoenix has sought to provide this type of learning experience.

For many people, University of Phoenix is synonymous with online education, even though the university began in 1976 as a campus-based institution that now has a physical presence in forty-one states, the District of Columbia, and Puerto Rico. In the early days, all students enrolled in classes at their local campus. In 1989, the university pioneered online education—students had the option to enroll in courses from anywhere there was a phone line. The technology consisted of a bulletin board program delivered to the student on a disk via the postal system. Students downloaded the program to their computers. All learning materials, including textbooks, were delivered by mail. Work was completed via a dial-up modem.

The online campus predated the dot-com revolution, and student enrollment was initially limited to those with the digital expertise and equipment. With the World Wide Web now generally accessible, the University of Phoenix has leveraged this to deliver a wide array of digital services to students. Students may take courses in a classroom or virtual classroom, giving them the choice to take courses best suited to their learning or personal needs. Students have the advantage of face-to-face instruction when that works for them or a virtual classroom when they find online study meets their learning styles, when they must travel, or if they need the flexibility of class anywhere, anytime.

Pervasive Technology

Today, technology is embedded throughout the students' experience. It even helps potential students determine if the University of Phoenix is the institution they wish to attend and if they are ready to do so. Prospective students interested in the university—in any modality—can sign on to the Visiting Student Center (VSC) to learn about the university and about themselves, taking a variety of assessments that include learning styles, readiness, and technology.

Technology has become a part of our everyday lives, so many prospective students believe they have the technological acumen required to complete either an online program or a local campus program. However, texting, gaming, and social networking do not provide all the skills required of today's college student. Visitors to the VSC are able to compare their skills to what are considered minimum expectations of the university.

Technology provides a robust array of scalable, digital resources to all students, regardless of their primary mode of delivery. There are a number of virtual student support services, learning assets, and tools available. The following are a description of some of them.

Student and Faculty Portal

Once enrolled, all students and faculty have access to the university portal, which allows them to perform a variety of administrative and support functions, and also to access academic materials, learning assets, and tools. For online students, the portal is the entry point for their courses. For students attending local campuses, the portal provides forums for learning teams and the ability to submit assignments and receive graded assignments with feedback from faculty between class meetings.

In 2001, the university made all course materials available electronically, including all textbooks, supplemental reading materials, multimedia files, and other support materials. This platform provided a means of developing and delivering curriculum and materials via a centralized database, giving curriculum developers the ability to easily adjust courses based on instructor/student feedback. Course-delivery scalability was essential as enrollments grew.

Course Builder

Course Builder is an interface utilized by faculty and curriculum developers to create, manage, and deliver curriculum. The portal allows for the integration of additional learning applications into students' course and program pages. Features within Course Builder include enhanced course-level customization, a structure that is aligned to best practices in instructional design, and an intuitive user interface. Course Builder upgrades included a more nuanced system for version control and archival of curriculum materials, allowing for more granular assessment and programmatic evaluation data collection/interpretation. Faculty have access to virtual resources that enable them to develop scalable, consistent curriculum.

University Library

With an average of 5,000,000 downloads each month, the university library is one of the most utilized learning assets available via the portal. The university library makes more than 300 licensed databases as well as 95,000 scholarly journals and periodicals accessible to students and faculty. These databases are commercially licensed products not available through an Internet search. Additional services available to students and faculty include "Ask a Librarian" and the Document Delivery/Interlibrary Loan service.

eBook Collection

The eBook Collection is an aggregation of more than 1,600 digitized textbooks licensed from the university's academic publishing partners. These texts have been converted to XML format to allow searching across the collection. This also permits licensed content to be disaggregated, allowing the more granular material to be repurposed in support of specific learning objectives. The entire eBook Collection is available to all students and faculty. Digital-rights management protocol is built in to protect intellectual property rights of authors and publishers.

Virtual Organizations

Virtual Organizations are realistic simulated environments that model businesses, schools, health care, and government. Students apply critical information-utilization and problem-solving skills to determine the economic health of an organization. Students use Virtual Organizations to examine complexities of organizations and to mine, analyze, and apply data. Using the data found within the company's or institution's websites, students must solve problems, even if only partial information is available, determine what they are looking for, in what area they might find it, and the context in which it is to be used. More than 50,000 unique users log in to Virtual Organizations in an average month.

Simulations

University of Phoenix began embedding simulations across the curriculum in 2004. Simulations are used as problem-solving exercises, class assignments, discussion starters, case studies, and tutorials. Simulations reinforce concepts and encourage practical application of material presented in course discussions and texts, and they provide students opportunities for higher-level learning. Students can hone their decision-making skills in safe environments. Scenario review and feedback are immediate.

e-Portfolios

The university has acquired licensed electronic portfolio (e-portfolio) software from TaskStream. The College of Education has made completion of the DRF e-portfolio a requirement for teacher education programs.

Remediation

Most studies indicate that close to 40 percent of students entering college require remediation in mathematics and/or English and writing skills. Due to the availability of assistive technology, remedial assistance can be made available to all students throughout their entire course of study. It is available in most cases twenty-four hours a day, seven days a week. The technology aiding in the just-in-time remediation includes centers for writing and math excellence:

Center for Writing Excellence. The university began providing online writing assistance in 1999. In 2002, the Center for Writing Excellence (CWE) emerged, an online writing lab designed to assist students in developing essential written communication skills. In 2004, the automated review and feedback system WritePoint was added. Since that time, the CWE has continued to add services for students wishing to improve their writing skills, including:

- WritePoint, an automated review system providing feedback on grammar, punctuation, and style points;
- CWE Review, review with feedback from faculty members;
- El Centro de Redacción (a Spanish writing lab);
- Tutorials and guides; and
- Turnitin plagiarism checker.

Center for Mathematics Excellence. Since 2006, the university has continually expanded just-in-time remediation. The Center for Mathematics Excellence (CME) website serves all members of the university with resources to assist quantitative teaching and learning. In an average month, more than 40,000 students access the CME homepage.

The center addresses needs of students who have not practiced math for some time or who suffer from math anxiety. This site helps address these issues, dispels math-anxiety myths, and suggests study and coping skills for those who struggle with math classes. Selected math and statistics courses include access to WorldWideWhiteboard web conferencing for online math assistance. Students may choose a coach to work with or they can observe coaches working with other students in real time. More than 4,000 live coaching sessions are conducted each month.

Student Success Workshops

Student workshops are three-day online minicourses designed to improve basic skills. Currently there are twenty-five workshops. All are free and require no additional purchase of materials.

Virtual Computer Labs

The University of Phoenix teaching/learning model has always focused on experiential learning. The College of Information Systems and Technology incorporated four different resources for tutorials and virtual labs: TestOut LabSim, Visual Logic, ToolWire, and Element K. Students work with tangible components in virtual settings, which provides hands-on learning and the freedom to experiment and test expertise in safe environments.

Multimedia Resources

The Instructional Materials and Technology Department provides multimedia resources for a variety of courses. These include purpose-built, interactive graphics with audio and/or video. These are used to present, explain, test, and assess important instructional objectives and to complement other instructional materials such as published content and textbook resources. The group creates custom as well as rapid-authored multimedia, including video productions as well as podcast-style lectures.

PhoenixConnect

Research indicates that social and emotional connections affect students' perceptions of relevancy; a lack of these connections can lead to disengagement.[3] To address this issue, the university established a proprietary academic social media site called PhoenixConnect in 2011. Students and faculty can interact to discuss academic topics, meet new friends with similar interests, reach out to alumni, or launch a professional group. In a matter of a few months, more than 450,000 students and faculty have begun using PhoenixConnect.

PhoenixConnect is organized into communities with over 10,000 discussion topics. The communities include:

- *Learning Communities*. Students and faculty can find information, post questions, or contribute to conversations about classes, programs, and academic interests.

- *Career and Professional Development*. Students can connect with others around specific professional areas, dialogue with experts, and get assistance with job hunting.

- *Campus Life*. Students and faculty who have similar extracurricular interests can connect with each other. Discussions include events in various areas, sports, and hobbies.

- *Support Communities*. Students can ask questions and share experiences about the university, their programs, or financial aid.

In addition to communities, more than a thousand student-generated groups engage around academics, professional networking, and extracurricular activities. Faculty and students maintain more than 3,000 blogs. Real-time chat is also available. Users can see who is online and can connect with each other. In the fall of 2011, the university began implementing group chat as an aid for student learning teams.

Administrative and Student Services Available via Online Portal

In addition to academic support services for students, administrative tasks can be performed online as well. These include the following:

- Reviewing contact information
- Registering for classes
- Paying tuition
- Meeting with a representative online
- Requesting transcripts
- Submitting assignments
- Receiving graded assignments with feedback
- Obtaining grades
- Registering for Student Success Workshops
- Accessing e-mail

Faculty use administrative services to submit grades to an online automated gradebook, which then sends the grades, comments, and assignments with feedback to the students and posts the final grade to the system. Faculty also receive and accept contracts via the portal and can sign up for faculty development activities, including faculty workshops. Of course, faculty also have access to all the academic assets that are available to the students.

Nursing Labs

In addition to virtual assets available through the student and faculty portal, in 2009 the university established nursing labs. The university's Licensed Practical Nurse to Bachelor of Science in Nursing (LPN-to-BSN) program, currently the university's only program dedicated to training and licensing new registered nurses (RNs), has incorporated high-fidelity nursing scenarios as a core component of its campus-based curriculum.

The four nursing simulation labs located in Arizona, Colorado, Hawaii, and California are equipped with high-fidelity simulations and manikins. Used in conjunction with simulated hospital rooms, these manikins are part of an innovative simulation program involving both students and faculty. Each simulation occurring in the lab is a medical situation carefully constructed by faculty to teach students a particular lesson.

The key advantage of high-fidelity training scenarios is that, unlike in traditional classroom-based lectures or on-site training with real patients, students get to learn and practice essential nursing techniques in critical-care situations without putting themselves or patients at risk.

The Role of Faculty in a Technology-Enhanced Environment

Too often, discussions and research about e-learning are centered on distance education. All educational systems, just like our lives, must be a blend of technology and face-to-face interaction to be effective. A single delivery system is not sufficient to engage students in learning, to inspire them to take responsibility for their learning, or to encourage innovative and creative thinking and promote quality outcomes. Today's students—the ones who have to work, who have children to care for, who all institutions need to serve—not only want this same kind of access to their learning resources and classes that they encounter in the real world, they *must* have it to succeed.

To accomplish this, faculty must be given the time and the resources to explore new technology approaches providing the requisite training and technical support to master these new skills, methods, and technologies for inclusion in their courses. If this does not occur, faculty may become impediments to implementing technology-assisted learning. Training does not simply entail learning how to operate the software, but rather gaining the knowledge of how and why it will assist learning.

The institution's concept of what a faculty member is and does must thus evolve as new institutional models appear. In recent years, the idea of the unbundling of faculty roles has achieved greater currency. University of Phoenix employs a core cadre of full-time faculty who oversee curriculum and instruction. The majority of the faculty are associate faculty, most of whom work full time in their professions and teach part time. University of Phoenix faculty are primarily a teaching faculty, rather than a research-oriented faculty as might be found at many traditional institutions.

The research faculty model assumes that research keeps faculty current in their fields and cutting edge in their approaches, ensuring students a sound educational experience. University of Phoenix recognizes research as a valuable scholarly pursuit, but for its students emphasizes the application of knowledge to real situations, the integration of knowledge across disciplines, and the disciplinary expertise necessary to effective teaching.

An unbundled model provides a system that rewards faculty according to their strengths and their ability to add value both to the student-learning experience and to the body of academic knowledge.

Academic Apps

In some ways, the future is already here with the introduction of the newest member of the University of Phoenix technology family—the University of Phoenix Mobile iPhone app. For busy students who are juggling work, life, and school, the University of Phoenix Mobile app, implemented in April 2011, makes it easier for users to be engaged wherever and whenever it is convenient for them.

The University of Phoenix Mobile app joins the growing list of academic application software available on iTunes for students on the go. With this free application, students and faculty with Apple iPhones or iPads are able to do the following:

- Participate in discussion forums.
- Draft and post to discussion threads, and reply to other students' posts.
- View, edit, and save drafts of discussion comments created on the classroom portal.

- View message flags, discussion questions, and class announcements.
- Receive real-time alerts when grades are posted and when the instructor posts new information.

Learning apps for other smartphones are currently under development.

Looking Forward: The Untapped Potential of Technology

What we have discussed, while representing significant advances for higher education, only scratches the surface of what current technology can offer. There is much more to be adapted from the current technological playlist for the higher education community. The most important cumulative result is that technology has the potential to increase student engagement by creating a more personalized learning environment that can incorporate adaptive features. In other words, the student learning environment can be designed to respond to the specific student.

A major source of potential here lies in ambient intelligence—that is, technology that knows the users, serves them, responds to them, and does so unnoticed. Ambient intelligence, for example, is what makes possible Amazon's recognition of users and the types of products they are interested in, and thereby puts those in front of users as soon as they log in, or perhaps even e-mails them with updates when new, similar products arrive.

This type of technology can be adapted to academic data sets in order to determine a student's learning profile and then adjust the learning environment to his or her needs. The more data points that can be gathered, the better the prescription is for learning. Once the strengths and challenges of a student are determined, programs can then be informed of skill enhancements, as well as appropriate levels and modes of content. In short, technology can make it possible to provide an individualized learning experience for every student.

Such technology not only serves the student directly, but also connects the student to faculty members in new ways so that they can mediate in a more deliberate manner than is currently possible. Faculty members will be able to see student information on online dashboards populated for each class. The information can include individual student needs and direct faculty members to resources to assist the students.

If courses are designed to include materials that are suited to different learning styles, faculty members no longer must teach to the middle of the class. Learning can and will adapt to each individual's needs. Faculty members

143

will know what the students have learned and what they have missed. Faculty members can use this feedback in a variety of ways. For instance, they can assist the students in specifically identified areas of concern. They can also alter their approach to address areas in which a large number of students are showing deficiencies.

When this highly individualized and interactive learning experience is combined with social networking, new levels of interdisciplinary, interprogram, and intercohort dialogue and collaboration are possible. In short, adaptive technology can enhance the student's experience, and it is expected to increase engagement and learning outcomes. However, technology is just the tool. The key to the successful utilization of technology is the empowerment of faculty members to excel.

Conclusion

In the twenty-first century, the University of Phoenix is a game changer in higher education in that it early on recognized the power of technology to increase engagement and learning outcomes. The University of Phoenix is fully cognizant that technology is just the tool. The faculty member remains critical. Technology is most valuable when it empowers faculty and students to excel. To that end, the University of Phoenix has been proactive in ensuring broad implementation of technology, which helps faculty and students ensure a successful learning experience.

Notes

1. Mark Longer Press Quotes, http://www.ubiq.com/hypertext/weiser/WeiserNews Quotes.html.
2. *Framework for 21st Century Learning* (Partnership for 21st Century Skills, March 2011), http://p21.org/documents/1.__p21_framework_2-pager.pdf.
3. Ibid.

Bill Pepicello *is president of the University of Phoenix. He previously held positions at Temple University, National University, and the University of Sarasota (now Argosy University). He serves nationally as a consultant-evaluator for the Higher Learning Commission of the North Central Association of Colleges and Schools and was appointed to the National Advisory Committee on Institutional Quality and Integrity (NACIQI).*

11

SUNY Empire State College: A Game Changer in Open Learning

Meg Benke, Alan Davis, and Nan L. Travers

The Learning-Focused Institution as a Game Changer

Introduction

THE STATE UNIVERSITY OF NEW YORK'S (SUNY) Empire State College was established in 1971 by Ernest Boyer[1] in a period of significant social and cultural change. Inspired by the works of John Dewey, Paulo Friere, Ivan Illich, and others, the college was fiercely radical and anti-establishment, and was determined to break all the shackles of tradition in order to better serve those traditionally underrepresented in higher education.[2] This included forgoing classes in favor of independent and group studies; rejecting traditional disciplinary departments; eschewing grades for narrative evaluations; and, with faculty mentors working with learners individually, devising unique and personalized degree programs that incorporated learning acquired beyond the academy. Unlike prescribed curricula and course outlines, co-developed learning contracts presumed that learners had unique goals and interests and were active partners in the design of their own learning.[3]

The college was thus "open" in every sense of the word and in ways that went beyond simply having open admissions or flexible delivery modes, as was the case originally at the UK's Open University, which also opened in 1971.

The college has resisted forces pushing its unique educational model toward traditional instruction. Along with other adult learner–focused institutions that began in the early 1970s and that have stayed true to their original mission (e.g., Goddard College, Evergreen State College), the college has withstood adaptation to more mainstream structures—for instance, to meet state and federal funding requirements. It began as a game changer, and has deliberately continued in that role.

While the college has diversified its approaches since 1971, adding considerable online capacity and programs that are somewhat more standard, the individualized mentor-learner model just described still informs its core values and operations. Today, the college is substantially more cost effective (both for the learner and taxpayer) than traditional four-year and graduate institutions, public or private. The college has a lower-than-average administrative overhead, shows increasing measures of learner success and persistence each year, and has the highest student satisfaction in its SUNY sector.

In its vision for 2015, SUNY Empire State College continues to challenge the norms of higher education. It thrives on innovation in order to remain resilient in a changing educational world and to fulfill its mission, currently stated as follows:

> SUNY Empire State College's dedicated faculty and staff use innovative, alternative, and flexible approaches to higher education that transform people and communities by providing rigorous programs that connect individuals' unique and diverse lives to their personal learning goals.

The thrust of the college's current work involves redefining and repositioning the college as an "open university" in a digital age by

- optimizing the affordances of emerging technologies to enhance the mentor-learning experience;
- building on the college's strength in the recognition, articulation, and accreditation of informal and alternative college-level learning;
- extending access to all forms of open educational resources and developing the supports for learners to use and integrate different resources;
- developing flexible and stackable structures that best match learners' needs, goals, and directions; and
- engaging in the wider discourse and scholarship of open education in all its manifestations.

Recognizing Learning No Matter Where It Occurs

A basic tenet of SUNY Empire State College is that learners have valuable college-level knowledge that can be assessed and credentialed toward their degree. For many learners, assessing and awarding credit for prior learning allows them to complete their degrees without repeating courses and incurring redundant expenses and loss of time.

The Council on Adult and Experiential Learning defines prior learning as "learning that a person acquires outside a traditional academic environment. This learning may have been acquired through work experience, employer training programs, independent study, non-credit courses, volunteer or community service, travel, or non-college courses or seminars."[4] Credit for prior learning can be awarded based on a number of assessment options. These include training or exams that have been preevaluated through outside organizations, such as the American Council on Education, through the college's own evaluation, or through an individualized prior learning assessment process.

Empire State College permits up to three-quarters of the bachelor's degree to be earned through a combination of transfer and prior learning assessment credit (provided that the learning is relevant to the degree sought). Prior learning assessment at the graduate level is more limited, but still possible in certain programs. The master of business administration allows up to one-half of the degree to be acquired in specific areas through an examination process, and the master of arts in adult learning includes individualized prior learning assessment. Empire State College has long recognized learning acquired outside the academy, and our learners have realized reduced costs and time to degree completion.

Individualized Learning Design

The learners' prior learning provides the foundation upon which Empire State College develops a personalized degree program within the broad guidelines for the majors. Learners collaborate with a faculty mentor in the design of their education, particularly in their degree program. The program might be unusual and unique, or more traditional and recognizable, depending on the learner's own educational and employment goals. The college's innovative, alternative, and flexible approaches provide learners with the opportunity to connect their unique and diverse lives to their personal learning goals.

Within this personal degree plan, a learner can design individualized, independent studies in partnership with an appropriate faculty mentor, either face-to-face or online. Learners are expected to be active partners in the design of the learning contract associated with any study, with the faculty mentor acting as a learning coach, posing questions, and helping the learner think through the issues. For example, to fulfill a general education requirement, a learner with an interest in fiber arts might design an independent study to explore the political and policy implications of fiber and fabric throughout the history of the United States.

In the college's mentor-learner model, learners examine what they have learned, where they want to go in their education, and what it takes to get there. Learners note that although the degree planning and prior learning assessment processes are difficult, they develop self-awareness as learners and the capacity to continue their learning in work and other educational settings. They also comment that the career exploration portion of degree planning helped them understand what was expected in their field and how to design their degree to meet those expectations. Employers have reported that our learners are very well prepared, and many progress in their careers and/or continue to further their studies.

As access to content and resources becomes ubiquitous, the role of the faculty mentor aligns closely with what Siemens[5] posits as the real value in higher education. What can be scaled and duplicated is content, but what is embodied in the Empire State College mentor remains vital to a college education: "personal feedback and assessment, contextualized and personalized navigation through complex topics, encouragement, questioning by a faculty member to promote deeper thinking, and a context and infrastructure of learning."

A Learning-Focused Institution

In modern higher education, almost all institutions strive to be "learner centered" or "learner focused" as opposed to "faculty centered." This rightly puts the learner in the middle of the educational process, and yet still maintains a clear separation between the roles of learners and faculty.

A key attribute of a game-changer college is being "learning focused," wherein the institution is organized and committed to learn and to adapt to new innovations and opportunities, and that emphasizes members of the faculty and learners as equal partners.

At SUNY Empire State College, faculty mentors are thoroughly engaged in all aspects of learning design. In doing so, they also learn, and they leverage this learning to better support new learners, to share ideas for new curricula with colleagues, and to be aware of trends in their own fields. "Curriculum development" is therefore a collective and continuous cycle of discovery and delivery: the faculty mentors remain current, and the institution can respond to changes in the educational needs of communities and the workplace. Others in the field of mentoring[6] discuss this process, which could be termed as relational or reciprocal mentoring.

Scholarship and Game Change

SUNY Empire State College fully embraces Ernest Boyer's expanded defini-tion of scholarship related to discovery, integration, application, and teaching.[7] Scholarship is thus not bounded by discipline, nor disconnected to teaching and learning, nor is it distinct from communities of practice. The supportive culture includes a Center for Mentoring and Learning, a Distinguished Professor of Men-toring, annual college meetings, publications, and new-mentor orientations, all designed to promote and disseminate engaged scholarship. Faculty recognition occurs through awards for excellence in mentoring and for excellence in con-necting community service with learning, and faculty reassignments are directed toward the improvement and evolution of mentoring.

In the Center for Distance Learning, the college supports collaborative projects that explore innovative ways of working with learners, such as deliv-ering science laboratories in online courses, or the use of mobile technology. Mentors, instructional designers, and librarians all contribute to the creation of online courses.

As innovations evolve, a learning-focused institution can integrate them with current practices. As a game changer and leader in open learning for the past forty years, SUNY Empire State College is undergoing a new era of inno-vation as it harnesses the affordances of emerging technologies to enhance its unique mentor-learning model and its expertise in assessing learning acquired outside the walls of the ivory tower.

SUNY Empire State College 2010/11 Key Data

	Head Count	Average Age
Undergraduate	18,656	36.0 yr
Graduate	1,128	39.7 yr
Total	19,784	

Percent Distribution of Learner Residency

Residence	Percentage
New York	87%
Other 49 States	10.0%
International	2.3%

Percent Enrollment Based on Gender

Male	Female
39%	61%

Average Advanced-Standing Credits Used within Undergraduate Degrees

	Bachelor's Degree	Associate's Degree
Transfer Credits	56 credits	21 credits
Prior Learning Assessment	36 credits	23 credits
Total Average Advanced-Stand-ing Credits	69 credits	29 credits

Looking Ahead: SUNY Empire State College as "New York's Open University"

The Open Movement

In the important and timely edition of the *EDUCAUSE Review* entitled "The Open Edition,"[8] contributions included those that explored the idea of the open faculty, the open course, the open student, open technology, and so forth. It did not include an article on open institutions such as SUNY Empire State College and the role they can play in demonstrating what can be achieved based on their decades of experiences as game changers in higher education. In fact, open education has a rich philosophical and political heritage.

> Open education involves a commitment to openness, and is therefore inevitably a political and social project. The concept of openness has roots going back to the Enlightenment that are bound up with the philosophical foundations of modern education with its commitments to freedom, citizenship, knowledge for all, social progress and individual transformation.[9]

The open education movement[10] now goes beyond open admission, distance education, and various forms of "broadcast" teaching. It includes the expansion of shared open resources and virtual peer-mentoring environments that provide learners with the opportunity to create global networks of peers who are engaged in the same areas of learning. It offers faculty the opportunity to connect with other experts in the field and to learn from the learners as they explore, ask questions, and critique emerging knowledge. Open learning provides each learner and faculty mentor with multiple networks and opportunities to grow as an educated person and as a member of a profession. In all these respects, open education, broadly defined, builds upon and extends SUNY Empire State College's mentored-learning approaches. It also inspires discourse on new theories of learning.

As digital devices and networks have evolved, they have become central to the ways in which we relate to each other, to ideas and information, and to how we construct our lives:

- The information age provided freely obtainable information outside of higher education, while the recently emerged "relational age"[11] completely shifts how people use information and gain knowledge.

- Once the exclusive domain for in-depth and purposed knowledge, higher educational institutions no longer hold the monopoly. People gather information for what they want or need, based on their own self-regulated choices, and connect that information to themselves, to others, and to the world around them.

- Siemens[12] noted a trend for increased informal learning across many different fields. Open educational resources can augment informal learning, increasing work-related knowledge sets for individuals without their having to attend higher educational institutions.

- Many of the processes previously handled by higher education can now be off-loaded to, or supported by, technology. "Know-how" and "know-what" are being supplemented with "know-where" and "know-when"— the understanding of where to find needed knowledge, and how and when to connect and relate different aspects of that knowledge.

The role of higher education institutions therefore now shifts, since they possess the expertise to recognize, assess, and accredit knowledge. They also provide effective frameworks within which people can learn to learn and to purpose and repurpose that learning into constructed and organized knowledge. Paired with open learning resources, institutions can provide opportunities beyond what they normally offer and for learners who have not been able to access higher education. The net result is that learners have richer educational opportunities—and at much lower costs.

SUNY Empire State College, like several other institutions, has offered an innovative MOOC (Massive Open Online Course), which manifested many of the dimensions of technology-enabled open education. Creativity and Multiculturalism, jointly offered by an arts mentor and a math mentor, was open to all comers, with credit (for a fee) or without, or for those wishing to document their learning for subsequent recognition through prior learning assessment. Further MOOCs are being developed in quantitative studies and diversity.

The connected and relational aspects of contemporary open learning call for an approach to education that strikes a balance between the opportunities afforded by emerging technology and the dangers of relentless, unexamined information. The college's Project for Critical Inquiry[13] aims for that balance by creating a single virtual space in which students, using a series of individualized learning contracts, are free to join, extend, repurpose, mash up, and adapt learning activities to suit their individual needs.

As a pedagogical commitment, critical inquiry stresses clarity of expression, rigorous critical thinking, and an understanding of the social, economic, and political dimensions of knowledge. Critical inquiry models encourage students to "follow the learning" while providing consistent access to faculty expertise and guidance. By providing students with an open, interdisciplinary forum in which to contribute to learning groups, the Project for Critical Inquiry also provides interesting opportunities for the identification and integration of prior learning. It is this faculty guidance around the examination of ideas that is the value added by higher education; the learners can access resources, but need support in developing judgment.

Prior Learning Assessment and Open Education

There are some gaps in the envisaged future of the open education movement. Learners using open educational resources can personalize their learning and create learning environments to match their own choices and needs, resulting in unusual, unique, and unpredictable paths. These learners also need to validate and accredit their college-level learning in order to have it transfer to other institutions of higher education and be accepted by employers.[14]

Consequently, higher education forerunners must expand the assessment of learning in open learning environments. With the higher levels of connectivity, experts from around the world can more readily engage. Networks of peers can share perspectives on each other's work or assess each other's learning, augmenting the feedback usually available from only one expert. For learning that emerges from the less prescriptive learning processes, institutions can apply prior learning assessment methods more broadly. Applying the retrospective analysis and reflection typically associated with prior learning assessment on this more emergent learning provides a valid and authentic assessment.

SUNY Empire State College is uniquely positioned to fill this gap. It has (1) a mentoring model designed to support learners to bring together multiple sources of study and exploration, as well as to guide reflection and deeper examination of that learning; and (2) ways to validate, assess, and accredit college-level learning, regardless of where or how the learning is acquired. The college is also exploring ways to incorporate Mozilla's Open Badges project as another way to document prior learning and for faculty to share expertise.[15]

Finally, as the open educational resources university's (OER university) first anchor partner in the United States, SUNY Empire State College is already working to meet the needs of OER learners in collaboration with like-minded institutions across the world through the OER university project. The project intends to support free access to OER learning materials to students around the world and coordinate assessment and credentialing through recognized educational institutions.[16] Participants from several continents are designing open courses, which will have methodologies in place for learning assessment and transfer.

Stackable Learning Accreditation

There is a significant national push to increase the rate of degree completion, with multiple projects being funded through the U.S. Department of Labor and private foundations. For example, through Lumina Foundation funding, the Adult College Completion Network[17] has been developed to support institutions engaging in various efforts focused on adults completing their degrees. In the recent report *College Completion Tool Kit*, the U.S. Department of Education[18] identifies prior learning assessment as a key strategy for augmenting the efforts to assist adult learners toward degree completion, especially those with work and family commitments who stop in and out of higher education numerous times. Regulators, legislative members, accreditors, employers, and others are committed to achieving degree completion and raising participation rates as federal research links the country's economic vitality to the education of its workforce.[19]

In response, SUNY Empire State College is developing certificate programs for undergraduate and graduate levels that "stack" in multiple ways toward a final degree. Similarly, the learning gained through an open education resource can be assessed for college-level learning, the credit applied toward stackable certificates, and the prior leaning assessment used to fold in emergent learning.

Unlike a credit bank, which just collects assessed learning onto a transcript, the stackable learning accreditation model allows for more modular curricular and credentialing opportunities. Such modular credentialing does not replace standard paths to degrees, but recognizes key accomplishments on the pathway toward learners' goals. This approach increases access to marketable college credentials and ultimately supports degree-completion initiatives.

For example, learners may have more than one certificate based on their learning in professional fields. In addition, a learner may take courses through multiple means to create a general education certificate. Together, the professional and general education certificates would stack and form a coherent bachelor's degree. These smaller and more agile packages can be used to address a region's economic development needs.

Barriers to the use of open education and individualized, stackable learning accreditation stem from traditional concepts of education and of conventional degrees. For example, federal and state funding sources are designed to support almost exclusively first-time, full-time learners taking conventional degrees. Also, with diminishing state aid, the financial burden of an education is becoming more and more the learner's responsibility. Spacing out educational costs through incremental accomplishments may be more attractive to many learners than the daunting debt of four continuous years at full-time rates. Open institutions such as SUNY Empire State College have been dedicated to removing barriers to quality higher education (with costs being one of the highest barriers) for those underserved.

The Role of Academic Technologies

Typically, the information technology departments within institutions of higher education have taken on a service/support role to the academics. Academics rely on the technology team to ensure that supportive structures are in place and processes run smoothly. In the digital-learning world, teaching, learning, and technology are increasingly interdependent. The role of technologists has therefore evolved over the last decade to include a greater responsibility for learning design, while the academic faculty and staff now have a greater responsibility to understand how technology functions and impacts the educational processes.[20] The emergence of technology to support the individualized degree-planning process is one example of how SUNY Empire State College has brought the two functions into a closer partnership.

The basic structure of the individualized degree plan at SUNY Empire State College is that of a portfolio, which has evolved over the years into a homegrown electronic system. Recently, a team of faculty mentors and professional staff from the academic, technology, and learner-support areas across the college developed projects using new e-Portfolio systems in teaching and learning, degree planning and prior learning assessment, career development, assessment, and institutional effectiveness.

The e-Portfolio provides an environment for learners to reflect, interrelate, and assess their learning using multimedia, concept maps, and other digital structures. The process of assessing degree plans and college-level prior learning is also eased: faculty mentors provide ongoing feedback directly within each learner's portfolio and develop dialogue around specific topics. Evaluators have access to the documented knowledge and can view how learners organize and relate their concepts. Assessment strategies are linked to institutional and program standards and learning outcomes for credentialing.

Technology-enabled open educational learning environments linked with the use of open educational resources and e-Portfolios provide a platform within which each learner can develop an individualized learning environment, including a repository of his or her work and reflections that create links within the learning and connect it with other learners and scholars, as well as with the workplace and the community.

Engaging in the Wider Discourse of Open Education

Openness as a paradigm, and open education as a movement, evolved from complex histories and collective aspirations of open source, open knowledge, and open access initiatives in higher education. They have strengthened as a result of enduring democratic aspirations for alternative education and the ideals of social justice, and also by the affordances and the increasing ubiquity of emerging technologies. Exploring more deeply the meanings and possibilities of openness, scholars must ask how open tools, resources, and knowledge can demonstrably improve educational quality[21] and must investigate "the transformative potential of open education."[22] In order to remain a "game changer," the college and its scholars must engage thoroughly in this discourse.

Conclusion

Higher education in general has been slow to recognize opportunities for innovation and transformation, with change generally occurring on the fringes.[23] Calls continue from inside and outside higher education to examine issues related to the value of the credit hour and links to learners' learning outcomes and success.

Innovation is not undertaken just for the sake of change. According to Brewer and Tierney, "Higher education needs to be more competitive and cost conscious. But, ultimately, a more innovative postsecondary industry will increase access to higher education, create a better educated workforce, and enable individuals to participate more fully in the democratic public sphere."[24]

Policy makers and Lumina, the Bill & Melinda Gates, and other foundations have supported initiatives to promote new models, enhance career readiness, and reduce time to degree completion. SUNY Empire State College has demonstrated transformative and disruptive approaches throughout its history. As "New York's open university," it remains a game changer by enabling learners to access open resources independently, engage through rich open learning environments with peer leaders and/or faculty mentors, document their college-level learning through e-portfolios for assessment, and stack credentials.

Acknowledgments

We would like to thank our colleagues at SUNY Empire State College who contributed in various ways to this chapter: Tai Arnold, Jill Buban, Dawn Riley, and Mitchell Nesler.

Notes

1. E. L. Boyer and American College Testing Program, *Emerging Learners . . . and the New Career Thrust in Higher Education* (Iowa City, IA: American College Testing Program, 1972); E. L. Boyer and F. M. Hechinger, *Higher Learning in the Nation's Service* (Washington, DC: Carnegie Foundation for the Advancement of Teaching, 1981); E. L. Boyer and M. Kaplan, *The Monday Morning Imagination: Report from the Boyer Workshop on State University Systems* (New York: Aspen Institute for Humanistic Studies, 1976).

2. R. F. Bonnabeau, *The Promise Continues: Empire State College—The First Twenty-Five Years* (Virginia Beach, VA: Donning, 1996).

3. L. Herman and A. Mandell, *From Teaching to Mentoring: Principle and Practice, Dialogue and Life in Adult Education* (London: RoutledgeFalmer, 2004).

4. Council on Adult and Experiential Learning, *Moving the Starting Line through Prior Learning Assessment* (2011), retrieved December 9, 2011, http://www.cael.org/pdfs/PLA_research_brief_avg_credit.

5. G. Siemens, *Connectivism: A Learning Theory for the Digital Age* (elearnspace, 2004), retrieved September 5, 2011, http://www.elearnspace.org/Articles/connectivism.htm.

6. N. H. Cohen, *Mentoring Adult Learners: A Guide For Educators and Trainers* (Malabar, FL: Krieger, 1995); L. A. Daloz, *Mentor: Guiding the Journey of Adult Learners*, 1st ed. (San Francisco: Jossey-Bass, 1999); M. W. Galbraith and N. H. Cohen, "The Complete Mentor Role: Understanding the Six Behavioral Functions," *Journal of Adult Education* 24, no. 2 (1996): 2–11.

7. E. L. Boyer, *Scholarship Reconsidered: Priorities of the Professoriate* (Carnegie Foundation for the Advancement of Teaching, 1990).

8. EDUCAUSE, "The Open Edition," *EDUCAUSE Review* 45, no. 4 (2010), retrieved December 9, 2011, http://www.educause.edu/EDUCAUSE+Review/ERVolume442009/EDUCAUSEReviewMagazineVolume45/209245.

9. M. A. Peters and P. Roberts, *The Virtues of Openness: Education and Scholarship in a Digital Age* (Boulder, CO: Paradigm, 2011).

10. M. A. Peters and R. G. Britez, *Open Education and Education For Openness* (Rotterdam: Sense, 2008).

11. N. L. Travers, "United States of America: PLA Research in Colleges and Universities," in *Researching Prior Learning*, ed. J. Harris, C. Wihak, and M. Breier (Leicester, UK: National Institute for Adult Continuing Education [NIACE], 2011).

12. Siemens, *Connectivism*.

13. F. F. VanderValk, *Project for Critical Inquiry* (2011), retrieved December 9, 2011, http://commons.esc.edu/criticalinquiry.

14. A. Kamenetz, *DIY U: Edupunks, Edupreneurs, and the Coming Transformation of Higher Education* (White River Junction, VT: Chelsea Green Publishing, 2010).

15. MozillaWiki, "Badges" (2011), retrieved December 9, 2011, https://wiki.mozilla.org/Badges.

16. WikiEducator, *Open Educational Resource University* (September 11, 2011), retrieved December 9, 2011, http://wikieducator.org/OER_university/Home.

17. WICHE, *Adult College Completion Network* (2011), retrieved December 9, 2011, http://adultcollegecompletion.org/content/adult-college-completion-network.

18. U.S. Department of Education, *College Completion Tool Kit* (2011), retrieved December 9, 2011, http://www.ed.gov/college-completion/governing-win.

19. A. P. Carnevale, "The American Response to Financial Crisis Lessons for Low and Middle-Income Countries" (presentation to the World Bank Forum on Maintaining Productive Employment in Times of Crisis, April 29, 2009, at Georgetown University, Center on Education and the Workforce), retrieved December 9, 2011, http://cew.georgetown.edu/resources/presentations.

20. T. Warger and D. Oblinger, "Surveying the Landscape," *EDUCAUSE Review* 46, no. 6 (November/December 2011), retrieved December 9, 2011, http://www.educause.edu/EDUCAUSE+Review/EDUCAUSEReviewMagazineVolume46/SurveyingtheLandscape/238377.

21. Toru Iiyoshi and M. S. Vijay Kumar, *Opening Up Education: The Collective Advancement of Education through Open Technology, Open Content, and Open Knowledge* (Cambridge, MA: MIT Press, 2008).

22. Ibid.

23. B. Wildavsky, A. Kelly, and K. Carey, eds., *Reinventing Higher Education: The Promise of Innovation* (Cambridge, MA: Harvard Educational Publishing Group, 2011).

24. D. J. Brewer and G. Tierney, "Barriers to Innovation in U.S. Higher Education," in *Reinventing Higher Education: The Promise of Innovation,* ed. B. Wildavsky, A. Kelly, and K. Carey (Cambridge, MA: Harvard Educational Publishing Group, 2011): 11–40.

Meg Benke *is Provost at SUNY Empire State College. Benke's work is dedicated to increasing access to higher education for adult learners through online education, and she advises universities on student services in online education programs. Benke is particularly focused on increasing employability of graduates and working to ensure that the outcomes of online and blended education match traditional education.* **Alan Davis** *is President of SUNY Empire State College. He has held academic leadership positions in a variety of traditional, online, and adult-focused institutions. He is president of the Canadian Society for the Study of Higher Education, a member of the Board of the Council for Adult and Experiential Learning, and serves on the Commission for Lifelong Learning for the American Council on Education.* **Nan L. Travers,** *Director of the Office of Collegewide Academic Review, oversees self-designed degrees, prior learning assessment (PLA), and ePortfolios. She serves on the board for LearningCounts. org and Prior Learning International Research Centre, and is the founding co-editor of* PLA Inside Out: An International Journal on the Theory, Research, and Practice in Prior Learning Assessment.

12

Athabasca University:
Canada's Open University

Dietmar Kennepohl, Cindy Ives, and Brian Stewart

THE PRIMARY DRIVING FORCES moving Athabasca University forward are its motto Learning for Life and its mandate to remove barriers to university-level education. By seeking to provide flexible education and serve nontraditional learner groups and needs, the university is very different from traditional campus-based institutions. Athabasca University (AU) is re-creating itself into a twenty-first-century university through its adoption and use of technology to expand the opportunities for its stakeholders. The growing needs of students, academics, and staff to learn and work in an integrated online environment is reflected in the institution's movement to a virtual campus with easy access to learning assets. Students are allowed to learn on their time at their pace in their place. For many, this is their only opportunity to access tertiary-level education.

The model that AU is inventing is responsive to the developing crisis in postsecondary education. New approaches and sector reinvention are necessary for creating knowledge-driven societies to meet the growing requirement for education to develop the citizenry and to be economically sustainable. The current higher education model, where operational costs rise at the real rate of inflation above all other sectors,[1] and where expectations of stakeholders for improved outcomes have increased—all occurring in a milieu of traditionally slow organizational change—cannot continue as is. AU has developed an approach that is cost effective,[2] pedagogically sound, responsive to student needs, and above all, adaptable to changing circumstances. In a world of uncertainties, change is probably the only certainty.

The Future Is Not What It Used to Be

AU has been one of the few universities worldwide already bridging the new educational future with its open- and distance-learning approach since its inception. This meant, in the 1970s and '80s, that it delivered print-based, independent study courses with telephone-tutor support.[3] Still, as newer technologies became available, they were experimented with and, if found useful, adopted. Assignments could be submitted electronically rather than through the postal system with the advent of e-mail, for example. However, adoption of new technologies usually varied across the university, with the technology essentially considered an add-on or modification to the basic working model. While appropriate and effective for its time period, this traditional approach to designing and delivering courses became entrenched and reinforced by years of policy, practice, and collective agreements. Wholesale system-wide changes were slow in coming, although individual examples of innovations could be found. Choosing one learning management system (LMS) for the entire university, for example, became a lengthy and complex debate, reflecting not only the politicized nature of course development and delivery, but also the widely divergent opinions across the academy itself.[4]

The incorporation of appropriate technology, as well as actual approaches to learning design, delivery, and support, has been the subject of continuing discussions. We have recently observed a substantial increase in willingness and momentum for change, with the focus having moved from accepting the necessity for change to reinventing the AU model. Two recent externally funded university projects ($14.5 million total) have catalyzed this acceleration: one for the digitization of all AU course content, and the other for increasing systems capacity and currency for research, collaboration, learning, content management, and student support.

A broad analysis of the literature indicates that critical success factors for integrating technology into teaching and learning are "organization-dependent, related to variables such as organizational mission, goals, culture and practices, as well as faculty and student perspectives."[5] AU's stated approach to institutional transformation is collaborative, informed by multiple perspectives, and focused on learning as the core business of the university. Effective integration of information and communication technologies (ICTs) depends on the successful coordination and implementation of a number of interdependent subsystems within the organization. This chapter describes AU's journey, which is ultimately a story of great change and reinvention, but also one of discovery. We share our approach to and perspectives of some of the serious difficulties we have found along the way, recognizing that these once-unique challenges, through their universalities, can offer lessons for many postsecondary institutions.

Our Infrastructure Really Is ICT

In 2009, AU was awarded a Knowledge Infrastructure Program (KIP) grant after years of lobbying both provincial and federal governments to consider ICT funding as capital rather than purely operational funding. While many other institutions applied KIP funding to physical buildings, AU's bricks and mortar is mainly its technology. This recognition from the government of ICT as capital infrastructure was a fundamental paradigm shift—it was not only essential to AU's model, but it served as an important next step for higher education as a whole.

AU's ICT Capital Plan is a ten-year development program inspired by the vision of an Online Knowledge Environment (OKE). The creation of a unique and compelling experience driven by world-class pedagogical research and practice, available through individualized access, with course delivery tailored to students' learning preferences to enable greater success, were some of the main tenets of the OKE vision. In order to improve services and supports throughout the organization, the capital plan essentially seeks to establish the OKE through the use of ICTs across learning, research, and administrative activities. Superficially, most innovations and projects that flow from this plan manifest themselves through changes in technology. However, they are often process or practice changes that also incorporate an ICT systems component at their foundation. Thus, ICT has come to play an increasingly important role throughout the operations of the institution and is creating a culture of innovation and a desire for change. ICT represents the overwhelming capital base of the institution. AU is seen as a virtual institution both internally and externally, one in which the traditional view of capital infrastructure, buildings, and land does not apply.

Course Delivery and Learning Support

It is crucial to have the appropriate supports in place for success, given that most AU courses are offered as *individualized study* courses (mainly undergraduate level) with year-round enrollment and that some students may only have minimal formal prerequisites or may have been away from their studies for many years. A long-standing strategic objective of the university has been to provide high-quality support in a flexible learning environment. The learning experience is greatly influenced by academic support, in addition to the full suite of administrative and student support services available online and by telephone (detailed later in this chapter). Still, some fundamental issues have had to be dealt with.

Learner preparedness: Academic supports are available in some cases before one even formally becomes a student.

- Degree Audit and Program Planning (a web-based advising/degree audit tool) enables students to perform "what if" scenarios based on their coursework to evaluate how transfer credits would apply to their program.

- Several self-diagnostic tests ("Am I Ready for … ?" series) are available to potential students to help determine if they are ready for a specific course or, more generally, for university-level study itself.

At an open university, students are not required to have formal prerequisites to register in entry-level courses, but they are still expected to perform satisfactorily once they enter. Because AU faculty and staff wish to reduce failure rates, this creates challenges. Furthermore, to ensure that students have a reasonable chance to obtain the education they seek and deserve, the teaching staff feel morally obligated to adequately advise and inform students attempting a course.

AU has also developed academic supports that are open to all students in the area of general education. This includes the Write Site, the Math Site, and Information Literacy, which all provide a wide variety of online resources (and in one case, personal coaching). However, at the heart of the AU model is the fact that (1) courses and programs are developed and overseen by research-active professors in those fields and (2) students have access to a tutor.[6] Enhancing student success is the aim in all cases.

Student engagement: Again, as with learner preparedness, the need to enhance student success and increase the traditionally low pass rates for students studying alone and online drives much of the discussion and debate at AU. Research links proactive student contact with persistence and student success.[7] In order to establish a relationship and encourage course completion, this used to mean telephoning or e-mailing a student. A critical factor in student success is student engagement, as has been repeatedly pointed to in wide-scale studies; as a result, benchmarking tools such as the National Survey of Student Engagement have become common. AU provides student engagement opportunities via well-designed interactive courses (discussed later in this chapter) and through individual communications with course tutors and online discussion forums with course colleagues as a result of the possibilities afforded by new technologies. The creation of an interface for the teaching staff portal and community (myAU Learning Management [Tutor] Tab) that highlights recent student activities (submission of assignments, forum postings, internal mail postings) and disseminates tutor-related information in an effort to increase tutor engagement with students is the outcome of one recent initiative.

Social networking: Studying alone and online is not a typical environment for many students. Traditional residential universities have spaces that enable a rich diversity of informal, nonformal, and formal interactions in a variety of places, such as cafes, lecture theatres, libraries, common areas—Oldenburg's "third places."[8] These physical social spaces provide many opportunities for learning and research, including the discovery of new ideas and people with relevant interests. Such spaces are unavailable or unevenly distributed in online institutions. The growth of social networks in society (e.g., Facebook, LinkedIn, Twitter) and in academic settings (e.g., University of Brighton's community@brighton and University of Manitoba's Virtual Learning Commons) has inspired AU to offer a secure social network for learners, alumni, staff, and faculty. The site (The Landing) increases social interactions among members of the AU community, offering more opportunities for collaboration, cooperation, and sharing through the use of an extendable online social software system. Pilot projects currently underway are leading to successful practices for incorporating The Landing into self-paced individualized study courses. These experiences are informing course design more broadly across the academy.

Student Support Services

The nature of services students are demanding has been impacted by the proliferation of postsecondary learning options.

- Students' perceptions of university education are moving toward a business orientation whereby they see themselves primarily as clients purchasing services rather than as students learning with faculty.
- Technology has increased access and 24/7 service is now expected.
- The nature and level of services can differ greatly for undergraduate and graduate students.

The AU model is characterized by openness, flexibility, breadth, and quality of programs in a distance and online learning framework, accessed through continuous enrollment at the undergraduate level. Taken together, these features demand an array of student services that not only meet changing expectations, but that also offer more immediate, effective, and customized services in the unique AU learning environment. This has prompted efforts in several vital areas.

Credit transfer, evaluation, and coordination: Because students have become more mobile, they are increasingly seeking credit for a combination of courses from a variety of institutions and a range of other learning experiences, so that advising, program planning, transcript evaluation, and prior learning assessment have become progressively more complex. In addition, maximum recognition of previous learning for students that can be applied to their program is allowed by the open nature of the university. Until recently, this had been done manually and was very time consuming. AU introduced a document workflow related to transfer credit evaluations, articulation agreements, and examination requests (Transfer Credit Administration System), which also provides automated and seamless updating of student records and allows students to preview transcript evaluation. Future integration with the provincial postsecondary application system (ApplyAlberta) will further expedite transcript receipt.

Pan-university collaborations: Student support areas at AU include registry, course materials, access for students with disabilities, prior learning assessment and recognition (PLAR), challenge for credit, financial aid, information center, technical support (Help Desk), examination services, transcript requests, transfer-credit evaluations, advising, program planning, counseling, library services, ombuds office, and student awards. Also, AU has offices at major collaborating residential institutions. These student support areas are distributed across the university in several units and together offer a wide variety of services. Unit heads from student services and learning support consult regularly in different pan-university collaborative working groups—which include the Contact Centre Group, AU Web Advisory Committee, and the Student Success Group—in an effort to pull everything together and offset any "silo effect." Coordinating efforts across the university and maintaining consistency in all student-facing operations is crucial. Four overarching principles articulated in the Student Success Group vision guide the initiatives: (1) enhance student experience and success, (2) cultivate a service culture, (3) integrate appropriate technology, and (4) maintain continuous evaluation and improvement.

Student relationship building: AU is introducing an ICT system (Student Lifecycle and Relationship Management Support Services) that tracks student contact information related to various constituents (prospective students, current students, alumni) with the goal of enhancing student engagement outside the classroom, improving service relationships, and informing strategic communication and business planning. This is being used in combination with other initiatives, including a call management system (Virtual Call Centre) to facilitate improved frontline service and provide information on patterns to stimulate further development. The relationship management system will provide insights into student behaviors, allowing future developments to better meet emergent demands and respond to student needs.

Paving the way: Many of the ICT innovations adopted by student services and learning support are not necessarily direct supports. They are instead meant to make various practical functions easier for the student and less of a distraction to learning. For example, students can arrange for invigilated examinations literally at any time anywhere in the world. Systems under the Exam Harmonization project will not only define and streamline the exam life cycle; they will provide efficient exam management. The Gradebook system integrates and enhances student grading functions in the learning management system (Moodle) with the student information system (Banner), allowing students to more easily submit assignments and eliminating duplicate grade entry by tutors. The Federated Search system enables students and researchers to browse and find information in multiple databases and resources during a single library search. Some innovations, while still essential to supporting students, are more administrative and thus unseen. Examples of this include AU's move to a single content management system (Alfresco) and its adoption of Desktop Virtualization, which transitions the desktops of personal computers onto a centralized server and enables staff to securely access their digital assets from any computer with an Internet connection, whether inside the AU workplace, on the road, or at home.

Finally, numerous common strategies employed by student services and learning support units are in place across the university. For example, technology is often used to automate routine work to free up more time for personalized high-touch interactions. Students can also directly access needed resources and information, affording them more control over their own learning environment. However, student services and learning support are not a concierge service for fulfilling any and all requests. The collection of services is meant to reduce barriers to university education and to facilitate an environment conducive to learning and personal growth. They provide a balance of what is wanted and what is needed to enable the success of independent self-directed learners.

Course and Curriculum Development

The early AU model used an instructional systems design[9] approach wherein courses were written by subject matter experts (authors) following a template created by instructional designers, edited for quality and consistency and produced as print-based materials by specialists in visual design and type-setting. Courses typically included study guides that provided commentary about readings from textbooks or collected articles, course manuals that described how students should work through courses, and assignment manuals. These materials were boxed and mailed to students.

A detailed seven-phase process guiding course-development activities included opportunities for curriculum alignment, peer evaluation of content, and regular revision of courses. This process, focused on the publication of content, worked well for many years.[10] As ICTs emerged, instructional designers were hired to help with experimental projects, create learning objects, and advise on the use of multimedia. At the same time, learning theory was evolving from positivist to relativist, and students' preferences were changing from accepting direct instruction to expecting to actively participate in their learning.[11] Greater possibilities for student interaction with content, with instructors, and with other students[12] were afforded by the new online technologies. The world changed, challenging the original course-development model.

Several academic units experimented with online student activities in early course-management systems. By the early 2000s, most graduate programs and programs in two undergraduate disciplines—Business and Nursing—were delivered online (with the exception of textbooks and exams). The pedagogical model of textbook wraparound or information delivery approaches in the self-paced programs saw few changes, however. In 2006, the LMS enterprise was consolidated—Moodle is an open source software, in line with AU's commitment to openness—and course materials were speedily converted to the online environment, at least initially.[13] Conversion did not involve much change, but it was a first step in the long process of influencing the culture and practices of both academic and administrative staff. While some staff resisted the conversion approach and viewed it as too threatening to traditionally successful models, others saw an opportunity to create more engaging courses and enhance the learning experience of students and felt the university was not moving fast enough into the online world.

Recent Course Design Innovations

In the late 2000s, AU began recruiting learning designers[14] to help influence the transition from print to online course development. As their experience with course conversions and the LMS grew, and examples of successful online courses were shared throughout the university community, more and more academics came to appreciate the need to rethink their approach to course design. Student feedback was also beginning to describe changing expectations. The learning designers focused their efforts on designing learning activities and aligning assessments with learning outcomes. Working with course professors and other subject-matter experts to redesign course materials into engaging and interactive learning environments that are also motivating and challenging, the learning designers identified the need for an educational development program that would share promising practices in online teaching and learning across disciplinary boundaries. Workshops, presentations, and open conversations covered instructional and learning theories, appropriate use of technologies for student success, assignment design, and examples of innovative course design at AU. These efforts supported new relationships with course professors and inspired greater confidence in the potential of online courses to meet the needs of both students and specific disciplines. As a result, new policies and processes for course development are expected soon.

The externally funded ICT infrastructure projects provided additional resources for experimentation in several areas, including learning analytics and open educational resources (OERs). A suite of complex online tools was designed to assist with analyzing student behavior in the LMS and with the development of interactive learning objects at the activity level. One application accesses data for formative evaluation of courses that use learning resources in new ways. Other applications include authoring interfaces that allow non-programmers to develop media-supported learning activities such as quizzes, tutorials, decision trees, and m-casts.[15] The digitization project supported the development of twenty-five interactive, multimedia learning objects and activities for seventeen of AU's largest enrollment courses. These "showcase" enhancements were designed to focus students' attention on difficult content or concepts in individual courses in order to increase their engagement and motivation. Formal formative evaluation is under way, but early feedback from tutors and students is promising. Producing reusable resources using core XML coding so that they could be easily adapted for other uses was another goal of the project. Most of the objects and their associated editors are now licensed with Creative Commons and have been released into the OER community. And we are already repurposing the objects in new courses.

These special projects also offered opportunities for faculty to get more involved in conversations about moving AU programs and services online, which has resulted in a greater understanding of and commitment to innovation in course design for online delivery. A higher level of engagement in and support for initiatives that are renewing the culture of teaching and learning services at AU and accelerating the adoption of change is one outcome. A heightened sense of collaboration among the various stakeholders in the teaching and learning enterprise is another.

The Future Is Here

Research programs are focused on the application of emerging technologies to improve student access to and success in AU courses in support of future developments in course design and learning support. Researchers at AU's Technology Enhanced Knowledge Research Institute are actively engaged in exploring advances in mobile learning, adaptivity and personalization, social networking, learning analytics, and open education. The design-based nature[16] of these research initiatives connects researchers directly with practitioners—both learning designers and professors—and helps builds community, further supporting an understanding of the need for change. New pedagogical approaches are already emerging. One is focusing on the use of OERs in course design, which is expected to reduce course development time and cost (AU is a founding member of the OER university[17]). Reusable learning designs will have a similar impact on production processes.

The results of learning analytics studies in particular will likely guide the design of course models in years to come. Analytics broadly promises that new insights can be gained from in-depth analysis of the data trails left by individuals in their interactions with others, with information, with technology, and with organizations. Learning analytics focus on course- and class-level activities, letting students access data about their learning progress and offering design teams ideas for iterative improvements of courses.[18] Our goal—to provide personalized learning environments—is achievable if combined with the data from administrative systems, especially grades and student demographic information from the student information system.

Student Perspective and Performance

Approximately one-third of AU students register for one or two courses in order to complete degrees at their home university or college. The demographics of these visiting students are analogous to those at traditional institutions. The rest of the students are nontraditional learners who tend to study part time, are often more mature, and already have job obligations and family commitments. AU regularly surveys its students to obtain feedback on course, tutor, and learning support, as well as on nonacademic services,[19] using the detailed information to improve services.

Overall satisfaction scores tend to be quite high, with 95.3 percent of students rating services as excellent or good and 97.7 percent who would recommend AU to friends.[20] The provincial government also conducts an

Table 1. **Athabasca University Graduate Student Satisfaction Compared with Mean Alberta Universities, 2010**[22]

	Quality of Teaching (%)	Quality of Program (%)	Overall Experience (%)
Athabasca University	94	97	97
Mean Alberta Universities	88	87	90

independent satisfaction and outcomes research survey (approximately two years after graduation) of all provincial postsecondary education institutions. In almost two decades of these surveys, AU graduates have consistently expressed high levels of satisfaction with the quality of the teaching, programs, and overall educational experience. The 2010 report is no exception,[21] as seen in Table 1.

In its last undergraduate student survey in 2008,[23] the Canadian Universities Survey Consortium rated Athabasca University as being as good or better compared with the national average in several areas, including satisfaction with teaching quality (88 percent vs. 88 percent) and overall educational experience—92 percent vs. 85 percent. (Since most of the thirty-one universities in the consortium are primarily classroom-based with online supports, the questions related to the in-classroom environment, social activities, and in-person perceptions of the professor generally scored lower than average.) Athabasca students reported higher levels of satisfaction with online instruction (95 percent) compared with students having taken online courses at other institutions (73 percent).

Similar to other universities, learners are evaluated by their submitted work, interaction with the teacher/tutor, and invigilated examinations. Although the open nature of the university does not require prerequisites to enter many courses, it does require students to meet rigorous standards to pass the course. Grades obtained in AU courses are comparable in distribution and in absolute terms to those at sister universities in the province,[24] which all use the same grading scale.[25] Other institutions in Canada and abroad commonly recognize bachelor degrees for entry into graduate programs and courses for credit transfer. AU is a formal member of the credit-transfer system in both Alberta[26] and British Columbia[27] and has the authority to be a university and grant degrees through Alberta's Post-Secondary Learning Act. It is also officially recognized by the Government of British Columbia. In 2006, AU became the first Canadian public university to receive accreditation in the United States, through the Middle States Commission on Higher Education (MSCHE), one of six regional organizations in the U.S. that accredits universities. No other public Canadian university holds this level of foreign accreditation.

The Participation Challenge

The completion and pass rates are the most distinguishing student performance features when compared with traditional residential universities. Students studying online as individuals (as opposed to being in a cohort) have significantly lower pass rates. This is especially true in an open course with minimal prerequisites. The course pass rate for undergraduate students at AU for the period 1996–2003 was 54 percent, comparable to other open distance-learning (ODL) universities.[28] However, AU's nonstart rates[29] are substantial, and when nonstart course registrations are excluded from pass rates, "The pass rates for … students at AU increase from 59% to 84%—a figure that likely approximates pass rates at conventional universities."[30] Though technically the nonstart students are not students who fail the course, AU and other ODL universities expend much effort toward understanding and, more importantly, increasing student retention and persistence in their courses by fostering more student engagement and designing better courses. For example, can ICTs be used to create a cohort "feel" to a course, but still allow the flexibility of individualized study? In the end, it is factors that the university has no control over—family, home, health, work—that are connected with nonstart behavior for many mature students.

In addition to internal and external pressures to increase pass rates, good news can be found on the participation front. AU provides a viable option for those in remote, rural, and northern communities, and reaches many underrepresented groups, especially aboriginal students and students with disabilities. Learners (79 percent) who may be mobile or who have family and job commitments and who wish to study part time from anywhere regularly take advantage of the tremendous flexibility offered. The fact that 74 percent of graduates are the first in their family to earn a university degree, a significantly higher number than at most universities, is the noteworthy result of the combination of open admission and rigorous course standards. This participation—where it is most needed—reflects AU's mandate to remove barriers to university-level education and is of great value.

Becoming a Twenty-First-Century University

Transforming a large academic organization is very much like trying to change the tires on a car while driving down the highway. Even if everyone can agree on what the final outcome might be, its realization is demanding and risky. Many visions of the twenty-first-century university have been proposed—often embracing features AU employs—and include being learner centered and open, having self-paced courses, offering continuous enrollment, incorporating appropriate technology and learning design, focusing on learning outcomes and not inputs, and providing strong student service and learning supports. What could other institutions learn from AU if they were to design themselves as a twenty-first-century university?

- Many of the proposed features that have been successfully implemented by AU do result in high student satisfaction and successful performance. They come with their own challenges, however.
- Preparing for and embracing changing technologies is vital. ICTs have become an integral and critical part of AU. They are no longer "add-ons."
- Effectively adopting ICT requires transparent governance allied with reliable processes and administration. ICTs are disruptive to a university's core business and require broad understanding and acceptance to be successful.
- Providing institutional infrastructure and fostering a culture that can accommodate unforeseen future changes are key to laying the groundwork for building a twenty-first-century university.

Becoming an educated person is what attending the university is still about. Universities prepare people for careers with skills that fuel the economy. However, developments such as the following have inspired us to rethink the concept of the university: the vast amounts of information now available; rapid changes in technology; the creation of new professions; the blurring of formal, informal, and nonformal learning; employers' desire for general education and soft skills; globalization and increased mobility; and changing learner expectations. While these factors will drastically change how, when, and where we learn in the future, they also bring us back to the idea that a particular area of study is essentially just a vehicle to a good university education. Learning to learn, rather than focusing on specific disciplinary content, is the solid emphasis at Athabasca University. It's about learning for life.

Notes

1. Schumpeter (blog), "Declining by Degree: Will America's Universities Go the Way of Its Car Companies?," *The Economist* (September 2, 2010), retrieved from http://www.economist.com/node/16960438.
2. L. Wagner, "The Economics of the Open University," *Higher Education* 1, no. 2 (1972): 159–83.
3. T. C. Byrne, *Athabasca University: The Evolution of Distance Education* (Canada: University of Calgary Press, 1989); L. J. Hughes, *The First Athabasca University* (Canada: Athabasca University, 1980).
4. B. Stewart, D. Briton, M. Gismondi, B. Heller, D. Kennepohl, R. McGreal, and C. Nelson, "Choosing MOODLE: An Evaluation of Learning Management Systems at Athabasca University," *The International Journal of Distance Education Technologies* 5, no. 3 (2007): 1–7.
5. C. A. Ives, "Designing and Developing an Educational Systems Design Model for Technology Integration in Universities" (unpublished PhD diss., Concordia University, Montreal, Canada, 2002): iii.
6. The general term *tutor* includes both individualized study tutors and academic experts/markers.
7. M. A. Drouin, "The Relationship between Students' Perceived Sense of Community and Satisfaction, Achievement and Retention in an Online Course," *Quarterly Review of Distance Education* 9, no. 3 (2008): 267–84; O. Simpson, "The Impact on Retention of Interventions to Support Distance Learning Students," *Open Learning: The Journal of Open, Distance and e-Learning* 19, no. 1 (2004): 79–95; V. Tinto, *Leaving College: Rethinking the Causes and Cures of Student Attrition*, 2nd ed. (Chicago: University of Chicago Press, 1994).
8. R. Oldenburg, *The Great Good Place: Cafes, Coffee Shops, Bookstores, Bars, Hair Salons, and Other Hangouts at the Heart of a Community* (Cambridge, MA: Marlowe & Company, 1999).
9. W. Dick and L. Carey, *The Systematic Design of Instruction* (Glenview, IL: Scott, Foresman, 1978).
10. L. R. Ross and A. Davis, "Going from Distance to Digital: Athabasca University's E-Learning Plan," in *At the Interface Project: Virtual Learning and Higher Education*, ed. D. S. Preston (Amsterdam, Netherlands: Rodopi, 2004), 8: 29–54.
11. R. A. Reiser and J. V. Dempsey, eds., *Trends and Issues in Instructional Design and Technology*, 2nd ed. (Upper Saddle River, NJ: Pearson Prentice Hall, 2007).
12. T. Anderson, "Toward a Theory of Online Learning," in *Theory and Practice of Online Learning*, 2nd ed., ed. T. Anderson (Canada: Athabasca University, 2008), 45–74, retrieved from http://www.aupress.ca/books/120146/ebook/02_Anderson_2008-Theory_and_Practice_of_Online_Learning.pdf.
13. Stewart et al., "Choosing MOODLE."
14. G. Conole, A. Brasher, S. Cross, M. Weller, P. Clark, and J. Culver, "Visualising

Learning Design to Foster and Support Good Practice and Creativity," *Educational Media International* 45, no. 3 (2008): 177–94.

15. *M-cast* is the term we are using to refer to multimedia webcasts. It includes podcast, vodcast, and webcast and allows for the anticipated development of other technologies as well.

16. T. Anderson, "Design-Based Research and Its Application to a Call Centre Innovation in Distance Education," *Canadian Journal of Learning and Technology* 31, no. 2 (2005): 69–83, retrieved from http://auspace.athabascau.ca:8080/dspace/bitstream /2149/741/1/design_based_research.pdf.

17. J. C. Taylor and W. Mackintosh, "Creating an Open Educational Resources University and the Pedagogy of Discovery," *Open Praxis Special Edition* (October 24–29, 2011).

18. M. Brown, "Learning Analytics: The Coming Third Wave" (ELI Brief, EDUCAUSE, April 2011), retrieved from http://www.educause.edu/Resources/LearningAnalytics TheComingThir/227287.

19. Office of Institutional Studies (OIS) Athabasca University. *Undergraduate Student Satisfaction with Non-Academic Services,* 2009 (OIS Report 20100202). Athabasca, Canada.

20. Ibid.

21. Alberta Advanced Education and Technology, *Alberta Graduate Outcomes Survey Class of 2007–2008 Final Report* (prepared by HarrisDecima, October 7, 2010), retrieved from http://www.advancededucation.gov.ab.ca/media/280913/ gos2010%28final%29.pdf.

22. Alberta Advanced Education and Technology, Comprehensive Academic and Research Institutions (Sector 1), 2010.

23. Canadian Universities Survey Consortium (CUSC), *Undergraduate Student Survey* (unpublished report, 2008).

24. J. D'Arcy, Registrar, Athabasca University, personal communication, August 13, 2011.

25. D. Jabbour, "From My Perspective: A New Grading System," *The Voice Magazine* 10, no. 49 (2002), retrieved from http://www.voicemagazine.org/search/searchdisplay. php?ART=317.

26. Alberta Council on Admissions and Transfer.

27. British Columbia Council on Admissions and Transfer.

28. R. Powell, *Openness and Dropout: A Study of Four Open Distance Education Universities* (M-2009: 23rd International Council on Distance Education World Conference on Open Learning and Distance Education, Maastricht, Netherlands, 2009), retrieved from http://www.ou.nl/Docs/Campagnes/ICDE2009/Papers/Final_ paper_262powell.pdf, Table 6; Open University, 2009; Open University (2009). Course results 2008. *Sesame* (242), 22–24. Retrieved from http://www3.open. ac.uk/events/3/2009922_43263_o1.pdf.

29. A "nonstart" is a student who registers in a course but has not submitted any assignments or done any examinations.

30. Powell, *Openness and Dropout*, Table 7.

Dietmar Kennepohl *is Professor of Chemistry and Associate Vice President Academic at Athabasca University. Most of his teaching experience has been in a distributed and online setting. He holds both university and national teaching awards. His current research interests include chemical education, main group, and green chemistry.* **Cindy Ives** *brings professional and teaching experience in university administration and distance education, with expertise in designing and developing effective course materials and faculty development. Her doctoral studies and subsequent professional responsibilities focused on ensuring the appropriate integration of technologies for teaching and learning through collaborative, multi-perspective and systemic planning, implementation, and evaluation processes.* **Brian Stewart,** *Vice President and Chief Information Officer at Athabasca University, provides strategic leadership to the application of information and communications technology (ICT). Stewart is charged with identifying and resourcing appropriate technologies to improve administrative effectiveness and efficiency; assisting the academic community's use of ICT; and facilitating the research and development of e-learning initiatives.*

13

Providing Quality Higher Education for Adults

Susan C. Aldridge

UNIVERSITY OF MARYLAND UNIVERSITY COLLEGE (UMUC) first opened its classrooms in 1947 as a special college at the University of Maryland, created specifically to serve the state's returning World War II veterans with GI Bill in hand. That was the spark that in many ways ignited America's adult-learning movement and paved the way for open-access institutions such as UMUC, founded in the belief that higher education should be available to anyone, anywhere, at any time—institutions that forged new trails in adult-focused curriculum design, instructional methodologies, distance delivery, and student service.

Consequently, by 1970, what had once been a "grand experiment" became a separate degree-granting institution within the University System of Maryland. Today, UMUC is the nation's largest public university and a truly global academic enterprise, with three divisions in Europe, Asia, and the United States serving 94,000 students in 28 countries. It also continues to forge new trails.

Having now spent sixty-four years educating adults, UMUC has come to appreciate how different its students are from students who go on to college right out of high school. For the most part, their families and careers are already well under way, which means they often come with a good bit of experience and a lot of responsibility in their lives. Adults also tend to be highly self-directed and problem-oriented learners, with clear academic goals in mind that are, more often than not, tied to professional advancement. Likewise, they have a strong penchant for experiential learning that is meaningful, as well as an intense need to apply what they are learning immediately and effectively.

That being said, they are looking for academic opportunities that help them bridge what they know with what they need to learn in a way that is both easily transferrable beyond the classroom and tailored to meet them "where they are" dispositionally and experientially. Moreover, they demand market-driven degree and certificate programs—full time and part time, online and in class—with options that include prior learning credits, accelerated program formats, and targeted career counseling.

Because the college day begins after rush hour ends for most of these students, their success depends on wraparound support services that are as easy to access as they are to use. They are also more likely to take a course or two at a time; "stop out" altogether when life gets in the way; or simply move on to other, more promising academic options when their needs go unmet.

Harnessing the Power of Technology

In searching for innovative ways to deliver high-quality, affordable academic programs beyond its physical campus in Maryland, UMUC turned to technology early on, investing in everything from instructional television in the 1950s to video conferencing in the 1990s. In 1994, the university launched its first proprietary, computer-based learning management system, with little more than a hundred enrollments in only a handful of courses. Since that time, we have built a full-blown virtual campus, which has grown to include nearly 235,000 enrollments in more than one hundred undergraduate and graduate degree programs and certificates that are offered entirely online. And while UMUC also offers face-to-face and hybrid courses, the majority of its students now prefer the online option.

With the advent of Web 2.0 and its highly interactive technologies, UMUC has come a long way since 1994, when its course modules were essentially a series of handouts, published and delivered online. As digital technology continues to evolve, it has proved to be both a flexible platform from which to teach and a dynamic tool through which to learn, while allowing individuals of all ages, abilities, ethnicities, and economic circumstances to move seamlessly in and out of the classroom, at different times, in different places, and for different reasons.

By harnessing the power of technology, UMUC can now connect a student in Okinawa, Japan, with a professor in Adelphi, Maryland, or transport a wheelchair-bound, Iraq War veteran into the virtual classroom from the comfort of his living room. Similarly, it can bring real-world practitioners, in any given field, on board to teach a class, conduct a webinar, or mentor a student, while at the same time providing our instructors with the training they need to do their jobs effectively.

Figure 1. **Ideal Learning Environment**

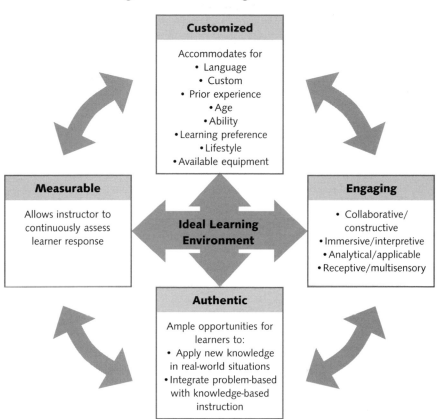

UMUC can furnish 24/7 access to high-tech, high-touch student-support services and a vast selection of digital library resources, which means that its students never have to wait in long lines to register for classes or stay up all night doing research in the far corners of a library. It can also facilitate online communities of practice, connecting students and faculty members from various institutions and organizations around the world, to create new knowledge, share information, and engage in cooperative problem solving.

More importantly, however, technology has made it possible for UMUC to create what research has repeatedly shown to be an ideal learning environment,[1] which allows students to take greater control over their learning process while also achieving at higher levels (see Figure 1).

Maximizing Student Success

While this ideal learning environment is certainly essential in meeting the academic needs of our students, curriculum plays an equally significant role in their ultimate success, particularly when it comes to the development of career-relevant programs and coursework. With that in mind, the academic model itself must be flexible enough to address the rapidly evolving needs of both a changing workforce and a changing world by enabling the university to adapt its curriculum, content, and instructional technologies as needed. This focus on relevance and flexibility thus became the driving force behind UMUC's ambitious undergraduate curriculum reengineering project.

The Project

In 2009, after conducting an exhaustive, five-year study on student engagement and persistence, UMUC realized it needed to take a long hard look at its undergraduate curriculum, especially given the dynamic and highly specialized nature of today's knowledge work. With this data in hand, UMUC's undergraduate division launched Project SEGUE (Supporting Educational Goals for Undergraduate Excellence) to develop and implement a transformational academic model that would

- generate a UMUC-defined curriculum, which when delivered within the ideal learning environment would enable our students to move more successfully from coursework to real work;
- streamline the degree completion process to boost student retention; and
- furnish students and faculty alike with a better process for tracking academic progress, while also measuring the value of a UMUC degree.

In framing the project, UMUC's undergraduate school identified one simple question that would guide its efforts going forward: *"What should our students be able to do 'out there' that we are responsible for teaching them 'in here'?"* That meant looking more closely at what employers were actually seeking in the college graduates they hired. In 2008, the American Association of Colleges and Universities published a national survey of more than three hundred business leaders, which laid the groundwork for subsequent inquiry. Those leaders polled indicated that today's employer is more likely to hire graduates who have studied at universities where educational achievement is measured using assessments of real-world and integrative, applied learning.

They also reported that student preparedness was lowest in the areas of global knowledge, self-direction, writing, critical thinking, and adaptability.[2]

Using this and other relevant research, the Project SEGUE leadership team members settled on a curriculum redesign process that would allow them to "begin with the end in mind."[3] As such, UMUC's undergraduate faculty would collaborate with industry experts to identify appropriate learning outcomes for each program and every course—which were aligned with real-world professional expectations—while also incorporating the application of complex abilities and knowledge. For example, outcomes for UMUC's legal studies program would better reflect activities that legal professionals regularly engage in (Table 1).

Table 1. UMUC's Legal Studies Program Outcomes

	Old	New
Program Outcomes	Recognize and discuss ethical considerations involved in the practice of law.	Apply knowledge of legal systems, concepts, and methodologies to efficiently and ethically support the resolution of legal disputes.
Course Outcomes	Explain the various forms of alternative dispute resolution and their common applications.	Draft a comprehensive interest analysis of a party to a dispute based on a client interview and development of evidence.

Once these more robust outcomes were in place, the faculty would then work backward, using the latest research in teaching and learning to build in effective learning experiences and assessments that provided ample opportunities for students to synthesize and demonstrate what they learned as they moved through their programs. Figure 2 shows what the end result would resemble.

The Process

Given the size and scope of Project SEGUE, the undergraduate dean created a complement of interdependent teams, tasked with developing a set of policies and procedures. These teams included a five-member SEGUE steering committee, a curriculum redesign group, a communication and linkages committee, and a student-success group. UMUC also hired The Learning

Figure 2. **Desired Learning Outcomes**

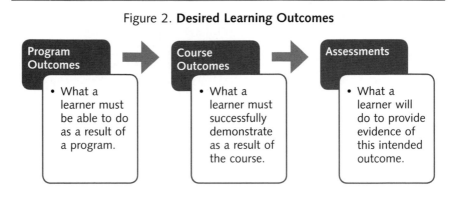

Organization, a consulting firm founded by Dr. Ruth Stiehl, professor emeri-ta at Oregon State University, and a group of college faculty members with broad-based experience in building internal capacity for curriculum redesign efforts such as this one. Working with undergraduate program directors and university instructional designers, these consultants covered all of the relevant bases, including (1) principles of outcomes-based design; (2) facilitation skills; (3) learning-assessment development; and (4) concepts, skills, and issues that support learning outcomes.

With 33 programs and some 1,200 courses to reengineer, there was no question that Project SEGUE would involve a large number of undergraduate faculty and staff. UMUC also wanted to complete this effort within a two-year time frame. Therefore, in choosing a curriculum-design process, the undergrad-uate division settled on one that was both efficiently organized and logically constructed, as shown in Figure 3.

UMUC began this process at the program level by assembling its un-dergraduate program directors to identify specific gaps in program content, common barriers to student progress, and persistent problems with course sequencing and integration. Using this information, they produced a series of program maps that outlined a standard path for degree completion, as well as key points for student-learning assessment.

After mapping each program, our program directors convened a group of outside experts from among both the university's industry-learning partners and its alumni to help articulate new learning outcomes for each program based on the twenty-first-century knowledge and skills our students would need in the real world of work. The revised outcomes subsequently became the foundation for a second series of program maps, which were used in de-veloping Program Outcome Guides (POGs). These guides serve as detailed

Figure 3. **SEGUE Program Design Process**

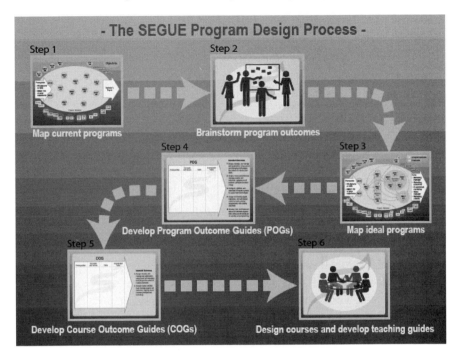

blueprints for measuring the extent to which our students successfully master course content while also meeting program objectives.

Once the program portion was complete, SEGUE leaders deployed teams of instructors in each academic program to tackle the course redesign process. These faculty teams began by matching industry-driven program outcomes with such other competencies as writing proficiency and technological fluency, cultural literacy, and systems thinking. In addition, to provide a context for this phase, they crafted an undergraduate learning model that is highly compatible with the foundational components of an ideal learning environment. Grounded in Chickering and Gamson's seven principles for undergraduate learning,[4] this model also incorporated subsequent research findings in cognitive science, including UMUC's own ongoing studies in the areas of adult and distance education.

Working from both this model and the outcomes alignment, our faculty teams went on to create Course Outcome Guides (COGs), which delineate specific learning outcomes for each individual course, along with appropriate learning content and "best practice" learning activities. They also revamped each course to fit within a three-term, eight-week format (rather than the conventional fifteen-week semester), which is standard for most adult-focused learning institutions. To better support UMUC instructors, these teams produced Course Teaching Guides (CTGs), as well, which are essentially road maps for effectively delivering the new curriculum—whether online, face-to-face, or a combination of both.

The Result

In the end, more than seven hundred UMUC faculty members worldwide voluntarily joined forces across divisions, departments, and disciplines to complete the project in two years, a record by most university standards. They were also able to reduce the sheer number of courses, which had grown by accretion over the years. On August 22, 2011, UMUC inaugurated its new curriculum. Although the weeks that followed were certainly stormy with respect to the weather in Maryland (thanks to a minor earthquake, followed closely by Hurricane Irene), the rollout itself was remarkably calm.

Given the scope of this launch, there were relatively few problems or concerns overall. Because our faculty members were trained in teaching the new curriculum, they were prepared to support their students throughout the semester. When issues did arise—for instance, a student struggling with the more accelerated pace of work—advisors and student-support specialists were on hand to provide help for as long as it took to get students over the hump. Instructors also stepped in to offer focused support in the classroom. With the initial rollout behind us, our institutional effectiveness team is now evaluating the new curriculum from both student and faculty perspectives to ensure rapid and continuous improvement as we move forward. Moreover, our virtual Center for Teaching and Learning is developing experiential online training modules for faculty members, which will provide additional support for teaching the new curriculum.

All in all, SEGUE has been an extraordinary exercise in synthesis in that it enabled the university to infuse its undergraduate programs and courses with all of the components our students must have to succeed: workforce-relevant skills, industry-driven knowledge, effective teaching and learning strategies, and ongoing assessment. It has also provided the faculty with a highly effective and easily replicable process for ongoing curriculum updating and refinement as needed to ensure that both content and outcomes remain relevant.

As a result, UMUC has created a transformational academic model that is program driven rather than course centered, learner focused rather than teacher directed, with a solid foundation in research-validated practices for effective teaching and learning, regardless of the delivery system. Even more importantly, however, it redirects the emphasis away from contact hours and toward quality learning outcomes in line with real-world professional expectations. Consequently, this new model furnishes our students with a learning experience that is far more coherent and predictable. Similarly, the new curriculum articulates and embeds career-relevant skills that will make our graduates more attractive to prospective employers.

The eight-week, three-term course format is a bonus as well, given that part-time adult students may now complete a UMUC degree within roughly the same time frame as any traditional full-time undergraduate—a critical success factor for busy working professionals. In fact, before introducing the new format, the undergraduate faculty conducted eight-week course-demonstration projects, which yielded very positive results. Not only did retention and course-completion rates increase, but student achievement was commensurate with the longer semester format.

UMUC is also better prepared to incorporate the ideal learning environments and next-generation learning technologies our students need to become competent and creative twenty-first-century knowledge leaders—individuals capable of engaging in collaborative and authentic knowledge exchange across cultures and disciplines while working and learning effectively in virtual teams and communities of practice.

Taking the Next Step

As is the case with higher education in general today, UMUC cannot simply rest on its laurels, but must instead remain at the forefront of teaching and learning strategies and technologies that benefit its students by facilitating ever-better learning outcomes. Therefore, with the new outcomes-based curriculum now in place, the undergraduate division is moving on to its next project.

Given that most adults return to college after being out of school for extended periods of time, their academic skills are sometimes rusty and their knowledge deficits, significant—both of which can be especially problematic in the online environment. In looking for ways to boost student success early on, UMUC's undergraduate faculty members have identified and tracked a series of "gateway" courses that serve as foundational building blocks for successful program completion and that represent 21 percent of online undergraduate enrollments in our stateside division.

Gateways include general introduction courses in accounting, business management, criminal justice, student-success strategies, history, sociology,

Spanish, and introductory writing, along with such STEM introductory cours-es as biology, information systems, economics, computing, natural sciences, math, psychology, and statistics.

Thus, by redesigning the learning environment to improve online achieve-ment in these courses, we can give our students a better chance to realize their academic goals. Carnegie Mellon's Open Learning Initiative (OLI) offers one exceptionally promising approach, based on the principles of adaptive learning. Generally, adaptive learning relies on "intelligent" technologies that recognize and respond to individual learning differences as and when they occur, there-by facilitating personalized instructional adaptations that have been shown to enhance learner outcomes.

Although American higher education has largely ignored existing research around *how* students learn best, OLI has incorporated these findings to de-velop e-courseware that is now being effectively implemented by colleges and universities across the country. Moreover, to ensure consistent results among all of its course materials, Carnegie Mellon has established a highly respected development team of learning scientists and software engineers, who work in consonance with faculty content and human-computer-interaction experts.

Using a variety of such innovative strategies as supported practice and targeted feedback, the OLI model fosters a far more interactive, flexible, and responsive e-learning environment. With that in mind, it establishes powerful feedback loops for continuous evaluation and improvement, which generate real-time data for mediating course design and instructional activities, ongo-ing student performance, and the science of learning. Faculty members then have the information they need to quickly measure a student's progress with an eye toward modifying or supplementing instruction as needed. Students are also able to consistently track their own performance and improve upon it as needed.

UMUC has already piloted an OLI statistics course, with excellent results. After administering a common final exam, we found that students who took this course actually achieved better outcomes in the same amount of time than those enrolled in the university's standard online statistics classes. In 2011, we received a Carnegie Corporation grant to partner with OLI, an effort that will not only build upon the current adult- and distance-learning research literature, but will contribute new knowledge as well.

Under this grant, UMUC and Prince George's Community College will work collaboratively with OLI to evaluate outcomes in three of its existing on-line courses—Introduction to Computer-Based Systems, Introduction to Biology and Lab, and Introductory Business Statistics—all of which are being adapted to meet the needs of each institution's adult-student population. In measuring results, we will compare learning outcomes between students enrolled in OLI courses and those enrolled in standard versions of the same course. Based on evidence we have already collected from UMUC's initial pilot, we expect that the OLI students will exhibit higher rates of performance and satisfaction, as well as greater knowledge retention.

Conclusion

As adults continue going back to college at record rates, it is safe to say that technology-enhanced learning and adult-focused education are not just passing fancies, but rather permanent—albeit rapidly evolving—dimensions of today's higher education landscape. Therefore, it is incumbent upon trailblazing universities such as UMUC to continue developing the appropriate metrics and collecting the necessary data to measure the impact of innovative strategies and technologies on its students, its faculties, and its institutions. By doing so, we can create a far more inclusive and empowering knowledge ecology in which information, ideas, and inspiration flourish and cross-pollinate, thereby ensuring even greater success for the students we serve.

Notes

1. C. Zhu, M. Valcke, and T. Schellens, "Collaborative Learning in a Social Constructivist E-Learning Environment: A Cross-Cultural Study" (proceedings of the 13th Annual Conference of the European Learning Style Information Network, Gent, Belgium, June 23–25, 2008): 617–30.
2. Peter D. Hart Research Associates, Inc., *How Should Colleges Assess and Improve Student Learning? Employers' Views on the Accountability Challenge* (survey of employers conducted on behalf of AACU, January 9, 2008), http://www.aacu.org/leap/documents/2008_Business_Leader_Poll.pdf.
3. Stephen Covey, *Seven Habits of Highly Effective People* (New York: Free Press, 2004).
4. Arthur Chickering, "Applying the Seven Principles of Good Practice for Undergraduate Education," in *New Directions for Teaching and Learning*, ed. Zelda Gamson (New York: Jossey-Bass, 1991).

Susan Aldridge *is Special Advisor to the University of Maryland University College, having served as the institution's President from 2006 to 2012. Dedicated to working professionals, UMUC offers face-to-face instruction and distance education in 28 countries at over 170 locations. Aldridge is a national and international speaker, writer, and expert on adult education. She serves on national education boards relative to adult, military, and distance education.*

14

University of the People

Shai Reshef

Introduction

Let us think of education as the means of developing our greatest abilities, because in each of us there is a private hope and dream which, fulfilled, can be translated into a benefit for everyone.

— John F. Kennedy

Millions of people around the world lack access to higher education either because it is too expensive or because cultural and geographical barriers prevent them from pursuing their educational goals. The University of the People, abbreviated as UoPeople, believes that education is a fundamental human right and that higher education should be universally available to qualified students, regardless of their personal or financial circumstances. This pioneering institution is the first nonprofit, tuition-free (although not entirely no-fee) online university. Since UoPeople's first semester began in September 2009, its programs have been available to students around the world.

The following are the three main points to understand about UoPeople:

- It was created to assist individuals who seek higher education, but currently are unable to attain it due to financial, geographic, or societal restraints.

- It is based in the belief that higher education is an essential catalyst for generating economic development and, just as important, for creating a more peaceful world through access to individual thought and heightened exposure to diversity.

- It seeks to serve as a model for universities and governments to encourage an industry-wide, global drop in education prices as it models the delivery of higher education at significantly less expense with its creative infrastructure. At its core, this innovative university hopes to create positive change in worldwide higher education through its disruptive effect.

Rationale for the Approach Taken by University of the People

Bringing together students from all walks of life, across cultures and nationalities—that is the ultimate learning experience.

—Shai Reshef, UoPeople founder and president

The need for education in general, and tertiary education specifically, is a growing global concern, especially for countries in the developing world where the education index is very low. (The education index is one component of the United Nations' annual Human Development Index and is measured by combining literacy rates with the gross enrollment ratio for primary, secondary, and tertiary participation.) Africa—most notably, perhaps—has a long history of low participation rates in postsecondary education. In Sub-Saharan Africa, despite rapid growth in tertiary education, recent estimates are that only 6 percent of eligible students have access to higher education.[1]

Socioeconomic conditions lead to significant inequality in access to higher education in both developed and developing countries. In regions that have been devastated by natural disasters, political conflicts, or social upheaval, colleges and universities are often severely affected, leaving few or no options for students who want to further their education. Haiti provides a striking example: the 2010 earthquake that ravaged that country destroyed twenty-eight of the thirty-two major universities in Port-au-Prince and the surrounding area, and the other four were severely damaged.[2]

The primary reason that millions of people are unable to attain higher education is that most people on the globe today can't afford the cost of going to college. This is an issue even in wealthy countries: in the United States, the cost of higher education has been steadily on the rise over the last three decades—growing four times faster than the rate of inflation—causing many students to find that a college degree is simply out of reach.[3]

In addition to the expense, in many regions of the world there simply aren't enough colleges to accommodate the number of students who would want to attend. Neither the private sector nor governments have the resources to build enough bricks-and-mortar colleges or universities to accommodate the need. Potential students may desire to study—and may even have the financial resources to attend a college or university—but there simply aren't enough institutions available to admit them.

Cultural factors can also limit access to higher education for some students. Even in the United States and other developed countries, family background, personal circumstances, or socioeconomic status lead to wide disparities in access to postsecondary education. In some cultures, women may be excluded from going on to college. In many areas of the world, notably Sub-Saharan Africa and the southern and western regions of Asia, even if women have access to higher education, they enroll at far lower rates than men.[4] Geography can also be a factor, especially for students who don't live close enough to a college or university to attend: Students whose families rely on them for financial or other kinds of support may be unable to relocate. Such students face limited possibilities for their future if their educational aspirations remain unfulfilled.

The main goal of UoPeople is to enable individuals to obtain a tuition-free higher education from wherever they are in the world, with the hope that these students will reap both personal and economic rewards. Evidence shows that obtaining an education is not only a path to employment, but can positively impact individual health, lifetime income, and other quality-of-life measures. In addition, access to higher education can produce many positive ripple effects for communities where college graduates work and live, such as improved economic stability and social awareness, as well as reduced crime rates. Education is linked to having a more informed and engaged citizenry and aids in the lowering of child mortality rates and in the promotion of child health.[5]

The Creation and Vision of UoPeople

> However futuristic it may seem, what we're living through is an echo of the university's earliest history. Universitas doesn't mean campus, or class, or a particular body of knowledge; it means the guild, the group of people united in scholarship.
>
> —Anya Kamanetz, author of DIY U

Similar to most online educational programs, UoPeople uses the power of networked technology to substitute for a traditional on-campus experience. And, just as other online education programs do, UoPeople combines technology with relevant pedagogical e-learning methods to bring college-level coursework to students around the world. UoPeople has developed its own information architecture for business processes, data management, and academics in order to reduce the cost of delivering its educational program to substantially less than that of a conventional education. The institution's business model is designed to keep operating expenses at a minimum while ensuring that the systems are scalable and sustainable as the university's student population grows.

The university relies on peer-to-peer learning using open source technology, open educational resources (OER) materials, and volunteers. By leveraging access to the Internet with the availability of free materials online—including resources from MIT and many other institutions under the Creative Commons license—UoPeople can provide quality postsecondary education for a fraction of the price of a similar program at a traditional institution. Thus, it is able to promote its mission of democratizing higher education and its vision that universal access to education promotes world peace and global economic development.

UoPeople's mission and vision are guided by the university's four core values:

- **Opportunity**—the belief that affordable education is a basic human right for all suitable applicants;
- **Community**—the creation of a diverse group of students and faculty from around the world engaged in a common learning enterprise;
- **Integrity**—an emphasis on personal and institutional professionalism, with the expectation that all participants are honest, responsible, and maintain a seriousness of purpose; and
- **Quality**—an academic program that is rigorous, suited to the challenges of today, and assessed on an ongoing basis.

The Academic Model Used by UoPeople

UoPeople is a bold venture designed to break the barriers to knowledge preventing many people from enjoying the benefits of the modern world. UoPeople is likely to create a new world of knowledge transactions.

—Dr. Y. S. Rajan, member, UoPeople Advisory Committee

The entire academic program of UoPeople is comprised of online courses. Students at UoPeople reside in nations all over the world. Students seeking admission to UoPeople are required to have a high school diploma and a sufficient command of English language skills. Each accepted applicant is required to take (and successfully pass) two orientation classes, Skills for Online Learning and English Composition 1, to ensure that they are prepared to complete their course of study. Courses are held within a virtual classroom. Each course is nine weeks long, with each weekly class component beginning on Thursday and ending on the following Wednesday. Courses are conducted in English only and each course section has an enrollment of up to about twenty students. Library services are available to students and faculty through the UoPeople Library and Resource Center, which offers access to the university's collection of electronic databases, resources, and online assistance from a staff of librarians.

A few key characteristics of the UoPeople educational experience distinguish UoPeople from other online higher educational programs.

First, the courses offered by UoPeople rely solely on text-based materials. Offering only text-based course materials and assignments may seem antiquated in an era when audio and video are routinely used to augment online learning, but UoPeople has deliberately chosen a "lower tech" and simplified approach. Opportunity and community are two of the university's founding principles, and UoPeople wants to be sure that all its students, wherever they are in the world and no matter what kind of computer technology or connectivity they have, will be able to access the materials required for their classes. This is especially important for students in developing countries, where the only access they may have to the online world may be from an Internet café or via a slow connection.

Second, each course is managed and conducted asynchronously, i.e., a student accomplishes his or her work for that particular course at any time and place during the week that is most convenient for that particular student. This arrangement provides students the flexibility to use the materials when and where they are able to within the framework of each week's class.

A third distinctive component of the UoPeople program is that the university (as of 2011) offers coursework in two fields: computer science and business administration. The founder of the university decided to focus on these two fields—at least initially—because computer science and business administration are relevant worldwide and because these fields directly lead to employment opportunities. The underlying principles in each of these fields can be applied in practical ways globally.

For typical UoPeople students, the classroom experience might follow a scenario such as this: Once they have successfully registered, students are given access credentials for their particular course, its virtual classroom, and the course materials. When students enter their virtual classroom, they will encounter students from a variety of other countries, exposing them to an array of diversity they may not have encountered before and assisting in creating cultural awareness and understanding. In addition to their peers, students will find lecture notes, weekly reading and homework assignments, and discussion questions. A critical part of the peer-to-peer learning model, the discussion questions are central to the academic work of each class. Each student reads the assignment and discussion question and downloads the materials for that week's class. Students read their assignments and assimilate the course material, then begin engaging in a dialogue about that week's assigned discussion question. As students from around the world contribute to this discussion, they bring their own perspectives—cultural or personal—as well as their own ideas about the reading assignment. Their ideas may be enlarged upon or even challenged as the conversation proceeds during the week.

Because this course structure is designed to encourage a peer-to-peer learning process, the role of the instructor is different from what it would be in a traditional classroom setting. Instead of serving as the all-knowing source of information for the students, the role of the faculty member at UoPeople is to monitor the class dialogue, answer any questions students have along the way, "coach" students through the course, and encourage their engagement with the material and assignments. As students gain familiarity with the process and with the materials, they tend to coalesce as a group, and the discourse then builds and develops naturally. At the end of each week, students take a quiz to demonstrate that they have successfully mastered the information covered in the week's assignment. When the ten-week period concludes, students take an examination to demonstrate that they understand all content of that particular course. At the end of the course, they receive a grade and are allowed to advance to the next course in their program.

The Financial Model Used by UoPeople

I am able now to do the studies I have always wished for and also cater to my family's needs. UoPeople stands out as far superior at a fraction of the cost.

—Alexander M., a UoPeople student from Papua, New Guinea

Although the university is tuition-free, there are modest fees including a one-time processing fee for an application. Starting in 2012, processing fees for examinations will also be implemented. These fees are necessary for the nonprofit UoPeople to remain sustainable and provide its education. The application fee is based on a sliding scale of $10 to $50, depending on the applicant's place of residence (students from countries with lower-income economies are charged less than students from more affluent places). For example, the application processing fee for a student in Afghanistan is $10, whereas the application processing fee for a student in the United Kingdom is $50. The examination processing fee will be based on the same sliding scale determined by the student's place of residence and set at $10 to $100. Based on these processing fee charges, a student's direct expenses to complete a full BS program at UoPeople would cost anywhere from less than $400 to less than $4,000. With these processing fees, UoPeople's financial model predicts that it will be sustainable at 10,000 to 15,000 students.

An Effective Model: Evidence and Aspirations

It's amazing that everything is available just on my fingertips: classmates from all over the world, qualified instructors, free textbooks, online library, technical support, student services, and a discussion forum. It's awesome.

—Marice S., a UoPeople student from Indonesia

In its second year (as of November 2011), the University of the People is still very much a developing institution. And although it is young, the administration, staff, and faculty of the university know that their efforts will significantly improve the employment prospects and socioeconomic status of their students and graduates. Ultimately, strengthening students' job prospects and economic status through education will benefit their families and communities as well. Business administration and computer science students will gain skills that can readily contribute to the economic development of their countries. UoPeople students also benefit from the diversity of the student body as new associations and global friendships flourish in virtual classrooms. Sharing space together in a virtual classroom and partaking in the diversity of ideas and opinions helps to heighten students' awareness of other cultures and can offer a very enriching learning opportunity. Outside the virtual classroom, fellow students might have considered themselves enemies, but with the affiliation and possible affinity of the online experience, students may come to understand that the "enemy" or the "other" is really not all that different from themselves. By encouraging diversity, the UoPeople model promotes peace, tolerance, and understanding among the peoples of the world.

The faculty members of UoPeople, most of whom serve the university as volunteers, come from all over the world, including top-flight academic institutions in North America (e.g., Yale, New York University, Columbia, Emory, Hofstra, and Rutgers), as well as from relatively newer institutions located elsewhere around the globe and online universities. These volunteer faculty members may be active or retired professors, master's-level students, or working professionals from the fields of business or computer science. UoPeople pays those academic volunteers who serve as instructors a modest honorarium in order to ensure commitment. It also relies on a small cadre of paid staff to supplement the academic volunteers and to keep programs running smoothly and consistently.

UoPeople benefits from its affiliation with the traditional academic community in other ways as well. Since 2009, UoPeople has been a research partner of Yale Law School's Information Society Project, a center devoted to studying the relationship between the Internet and new technologies, especially as it affects law and society. In 2011, New York University announced that it would consider eligible UoPeople students for acceptance to its campus in Abu Dhabi. In another show of support, Hewlett-Packard (HP) invited UoPeople students to become online interns with HP's Catalyst Initiative, a program aimed at supporting projects to improve STEM education (science, technology, engineering, and math).

UoPeople has attracted support from a number of countries and nonprofit agencies, including the United Nations, the World Economic Forum, Ashoka, and the Clinton Global Initiative. It has garnered widespread press coverage from the *New York Times,* CNN, ABC News, *The Guardian,* and as many as one thousand other national and international news outlets. In 2010, *The Huffington Post* named Shai Reshef one of its "Ultimate Game Changers in Education," and in July 2011, the university's innovative model was profiled in *The Chronicle of Higher Education.* Furthermore, UoPeople's model has been presented at many conferences. The university's Facebook page—which, as of November 2011, has a fan base of over half a million Facebook users—promotes its programs and philosophy and encourages its students with inspirational messages about achievement and education.

As of November 2011, UoPeople has accepted over 1,200 students from 121 countries. In a continuing effort to evaluate and assess all aspects of its academic model, the university actively solicits feedback from its students. At the end of each term, students are asked to complete an extensive survey about the quality of the course, materials, instruction, and technology. In a survey conducted in May 2011, 97 percent of students reported that they were satisfied with their studies at the university, and 88 percent said they believed their educational goals would be achieved at UoPeople. But the question that matters most is, "Would you recommend the UoPeople to your peers?" In the May 2011 survey, 95 percent answered that question in the affirmative.

An Example from the Field: The Haiti Project

> *After high school, I could not go to university because it was too expensive. Every day, I would stand in the street talking with my friends about what we would do if we had money. We hoped that 2010 would be better, but then the earthquake destroyed every-thing, houses, businesses and many lives. Since that day, I have been sleeping in the street, under a tent, and nobody cares about my education anymore. University of the People is better than food and a tent. And education is even better than a visa or a green card.*
>
> —Elysee, a UoPeople student from Haiti

UoPeople's groundbreaking work in Haiti following the devastation of the 2010 earthquake—which destroyed twenty-eight out of the country's thirty-two universities—serves as a fitting example of the university's commitment to its mission. In Haiti, UoPeople implemented a dedicated project using technology to help address the country's need for educational services. The project will give 250 Haitian students the opportunity to pursue their education online. As part of the project, UoPeople has formed partnerships with local NGOs to pro-vide hardware and connectivity (including computers, electricity, generators, high-speed Internet access, and security) at student computer centers in vari-ous locations. As of November 2011, over eighty students have been admitted to the university as part of the Haiti Project and have undertaken their course-work in the Port-au-Prince and Mirebalais computer centers. Because many students have been left extremely poor following the earthquake, UoPeople, in conjunction with a local partner at one of the centers, has created a feed-ing program where students study for four hours a day and are provided a free meal. Fund-raising to raise money to support additional students and/or implement additional feeding programs is ongoing. In establishing a local op-tion for students to pursue their education, this initiative also attempts to stem the "brain drain" migration, which has seen some of the brightest and most talented Haitians leave their homeland in search of better educational or oc-cupational opportunities. By making higher education available for the people of Haiti, UoPeople is providing much-needed skills in these communities and encouraging efforts to rebuild areas in this devastated country.

UoPeople's Future Expectations: Challenges and Opportunities

Think what a world we are becoming—a world where money is not required in order for individual and collective intelligence to be expressed and compounded. Removing money from the equation, we will see in a very short time what universal affordable education will achieve in changing, brightening and modifying the world we live in. —Shai Reshef

Although it shows promise as an alternative to the standard higher educational model, and although its first several terms have been successful, UoPeople faces many challenges as it strives to fulfill its mission of bringing quality and affordable education to deserving students.

The clearest challenge UoPeople faces concerns sustainability: to prove that it can in fact break even with 10,000 to 15,000 students as it believes, and then to continue to remain financially viable as it expands further. A distinct second challenge is the scalability of relying on academic volunteers. At present, UoPeople pulls from a pool of over 2,000 volunteers; this is sufficient to meet its November 2011 needs with 1,200 accepted students. At 10,000 or even 100,000 students, this dependence on volunteers may need to be reevaluated. The third challenge for UoPeople is whether it can effectively raise grant money to progress further with its mission of democratizing higher education.

After sustainability, the next major hurdles are simply delivering online education and building up student recruitment. In addition to the basic challenge of delivering online education, there is the matter of reaching students in parts of the world where there is simply a lack of technology infrastructure. UoPeople's offerings do not require audio or video capability, which makes the course materials more accessible to students living in areas without ubiquitous Internet access or broadband network capacity. And, even when sufficient infrastructure exists, not everyone in the world has convenient access to the Internet. UoPeople is addressing this problem by establishing local student-computing centers. As previously mentioned, the university has already launched pilot computing centers in Haiti as part of a dedicated project there, and it has plans for similar centers in other locations, including Bangladesh, the Dominican Republic, Liberia, Palestine, and Zimbabwe—all areas where technology infrastructure is lacking. Regarding student recruitment, UoPeople also will be working with local NGOs to better reach those students who otherwise wouldn't know that a tuition-free option exists for them.

Another challenge for distance learning or online programs is the issue of credentialing and accreditation. While many students study just for knowledge and self-improvement, accreditation is highly important for the future job prospects of graduates. At the present time, UoPeople offers associate's (AS) and bachelor's (BS) degrees in the areas of computer science and business administration, but is careful to inform students that the university is not accredited. The university is working on becoming accredited by the U.S. Department of Education, but the university cannot promise when, or if, its programs will be accredited.

One of the biggest challenges facing online education is establishing the model as equivalent to—possibly even superior to—more traditional forms of education. A 2010 meta-analysis done by the U.S. Department of Education found that students who had all or part of their educational courses delivered online performed better, on average, than those taking the same courses in a physical classroom environment. Other studies support this claim as well. As a result, online education is gaining acceptance, but the continuing challenge, perhaps, is in getting society—educators, students, accrediting bodies, etc.—to understand that online education is not something "less than" a traditional education; nor is it just a low-cost alternative to the "real thing." Rather, the focus should be on the possibilities for new and effective models of teaching and learning, including models of peer-to-peer learning, where students learn collectively and where there is less reliance on the all-knowing teacher imparting a one-way flow of information to the class. These new online delivery formats and more creative and interactive models—where the line is blurred between student and teacher—can have a positive effect on the learning experience.

Replicability by Other Institutions and Programs

Universities need to be designed with both the global and the local sphere in mind, in order to widen participation and dialogue.

—Shai Reshef

Individual parts of the education delivery model employed by UoPeople (i.e., peer-to-peer learning using open educational resources and open source technology) are already being used to varying degrees in multiple settings as part of the ongoing evolution of education. However, UoPeople hopes to scale in such a way as to reach underserved markets in a cost-efficient and effective way and, in so doing, serve as an all-encompassing example for others to follow worldwide. One of UoPeople's main goals is for its model to be used and replicated in other educational settings, such as by NGOs or by governments anywhere in the world that provide higher education. UoPeople is eager to share its model as a way of reaching greater numbers of students who have the desire and motivation to be educated but whose personal, geographical, or financial circumstances make it difficult or impossible for them to do so. By sharing its model, UoPeople's ultimate mission of democratizing higher education access globally will have a better chance of realization.

Conclusion

> *[For] a man who comes from a poor country, UoPeople represents a dream that allows me to reach my goal of completing a bachelor's program. I consider UoPeople my global family in this global world.* —Valery, a UoPeople student from Haiti

The University of the People's mission is the promotion of higher education as a way of promoting peace around the world. In a higher education landscape that's in the midst of change and uncertainty, the University of the People offers great promise for students who have limited access to postsecondary education. UoPeople is demonstrating that quality higher education opportunities can be made available to people all over the world—and at a lower cost—thus helping individuals expand their potential, achieve their dreams, and work toward economic stability for themselves and their community. Furthermore, it provides universities and governments alike a model to look toward, and hopefully adopt, for democratizing access to higher education globally. As Professor Jack Balkin of Yale University, one of UoPeople's advisors, pointedly observes, "Harnessing new technologies to deliver low-cost education to people around the world is a daring venture. It is the kind of experiment that everyone should want to succeed."

Notes

1. UNESCO Institute for Statistics, *Global Education Digest 2010: Comparing Education Statistics Across the World,* Table 8.
2. Interuniversity Institute for Research and Development, *The Challenge for Haitian Higher Education: A Post-Earthquake Assessment of Higher Education Institutions in the Port-Au-Prince Metropolitan Area* (March 2010).
3. The Education Trust, *Priced Out: How the Wrong Financial-Aid Policies Hurt Low-Income Students* (2011).
4. UIS Fact Sheet, *Trends in Tertiary Education: Sub-Saharan Africa* (2010).

5. L. Lochner, "Non-Production Benefits of Education: Crime, Health, and Good Citizenship" (NBER Working Paper No. 16722, issued January 2011).

Shai Reshef *is Founder and President, University of the People (UoPeople)—the world's first tuition-free, nonprofit, online academic institution dedicated to the democratization of higher education. Reshef has 20 years' experience in international education and has been recognized on behalf of UoPeople for opening access to education. He holds an M.A. from University of Michigan.*

15

The Open Learning Initiative: Enacting Instruction Online

Ross Strader and Candace Thille

NEW TECHNOLOGIES ARE OFTEN USED to replicate current systems, without much thought given to how the affordances of the technology can help design a better system. Higher education has been particularly guilty of this lack of imagination. Since the days of "distance education" delivered over closed-circuit television, we have too often sought to use technology simply to replicate the traditional lecture-based classroom model. Technology has brought about significant change in many sectors of our economy, yet the primary delivery system for knowledge in our country has largely remained unchanged.

Why is this? Is it that the traditional lecture-based model works so well that we have no need to look for anything better, and that we are best served by using technology merely to replicate and augment this system that has been in place for hundreds of years? Our process for higher education worked well in the context for which it was constructed—when we could safely assume that we were teaching small classes of students with fairly homogeneous background knowledge, relevant skills, and future goals. However, that context has changed. We now teach vastly larger numbers of students who have a much greater diversity of background knowledge, relevant skills, and future goals.

Technology has clearly provided us with some benefits. Students today do not always have to be physically present in the classroom—instead, we use technology to provide them with "anytime, anywhere" access to video-recorded lectures, electronic textbooks, or audio-based podcasts. We set up online discussion forums so that our students can communicate and collaborate more easily and efficiently. Because of technology, we now have the ability to create elaborate computer simulations of phenomena that are too large or too small to physically observe. However, at the core of all of these uses of technology is still the same underlying model: the primary mode of knowledge transfer is that of a student sitting and listening to an instructor giving a lecture.

Limitations of Traditional Instruction

Problem No. 1: Many Instructors Teach to a Certain Percentile of the Class

As the diversity of the student population increases, instructors are forced to make increasingly tough choices about the level at which their teaching is targeted. Some instructors teach to the top students in the class, and most of the students in the class struggle to keep up. Others strive to ensure that the needs of every student are met, which unfortunately can result in an uninspiring, even tiresome experience for many of the students in the class. Others seek to hit a middle ground, which can result in both of these problems—half the class is lost and half the class is bored.

Problem No. 2: Students Frequently Do Not Receive Immediate Feedback Crucial to the Learning Process

In order to learn the material, most students listen to instruction in the classroom and read textbooks. To demonstrate their level of competence, they turn in homework and take quizzes. By the time they receive feedback on their work, the chance to correct any misunderstandings or reinforce correct responses has often passed. The main reason that human tutors can be so effective in working with students is that they are able to provide immediate, targeted feedback at the right points in the learning process.[1]

Problem No. 3: In All but the Smallest Classes, the Student's Knowledge State Is a Black Box to the Instructor

Instructors might have brief glimpses into this black box through homework and quizzes, but again, this information typically arrives too late to be of use while the instruction is being given—the point at which it would be most valuable. Depending on the instructor's ability to interpret students' facial expressions, he or she may have little or no understanding of how well students are grasping the concepts being presented. In large lecture halls, the instructor is deprived of the benefit of even this level of feedback beyond the first few rows.

Problem No. 4: Degrees Favor Time Spent in a Classroom over Demonstration of Competency

Students come to our colleges and universities with a wide range of backgrounds and abilities. Yet we force them into a one-size-fits-all four-year plan toward a degree, with very little flexibility. In addition, degrees do not so much certify that the student has mastered a given set of competencies and is now proficient in a particular field as they certify that he or she was in the right place at the right time for four years running.

Problem No. 5: There Is Great Inefficiency in Creating Instruction within Higher Education

By and large, instructors create their own course materials for their own lectures. Knowledge gained by an experienced instructor about how best to teach the material is typically lost when that instructor retires or moves on and a new instructor begins the cycle again. This model is not as problematic in specialized graduate courses where faculty can bring their expertise on a given topic to bear in a way that few others could. However, it is terribly wasteful in large undergraduate courses, where there are thousands of instructors across the country—all developing what are essentially the same materials year after year.

Unfortunately, most of these limitations persist even with the use of new technologies. The Open Learning Initiative (OLI) was created in 2002 with a grant from the William and Flora Hewlett Foundation to address these challenges: Rather than simply moving artifacts of the traditional classroom-based model to the web, how can we use technology to enact instruction in this new online environment, and what benefits can we derive from this new use of technology?

The OLI Approach

To answer these questions, OLI put together a team of content experts, learning scientists, human-computer interaction experts, and software engineers. We started with one of the most widely used undergraduate courses: Introductory Statistics. We took advantage of work that had been done in the field to identify a common set of learning outcomes that students should be able to achieve after taking the course. We set out to create an online course environment that would bring to bear not only the affordances of the new technologies, but also everything that the state of the science had to tell us about human learning.

The collaboration among this diverse group of experts led us to a method of instruction that is repeated throughout an OLI course for each concept. Instruction on every concept starts with one or more student-centered, observable learning objectives. We then present expository content in the form of text, images, simulations, short (3–5 minutes) videos, and worked examples where appropriate (Figure 1).

Interspersed with the exposition are interactive tasks that support students to engage in authentic practice with the concepts and skills they are learning. The tasks are presented in a supported environment with hints available to the students if they are struggling. They receive feedback that reinforces correct responses and targets common student misconceptions (Figure 2).

Finally, we offer students a chance to do a quick self-assessment and reflect on what they have learned, so that they can decide whether they should move on or whether they need additional practice (Figure 3).

A key attribute of the OLI environment is that while students are working through the course, we are collecting analytics data and using those data to drive multiple feedback loops (Figure 4):

- Feedback to students: We provide the student with timely and targeted support throughout the learning process. This support is in the form of corrections, suggestions, and cues that are tailored to the individual's current performance and that encourage revision and refinement.

- Feedback to instructors: The richness of the data we are collecting about student use and learning provides an unprecedented opportunity to give instructors a clear picture of the student's current knowledge state. As a result, instructors are able to spend less classroom time lecturing and more time interacting with students in ways that take advantage of the instructor's unique expertise and interests targeted to student needs.

- Feedback to course designers: Analysis of these interaction-level data allows us to observe how students are using the material in the course and assess the impact of their use patterns on learning outcomes. We are then able to take advantage of that analysis to iteratively refine and improve the course for the next group of students.

- Feedback to learning science researchers: Finally, there is a feedback loop for learning science researchers who use information gathered by the OLI environment to create and refine theories of human learning. In addition to building on what we know about learning, our courses serve as a platform in which new knowledge about human learning can be developed.

Figure 1. **Learning Objective, Expository Content (Engineering Statics)**

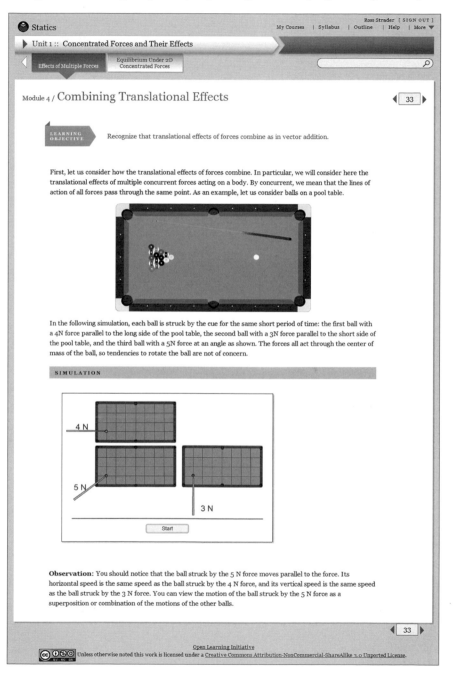

Observation: You should notice that the ball struck by the 5 N force moves parallel to the force. Its horizontal speed is the same speed as the ball struck by the 4 N force, and its vertical speed is the same speed as the ball struck by the 3 N force. You can view the motion of the ball struck by the 5 N force as a superposition or combination of the motions of the other balls.

Figure 2. **"Learn by Doing" Activity with Hints and Targeted Feedback (Introductory Psychology)**

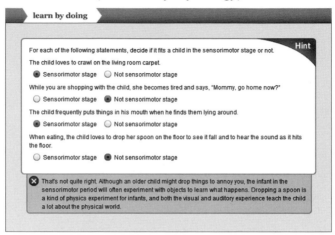

Figure 3. **"Did I Get This?" Activity That Allows Students to Self-Assess Before Moving On (Introductory Psychology)**

Figure 4. **OLI Feedback Loops**

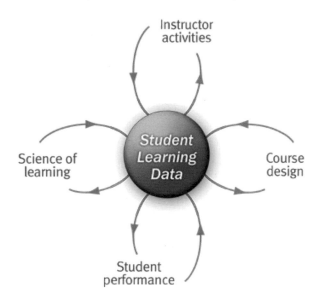

Effectiveness

To evaluate the effectiveness of the OLI approach, evaluators inside and external to the OLI project have conducted studies comparing students using OLI in hybrid mode (instructor-led class using OLI) to students in a traditional classroom environment. In an accelerated learning study using the OLI statistics course, students learned a full semester's worth of material in half the time and performed as well as or better than students learning from traditional instruction over a full semester. Furthermore, there was no significant difference in information retention between OLI students and traditional students in tests given more than a semester later.[2]

Similar results were achieved in a community-college accelerated learning study with a different course (OLI Logic & Proofs). Students in the OLI course learned 33 percent more material than students in traditional instruction and performed at higher levels on shared material.[3] In a study conducted on the OLI chemistry course at Carnegie Mellon University, the number of student interactions with the virtual lab was shown to outweigh all other factors—including gender and SAT score—as the predictor of positive learning outcomes.[4]

How the OLI Approach Can Address the Limitations of Traditional Instruction

Problem No. 1: Many Instructors Teach to a Certain Percentile of the Class

One of the advantages of online education is that students are able to move through the material at their own pace. Technology also makes it easy to provide multiple levels of instruction and many pathways through the same material. Students who come into the course with background knowledge or who are quick learners are able to achieve a given learning objective and move on. Students who need more time with the material are able to work through it at a slower pace and are able to access additional content—alternate explanations, more worked examples, and more practice activities. Depending on his background, a given student may move quickly through one part of the course but need to spend more time in another part.

Since we maintain a model of the student's knowledge state behind the scenes—a model driven by the student's work in the course—one can imagine that we could deliver course content in a completely adaptive manner. We could keep giving the student more instruction on a concept until she has achieved the learning objective, and then allow her to move on to the next topic. However, we feel that to do so would actually be a disservice to the student, as we would not be helping her to develop the metacognitive skills necessary for guiding her own learning. Thus, one of our goals at OLI is for students to become able to assess for themselves when they need more practice and when they are ready to move on—in essence, we would like them not only to learn statistics, or biology, or psychology, but also to *learn how to become better learners.*

Problem No. 2: Students Frequently Do Not Receive Immediate Feedback Crucial to the Learning Process

One of our goals in creating an OLI course is that the interactions the student has with the course should, to the extent possible, model the types of interactions that student would have with a human tutor helping him work through the material. Rather than presenting the student with a large amount of content to listen to or read through as he would with a traditional lecture or textbook, we introduce him to a concept with a limited amount of expository content. We then let him move immediately into activities where he is working with the concept.

In these "Learn by Doing" activities, the student is not expected to have mastered the material—indeed, we expect her to make mistakes. During the authoring process, we work to capture the common mistakes that students make when learning a given concept. This can be done through conversations with faculty who have extensive experience teaching the course, or by analyzing artifacts of student work, e.g., homework and quizzes. We then write feedback targeted toward those common student mistakes. When a student chooses an incorrect answer, the feedback explains why the answer is incorrect and corrects that misconception—just as a human tutor would if he were helping the student work through the material. When done correctly, this can be very powerful. One student who received such feedback while working through an OLI course was overheard to say, "How did the computer know what I was thinking?" The experience that student had is what we strive for when authoring feedback.

Problem No. 3: In All but the Smallest Classes, the Student's Knowledge State Is a Black Box to the Instructor

We use the model of the student's knowledge state that we maintain behind the scenes to drive a dashboard-style display for the instructor.[5] This display gives a high-level overview of how students in a class are performing on the learning objectives for each module in the course (Figure 5). This gives instructors using OLI a rich view into what has always been a black box. Before going into class, instructors can see quickly the concepts students are grasping and the concepts with which they are struggling. This enables instructors to spend their time with students in a way that better utilizes their expertise. Instead of spending valuable class time going over concepts that students were able to learn outside of class, they can address problems students are having. They can also focus on richer aspects of the material that they might not have had time to cover in a traditional instruction model.

Problem No. 4: Degrees Favor Time Spent in a Classroom over Demonstration of Competency

A trend with online education in general—not just OLI—is a focus on demonstration of competency as opposed to the more traditional "seat time" measure. In OLI, learning objectives are at the core of everything we do. They are the focus of the instruction that is presented and are what students are asked to evaluate themselves against when measuring their learning. These objectives are the primary way in which information about students' knowledge states is presented to instructors. They are the driving force in our

Figure 5. **Instructor Dashboard for Module 1 of the OLI Statistics Course**

Module 1

Examining Distributions ▷

ESTIMATED LEARNING LEVEL Learning Objectives

Summarize and describe the distribution of a categorical variable in context.
[» Show Details...]

Generate and interpret several different graphical displays of the distribution of a quantitative variable (histogram, stemplot, boxplot).
[» Show Details...]

Summarize and describe the distribution of a quantitative variable in context: a) describe the overall pattern, b) describe striking deviations from the pattern.
[» Show Details...]

Relate measures of center and spread to the shape of the distribution, and choose the appropriate measures in different contexts.
[» Hide Details...]

Estimated Learning by Student ⓘ

50 students
1 dot <= 2 students

Class Accuracy by Sub-Objective ⓘ

	% correct
Predicting...	38
Mean vs median	38
Compute median	37
Identify outlier	27
Select appropriate...	27

0   % correct   100

Compare and contrast distributions (of quantitative data) from two or more groups, and produce a brief summary, interpreting your findings in context.
[» Show Details...]

Apply the standard deviation rule to the special case of distributions having the "normal" shape.
[» Show Details...]

course-development teams as new content is authored. While OLI is not a credit-awarding entity, we strive to create the most efficient process for our students in much the same way that Western Governors University does. Students who have had previous exposure to the material or who are able to learn it quickly can demonstrate competency and move on. Students who need to spend more time on a concept are afforded that option. Our goal is not for every student to complete every activity in an OLI course. Rather, our goal is for students to work enough with a given concept that they achieve that learning objective and then move on.

Problem No. 5: There Is Great Inefficiency in Creating Instruction within Higher Education

Technology can help us solve this problem and maximize productivity by enabling us to create courses that meet the needs of students and faculty across many institutions. This will allow us to eliminate the current redundancy in creating instruction that is rampant across higher education. For example, introductory statistics courses are taught at almost every community college and university across the country. Hundreds of instructors each year spend time creating instruction similar to that created last year at other institutions and that will be re-created next year at still other institutions. Instead of spending resources on thousands of separate introductory statistics courses, we think it makes more sense to bring content experts from a wide range of colleges and universities together to create a small number of statistics courses that will meet the needs of students at all of those colleges and universities.

Challenges

Moving to new outcomes in higher education is not without its challenges. The main challenge we find is that when we combine the affordances of technology with what we know about human learning, the opportunity we have for changing the way we approach instruction is significant enough that it necessitates a fundamental shift for both students and instructors. For students, the focus on learning objectives rather than on simply completing a certain amount of assigned work makes them more responsible for their own learning. They are not always comfortable with this new competency-based model. While there is much to be gained in helping students improve their metacognitive skills and become better learners, this represents a fundamental shift for them, and they need support in making the change. The key to this change is the underlying contract that we have with the student; we will help them to avoid wasting time by enabling them to maximize their productivity in achieving their goals.

For instructors, the challenge is in moving away from the historical activity-based model ("students who do more, learn more"). The new model is one in which the amount of work students must do depends on their diverse backgrounds and skill sets, with each student doing as little or as much as necessary to achieve the learning objectives. Instructors are accustomed to using participation as a proxy for learning. Technology enables us to move beyond that system and actually measure and report learning. However, it is sometimes difficult for many instructors to fully embrace this new approach, as it represents a dramatic change in the way they teach. We have found that instructor training and participation in communities of use are very helpful to instructors in making this shift.

Another challenge we face with instructors is the "expert blind spot" problem, wherein expertise in a subject area may make educators blind to the learning processes and instructional needs of novice students. The educators themselves often are entirely unaware of having such a blind spot.[6] Even when provided with evidence that a given set of instruction and activities on a concept does result in achievement of the learning objective, instructors will sometimes be reluctant to use the material because it is not explained in the same way that they would explain it. This problem is also rooted in the existing structure of higher education, where instructors develop the material for their courses more or less on their own. Our challenge is to help them to understand that OLI really focuses on what students do outside of class, and that we can give instructors better information to help them design their in-class instruction.

Conclusion

At OLI, we believe that technology can be harnessed to make significant improvements in higher education in terms of cost, productivity, and learning, and we believe that we are on the right path toward making that change happen. In 1991, Herb Simon, a Nobel laureate from Carnegie Mellon University, said that, "Improvement in post-secondary education will require converting teaching from a 'solo sport' to a community-based research activity." Information and communication technologies can now be used to provide meaningful, actionable feedback to students, instructors, instructional designers, and learning scientists. This information is not available in the traditional "teaching as a solo sport" model. To date, these technologies have not been widely used for such purposes. Once they are, the long-hoped-for transformational impact of technology on education becomes a reality.

Notes

1. B. Bloom, "The 2 Sigma Problem: The Search for Methods of Group Instruction as Effective as One-to-One Tutoring," *Educational Researcher* 13, no. 6 (1984): 4–16.
2. M. Lovett, O. Meyer, and C. Thille, "The Open Learning Initiative: Measuring the Effectiveness of the OLI Statistics Course in Accelerating Student Learning," *Journal of Interactive Media in Education* (2008), retrieved from http://jime.open.ac.uk/2008/14/.
3. C. D. Schunn and M. Patchan, *An Evaluation of Accelerated Learning in the CMU Open Learning Initiative Course Logic & Proofs* (technical report by Learning Research and Development Center, University of Pittsburgh, Pittsburgh, PA, 2009).

4. K. Evans, D. Yaron, and G. Leinhardt, "Learning Stoichiometry: A Comparison of Text and Multimedia Formats," *Chemistry Education Research and Practice* 9 (2008): 208–18.
5. M. Lovett, J. Rinderle, J. Brooks, C. Thille, and R. Strader, "Creating a Learning Dashboard for Instructors in OLI" (unpublished).
6. M. J. Nathan and A. Petrosino, "Expert Blind Spot among Preservice Teachers," *American Educational Research Journal* 40, no. 4 (2003): 905–28.

Ross Strader *is Associate Director of the Open Learning Initiative (OLI) at Carnegie Mellon University. His work focuses on the intersection of technology and the learning sciences, looking at ways to bring learning research to bear on technology-based, student-centered learning environments. Strader has won the Carnegie Mellon Graduate Student Teaching Award and received Carnegie Mellon's Andy Award for Innovation.*
Candace Thille *is the Founding Director of Carnegie Mellon OLI and co-director of OLnet. She serves as a redesign scholar for NCAT; as a Fellow of ISDDE; on the Executive Advisory board for HP Catalyst; as co-author of the National Education Technology Plan; and on the PCAST working group to improve STEM education.*

16

The Postmodality Era: How "Online Learning" Is Becoming "Learning"

Thomas B. Cavanagh

Introduction

ACCORDING TO THE National Center for Education Statistics, between 2000 and 2008, the percentage of undergraduate students taking at least one online class grew from 8 to 20 percent.[1] The Sloan Consortium states that approximately 5.6 million students enrolled in at least one online course during fall 2009, and nearly thirty percent of all higher education students now take at least one course online.[2] Clearly, the percentage of students taking one or more courses online is trending upwards, reflecting an increased reliance on the flexibility they afford.

Juxtapose these online learning growth trends with the following statistics: of the 17.6 million undergraduates currently enrolled in American higher education, only 15 percent attend four-year institutions *and* live on campus. Thirty-seven percent are enrolled part time and 32 percent work full time. Only 36 percent of students who are enrolled in four-year institutions actually graduate in four years.[3]

What these statistics indicate is a blurring boundary between the traditional and nontraditional. Even classically traditional students at classically traditional institutions, such as Jennifer, increasingly require nontraditional flexibility to meet their educational goals. Online learning has become the catalyst for this change and it is forever altering the landscape of higher education. Classifying a student as "main campus" or "extended campus" or "distance" becomes meaningless in an environment where students take whatever courses they need in whatever location or modality best suits their requirements at the time. These students are unconcerned with categorical labels—they are concerned with getting the courses they need in the formats that fit their lifestyles, whether they are a working adult or an undergraduate who travels frequently as part of the volleyball team. The Sloan Foundation has dubbed this concept "localness," meaning that student access to education is always local to them, even if they do so through online learning. Students may take courses at an institution's main campus, regional or extended campus, completely online, or in a blended format. Institutions can support "localness" by constructing programs that are flexible and that deliver courses in multiple modalities.

> Most traditional, non-profit institutions with large commuter, non-residential and part-time student populations are well-known and trusted within their localities. When online learning burst into the academic consciousness in the mid-90s there was a rush by many of these institutions to downplay their locality, and to emphasize their role in meeting the needs of all kinds of geography-independent and global student populations. However, many of these same institutions eventually came to realize that many of their local and in some cases *even their residential student populations were as interested in enrolling in online learning courses as were students living afar*. The institutions are known in their local regions; that's not the issue. What is not always known is that they are offering a "quality" online or blended product.[4] [emphasis added]

Some research indicates that even in end-of-course evaluations, students do not consider modality an important factor in their course-taking experiences. According to Dziuban and Moskal,[5] "When students respond to the end-of-course evaluation instruments for online, blended, and face-to-face courses . . . they do not differentiate the instructional idiosyncrasies found in the three modalities."[6] Students are able to translate specific end-of-course evaluation questions to apply to any of the three modalities without any problem. The modality is not a factor. Further, the same study indicates that course mode is not an effective predictor of success or withdrawal within a course. "Historically, students who have done well in courses do well in any mode; a course is a course."[7] To these students, *a course is a course*; modality makes no difference.

The postmodality blurring of boundaries between traditional and nontraditional is being hastened by the intersecting dynamics of these student preferences for flexibility and convenience with the desire for efficiency by system and state policy leaders. The University System of Maryland now requires undergraduates to complete twelve credits in alternative-learning modes, which include online learning. Texas has proposed a similar rule with a 10 percent threshold. The Minnesota State Colleges and Universities system is advocating that 25 percent of all student credits be earned online by 2015.[8] When top-down systemic mandates such as these align with the bottom-up preferences of students to have maximum flexibility in their course-selection practices, a powerful force for change across all of higher education is created. Online learning has catalyzed these forces into a movement that university administrators and faculty members are trying to address in a variety of ways, depending upon the institutional mission and available resources. This chapter will highlight several examples, from several different types of schools.

University of Central Florida

If there is a "ground zero" for this postmodality phenomenon, it may be the University of Central Florida in Orlando. When UCF began its online learning enterprise in the mid-1990s, it quickly discovered that 75 percent of online students were already on campus or lived nearby. That gave rise to the university's blended learning initiative, which mixes both face-to-face and online elements. UCF has grown rapidly, with enrollment expanding from 21,000 in 1991 to 58,600 in fall 2011, and it now ranks as the nation's second-largest university. Constructing physical classrooms quickly enough to keep pace with this growth has been a challenge, exacerbated in recent years by reduced state funding. By some estimates, the university is 40 percent short of classroom space. Offering online learning has become a key strategy for fulfilling UCF's institutional mission of educational access. As more and more students choose to attend UCF, the institution has expanded the ways that they can access courses and services.

Students at UCF, such as Jennifer, make little distinction between face-to-face, online, and blended courses when registering for a particular semester. As illustrated in Table 1, UCF students mix and match modalities in a variety of ways. Of particular note is that during fall 2010, almost 2,700 students took face-to-face, online, and blended courses *at the same time*. This is the definition of student behavior in a postmodality era. These students are not "online" or "distance" or "main campus"—they are simply students. In fact, UCF's online learning unit is intentionally called the Center for *Distributed* Learning, eschewing the more commonplace "distance" for "distributed" in recognition of its students' "localness" and course-taking preferences.

UCF's students don't even draw much distinction between "main campus" face-to-face classes and "regional campus" face-to-face classes. The university maintains a network of ten regional campuses located throughout central Florida, from Ocala to Daytona Beach to Palm Bay. Students will not only register for courses in various modalities but will also register for courses at various

Table 1. **UCF Student Head Count by Modality Combinations (Fall 2010)**

Total UCF Students	56,129
Students in Face-to-Face (F2F)	49,510
Web OR Blended	23,741
F2F + Web	12,157
F2F + Blended	8,827
F2F + Web OR Blended	18,288
F2F + Web + Blended	2,696
Online Exclusive (excluding video-lecture capture)	4,109 Summer 2011: 6,972 (Online exclusive students always increase during the summer semesters.)

locations, depending upon what they need and the times at which they need it (Figure 1).

As indicated in Figure 1, during fall 2010, 478 students took courses on the main campus, at one or more of the regional campuses, and online. Additionally, 764 students took courses on the main campus, at the Rosen campus (which is a separate residential campus located near Orlando's attractions area and is not part of the regional campus system), and online. These students are unconcerned with labels of "main," "regional," or "distance." They are highly mobile, often changing their location/modality mix from term to term. In tracking these numbers over several years, researchers discovered one undeniably clear trend: growth in online learning continues to far outpace all other university growth. During the 2010–2011 academic year, overall online-student credit-hour production increased 32.2 percent, while classroom-based student credit-hour production increased 4.1 percent. Online learning now represents 30.2 percent of UCF's total student credit-hour production. While UCF offers nearly sixty exclusively online programs, the vast majority of these online credits are produced by students in traditional (not online) programs. Of the top-ten programs (graduate and undergraduate) for students taking online courses,

- only three completely online undergraduate programs are represented and none are in the top three, and
- only five completely online graduate degrees are represented and only one is in the top three.

Figure 1. **UCF Head Count by "Location" (Fall 2010)**

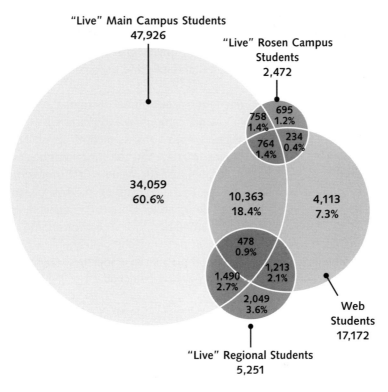

"Live" Main Campus Students
47,926

"Live" Rosen Campus
Students
2,472

758
1.4%

695
1.2%

764
1.4%

234
0.4%

34,059
60.6%

10,363
18.4%

4,113
7.3%

478
0.9%

1,490
2.7%

1,213
2.1%

2,049
3.6%

Web
Students
17,172

"Live" Regional Students
5,251

Note: Students in "blended" courses are not included in the "web students" category.

What this indicates is that students from all majors, both graduate and undergraduate, traditional and online, all across the university, are integrating online courses into their studies, leveraging the flexibility offered by technology to meet both their educational goals and lifestyle needs, whether they are a traditional student in a dorm on campus or an adult learner with a mortgage forty minutes away by interstate highway.

Embry-Riddle Aeronautical University

A very different sort of institution from UCF is Embry-Riddle Aeronautical University (ERAU). Yet ERAU finds itself with a student population just as illustrative of a postmodality mind-set. Founded only twenty-two years after the Wright brothers' first flight, ERAU is a private, nonprofit university best known for its emphasis on education and research related to aviation and aerospace. The university is comprised of three distinct campuses: a residential campus in Daytona Beach, Florida, with approximately 5,100 students; a residential campus in Prescott, Arizona, with approximately 1,700 students; and Embry-Riddle Worldwide, global teaching centers and online offerings with approximately 27,260 students. The university's total unduplicated head count is 34,532 (fall 2009–summer 2010).

Where ERAU finds its students most exhibiting postmodality course-taking behavior is within its Worldwide campus. Headquartered in Daytona Beach, Florida, ERAU's Worldwide campus consists of both its online operation (Worldwide Online) and approximately 150 teaching locations throughout the United States, Canada, Europe, and the Middle East (many of which are affiliated with U.S. military bases). Distance learning at ERAU began in the 1970s with correspondence courses designed to support the highly mobile military student. That distance-learning operation has since evolved into a significant online initiative, with thirty-seven different completely online programs, from undergraduate certificates of completion to associate's, bachelor's, and master's degrees. The university also recently launched an online/low-residency Ph.D. in Aviation.

On its website, Embry-Riddle Worldwide specifically advertises that it offers "five ways to learn." These five modalities are as follows:

- Classroom Learning, which is traditional face-to-face instruction in a synchronous, physical location
- EagleVision Classroom, which is a synchronous web-video conferencing platform that connects multiple physical classrooms into a single live, real-time classroom
- EagleVision Home, which is a synchronous web-video conferencing platform that connects individual users for live online learning
- Online Learning, which is completely online, asynchronous instruction facilitated through a learning management system
- Blended Program, which combines elements of Classroom and Online Learning

Here is how the university describes its approach to serving its postmodality student:

> At Embry-Riddle Aeronautical University—Worldwide, our goal is to give you exactly the education you need, exactly the way you need it. That's why, in addition to offering the industry's most sought after

degrees and programs, we offer you more ways to take courses and complete those programs. Each of our learning modalities, while distinct in its delivery and operation, provides the same high-quality information, instruction, and opportunities for interaction with faculty and fellow students. Simply pick the one that fits your learning and lifestyle best, and embark on the road to educational success.[9]

This is "localness" writ on a large, global scale. ERAU's students are especially mobile, literally traveling the world as pilots, military service personnel, and other aviation-related professionals.

While the Worldwide campus students might primarily be considered "nontraditional," their course-taking behavior mimics that of the more traditional students at UCF. As described in Table 2, ERAU's Worldwide campus students are not only creating their own mix of modalities, but they are doing so at a growing rate. The registrations listed in Table 2 represent duplicated head count, meaning that a single student taking more than one course is likely represented in more than one category. Of particular note in Table 2 is the year-to-year growth in the Blended Program and the EagleVision modalities, contrasted with the decline in Classroom Learning registrations.

This growth (and decline) indicates a shift away from the "traditional" forms of instruction to technology-enabled modalities, enabling the kind of flexibility ERAU's mobile students need. As the university continues to expand both overseas and domestically, this type of postmodality flexibility has become a key strategy for achieving institutional goals.

Table 2. **ERAU Worldwide Campus Course Registrations by Delivery Modality**

	2009–10	2010–11	% Growth
Blended Program	1,140	1,763	54.65
Classroom Learning	42,747	38,577	–9.76
EagleVision Classroom	4,219	5,625	33.33
EagleVision Home	3,080	5,870	90.58
EagleVision/Blended Program	917	1,389	51.47
Online Learning	37,606	39,478	4.98
Total	89,709	92,702	3.34

Table 3. **University of Wisconsin–Milwaukee Student Head Count by Modality**

	Fall 2010	Fall 2011
Number of students taking at least one fully online course	6,181	7,017
Number of students taking exclusively fully online courses	1,299	1,363
Number of students taking at least one blended course	1,918	1,783
Number of students taking exclusively blended courses	74	58
Number of students (unduplicated) taking a blended OR online course	7,707	8,329
Number of students taking a combination of face-to-face AND fully online courses	4,881	5,654
Number of students taking a combination of face-to-face AND blended courses	1,844	1,725

University of Wisconsin–Milwaukee

The University of Wisconsin–Milwaukee (UWM) is similar to UCF in that it is a relatively large state university. With almost 31,000 students, UWM sits in an urban location, which complicates its ability to grow physically. Online and blended learning have proved to be key strategies for the university to serve its students. UWM Online was the recipient of an Alfred P. Sloan Foundation Localness Blended Learning grant (as was UCF) and has leveraged that funding to expand its blended-learning initiative.

When examining UWM student course selections, we again see evidence of postmodality behaviors (Table 3). Of UWM's 7,017 students taking at least one fully online course (fall 2011), 5,654 of them are also taking face-to-face courses. Of the 1,783 students who are taking at least one blended course, 1,725 of them are also taking traditional face-to-face courses. When comparing these numbers to previous terms, as at UCF and ERAU, we see the amount of course-taking variety continuing to grow.

UWM Online's website describes its localness philosophy thusly:

> UWM offers the opportunity for you to take both online and on-campus courses and programs. It's your option. Some students like entirely online while others choose the combination of both online and in-person courses. Either will provide a quality, student-centered experience. For most students looking to save time and for students who

prefer a more flexible learning and study environment, online classes and programs are often a preferred option.[10]

Similar to UCF and ERAU, UWM has structured its online support infrastructure in a manner conducive to student choice. The university has positioned itself to meet the needs of students who are increasingly unconcerned with the labels of modality and location.

Rio Salado College

Part of Arizona's Maricopa Community College system, Rio Salado College was founded specifically to be innovative and to meet the needs of the nontraditional student. Founded in 1978 as a "college without walls," the institution has grown into a well-known practitioner of online learning, leveraging technology to serve students both local and distant.

When examining the course-taking behavior of Rio Salado students (Table 4), it is interesting to observe that a college now known primarily as an online institution sees 25 percent of its students taking courses in traditional classrooms in one of the college's fifteen locations in and around Phoenix and Tempe. It is also noteworthy that more than 2,000 Rio Salado students are concurrently taking courses in multiple modalities, a figure not too different from UCF's 2,700 students (each institution's total student head count is comparable).

Table 4. **Unduplicated Head Count of Rio Salado Students Enrolled by Modality (Academic Year 2011)**

Modality	Credit Students	Noncredit Students	Total
Blended (Hybrid)	51	2	53
In Person	14,463	286	14,749
Independent Study	122	0	122
Internet	40,481	436	40,917
Mixed Media	176	0	176
Print-Based	1,002	13	1,015
Multiple Modalities	2,002	29	2,031
Total	**58,297**	**766**	**59,063**

What these figures indicate in the context of a postmodality discussion is that where UCF's traditional students are leveraging technology to achieve nontraditional flexibility, Rio Salado's nontraditional students are doing the same to choose more traditional course options for supplementing their online coursework. Postmodality behavior works both ways—originating from either the traditional or nontraditional student populations. This phenomenon is consistent with the institution's stated mission:[11]

> Rio Salado College transforms the learning experience through
> - choice, access, and flexibility;
> - customized, high-quality learning design; and
> - personalized service and organizational responsiveness.

"Choice, access, and flexibility" are at the core of localness and are the driving forces behind postmodality behavior.

K–12 Perspective

If the alignment of student preferences and state-level initiatives (enabled by technology) has created a higher education ecosystem supportive of postmodality course-taking behavior, then the future growth of that environment may actually lie outside of higher education. Postmodality course-taking behaviors are occurring at a rapidly growing pace in K–12 schools all across the country. Among the statistics compiled by the International Association for K–12 Online Learning,[12] the following are particularly relevant to this discussion:

- Supplemental or full-time online-learning opportunities are available statewide to at least some K–12 students in forty-eight of the fifty states, plus Washington, DC.
- Twenty-seven states, as well as Washington, DC, have statewide full-time online schools.
- 75 percent of school districts had one or more students enrolled in an online- or blended-learning course.
- 72 percent of school districts with distance-education programs planned to expand online offerings in the coming year.
- 82 percent of high school administrators interviewed in the United States had at least one student enrolled in a fully online course and 38 percent had at least one student enrolled in a blended or hybrid course.
- iNACOL estimates a total of 1,500,000 K–12 students were enrolled in online-learning courses in 2009.

- In 2010, over 4 million K–12 students participated in a formal on-line-learning program. This includes 217,000 students in cyber charter schools. Online-learning enrollments are growing by 46 percent a year, and the growth rate is accelerating.

In addition to the local preferences and desires of students and schools/districts to have online course offerings, statewide, systemic forces are also acting upon the K–12 ecosystem. States such as Michigan, Alabama, and Florida now require all high school students to take at least one online course in order to graduate. Idaho recently approved a plan to become the first state to require two credits to be completed online for high school graduation. These states are actually mandating postmodality course-taking behaviors, compelling secondary students to take online courses in addition to their traditional, face-to-face high school classes. Based upon the growth of K–12 online learning (46 percent a year, as cited above) in an environment where these state requirements did not yet exist, it can only be assumed that the growth of online learning in this sector will now grow even more quickly.

Florida has not only established a requirement for high school students to complete at least one online course to graduate, it has also mandated that each of its sixty-seven K–12 school districts provide virtual-learning options to its students. Further, it is now possible for a student in Florida to complete his or her entire kindergarten-through-high-school experience completely online at state expense as a fully funded public school option. In practice, however, students are mixing and matching various modalities. "Most students who participate in virtual education do so to supplement their work in traditional schools. Last year, more than 115,000 students across the state took at least one course with the Florida Virtual School."[13]

As these students arrive on our postsecondary campuses, they will already be accustomed from their high school experiences to taking a concurrent mixture of face-to-face, online, and blended courses. They will expect (perhaps even demand) that same flexibility and choice from their colleges and universities.

Conclusion

During a panel of presidents at the 2011 EDUCAUSE Annual Meeting, James J. Linksz, president of Bucks County Community College in Pennsylvania, described how his institution's students move back and forth between face-to-face and online modalities. He estimated that approximately 20 percent of his college's student credit hours are generated online and that about double that number of students have taken one or more online courses. This type of behavior has become commonplace at both community colleges and universities, at institutions serving both traditional and nontraditional students alike.

Demand for online and blended courses continues to grow at a rapid pace. Faculty and administrators who have not already done so need to recognize postmodality student preferences and behaviors on their own campuses and respond accordingly with a supportive infrastructure. Institutions will need to expand campus information systems to make it easier for students to select and register for online and blended offerings. Academic support services, including advising and library assistance, will need to be reconfigured to address online, asynchronous learners. On-campus classrooms will potentially need more multimedia and network capability to help bridge the online and on-ground environments for students moving seamlessly between the two. Campus technology infrastructure may need to be expanded to accommodate greater numbers of students conducting online coursework from on-campus facilities and using on-campus bandwidth. Finally, faculty and course-development services will need to be expanded to prepare and support faculty who will also be moving back and forth between modalities just as their students do. It is not uncommon for a single faculty member at UCF to concurrently teach face-to-face, online, and blended courses, mirroring the course-taking behaviors of his or her students.

For students like Jennifer, and her younger peers currently in middle and high school, online learning is no longer a novelty. It is simply a regular part of their education. They are increasingly unconcerned with the distinctions between face-to-face and online learning, instead choosing individual courses that meet their particular needs at any given time, regardless of modality. This postmodality behavior, enabled by instructional technology, has become their normal routine. Going forward, meeting the needs of these students with institutional ecosystems that support, encourage, and enable them to succeed will become key components of college and university strategic plans.

Notes

1. A. W. Radford, "Learning at a Distance: Undergraduate Enrollment in Distance Education Courses and Degree Programs," U.S. Department of Education National Center for Education Statistics (2011), retrieved from http://nces.ed.gov/pubs2012/2012154.pdf.
2. I. E. Allen and J. Seaman, "Class Differences: Online Education in the United States,

2010," Babson Survey Research Group and The Sloan Consortium (2010), retrieved from http://sloanconsortium.org/publications/survey/pdf/class_differences.pdf.

3.   R. Hess, quoting NCES in blog, "The Changing Face of Higher Education," *Education Week* (October 7, 2011), retrieved from http://blogs.edweek.org/edweek/rick_hess_straight_up/2011/10/the_changing_face_of_higher_education.html.

4.   A. F. Mayadas and A. G. Picciano, "Blended Learning and Localness: The Means and the End," *Journal of Asynchronous Learning Networks* 11, no. 1 (2007): 3–7, retrieved from http://www.eric.ed.gov/PDFS/EJ842682.pdf.

5.   C. Dziuban and P. Moskal, "A Course Is a Course Is a Course: Factor Invariance in Student Evaluation of Online, Blended and Face-to-Face Learning Environments," *Internet and Higher Education* 14, no. 4 (2011): 236–241, http://dx.doi.org/doi:10.1016/j.iheduc.2011.05.003.

6.   Ibid., 239.

7.   Ibid., 240.

8.   M. Parry, "Tomorrow's College," *The Chronicle of Higher Education* (October 31, 2010), retrieved from http://chronicle.com/article/Tomorrows-College/125120/.

9.   Embry-Riddle Aeronautical University Worldwide, "Five Ways to Learn" (2011), retrieved from http://worldwide.erau.edu/why-worldwide/five-ways-to-learn/index.html.

10.   UWM Online, "Frequently Asked Questions about Online Learning" (2011), retrieved from http://www4.uwm.edu/future_students/online/faq.cfm.

11.   Rio Salado, "College Culture" (2011), retrieved from http://www.riosalado.edu/about/research-planning/culture/Pages/default.aspx.

12.   iNACOL, "Fast Facts about Online Learning" (2011), retrieved from http://www.inacol.org/press/docs/nacol_fast_facts.pdf.

13.   L. Postal, "Is Florida's Virtual-Learning Push Visionary—Or 'Blizzard of Hype'?," *Orlando Sentinel*, September 11, 2011, 1A & 6A.

Thomas B. Cavanagh *has over 17 years of e-learning experience in both industry and higher education. A regular speaker at professional conferences, he is an award-winning instructional designer, program manager, faculty member, and administrator. He is currently Assistant Vice President of Distributed Learning at the University of Central Florida.*

17

Going the Distance:
Outsourcing Online Learning

Susan E. Metros and Joan Falkenberg Getman

Setting the Stage

ONLINE LEARNING AND GAME CHANGING are rarely synonymous. Online learning evolved from early iterations of distance learning in which educational content was delivered remotely, initially through written correspondence. In the mid-1960s, distance-learning delivery advanced with the advent of analog communication technologies such as radio and closed-circuit television. More recently, educational institutions employed digital telephony, using computers and the Internet, to offer courses to off-campus populations via two-way videoconferencing. Today, with major advances in networking and computing technologies, current modes of online learning link faculty and students both synchronously and asynchronously.

While online learning technologies have advanced dramatically, the quality of the teaching and learning experience online has not. Much online learning still emulates the one-way communication of correspondence and television by capturing the classroom lecture or requiring students to slog through tomes of uploaded written material.

Online Learning at USC

The University of Southern California has been a leader in distance learning since the early 1970s. Established in 1974, the Viterbi School of Engineering's Distance Learning Network (DEN) offers over forty online master's degree programs, graduate certificates, and continuing-education courses. Prior to 2008, all distance-learning programs, including DEN, were designed and delivered internally by USC personnel. Master's degrees and certificates in gerontology, geographic information science and technology (GIST), pharmacy, and medicine were designed and managed in-house by individual schools and departments and delivered primarily using traditional videoconferencing technologies.

In 2008, USC expanded its online learning options to education students earning a master of arts in teaching (MAT) and, most recently, for master's degree programs in social work, public policy, communications, library and information science, and public health. USC's executive leadership understood that to remain current and competitive, it would need to extend USC's breadth and reach beyond the residential campus. It also understood that it needed to target and attract a new demographic of highly qualified and professionally driven adult learners.

Economically, online learning presented one of few ways left for a university to tap new revenue sources. The provost encouraged deans to talk with their faculty, students, staff, alumni, board of counselors, and professional communities to determine if online learning was an academically and financially viable option for their discipline and their school.

Outsourcing as a Game Changer

Rather than build capacity to offer and operate online-learning programs within the individual academic units or even coordinate full-service support centrally, USC chose to outsource the development and delivery of fully online, Internet-delivered degrees to for-profit vendor partners. The decision to outsource distance learning is a game changer because it not only introduced a new model for the development and delivery of online degrees at a private research university, but it reimagines the actual teaching, learning, and even practicum/residency placement experience. USC's new online programs are technologically sophisticated, exceptionally interactive, and accessible anywhere and anytime. The courses do not solely rely on text-based content, lecture capture, nor high-stakes testing, but instead take advantage of professionally produced, multimedia-rich learning modules that use Web 2.0 technologies, interactive case studies, graphic simulations, live web-based discussions, real-time cohort collaboration, high-profile guest lectures, and group-based projects.

The decision to outsource online learning was not without controversy, especially since the DEN model has been so successful in the past. However, DEN requires a large in-house staff to develop course content and manage the administrative, marketing, technical, and user-support components of the program. It also entails maintaining a customized learning management platform and dedicated, state-of-the-art studio classrooms. Furthermore, unlike students in other disciplines, engineers are familiar with and at ease with online-learning delivery and often are sponsored by their companies to attend courses remotely to earn advanced degrees.

The argument in favor of bolstering central resources to support online learning was seriously considered but deemed problematic. The USC Information Technology Services' Center for Scholarly Technology (CST) assists the campus community in integrating educational technologies into teaching and learning by offering design and assessment services, learning management system support, training and workshops, and presentations and events. However, the CST's small staff of six instructional technologists and media and assessment specialists is too small to support scores of fully online, full-service degree offerings. The CST does play an essential role of readying the faculty and the institution to participate in an outsourced online-learning relationship (see sidebar).

USC's online master's degree programs offer students the same high standard of academic rigor on which the residential programs pride themselves. The programs are reviewed and approved by regional accreditation agencies and, if applicable, discipline-specific professional accreditation agencies. Students must meet USC's highly selective admission standards and are eligible for the same financial aid and scholarship awards as their residential counterparts. Online students pay the same tuition as residential students; USC does not differentiate tuition for its online degrees. Students are encouraged to be an active member of the tight-knit "Trojan Family" community by joining student clubs and participating in student government and other extracurricular activities. The schools also are exploring ways to remain closely connected to their virtual graduates through on-campus, location-based, and online alumni activities. Interestingly, the vast majority of online students choose, at their own expense, to partake in the campuses' graduation ceremonies.

Online Integrators

To date, USC has partnered with two online integrator companies, 2tor and EmbanetCompass, for turnkey support of their current and proposed online degree programs. Both are privately owned and specialize in full-service support for postsecondary online learning degree programs. Full-service support includes needs assessment, marketing strategy, student and staff recruitment, admissions and enrollment support, educational content design and conversion, technology

Cont'd on p. 235

Faculty and Institutional Readiness: From an Educational Technologist's Perspective

Joan Falkenberg Getman, director for USC's Educational Technologies and the Center for Scholarly Technology, leads a support team that is tasked with preparing faculty to teach with technology:

I lead an educational technology organization that supports instructors who want to teach with technology. Today, in the fall of 2011, I am fairly certain that the instructor who opts NOT to use technology is in a very, very small minority. However, teaching with technology experience definitely evolves along a continuum.

The eLearning Continuum

At one end is the instructor who has a syllabus on his or her course website in the institution's learning management system (LMS)—period. At the other end of the spectrum is the instructor who is responsible for students who only ever connect online. In between those two points is a long stretch of fertile ground where my team and I spend most of our time. While it is not our stated goal, the programs, services, and resources we offer advance the readiness of faculty who choose to move out of the physical classroom and teach in a completely online environment. It is critical that a constant anywhere on the continuum is academic rigor. The X factors are the technologies that comprise the virtual learning environment, the physical distance between students and instructors, and the balance of synchronous and asynchronous activities.

Instructors who teach with technology often begin simply with web-enhanced courses that encourage students to access online resources. Migrating a web-enhanced course to one that is more of a" blended" format leads to more of the course being mediated by technology, but it does not necessarily mean a change in the balance of traditional "seat time." An example of this is the "flipped" or "inverted" classroom in which students are engaged in new online activities and assignments while maintaining the same amount of in-class meeting time. The innovation in the flipped course is that instructors shift the kinds of activities that students do synchronously in the physical classroom and the kind of work they are expected to do online and often by themselves, asynchronously. For example, students might access recorded lectures and self-assessments online, while in-class time is spent on collaborative problem solving or drilling deeper into concepts or skills that students find particularly challenging. The next significant threshold is changing the amount of seat time and moving the course to a virtual learning environment until eventually you reach the end of the continuum, where the majority, if not all, of the students' experience is online, with a minimal number of face-to-face meetings (if any at all). The number of faculty who teach further along the continuum drops dramatically at an institution such as USC, where the emphasis is on residential instruction.

Layering On and Teaming Up

Faculty tend to be self-sufficient; they are used to teaching in a "closed" classroom and preparing at their own pace with a small, agile group of support providers. An instructor might work alone or at most with one to three other people and campus organizations to teach in a traditional face-to-face course. Even with a field placement, the "support team" might only involve an administrative assistant, a librarian, and—for a technology-enhanced course—an instructional technologist.

As instructors move more of their teaching online, the layers of technology that exist between instructors and students increase. Accordingly, the support team also increases in diversity of skills, services, and size. The ultimate challenge in becoming an online instructor may be that the online classroom is transparent. In addition to using potentially new and unfamiliar technology, faculty are asked to expose their teaching to this large team of professionals and adhere to a very tight schedule. This is especially true when instructors are in the role of subject-matter experts who provide course content that will be transformed and formatted into engaging online material by the vendor's instructional design and production team.

Distance-learning providers offer full-service support from student recruitment to graduation; they provide marketing, content development, student assessment, statistical tracking, and technical support along the way. But regardless of the complex scaffolding and comprehensive support vendors provide, if instructors are unfamiliar with the technology, new to the advantages and idiosyncrasies of a virtual learning environment, and used to preparing on their own, teaching online can be a difficult, time-consuming process for everyone.

This is the place where readiness matters.

It seems that instructors who have taught with any level of technology prior to teaching an online course are better positioned to adapt to the nuances of different distance-learning platforms. These instructors are also more comfortable with virtual communication and collaboration, enabling them to engage with students more quickly. And in most cases, faculty who have taught with technology have established at least a few collaborative relationships. Educational technology organizations and faculty support providers are well positioned to lay the foundation for a successful distance-learning vendor partnership that produces consistent, high-quality online courses.

Standards, Opportunities, and Incentives

As mentioned earlier, the CST is a small unit situated in the Office of the Provost's division for Information Technology Services (ITS). Upon request, our group will consult with faculty who wish to develop their own distance-learning programs and courses, but we are very clear about the enormity of such an undertaking and the importance of connecting with other support providers to ensure that they have coordinated all the resources, services, and technologies to launch an online offering.

Outsourcing distance learning frees up campus instructional designers and technology consultants. What it means for my organization is that we do not end up "mass producing" distance-learning course after distance-learning course. Instead, we are able to work at a more strategic level. We focus on increasing faculty readiness by providing opportunities for exploring pedagogical strategies, gaining firsthand experience with different technologies, and developing a shared vocabulary. We also support institutional standards for academic rigor.

We have contributed to institutional readiness by taking a subset of questions from a form required for regional accreditation approval. The form is the Western Association of Schools and Colleges (WASC) Distance Learning template and must be completed by the university prior to offering a fully accredited online degree program. By asking schools to respond to select questions very early in the process of deciding whether to offer an online degree, faculty can determine if their proposed course and curriculum are ready to go online and if they can offer an educational experience that meets the same academic standards as the residential program. The "readiness" checklist is designed in such a way that the information faculty provide will go toward completion of the final WASC application if they continue to move ahead in the process.

The University Committee on Curriculum has also asked us to collaborate with it in developing a syllabus "template" that accounts for traditional courses as well as the courses that have varying degrees of online components. It is designed to address the nuances of teaching and learning online—from the technologies students are expected to use to describing the different online locations they will need to access during the course (e.g., the course website, web conferencing information, blog, etc.). The expectation for the template is that it will guide instructors to think about their course activities, assignments, assessments, and communications so that students can expect the same quality whether the course is online or residential.

One of our most interesting and rewarding activities is managing our faculty incentive program. With generous funding from the Office of the Provost, the Center for Scholarly Technology is able to award several different kinds of teaching-with-technology grants. One example is the C3 (Course Continuity in a Crisis) program, which asks faculty to create a "Plan B" assignment and at some point in the semester to announce a mock campus closing that requires the instructor and students to meet online. There are two requirements: (1) the instructor must use Blackboard (USC's current LMS) for the course website, and (2) the instructor and his or her students must use the technologies that will support their Plan B assignments early in the semester to gain experience with them prior to the "campus emergency." In many cases, instructors have created assignments that could potentially contribute to the community's documentation of or recovery from a crisis situation. Program evaluations indicate that instructors and students underestimate what it takes to go from meeting face-to-face to gathering together online. This opportunity to experience online teaching and learning with support for alignment of teaching strategies and technologies surely contributes to faculty readiness to teach a distance-learning course.

infrastructure and delivery hosting, assessment tools, and comprehensive training and community support services. Both vendors require a contractual commitment for at least 8–10 years or longer and are based on a tuition-split financial model. All course content remains the intellectual property of the university, and all academic decisions remain the strict province of the university, under the auspices of the faculty, its governing boards, university curriculum committees, and appropriate administrative officials.

An essential component of an institution/vendor partnership is clearly defining and delineating the roles and responsibilities of each partner early in the relationship. The contractual agreement captures much of this division of labor, but there are additional duties that must be assigned to either the institution or vendor (Table 1).

Table 1. **Roles and Responsibilities**

I. PLANNING AND DEVELOPMENT

1. Needs Assessment

Academic Institution	Vendor Partner
• Identify and help survey target audiences and provide data on competitive programs	• Conduct a needs assessment to analyze market to determine audience viability and program profitability

2. Business Planning

Academic Institution	Vendor Partner
• Jointly participate in developing the business plan • Jointly establish a revenue pro forma and associated budget • Negotiate and ratify the contract	

3. Marketing and Promotion

Academic Institution	Vendor Partner
• Approve recruitment/marketing strategy and plan	• Develop and execute recruitment/marketing strategy and plan
• Approve and collaborate on website design, social media site, and other marketing collateral	• Develop and manage a marketing website, social media site, and other marketing collateral
• Monitor marketing practices	

4. Curriculum, Course, and Content Design and Production

Academic Institution	Vendor Partner
• Assess faculty readiness • Design the curriculum and courses • Obtain all internal curriculum approvals • Approve all content conversion • Ensure faculty are available to consult on courses and serve as subject-matter experts (SME) • Review and approve synchronous course components and asynchronous course content	• Provide faculty with instructional technology design support • Convert course content to online format • Procure copyrights • Advance funding for faculty SMEs (vendor specific) • Build and test synchronous course components, develop and produce asynchronous course content

5. Teaching

Academic Institution	Vendor Partner
• Determine appropriate faculty configuration for program • Hire additional faculty • Supervise teaching • Evaluate quality of instruction and make improvements	• Assist in identifying prospective instructors

6. Host Sites and Field Placements (Program Specific)

Academic Institution	Vendor Partner
• Assist in identifying host sites • Approve hosts sites and field staff • Approve student placements • Orient field staff on program's curricular components • Manage, monitor, and assess field staff/student relationships	• Identify and secure host sites • Search for and place field staff • Identify and secure student placements • Orient and train field staff on using technology platform

7. Training and Support

Academic Institution	Vendor Partner
• Provide faculty and staff with pedagogical and readiness support • Provide students with academic and career advising	• Provide faculty support for teaching online • Orient and train faculty, students, and staff on using technology platform • Provide 24/7 student technical support

8. Student Evaluations

Academic Institution	Vendor Partner
• Jointly establish metrics and design surveys and assessments • Jointly improve program based on findings	
• Analyze, interpret, and disseminate evaluation results • Secure IRB clearance and design research studies (optional)	• Administer online student formative and summative evaluations • Participate in research studies (optional)

Table continues →

Table 1. **Roles and Responsibilities,** *continued*

II. ADMINISTRATIVE

1. Leadership and Strategy

Academic Institution	Vendor Partner
• Provide program's strategic vision and direction	• Contribute to the planning efforts
• Establish a plan that clarifies the program's goals, project scope, governance, timeline, etc.	

2. Accounting

Academic Institution	Vendor Partner
• Oversee the financial components of the program	• Provide enrollment projections and cost accounting
• Collect tuition and fees and pay vendor partner	

3. Recruitment and Retention

Academic Institution	Vendor Partner
• Jointly develop and implement a recruitment and retention plan	
• Establish admission requirements	• Recruit qualified students
• Monitor and audit recruiting processes	

4. Academic Approval and Accreditation

Academic Institution	Vendor Partner
• Initiate, coordinate, and complete regional and professional accreditation approvals	• Gather relevant data and resources

5. Admissions, Registration, and Fees

Academic Institution	Vendor Partner
• Review applications and make admission decisions	• Hire, train, and retain a staff of admissions counselors
	• Prepare qualified candidate application dossiers for institution's review

6. Financial Aid

Academic Institution	Vendor Partner
• Jointly counsel prospective students on financial aid information and options	
• Administer financial aid programs and disperse funds	

7. Program and Partnership Evaluation

Academic Institution	Vendor Partner
• Jointly establish metrics and design surveys and assessments • Jointly improve program based on findings	
• Perform mid contract vendor-performance review (vendor specific) • Administer evaluations, interpret and disseminate evaluation results	• Track longitudinal data on student satisfaction and program performance

8. Policies and Legalities

Academic Institution	Vendor Partner
• Comply with institution's policies and guidelines • Comply with local, state, and federal laws and rules including FERPA, HIPPA, HEOA, ADA, etc. • Abide by laws/policies pertaining to recruiting and enrolling international students • Monitor and report on all levels of government activity related to online learning	
• Pay state authorization fees and other related expenses • Execute the clauses in the contract that require the vendor to audit specified operations (SAS 70 audit, "ethical hack," penetration testing, and other independent reviews)	• Seek and maintain state authorizations • Provide periodic reports on contractually specified auditable operations

9. Credentials and Graduation

Academic Institution	Vendor Partner
• Confer degrees	

Table continues →

Table 1. **Roles and Responsibilities,** *continued*

III. STUDENT SERVICES

1. Academic Advising and Career Counseling

Academic Institution	Vendor Partner
• Jointly provide students with career counseling and placement options	
• Provide students with academic advising	• Provide students with nonacademic advising
• Identify and counsel students on probation or with conditional status	• Use LMS platform's analytics to monitor student progress and identify students at risk
	• Gather and share labor market statistics for career counseling
	• Provide online tutoring tools/services (optional)

2. Student Health

Academic Institution	Vendor Partner
• Provide access to health-education resources	• Use technology platform to encourage and promote healthy behaviors
• Provide elective health-insurance options	

3. Student Culture

Academic Institution	Vendor Partner
• Identify ways to build community and include online students in campus-based extracurricular activities	• Provide social networking tools so that online students can participate in campus-based communities and extracurricular activities
• Include online students in university communications	• Provide tools to support communication

4. Special Needs

Academic Institution	Vendor Partner
• Identify and address special needs	• Provide an ADA-compliant platform and tools
	• Develop technologies using the Universal Design for Learning (UDL) framework

5. Bookstore and Library Resources

Academic Institution	Vendor Partner
• Provide resource ordering information • Identify and provide access to library resources and e-reserves	• Integrate library resources into LMS platform • Provide online access to bookstore and other resource sites

6. Testing and Grades

Academic Institution	Vendor Partner
• Replace online high-stakes testing with other forms of assessment • Submit final grades to registrar	• Provide process for verifying students' identification • Provide secure online tests and assessments environment. If necessary, arrange for exam proctoring

7. Alumni and Lifelong Learners

Academic Institution	Vendor Partner
• Manage alumni relationships	• Use LMS platform to build and maintain an active alumni community • Assist in mining relevant alumni data

IV. TECHNOLOGY

1. Technology Infrastructure

Academic Institution	Vendor Partner
• If internally hosted, provide a robust, secure, and scalable LMS platform and network connectivity	• If externally hosted, provide a robust, secure, and scalable LMS platform and network connectivity • Provide and test business continuity and disaster-recovery plans • Comply with the institution's information technology protocols and policies

Table continues →

Table 1. **Roles and Responsibilities,** *continued*

2. Technology Support

Academic Institution	Vendor Partner
• If internally hosted, provide 24/7 technical support for students, faculty, and staff	• If externally hosted, provide 24/7 technical support for students, faculty, and staff
• Establish service-level agreements (SLAs) based on industry-standard requirements for externally hosted services	• Abide by SLAs based on industry-standard requirements
• Track technology issues/solutions	• Report and mitigate major issues/ solutions

3. Distance-Learning Facilities

Academic Institution	Vendor Partner
• If required, provide video conferencing, classroom space, and staff support	

The deans, in consultation with their staff and faculty, choose which vendor they prefer to work with and the Office of the Provost negotiates the contract on their behalf, with direct input from Admissions and Planning, Academic Operations and Strategy (Budget), Information Technology Services, and general counsel. The school's choice is usually based on a variety of variables—how quickly it is willing to build program capacity and how big it wants the program to be; the complexity of the technology platform; its faculty's predisposition toward programmatic innovation; the strength of the support structure; the terms of the agreement; and sometimes just the personality fit.

One of the biggest advantages of outsourcing online learning is that the vendor partners invest a generous amount of capital funding up front, assuming the majority of financial risk. They also have the ability to retain an agile and talented workforce with expertise to support the full spectrum of designing, marketing, programming, delivering, and assessing online programs. Furthermore, they recruit year-round and can "staff up" to offer prospective students multiple start dates to accommodate their work schedules and often help them complete a degree quicker than if they enrolled in the residential option.

2tor is relatively new to the market; USC was its first client in 2008. 2tor conforms to a business model based on partnering with a limited number of carefully screened, preeminent universities to offer one-of-a-kind, large-enrollment online degree programs. To date, it has partnered with only two other institutions in addition to USC and promises exclusivity in the marketplace, agreeing not to partner with any other institutions to offer the same degree. 2tor is headquartered in New York City with offices in Maryland, but each of its programs is assigned its own dedicated local community manager with a sizeable staff. Both of USC's programs that have partnered with 2tor have over fifty staff colocated with university staff in the Los Angeles area. One of 2tor's advantages is that it has built and perfected an innovative and robust LMS based on Moodle's open source architecture. This "learning platform" incorporates dynamic Web 2.0 technologies with a Facebook-like social networking interface. 2tor states that it makes an up-front minimum investment of over $10 million in each program; a large portion of that funding is invested in marketing and recruiting, technology infrastructure, and providing students with customized, just-in-time support.

EmbanetCompass has been in business since 1965 and has 34 academic partners and supports over 107 academic programs at a wide variety of higher education institutions. The Compass-Knowledge Group, a pioneer and provider of distance-learning services to nonprofit higher education institutions, merged with Embanet in 2010 to create EmbanetCompass. Different from 2tor, EmbanetCompass professes to be "LMS-agnostic" and develops high-quality, professionally produced content, available through the institution's internal LMS or on one of EmbanetCompass's hosted, fully functional LMS systems. EmbanetCompass provides the institution with a local community liaison and an instructional technologist, but supports the program with assigned staff from its headquarters in Toronto. It provides upfront funding to the university to provide faculty with incentives to serve as subject-matter experts, working with its staff to convert traditional courses to an online format. EmbanetCompass prides itself in offering a unique and robust support network that includes enrollment advisors to guide students through the application process, student-services managers to serve as personal advisors, program facilitators to help with matters involving course content and requirements, and technical support staff available 24/7.

There are a limited number of other companies offering online-integration services. Deltak, established in 1996, and the Learning House have both been in business for almost a decade. Deltak offers end-to-end support for over seventy degree and certificate programs, partnering primarily with small and midsized nonprofit postsecondary institutions. The Learning House, recently acquired by Weld North Holdings LLC (Weld North), has helped more than ninety institutions successfully launch and maintain their online programs. Also working primarily with independent small and medium-sized colleges and universities, the Learning House provides a package consisting of six core services, each designed to support unique aspects of implementing and managing online degree programs. The core services include curriculum and course development, program marketing and enrollment management, technology infrastructure, faculty and staff training, technology support, and consulting.

Two other contenders include Bisk Education and Colloquy. Bisk consults with universities to expand enrollment, increase revenue, and advance their mission through the development of online programs; it also works in tandem with its University Alliance division, which facilitates the delivery of these programs, overseeing marketing, recruitment and enrollment, program delivery, and support. Colloquy, a wholly owned subsidiary of Kaplan, Inc., subscribes to a proprietary 360° methodology that professes to address each step in the distance learning process including insight, design, marketing, recruiting, and student success services.

SunGard Higher Education's Online Learning Services, while not a full-service provider, assists institutions in evaluating, building, or enhancing their fully online or hybrid-degree and non-degree programs. It will assess and document technical and operational readiness, design academic programs for online delivery, support students and train faculty, and manage the institution's technology infrastructure.

Pearson eCollege, The New York Times Knowledge Network, and other publishing companies have considered the online integrator market, but to date have concentrated on developing and distributing online courses and educational content, providing virtual tutoring services, and marketing LMS and content-repository solutions.

A new addition to the market, Educators Serving Educators (ESE), a division of Excelsior College, is an innovative not-for-profit corporation that works with accredited, higher education institutions to develop and deliver online programs and courses. Employing a different type of model, ESE "teaches you to fish" so that an institution can gain the experience and skills to establish and maintain its own online learning unit. ESE specializes in assisting institutions that serve individuals traditionally underrepresented in higher education.

Online Learning at USC

The University of Southern California's online learning programs are under the umbrella of USCNow, a portal to USC's online professional master's degree programs. USCNow provides web access to all of USC's online programs. In addition, the site provides prospective students up-to-date information on admission and enrollment, financial aid, technical requirements, and international student requirements. Current students can find out more about registration and academic and career advising.

USC's Rossier School of Education was the first school to enter into an outsourced agreement, partnering with 2tor, to launch a master of arts in teaching (MAT) degree. The target audience for the MAT@USC degree was traditional preservice teacher candidates, who typically enroll within five years of graduating from their undergraduate institution, and career changers, who often enroll ten or twenty years after their undergraduate experience. Rossier previously offered a residential MAT program that, in 2008, served approximately eighty students. The MAT@USC was launched in June of 2009 and in two and a half years has grown from approximately 80 residential students to enroll over 1,500 online students. Faculty were concerned that the popular online program might cannibalize and decimate the residential program, but just the opposite happened. Because of the growth and visibility of the online program—and the fact that USC negotiated the rights to use the online content in the on-ground courses—the residential program enrollment has increased.

One of the more innovative online components of the online MAT degree is the way in which students complete their fieldwork and the guided practice required for teacher certification. USC, in partnership with 2tor, has built relationships with thousands of schools across the world. In the traditional student-teaching model, a student is assigned to a local classroom and supervised and evaluated by that class's teacher. During the fieldwork phase of the online degree program, students are still placed in local classrooms, but USC provides them with a digital video camera so that they can record their teaching. They upload the recorded segments to share not only with their supervising teachers, but also with USC faculty, guest experts, and their student cohort peers—greatly expanding the circle and quality of feedback.

Rossier has since launched a second MAT degree with a specialization for teachers of English to speakers of other languages (MAT-TESOL). The school continues to work with 2tor on other specializations within the MAT degree and on a fully online master of education (MEd) degree (see Figure 1).

With the success of the MAT@USC degree, the USC School of Social Work chose to partner with 2tor and within one year has created the first fully online, evidence-based master of social work (MSW) degree with close to a thousand students enrolled from across the country and internationally. Taught by renowned faculty and leaders in the field of social work, the MSW@USC curriculum mirrors the academic rigor of the on-site program. Available through the school's Virtual Academic Center, students participate in various web-based learning activities and hands-on supervised traditional field instruction in their local communities. Professionally produced case-study vignettes allow students

Figure 1. **The MAT@USC Web Portal**

Figure 2. **An Enhanced Faculty Lecture from the USC's School of Social Work's MSW@USC Online Degree Program**

to observe a "client's" behavior. Faculty lectures are recorded in front of a green screen so that they can be graphically enhanced (see Figure 2).

The School of Social Work is currently collaborating with USC's Institute for Creative Technologies (ICT) to develop social worker/virtual-client clinical simulations. ICT is a leader in producing virtual humans, computer training

Figure 3. **The USC's School of Social Work's MSW@USC's Virtual Client Clinical Simulation**

simulations, and immersive experiences for decision making. Online students engage with the ICT-produced artificially intelligent interactive agents (see Figure 3). The technology provides students with a chance to advance practical interviewing skills with realistic client interactions. The virtual clients can speak, express body language, show emotion, and offer immediate feedback.

The USC Annenberg School of Communication and Journalism chose EmbanetCompass as its online integrator partner and, in the fall of 2011, launched a fully online master of communication management (MCM) degree. The on-campus communication management degree program is designed for recent college graduates and working professionals who want the traditional graduate school experience of attending classes at USC's urban Los Angeles campus. The online MCM degree is different in that it is designed for mid-career professionals whose work schedules preclude them from enrolling in an on-campus program. By using the latest online education technologies, the same USC Annenberg faculty who teach in the on-campus program are able to teach these nontraditional students. Students have access to course materials at their convenience, paired with the opportunity to interact online with other students and faculty to complete assignments and participate in class discussions. The program is hosted on EmbanetCompass's Moodle platform and makes extensive use of multimedia-based content and Google Apps e-textbooks that allows faculty and students to dynamically update material

Figure 4. **An E-Textbook from the USC Annenberg School of Communication and Journalism's MCM Online Degree Program**

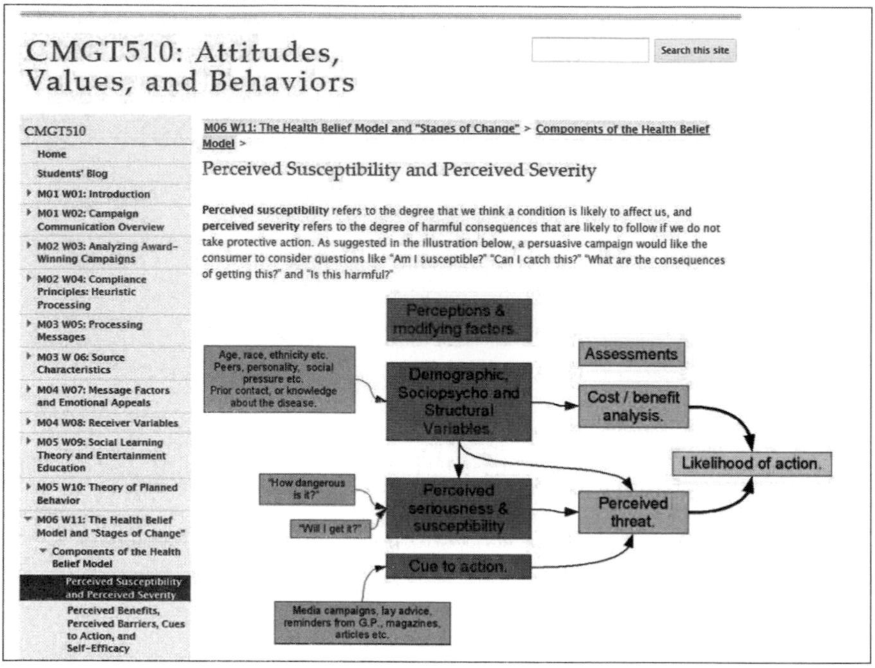

and examples together (see Figure 4). Students also are invited to attend special programs on the USC campus in Los Angeles during the course of their studies and are encouraged to participate in USC's campus commencement when they graduate.

In the fall of 2011, the USC Sol Price School of Public Policy also partnered with EmbanetCompass to launch a fully online master of public administration (MPA). MPA is a unique and multidisciplinary environment within the Price School that integrates all the major disciplines bearing on management and leadership in today's modern interconnected socioeconomic and political environment. The program connects cutting-edge research to the practice of public policy and management, equipping students with the skills required for the challenges and opportunities of the ever-changing nature of public administration. Similar to the on-campus program, online MPA students choose a specialization in local government or nonprofit management. The Price School also hosts the degree on EmbanetCompass's Moodle platform and students learn through authentic case studies and other interactive exercises (see Figure 5).

USC also engaged EmbanetCompass to provide à la carte recruiting and

Figure 5. **An Online Case Study from
the USC Price School of Public Policy's MPA Online Degree Program**

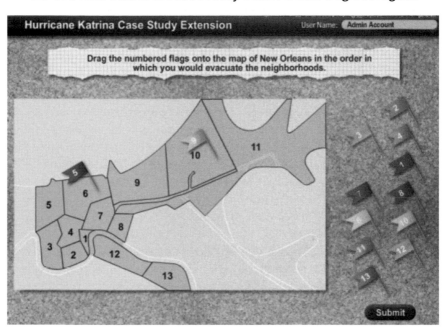

marketing services for the USC Davis School of Gerontology and the USC Dornsife College of Letters, Arts and Sciences' Geographic Information Science and Technology (GIST) program. USC developed, delivers, and maintains these online programs in-house. EmbanetCompass conducted market assessments and, based on their findings, rebranded and repositioned the programs, resulting in significant increases in enrollments.

Challenges

Outsourcing online learning is not without its challenges and detractors. There are tensions between the seemingly entrepreneurial goals of the administration condoning new kinds of partnerships and traditional academic values. The university leadership has met with faculty and alumni to address concerns ranging from instructors being replaced by technology to traditional on-campus programs degrees losing value.

Another problem that surfaced was the need to quickly identify and hire highly qualified instructors to teach in online programs that were expanding much more rapidly than the university and vendor partners ever anticipated.

Schools had to increase staffing to meet the influx of admission applications and to support the unique academic and social needs of nontraditional students interacting with the university from a distance. Admissions and Planning had to reengineer online processes to streamline access.

The line between online and "on-ground" students is blurring as faculty want their on-campus students to have seamless access to the vendor partner's technology platforms and online educational content modules. While beneficial to students, it plays havoc with traditional university policies and complicates internal and other required tracking and reporting procedures.

This highlights a bigger issue. Programs are hindered by university policies and procedures established exclusively for a time when the only delivery modality was face-to-face in the lecture hall or classroom. What constitutes seat time? Who owns course content? What activity, transportation, or health care fees should be levied upon a student who may flip between online and on-ground or may never set foot on campus?

Finally, the technology is not always facile and reliable. Online programs don't need to conform to fifteen-week semesters with specific start dates, yet it is not easy to reprogram an institution's student information system to support more and varied start dates, especially when the government's financial-aid award dates are static. Some of the programs had major issues with network bandwidth, especially during synchronous course sessions when students relied on the wireless connectivity in their homes. The program leaders had to reduce section size and require hard-wired Ethernet connections. In some cases, the vendor partners initially miscalculated the amount of support faculty would need to redesign their courses and to teach in an online environment.

Conclusion

Developing and delivering a full-service online learning program is a big job and most institutions are not equipped to do it on their own. If a school chooses to throw its hat in the ring, an important success factor is strong executive-level support. A less obvious predictor of success is faculty engagement and readiness, which can be fostered and encouraged with opportunities and incentives to teach with technology beginning with their campus-based courses. This proactive approach also builds collaborative partnerships that ease the instructor's transition to the teamwork involved in distance learning.

It is important to keep an ongoing dialogue with the academic community. The Center for Scholarly Technology publishes a quarterly newsletter with online learning updates, and the university convenes an online learning council made up of directors of online learning and curricular deans both from schools with active programs and schools considering establishing programs.

Finally, the partnership with the vendor goes beyond the business-as-usual relationship. The vendor's staff are agents of the university and represent themselves as university employees whether they are recruiting prospective students or resolving technology issues on a Help Desk call. It is essential that the institution partner with a company that it trusts, respects, and is comfortable working with over the many years of the contract and beyond.

Additional Resources

- USCNow: http://uscnow.usc.edu/
- USC Center for Scholarly Technology: http://cst.usc.edu
- 2tor: http://2tor.com
- EmbanetCompass: http://www.embanet.com
- Deltak: http://www.deltak-innovation.com
- The Learning House: http://www.learninghouse.com
- Bisk Education: http://www.bisk.com/about-bisk-education
- Colloquy: http://www.colloquy360.com
- SunGard Higher Education's Online Learning Services: http://www.sungardhe.com/Solutions/Online-Learning-Services
- Pearson eCollege: http://www.ecollege.com
- The New York Times Knowledge Network: http://www.nytimesknownow.com
- Educators Serving Educators (ESE): http://www.eseserves.org

Susan E. Metros *is Associate Vice Provost and Associate CIO for Technology Enhanced Learning at the University of Southern California. She holds faculty appointments in design, education, and communications. Her research focuses on leadership, visual and multimedia literacy, and the role technology plays in transforming education to be interactive and learner-driven.* **Joan Falkenberg Getman** *is Director for Educational Technologies and the Center for Scholarly Technology (CST) at the University of Southern California. Getman's experience includes video production, curriculum development, and evaluation-driven strategic planning. Her research focuses on authentic learning, assessment, and strategies that enable learners to be visual storytellers.*

Case
Studies

Royal Roads University: Using Synchronous Web Conferencing to Maintain Community at a Distance

Mary Burgess

Setting the Context

ROYAL ROADS UNIVERSITY, located in Victoria, British Columbia, was established as a special-purpose institution in 1995 with a mandate to provide applied and professional learning. Academic programs at Royal Roads are designed using a learning-outcomes approach and a blended delivery model consisting of short residencies and online delivery using a variety of learning technologies, including the Moodle Learning Management System and Blackboard Collaborate.

In 2010, the Royal Roads University MBA program embarked on a new way of connecting with students at a distance in sessions called Virtual Experience Labs (VELs). The VELs have had a significant impact on students and faculty in the program, as they enable the use of a team-based, collaborative-learning model and bring to the forefront the professional experience of our adult students—all at a distance using synchronous technologies. The creation and fostering of a learning community is a core pillar of our learning model. In the past, we had only been able to create these robust, intense learning and community-building experiences in our face-to-face residencies. Unfortunately, many prospective students were not able to enroll in the MBA program due to an inability to attend the number of residencies required. Developing learning experiences using synchronous technology has increased access to our programs, and, after some tweaking in the initial stages, both faculty and students are finding the VELs a rewarding and empowering experience.

Rationale

In early 2010, the twenty-four-month MBA program was shortened to eighteen months to improve accessibility to prospective students. Until that time, the program had included 3 three-week residencies; one at the beginning, one in the middle, and one at the end, with twelve-week distance courses delivered mostly asynchronously via Moodle in between the residencies. The residencies included instructional sessions and community-building activities to help strengthen the bond students felt with each other, with faculty, and with the institution. On a twenty-four-month cycle, the number and length of residencies was difficult but doable for students. When the program was compressed, however, many prospects did not ultimately enter the program because taking that amount of time away from work and family over eighteen months rather than twenty-four was not something they could accommodate.

A solution that maintained the vital link built during face-to-face sessions but that enabled enrollment was sought. Key to that solution was an increase in student access to the MBA program without compromising our core learning model, which focuses heavily on the fostering of a vibrant and supportive learning community.

In response to the problem being faced by the MBA program and similar issues being experienced by other programs at the institution, the Royal Roads University Centre for Teaching and Educational Technologies wrote a thought piece entitled "Rethinking Residencies." The paper offered alternatives to face-to-face residencies, including doing them online using synchronous tools.

Concurrently, a license for what was then Elluminate Web Conferencing System (now Blackboard Collaborate) was being procured for Royal Roads.

The pieces were in place to give something new a try!

Description of the Virtual Experience Labs

The Virtual Experience Labs were created to ensure the continual fostering of the learning community, so they are not content driven.

There are two types of delivery for the VELs. One uses a half-day conference model to allow students to present to their peers on a topic in their field of expertise, and one facilitates collaboration and connection related to a capstone project called the Organizational Management Project (OMP).

The conference model, facilitated by MBA instructor Amy Zidulka, provides a forum for students to practice presenting content and receiving feedback from their peers and faculty. The average age of students in the program is forty-one, and they typically have at least seven years' experience in their field. This model provides a golden opportunity for students to learn from each other as well as from their instructor. During the VEL, presenting students moderate Blackboard Collaborate sessions within breakout rooms, and their peers provide them with feedback, including a vote of "Best in Conference," which takes place at the end of the day. The instructor also provides feedback to the students.

The OMP model, facilitated by MBA instructor Don Caplan, is focused on ensuring that students working on their capstone projects have the support they need, both from faculty and peers. Potential for attrition at this point in the program is at its highest, so continuing to foster the learning community is key to the successful completion of the projects and ultimately the program. In these sessions, content is presented using uploaded slides; students then break into groups to discuss their research questions, methodology, and proposals and to provide each other with feedback. Depending on where in the research process students are, the instructor also brings in experts; at one stage, a librarian is brought in to field questions; at another, an expert in ethical reviews and research methods joins in. Tools such as polls are used to gauge topics of interest, and external video is also utilized as additional content.

Is It Working?

Following the VELs, students fill out an online survey and are asked specifically, "Do you feel more connected?" The response has been overwhelmingly yes. This indicates that the goal of maintaining the learning community has at least in part been met. Although a cohort has not yet graduated who has gone through this model, early signs point to positive results.

Challenges

Ongoing problems with the technology continue to drive a need for improvement. Because issues can stem from such a variety of sources—the headset being used by a participant, the bandwidth available to another, upgrades to software that require new learning, just to name a few—it's unlikely the VELs will ever be akin to physically being in a room together. Thus, managing expectations becomes one of the challenges. In addition, the early stages of this initiative were not well resourced. Innovation is messy and teaches lessons at every step. For instance, we are now aware of the difficulties for faculty members managing a synchronous online classroom of fifty students while dealing with technology at the same time. A technical-support person is now in the room with the faculty member at all times, providing much-needed relief from the back channel of the chat room and instead affording the faculty member the ability to focus solely on facilitating learning.

Applicability to Others

Other institutions using a distance-delivery method could certainly make use of this technology and the community-building model. In our experience, students in the program find the continual focus on the learning community helps keep them connected, and thus the tendency for the distance student to become isolated is significantly reduced. Expert facilitation, of course, must accompany appropriate learning technologies in order to ensure a positive experience.

Conclusion

Incremental improvements are continuing, and the overall feeling is that the goal of maintaining the learning community when students are at a distance is being met.

Mary Burgess *has been working in the IT sector for fourteen years. She is currently the Director of the Centre for Teaching and Educational Technologies at Royal Roads University. Burgess holds a B.A. in Liberal Studies, a Certificate in the Applied Management of Information Technologies, and an M.Ed. in Learning Technologies.*

The Open Course Library of the Washington State Colleges

Tom Caswell

THIS CASE STUDY describes an initiative of the Washington State community and technical colleges called the Open Course Library (OCL). The Open Course Library is a large-scale curriculum redesign effort leveraging a variety of existing open educational resources (OER) as well as original content by our faculty course designers. Our state agency invested in the development of educational content and requires that the resulting digital course materials be shared under a Creative Commons open license. This case study begins with background on our college system, our Strategic Technology Plan, and the formal adoption of an open licensing policy.

The State Board for Community and Technical Colleges (SBCTC) is an organization that provides leadership and coordination for Washington's public system of thirty-four community and technical colleges. Based on the 2009–10 Annual Enrollment Report, the number of students attending our colleges is 470,000 and climbing. This is the highest enrollment level in SBCTC history, with most of the increase due to growth in e-learning—more students are able to fit school into their busy schedules by attending hybrid and fully online classes.

In 2008, SBCTC released its Strategic Technology Plan to provide clear policy direction around a single goal: mobilizing technology to increase student success. One of the guiding principles of the plan is to "cultivate the culture and practice of using and contributing to open educational resources." With a clear plan in place, our next step was to provide opportunities, incentives, and policies to promote OER in our system. On June 17, 2010, SBCTC's nine-member board unanimously approved the first state-level open licensing policy. It requires that all digital works created from competitive grants administered through SBCTC carry a Creative Commons Attribution-only (CC BY) license.

This license allows educational materials created by one college to be used or updated by another college in our system as well as by other education partners globally. Allowing the free flow of all educational content produced by SBCTC competitive grant funds is an efficient way to participate in the OER movement while maintaining a focus on the specific needs of Washington's community and technical college students.

Building on the Strategic Technology Plan, eLearning director Cable Green launched the Open Course Library in 2010, an initiative to design and openly share eighty-one high-enrollment, gatekeeper, and precollege courses. The goals of the OCL project include

- lowering textbook costs for students,
- providing new resources for faculty to use in their courses, and
- fully engaging in the global open educational resources discussion.

OCL participants are selected through a competitive grant-proposal process. Each winning faculty member or team of faculty designs one course. Each of the eighty-one course teams is directly supported by a librarian, two instructional designers, and an eLearning director. All teams receive additional support from two institutional researchers, two accessibility specialists, and a multicultural expert.

Open Course Library development will occur in two phases. The first forty-two courses developed in Phase 1 were released in fall 2011 and are available at http://opencourselibrary.org. In the first four months the site has received over 25,000 visits from 125 different countries. The remaining courses will be designed in Phase 2 and completed by early 2013. Each phase is spread over four college quarters. In Phase 1, the first two quarters (summer/fall 2010) were spent designing course objectives, finding appropriate OER content, and creating assessments that aligned with the content. Faculty course designers worked closely with their assigned instructional designers (IDs) during this time to ensure that assignments and assessments are tied to course objectives. Faculty pilot taught their newly designed college course during the third quarter (winter 2011). They used feedback from two peer reviews and the course pilot to make updates to the course during the fourth quarter (spring 2011). Phase 2 will follow the same, four-quarter time line and will benefit from lessons learned in Phase 1.

It is important to emphasize that SBCTC will not mandate the use of Open Course Library materials within the Washington State colleges. While faculty course designers are asked to adopt the courses they have designed, adoption by other faculty is optional.

Another important consideration is how we will share the eighty-one OCL courses. Internal sharing is currently done through our existing WashingtonOnline learning management system. We will include a copy of the full course as a system-shared course so it can be viewed and copied by faculty at any of our thirty-four colleges. We are also exploring the use of Google Docs to make copying and modifying OCL course materials even easier. For external sharing, we have partnered with the Saylor Foundation, the Connexions Consortium, and the Open Courseware Consortium. At http://www.saylor.org/sbctc-saylor-courses/, visitors can search and view OCL course content adapted for self-learners. Because our course materials are openly licensed, anyone will be able to access, modify, adapt, translate, and improve them.

As student advocacy groups continue to make textbook affordability a top priority in Washington State—as well as nationally—the Open Course Library stands as a clear response to that call. The cost of making a million digital copies of an open textbook is essentially the same as the cost of the first copy. Print-on-demand solutions are making paper copies very affordable as well—often under $10.

Student feedback from the forty-two pilot courses was positive. Sixty-two percent of students surveyed stated they learned more from open materials. Eighty percent of students rated the redesigned content as either "good" or "excellent" on a five-point scale. In addition to this positive student-survey feedback, we were not surprised to learn that students were grateful they didn't have to pay $200 for a textbook.

Beyond the content-development process, we seek to expand our system-wide culture of open content sharing. Future challenges include

- driving awareness and adoption of Open Course Library materials; and
- creating a sustainable model for faculty to use to revise and update versions of OCL courses, as well as to add new courses.

We are working through a variety of channels to raise faculty awareness of OCL, including our new faculty institutes, faculty trainings, regional conferences, and workshops.

We will continue to seek technologies to support and simplify open sharing of learning content among faculty. Whenever possible, we will use existing workflows. For example, we have introduced lecture-capture software that makes it easy to record and share lectures or portions of lectures. These recordings can be made public and shared widely with just a few clicks. Another step we are taking will facilitate open sharing for faculty who use our system-wide learning management system (LMS). We have also included an open publishing feature requirement in our upcoming LMS search. Faculty will be able to attach a Creative Commons license and share their course content directly on the open web if they choose. This kind of sharing will likely attract prospective students and alumni alike, allowing them to preview and also review materials from open courses.

The Open Course Library is a significant step for our system as we strive to establish efficiencies and encourage a culture of open sharing in Washington's colleges. By sharing both the content and the process, we make two bold contributions to the open educational resources movement and set Washington State apart as a leader in that movement.

Tom Caswell *is Open Education Policy Associate at the Washington State Board for Community and Technical Colleges (SBCTC). His current projects include running the Open Course Library, piloting a community college Open Learning Initiative in Washington, and supporting the OPEN initiative for Department of Labor C3T grantees. Previously, Caswell was Strategic Outreach Manager for the OpenCourseWare Consortium.*

Austin Peay State University: Degree Compass

Tristan Denley

STUDENTS ENTERING HIGHER EDUCATION face the sometimes daunting task of navigating their way through a degree program. Confronted with a wide array of course options that could satisfy degree requirements, which is the best way to success? In what order should the courses be taken? Course descriptions often give few clues about what the course will entail, containing instead many technical terms that are introduced in the course itself. Advisors are well equipped to provide valuable advice in their own field. But most programs require students to take courses from across the full spectrum of the university, and advisors find themselves challenged to offer useful advice in disciplines far from their own.

All of this assumes that the student has chosen a major that is a good fit. In fact, a sizable proportion of students begin their college career undecided or in a major that they later realize is not what they expected. Complete College America recently reported that students on average take up to 20 percent more courses than are needed for graduation—not because of desire for a diverse curriculum, but because they had to rethink their plans several times. In an environment in which time to degree has considerable implications for a student's likelihood of successfully graduating, a semester of extra coursework plays a crucial factor.

What seemed to be needed was a system that could use the perspective of the past to begin a better-informed conversation between student and advisor. This system would allow advisors and students to make plans for future semesters, equipped with data on courses or even majors in which past students with similar programs, grades, and course histories had found success.

Degree Compass System: How It Works

Inspired by recommendation systems implemented by companies such as Netflix, Amazon, and Pandora, Austin Peay State University (APSU), in Clarksville, Tennessee, developed a course-recommendation system called Degree Compass that successfully pairs current students with the courses that best fit their talents and program of study for upcoming semesters. The model combines hundreds of thousands of past students' grades with each particular student's transcript to make individualized recommendations for current students.

This system, in contrast to systems that recommend movies or books, does not depend on which classes students like more than others. Instead, it uses predictive analytics techniques based on grade and enrollment data to rank courses according to factors that measure how well each course might help the student progress through a chosen program. From the courses that apply directly to the student's program of study, the system selects those courses that fit best with the sequence of courses in the student's degree program and are the most central to the university curriculum as a whole (see Figure 1). That ranking is then overlaid with a model that predicts the courses in which the student is most likely to achieve the best grades. Through this method, the system makes its strongest recommendations for courses that are necessary for a student to graduate, that are core to the university curriculum

Figure 1. **Degree Compass**

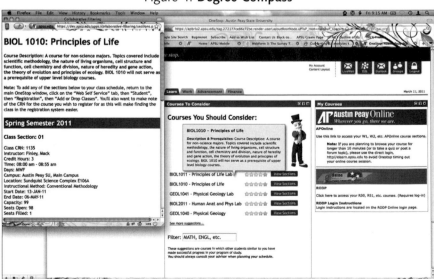

and the student's major, and in which the student is expected to succeed academically.

Each student's recommended course list is conveniently displayed in a web-based interface on the secure side of the university portal. This interactive interface provides information on each recommended course's curriculum and requirements and what role that course plays in the student's degree program, as well as class availability in upcoming semesters. This same information is also available on PeayMobile, the APSU mobile application (see Figure 2). Faculty advisors can access Degree Compass as a tool for academic advising to supplement the material available to faculty members when they provide advice to their advisees.

Degree Compass also provides a number of enterprise-scale reports that provide strategic information to department chairs and advisors. These reports provide data that enable targeted interventions. For instance, one report allows the institution to enhance its Early Alert System at the outset of the semester by using projected course grades to identify students who would benefit from tutoring support or academic mentoring.

Figure 2.
Degree Compass on Mobile Device

Does It Work?

The main factor in student success and progression lies in the system's ability to place students in courses in which they will be most successful. Faculty and students both welcome the additional information and interact comfortably with the interface.

The grade-prediction model provides an accurate estimate of the final grade a student is likely to receive. When the model's predictions are retrospectively compared with real student grades, we found that 90 percent of the time the model correctly predicted courses in which students would achieve a C or better—on average, it was able to successfully predict grades of C or better to within 0.56 of a letter grade. Moreover, when students' actual grades from their semester courses were compared, grades in courses that were recommended averaged 0.46 of a letter grade better than those in courses the system did not recommend to the student.

Challenges Faced

The main challenge with this system was creating a mathematical model to successfully estimate a student's future grades to an acceptable tolerance, based on the student's transcript and the university's legacy grade data. A secondary challenge was designing a system to sequence courses in a natural order, based on both a given major and the university curriculum as a whole. Once these models were designed and tested, the system then had to be taken to full scale, seamlessly interacting with APSU's course management system.

Course selection is crucial to student success, but so too is the choice of major. The APSU team is currently refining a feature that will allow Degree Compass to suggest majors based on each student's academic record and predicted future grades. We hope that this will be implemented at APSU later this spring.

Can It Work Elsewhere?

As APSU explores replicating Degree Compass at other institutions, the challenges of interfacing with other computer systems and adapting to the curriculum structure of other institutions remain to be fully resolved. Recently, the system played a central role in Tennessee's successful Completion Innovation Challenge application, which received a $1,000,000 award from Complete College America and the Bill & Melinda Gates Foundation to support implementation of Degree Compass at three other campuses in Tennessee—one university and two community colleges. Students, advisors, and administrators at these sister institutions in Tennessee will be able to use the system's features in spring 2012 to create schedules for fall 2012.

One of the major challenges in higher education today is to influence student success, progression, and graduation statistics. If we are to meet President Obama's commitment to having the highest proportion of students graduating from college in the world by 2020, we will need to be able meet this challenge. This system is already making an impact at APSU, and the results from the replications to three other campuses this spring will show how effectively it might be a factor on other campuses. It is our hope that in 2012 we will be able to implement Degree Compass at other universities and community colleges across the nation.

Tristan Denley *earned his Ph.D. in Mathematics from Trinity College Cambridge and held positions in Europe and North America before becoming Provost at Austin Peay State University in 2009. His work implements a wide variety of college completion initiatives, spanning pedagogy redesign and the role of predictive analytics and data mining in higher education.*

Yakima Valley Community College: Using Near-Real-Time Data to Increase Student Success

Wilma Dulin, Sheila Delquadri, and Nicole M. Melander

Overview

IN JULY 2006, YAKIMA VALLEY COMMUNITY COLLEGE (YVCC) joined the Achieving the Dream national reform network and began the process of transformation. Over the next four years, YVCC moved from an institution with very limited research capability to one with an Office of Institutional Effectiveness (OIE) dedicated to gathering and analyzing data on student outcomes—and to putting that information in the hands of faculty members.

Initially, YVCC's data analysis focused on course pass rates and sequence completion in English and math. Students who lack proficiency in basic English and math often have difficulty in a wide variety of other courses, and this affects success throughout the college. As the college began to ask questions about success, common data elements needed by all departments were identified. The OIE created a web-based data analysis tool with pivot table functionality that enabled YVCC personnel to access data related to placement, enrollment, and course completion. The data are disaggregated by ethnicity, gender, location, and mode of instruction. Faculty and their department heads use these data to analyze curricular areas, to strategize activities to increase student success, and to help monitor their own progress toward accreditation goals. Data are updated regularly, providing near-real-time information.

Because the data pulled was consistently provided from replicable sources, confidence in the accuracy of this data has increased. Now, data is required before YVCC invests in student-success strategies, including the development of course schedules that are based on course-taking patterns and success rather than just on past enrollments.

Examples

Data on student success have impacted faculty decision making and enrollment management in three different areas at YVCC.

Placement Data Available to Advisors

In 2006–07, YVCC analyzed data on first-quarter and first-year retention and conducted focus groups with students, faculty, staff, and community members on "barriers to success." The most frequently cited barrier was the lack of clear academic guidance.

In spring 2008, YVCC created a new intake process that includes an online orientation to placement testing and a two-hour mandatory "New Student Orientation and Registration" session. Each summer before orientation, the registrar provides the (faculty) advising team with placement data on incoming students. The advisors use the data to determine whether courses available are appropriate given the students' achievement levels. Courses are added or eliminated from the schedule accordingly.

Completion Data Available to Faculty

In any given year at YVCC, more than 50 percent of entering students are required to take developmental English, and more than 85 percent are required to take one or more levels of developmental math. An OIE analysis revealed that students who begin at the lowest levels of math have very low rates of earning quantitative course credits required for degrees. YVCC conducted focus groups with developmental students to redesign developmental courses, and three significant changes were made:

1. The Math Department created four different pathways to courses meeting the quantitative degree requirement, and it also created a new course to help students transition directly into a math pathway—if students do not have the skills to directly enter one of these four pathways, they can take this new course that will enable them to enter one of the four pathways.

2. Faculty members analyzed completion rates in precollege course sequences and determined that proper placement required more than scores from the COMPASS English test. They asked for a writing sample and basic skills tests (Comprehensive Adult Student Assessment Systems) from incoming students to assess proficiency in reading,

math, listening, speaking, and writing in order to place students in one of three levels of English coursework.

3. Student Support Services (SSS) was redesigned in the fall 2010 so that entering students were required to attend a new SSS Student Orientation session and to enroll in their first quarter in an SSS Learning Community.

Correlated Enrollment and Placement Data Available to Faculty

The OIE has conducted numerous analyses of the effectiveness of placement cut scores and prerequisites on student success. For example, a detailed analysis of enrollment data was matched with COMPASS placement data in English and math. It was discovered that success in psychology was significantly correlated with placement into English 101 and Intermediate Algebra. Based on this, a decision was made to add these as prerequisites for Psychology 100.

Results

The results of the strategies described above are summarized in Table 1.

Challenges

YVCC faced a number of challenges. The following have recurred in other initiatives related to the shift to an evidence-based culture.

1. **Faculty Are Not Data Analysts:** Faculty members are experts in their fields of study, yet they have only limited ability to analyze data or understand the difficulty of retrieving information in particular ways. It takes time for faculty members to learn how data are gathered, stored, and reported.

2. **Transparency Is Threatening:** Faculty worry that data will be used for their own evaluation or that certain faculty will be singled out based on results. Policies and procedures are needed to address these concerns.

3. **A Single Version of the Truth:** Data on the same topic (e.g., the same question) may vary from one data source to another due to the timing of the data extract, the cohort of students captured in a

Table 1. **Results of the Three Strategies**

Strategy	Outcome	Measures	Supporting Data
ADVISING New-Student Orientation and Advising	More students enroll in the courses they need and courses they can complete; higher student satisfaction and retention.	Tracked via "Incoming Student Survey" and "Annual Fall Student Survey"; tracked quantitatively via first-quarter and first-year retention.	More than 90 percent of new students reported positive perceptions of the intake process; first-quarter and first-year retention rates both increased 4 percent.
SCHEDULING Precollege Course Design and Management	Significantly more students enroll in precollege math. These students more smoothly transition to credit-bearing courses.	Precollege math enrollment levels.	YVCC hired two additional math instructors in 2010–11 due to increased enrollment.
	More accurate placement for students requiring developmental English.	Placement levels and course completion for precollege English.	20 percent of students place at a higher level of English without a decrease in student success.
	Higher retention of SSS students participating in learning communities.	Enrollment of SSS students in math.	80 percent of first-quarter SSS students enrolled in math compared to 58 percent of matched cohort.
SCHEDULING Placement and Prerequisites	More students succeeding in courses and fewer dropping courses; smoother course enrollment patterns.	Course grades Course drop rates Faculty satisfaction	Completion of "C or better" improved from 64 percent to 75 percent, and course drop rates were cut from 16 percent to 7 percent in Psychology 100.

particular data source, and/or the phrasing of a research question. Protocols and documentation address frustration with these data challenges.

Lessons Learned

In the course of this process, YVCC learned a great deal and came away with the following main lessons:

- **Determine Intent:** Understand the intended use of the data by the faculty member. Communicate data sources, meanings, and limitations. Spend time up front understanding the data requested. Understand what the requestor anticipates the data will reveal.

- **Document Data Sources:** Document data sources, including the actual "pathway" to the data. Archive reports for "look back" capabilities.

- **Develop Data-Governance Policies:** Develop data-access policies and notification protocols. Define data ownership—particularly course-level data owned by faculty.

Wilma Dulin *has been a faculty member at YVCC for twenty-three years. In addition to teaching student development courses aimed at underprepared first-generation college students, she directs the Office of Institutional Effectiveness and serves as the Title V Activity II Diversity co-coordinator. She was co-leader of the initial YVCC Core and Data teams and now convenes the Institutional Effectiveness Team.* **Sheila Delquadri** *has eight years of experience as a data coordinator for a variety of programs, including GEAR UP, Title V, ATD, and other student-success programs. She serves as the research analyst for the Office of Institutional Effectiveness. She was an original member of the Core and Data teams and continues to oversee research design and data collection.* **Nicole M. Melander** *is Chief Technology Officer (CTO) for Achieving the Dream, Inc. (ATD). In this role, she ensures programs are informed and supported by cutting-edge technology. Melander previously worked at Oracle Corporation, Microsoft, and Deloitte Consulting, where she acquired in-depth knowledge of social media, educational technologies, e-business software, and large database systems.*

Ball State University

Jo Ann Gora

USING TECHNOLOGY to take learning beyond the classroom, connecting the traditional classroom to the world, is Ball State University's educational niche. Underlying this approach is the assumption that the best instruction requires leveraging the best technology, but it also necessitates the creation of rich learning experiences that enable students to pull the world to them, irrespective of place.

Immersive learning stands as the centerpiece of Ball State University's current strategic plan, in which interdisciplinary teams work with a faculty mentor as they solve real-world problems and deliver a meaningful product to a business, community, or nonprofit organization. This initiative, enhanced by an emerging media emphasis (http://www.bsu.edu/Academics/Centersand Institutes/EmergingMedia), has included more than 12,000 students participating in at least one of the more than 750 immersive-learning projects since 2007.

Perhaps no other example better illustrates the possibilities for the enhancement of learning through technology than the experience known as Polyark/World Tour in the College of Architecture and Planning. Juniors and seniors in that college take a global tour every other year (http://cms.bsu.edu/ Features/Global/ImmersiveLearning/Polyark). In spring 2010, forty students majoring in architecture, landscape architecture, and urban planning visited twenty-three countries and fifty-six cities including Paris, Madrid, Cairo, Beijing, and Istanbul, led by three of their professors. Dating back to the 1970s, the experience focuses on the development of a rich vocabulary by which students can better contextualize, design, and interpret their surroundings.

During each World Tour, the students have daily assignments in each locale related to the components of theory, design, analysis, and collaboration, which mimic the professional experience. Students continually explore the relationship

---

between culture and the surrounding physical environment, testing their observations both as field researchers and architectural practitioners. However, the *methods* that students use to complete those assignments and share their observations and field study have changed drastically in the last few years.

For many years, students' tools were the sketchbook and notepad, with the occasional use of still photography. The fact that the film had to be developed in order to share the images with other team members was a limitation for completing assignments. Typically, students returned after weeks abroad and gathered their notes, journals, sketches, and photographs, and only then could begin assembling architectural presentations based on their findings. Each student was also required to apply content learned to the development of a proposed project for the student's hometown, which produced another presentation of architectural renderings.

In recent years, the use of technology has revolutionized this process. Students increasingly use today's digital tools, including smartphones, point-and-shoot digital cameras, and laptops to gather their data in the field. These devices are small, lightweight, and versatile, and they also can be used as scanners and recorders to convert field notes to classwork assignments and design projects.

The profusion of Wi-Fi connectivity, even in so-called underdeveloped countries, means that today's Polyark students can upload their findings more frequently and quickly. This enables them to share information with other team members and with their fellow students and faculty back on campus. Additionally, two-dimensional photographs or drawings of polygons can be quickly transformed via software into three-dimensional images, allowing for immediate manipulation. Utilizing digital media allows the student to arrive at solutions much faster than through traditional analog media.

Polyark students develop their work using a combination of analog and digital tools, a necessity as the course takes place in the field and is subject to all the complications of field study, including weather. However, students are required to submit their daily assignment to their faculty in digital form. That classwork is posted to a centralized website from the road in real time. Faculty members review the students' work, relying on digital tools to provide comprehensive feedback to the student and the greater global-tour community.

An additional, immediate connection between those students on the trip and their colleagues back at the university is made possible via a daily blog, housed at the World Tour website, http://www.bsu.edu/worldtour/polyark18/courses/journal.html. Instead of waiting until they return to campus to share their journal notes with classmates, the Polyark students can now do so electronically in real time from halfway around the world.

The various forms of emerging media have changed the course content as well. World Tour faculty organizers now require that students work on two simultaneous projects—one a detailed analysis of a design encountered in one of the cities visited, and one a parallel design to be developed for use in the student's hometown. Obviously, it is much easier to electronically adapt and apply designs when completing these requirements than it was when everything was accomplished with notebook and sketchpad. College of Architecture and Planning faculty are incorporating iPads into next spring's World Tour for use as an all-in-one communication and graphics device, thereby taking this process to the next level.

Using emerging technology to provide students with a fuller, more meaningful academic experience is certainly applicable for other institutions and programs. In fact, the model has spread to several other courses in our College of Architecture and Planning. Every other year, those students and faculty complete a ten-week field study and collaborate on design and planning in southern Asian cities. Called CAP Asia (http://www.bsu.edu/Academics/CollegesandDepartments/CAP/Activities/StudyAbroad/CAPAsia), this program employs many of the same technological breakthroughs to enhance teaching and learning both for students on the trip and for their colleagues on campus.

In addition to CAP Asia, architecture faculty and a team from Ball State's Institute for Digital and Intermedia Arts also were instrumental in developing the Las Americas Virtual Design Studio (http://www.bsu.edu/Academics/CentersandInstitutes/EmergingMedia/Videos/DigFab). This collaborative exchange enabled more than thirty Latin American architecture programs and Ball State to work on an annual common design project. By using a virtual reality program for enhanced collaboration, nearly two hundred students and faculty members developed designs to convert a large Indianapolis hotel into a "surge" medical facility that would treat the wounded in a natural disaster.

The impact of emerging technology on academic experiences is demonstrated in many ways. The College of Architecture and Planning has received numerous national awards, including being named by *Architect* magazine as one of the top three institutions nationally in digital design, a talent honed by the students in Polyark/World Tour. Ball State alumni work for many of the world's leading architectural firms, including HOK, Skidmore, Owings & Merrill, Frank Gehry Partners, and RTKL Associates, and several recent graduates have used their experience in digital design to land that first job. For instance, Tyler Kirages, a 2011 graduate with a bachelor's degree in landscape architecture, now works for the prestigious firm of DTJ and Associates in Boulder, Colorado, in part because of his digital work at Polyark.

For decades, Ball State University students have learned collaboratively, further blurring the lines between traditional faculty and student roles. The emphasis on emerging media across campus enhances these efforts while simultaneously extending their reach. The integration of fieldwork with emerging technologies is a powerful tool that prepares these students with an education that readies them for the knowledge-based, global economy they will experience after graduation.

Jo Ann Gora *became the fourteenth President of Ball State University in August 2004. Under her leadership, the university has dedicated more than $25 million to its emerging media efforts since 2008. In 2009, she earned the Mira Trailblazer Award from TechPoint for her significant and lasting contributions to technology innovation in Indiana.*

Mozilla Open Badges

Erin Knight and Carla Casilli

MOZILLA OPEN BADGES is an initiative exploring alternative ways for learners to receive recognition for skills and achievements gained outside of the school environment, such as open credentialing and accreditation for all types of learning, including informal and interest driven. We are working to build an ecosystem wherein badges can be issued for this learning regardless of where or how it happens. These badges can be carried with the learner and combined to form living transcripts of skills and competencies that tell a more complete story about the user.

What Is a Badge?

A "badge" is a symbol or indicator of an accomplishment, skill, quality, or interest. From the Boy and Girl Scouts to PADI diving instruction, to the more recently popular geolocation game Foursquare, badges have been successfully used to set goals, motivate behaviors, represent achievements, and communicate success in many contexts. We are exploring the use of digital badges—online representations and records of achievements and skills—for learning contexts.

Need for New Kinds of Learning

In today's world, learning can look very different from how it was traditionally imagined. Learning has evolved from simple "seat time" within schools to extend across multiple contexts, experiences, and interactions. It is no longer just an isolated or individual concept, but is instead inclusive, social, informal, participatory, creative, and lifelong. It's no longer sufficient to think of learners simply as consumers—now they are active participants and producers in an interest-driven learning process. A "learning environment" no longer means just a single classroom or online space, but instead encompasses many spaces in broader, networked, distributed, and extensible environments that span time and space. And across these learning environments, learners are offered multiple pathways to gain competencies and refine skills through open, remixable, and transparent tools, resources, and processes. In this connected learning ecology,[1] the boundaries and walls are broken down, expanding the potential learning landscape for each learner.

Much of this shift is due to the fact that our world is very different than the one in which the current education system was developed and standardized. With the advent of the web and its core principles of openness, universality, and transparency, the ways that knowledge is made, shared, and valued have been transformed, and the opportunities for deeper and richer learning have been vastly expanded. By enabling increased access to information and each other, the open web has provided an effective platform for new ways to learn and new skills to achieve.

And yet in the current formal education and accreditation systems, much of this learning goes undetected and unrecognized. Institutions still decide what narrow types of learning "count," as well as who has access to that learning. We know that lecture-based learning and multiple-choice exams represent a tiny fraction of what we learn during our lives, and yet these are the types of learning that are formally recognized and overwhelmingly required for advancement. Without a dependable, recognized way to capture, promote, and transfer all of the learning that occurs within this new, more broadly connected learning ecology, we limit that ecology by discouraging self-driven engaged learning, isolating or ignoring quality efforts and interactions and ultimately preventing learners from reaching their full potential.

Badges can play a crucial role in the connected learning ecology by acting as a bridge between contexts, making these alternative learning channels and types of learning more viable, portable, and impactful. Badges can be awarded for a potentially limitless set of individual skills—regardless of where each skill is developed—and a collection of badges can begin to serve as a virtual résumé of competencies and qualities for key stakeholders, including peers, schools, or potential employers. Specifically, badges support capturing and communicating learning paths, signaling achievement, motivating learning, and driving innovation and flexibility, as well as building identity, reputation, and kinship. Thus, badges can provide a way to translate all types of learning into a powerful tool for getting jobs, finding communities of practice, demonstrating skills, and seeking out further learning.

Figure 1. **Mozilla Open Badge Infrastructure**

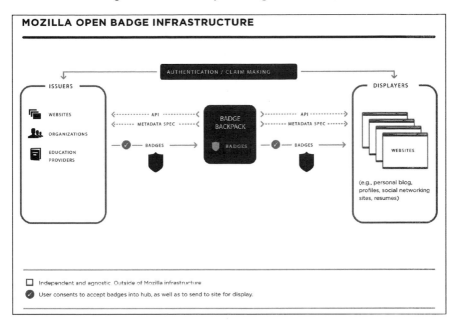

The Open Badges Approach

To contribute to and support this important and still-incipient ecosystem, the Mozilla Open Badges initiative is both developing badge systems for Mozilla and affiliate programs, as well as building the core infrastructure to support the ecosystem (see Figure 1).

The initial badge system developed was for the School of Webcraft, a partnership between Mozilla and Peer 2 Peer University (P2PU), offering free peer-learning courses and study groups on web-developer training. We designed a pilot that consisted of fourteen badges, including hard-skill badges such as *JavaScript*, value badges such as Accessibility, social or peer badges such as Good Collaborator, and participation badges such as Active Responder and Peer Editor.[2] The goal was to use badges to capture hard and soft skills that are important for web developers, as well as to guide community-beneficial behavior. We also implemented various approaches to assessment that reflected the nature of the community and learning experiences that were occurring. All hard skills were assessed through authentic challenges that immersed learners in the technology or allowed them to use existing work, and submitted work was either peer assessed for basic-level skills, or "guru" or "has-the-badge" assessed for expert level. Peer assessment was a critical part of the pilot since P2PU is built around peer learning and because web development is such a social discipline. Peer badges were also built around the peer-to-peer interactions and were awarded directly from one peer to another. Finally, participation badges were based on stealth assessment and data-tracking logic built into the learning environment. While the sample size was small due to constraints of the course cycles, the pilot resulted in a solid proof-of-concept of the potential for badges and these approaches to assessment. Learners liked the experience and reported seeking out specific learning opportunities in order to earn badges, as well as learning through the peer-assessment process (their only main complaint was that they wanted more badges). They also used badges to find mentors and to better understand their role in the community. We are currently building on this pilot to include more badges and expand the notion of challenge-based assessments. We are also working to build a Mozilla core set of web-literacy badges that will be rolled out through School of Webcraft as well as other learning platforms.

The other piece of the Open Badges initiative is the ecosystem infrastructure. The Open Badge Infrastructure (OBI) will provide the underlying open technology and standardization to support badge issuers and badge displayers, while also providing a repository for badge collection and management for each learner. The OBI includes a badge metadata specification, which defines what information must be included with a badge when issuers push badges in and displayers pull badges out. This specification ensures that each badge will carry with it all the information needed to understand that badge throughout the ecosystem. Information such as issuer, issue date, expiration date, and badge criteria are embedded within each badge—each badge thus becomes not just an image, but instead is a gateway to the evidence and value information behind the badge. The OBI also includes the Badge Backpacks, which are personal badge repositories for each learner. As learners earn badges from an array of issuers and across skill types, those badges are then collected into their Badge Backpack, where the learner can combine and manage the badges, set privacy controls, and share badges with displayer sites and organizations. OBI, then, supports learning across a multitude of issuers in the ecosystem and allows learners to translate the value of that learning into real results such as jobs, credits, or other kinds of advancement.

For more on the Open Badges initiative, see http://openbadges.org.

Evidence of Effectiveness

From our work with a broad set of other organizations, educators, developers, and researchers to test this brand-new experiment, it has become clear to us that learning is happening everywhere—not just within formal accreditation systems—and that a great deal of this learning is currently unrecognized. Our conversations with employers have revealed that they are looking for a new, more granular evidence-based system to help them better vet employees and understand their skill sets, particularly their social skills. Our pilot efforts have demonstrated that badges can motivate learning and build reputation within communities. And, the combination of overwhelming demand and positive feedback we have received tells us that there is interest in exploring this initiative further. Still, while there is a great deal of evidence pointing toward the potential success of these efforts, we are still very much in the early building stages. This is ultimately not a Mozilla-only project, but a much wider community project, and it will rely heavily on this wider community for success.

There are many unanswered questions and challenges to be confronted. Most of these will have to be tackled through the exploration process—by being as open and transparent as we can about our own work, assumptions, research and findings, and so forth.

This effort is about building an ecosystem. We are providing the infrastructure and one example of a badge system. Ideally, many learning institutions and providers will become part of this ecosystem by building their own badge systems. Because our aim is to support learners wherever and however they are learning, we believe that the more organizations, groups, and individuals that participate in the ecosystem, the better.

Notes

1. Our approach to badges aligns with the principles of "connected learning" being defined by the MacArthur Foundation's Digital Media and Learning Initiative. "Connected learning" is (1) participatory, demanding active social engagement and contribution in knowledge communities and collectives; (2) learner centered, empowering individuals of all ages to take ownership of their learning linked across a wide range of settings—in school, at home, and informally with friends and peers; (3) interest driven, propelled by the energies of learners pursuing their unique passions and specialties; and (4) inclusive, drawing in people from diverse backgrounds and walks of life across generational, socioeconomic, and cultural boundaries.
2. The pilot environment can be accessed through http://badges.p2pu.org.

Erin Knight *currently spearheads the learning and badge work at Mozilla, overseeing the building of learning pathways for webmaker skills, as well as the development of the Open Badge Infrastructure. She lives in Portland, Maine, with her husband, new baby son, and two chocolate labs.* **Carla Casilli** *leads Mozilla's Open Badge Infrastructure project and acts as the liaison to Mozilla's Learning Group. She oversees communication outreach efforts and strategizes on badge assessment, implementation, and application. Casilli has an M.A. in media psychology and social change and a B.F.A. in graphic design and writing.*

STAR: Using Technology to Enhance the Academic Journey

Erika Lacro and Gary Rodwell

Introduction

INCORPORATING TECHNOLOGY INTO EDUCATION continues to be at the forefront of research focused on improving student success. As the nation struggles with getting more students educated and prepared for work, institutions are attempting to combine and integrate technologies that successfully support student learning and success. A large portion of technology adoption has focused on the classroom support of students in their learning, such as the emporium model and classroom online assessments. Other uses of technology have concentrated on information dissemination and advising/degree attainment support for students.

The STAR Academic Journey

In 2005, the University of Hawaii at Manoa, the largest of the ten-campus University of Hawaii (UH) system, embarked on the development of a cross-institution, online advising/degree attainment support system called the "STAR Academic Journey," knowing that the future of higher education growth (i.e., enrollment) within four-year institutions would most probably not come from high school graduates but from transfer students from community colleges, coupled with the tenet that while the United States has excelled at providing access to higher education, especially at the community college level, we have not fared as well with ensuring college retention and completion.

Hence the need to design a real-time "academic journey system" that could span all of the campuses within the UH system with the express goals of

- engaging students in real time as they are making course choices and helping them to understand the effect of their choices on the degree program they are currently pursuing, including future aspirations irrespective of the UH institution(s) at which they are taking the course(s);

- allowing students to see in real time what courses they could take at any UH campus that would meet a "particular degree requirement" at their home institution and then "dragging and dropping them" into their academic plan;

- increasing retention rates by contacting advisors and letting them know which students are most off-track with the courses they are taking and the degree requirements (combined with leading indicators in the future);

- increasing transfers from community colleges to four-year institutions by letting students know not only how far along they are with their community college degree but also how far along they are with a four-year degree should they choose to carry on to a four-year campus (in addition to allowing students to do a "what if" for any degree at any campus);

- providing a tool that aids unit understanding of the demand for students' courses so that they can then plan accordingly (not just based on students in their major);

- allowing struggling students to automatically transfer credits from the four-year institution back to the community colleges so that they may be eligible for a community college degree when they would have otherwise dropped out without any degree;

- decreasing the time to graduation and increasing graduation rates, thereby decreasing the burden of the cost on the student, state, and the federal financial aid support programs, while ensuring no decrease in the quality of the education;

- creating a symbiotic relationship between advising and counseling staff, allowing advisors to engage the students in deeper conversations and enabling the mechanics of getting the degree program to the academic journey software;

- ensuring a simple and highly automated technical process for entering "degree rules" (what courses fulfill a requirement) that requires a maximum of one to two full-time employees entering in the rules for all ten campuses and 60,000 students;

- being able to process up to a maximum of one hundred hits per second (twenty hits per second, steady state) with a turnaround of 5 seconds, so that all 60,000 students could be processed in less than one hour; and

- technically functioning as an "intelligent cloud," thereby reducing required technical staff to two full-time employees and ten student helpers.

Six years later, students have flocked to the STAR system, which receives almost a million hits a semester—an average of about fifteen hits per semester by a student. Faculty and staff absorption rates have not been as stratospheric.

Other Features

Utilizing learner analytics and data mining of student trends, the STAR system is just at the tip of the iceberg of uncovering how this intelligence can help guide students. For example, the "Giving Tree" feature in STAR lets students know of scholarship opportunities (based on intelligent mining of the student and scholarship criteria).

Future Developments

The mission of the STAR project now includes a number of future developments. Capitalizing on learner analytics, other planned enhancements to STAR include development of a one-stop shop for students across a specific region, such as those belonging to the Western Interstate Commission for Higher Education (WICHE). This would allow students from other states to explore degree paths and transfer options across regions. A current initiative under way by the Western Alliance of Community College Academic Leaders (WACCAL) is working to establish a western states "core requirements" agreement. Students could potentially explore how their credits earned would apply to other degrees at other colleges and build a road map for on-time completion. In addition, serving as a one-stop shop, STAR could provide resources on scholarship options, online tutoring resources, and social networking interfaces, allowing students to further explore and make better-informed decisions.

Other features in the development phase include social networking interfaces that would be accessed through STAR. Online tutoring resources are in place and will be positioned as a separate module through STAR, thus making

Figure 1. **STAR CIP Model**

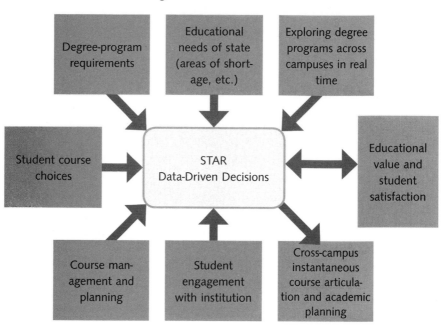

STAR the primary portal for students. Once these activities are launched, decision makers will have the ability to monitor and evaluate the use and success of the social networking activities.

The STAR Model and Continuous Improvement Process

The STAR Continuous Improvement Process (CIP) model (see Figure 1) identifies the inputs necessary to achieve student success and the long-term educational value to graduates. STAR has the ability to provide intelligent data sets that will assist college administrators in decision making related to course scheduling and in identifying trends.

Key to the success of this unique product is the constant engagement of students. Student surveys of user satisfaction are routinely employed to gauge feedback and to identify areas for improvement. The sustainability of the STAR improvements is based upon student programmers. Having students involved in the programming of the product not only benefits their financial status but also allows for important student feedback into the needed modules or features available in STAR.

Conclusion

STAR is a proven, enterprise-level software program developed by the University of Hawaii that addresses the implementation of software academic advisory tools that engage students by offering them "borderless" access to web-based, accurate information about course registration, automatic admission and reverse-transfer policies, scholarships, and social networking. Students entering college are more technologically savvy than ever. They expect dynamic, integrated systems available 24/7 to assist them through their academic endeavors, providing information-rich guidance. The University of Hawaii, specifically, has found this system to be an excellent tool for students and an important continuous improvement model. With a goal of increasing degrees and certificates awarded by 25 percent by 2015, the STAR tools improve student access to information while tracking and evaluating student patterns and utilizing data for decision making.

Erika Lacro *is Vice-Chancellor for Academic Affairs at Honolulu Community College. She joined the University of Hawaii at Manoa in 2001 and transitioned to Honolulu Community College in 2007. Previously, Lacro worked in several management positions in the Hawaii hotel industry. She holds bachelor's and master's in Travel Industry Management and is pursuing her Ph.D. in Communication and Information Sciences.* **Gary Rodwell** *is the director of Academic Technology for the Office of the Assistant Vice Chancellor for Undergraduate Education, the STAR Academic Journey architect, and lead programmer. He works collaboratively with students, academic programs, and the administration to develop broad technology-based resources, ensuring consistent application of the campus-wide strategic vision, initiatives, and academic policies, while adhering rigorously to a management methodology of knowledge sharing, transparency, and accountability.*

OpenCourseWare

Mary Lou Forward

OPENCOURSEWARE (OCW) and open educational resources (OER) are based on the simple yet powerful idea that free and open sharing in education can drive improvements in teaching and learning around the world. Sharing this common assumption, OCW, OER, and open education in general are proliferating.

Development of the OCW Movement

In 2000, when online distance-education programs were proliferating, a faculty committee at the Massachusetts Institute of Technology (MIT) recommended that MIT use the Internet not for paid educational programs, but to share all its classroom-based educational resources with the rest of the world for free, using an open license similar to that used by the open and free software movement. The scale of this institutional commitment—to openly share resources of its full curriculum—had never been made before.[1]

Other universities began to see the power of open sharing and began to share their own courses. To support this growing movement, the OCW Consortium was formed in 2005 (http://www.ocwconsortium.org). The consortium works to coordinate and support those who use, produce, and innovate with OCW and OER around the world.

OCW Users

Initially it was thought that OCW would primarily be a resource for faculty to exchange ideas and course materials. It quickly became apparent, however, that OCW supports formal and informal learning. Millions of people worldwide are now accessing high-quality educational materials for a variety of reasons, creating impacts well beyond the envisioned sharing of materials among faculty.

OCW content is freely and openly available and often hosted in multiple ways (on a university's OCW server, in repositories, through content providers, etc.). This presents challenges to collecting information about who is using OCW. Voluntary surveys of users are now being conducted more regularly by OCW projects. These survey results present interesting snapshots of the global audience for OCW and the ways it is being used. For example, surveys conducted in 2011 by the OCW Consortium and Education-Portal.com show that a significant percentage of users are not currently involved in formal education as faculty or students (see Figures 1 and 2).

An interesting difference in the audience for these surveys offers more information about general awareness of OER. The OCW Consortium site mainly attracts people who are looking for OER (see Figure 3), while the Education-Portal.com site attracts those who are looking for information on free courses. Responses on the use of OCW clearly show this difference, as a high percentage of respondents from the Education-Portal.com survey have never heard of OCW or have never used OCW (see Figure 4). Among those who have used OCW, more respondents said they use it to improve knowledge and skills for work than use it to help with formal studies. This could have interesting implications for workforce-development education.[2]

A survey of users of translated OCW materials by researchers at the University of Illinois at Urbana–Champaign revealed similar results. The Opensource Opencourseware Prototype System (http://www.myoops.org) has coordinated the translation of over 1,600 OCW courses into traditional and simplified Chinese. When asked to select all reasons for using these materials, 68.2 percent of respondents selected "to extend my professional knowledge," 62.8 percent selected "to increase knowledge of personal interests," 31.4 percent responded "to answer questions related to my profession," and 25.9 percent responded "for academic studies."[3] Other surveys from OCW projects around the world show similar user profiles.[4]

Impact of OCW

OCW for Professional Development

In California, teachers of single subjects at the middle- and high-school levels are required to show competency either by completing an approved preparation program or by passing the appropriate single-subject California

Figure 1. **Occupation of Survey Respondents—OCW Consortium**

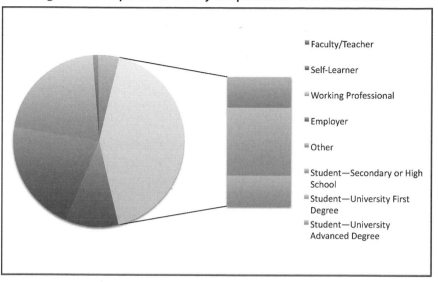

Figure 2. **Occupation of Survey Respondents—Education-Portal.com**

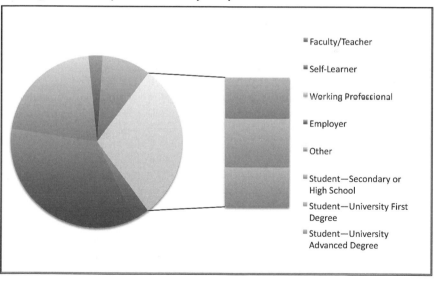

Subject Examination for Teachers (CSET). To assist practicing teachers in obtaining this credential, the University of California–Irvine (UCI) created preparation resources for CSET subject areas, available to anyone via its OCW site (http://ocw.uci.edu/collections/index.aspx). Beginning in October 2011, it

Figure 3. **Uses of OCW—OCW Consortium Survey Results (respondents could select multiple uses)**

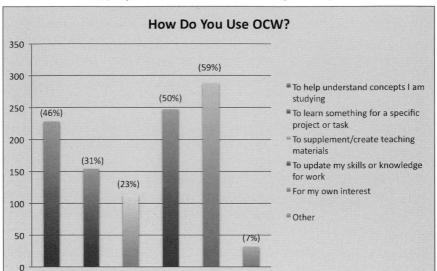

Figure 4. **Uses of OCW—Education-Portal.com Survey Results (respondents could select multiple uses)**

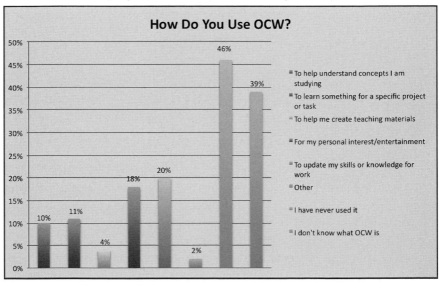

offered teachers the opportunity to join a peer-run study group based on these materials.

Among the users of UCI's CSET preparation resources was Charles Reynes, an experienced educator seeking additional credentials. He said, "I am a 2007 California Teacher of the Year and a recipient of the 2008 Presidential Award for Excellence in Math and Science Teaching, yet I do not hold a degree in science. In order to supplement my multiple-subject credential with a Foundational Level Credential, I decided to take the CSET science tests, 118 and 119. This website was an invaluable study tool. I worked through every lesson and passed both exams on my first try. Anyone wishing to pass the CSET exam would do well to work through this fabulous online program."[5]

The African Virtual University (AVU) provided professional development through the creation and use of OCW. With the objective of developing a Pan-African teacher education program in mathematics, science, and ICT, AVU brought together 12 universities, 146 authors, and peer reviewers from 10 countries to develop curricula for bachelor of education programs in five subjects. Working in collaborative teams across institutions and languages, participants developed seventy-three modules, all of which are openly available in French, Portuguese, and English on AVU's portal (http://www.avu.org). AVU has recently received funding to develop more resources using this model. Through this strategy, AVU is using the collaborative development of OER to address identified needs and drive professional development for both the creators and users.

OCW for Educators

Educators use OCW to get materials and ideas for their teaching, as was originally envisioned. One example of this is James Wixson, an advisory engineer in systems engineering at the Idaho National Laboratories and affiliate instructor for the University of Idaho. In designing a new course on product development, he performed research that led him to MIT's OCW course 15.783J—Product Design and Development (http://ocw.mit.edu). Since the materials were openly licensed, Wixson used them as the basis for his course design, making modifications that reflected his own interests and background. The resulting new course was openly shared via Wixson's university web page.[6]

OCW has led to new collaborations among educators who previously were unknown to each other. Delft University of Technology (TU Delft) in the Netherlands has a very strong water management/water engineering program. OCW courses in the program include videos of lectures and written course materials (see http://ocw.tudelft.nl). Fundamental theories of water treatment are fixed, but examples of how these theories apply to different locations around the world can vary greatly. Faculty from the Institut Teknologi Bandung (Indonesia), Tshwane University of Technology (South Africa), and the National University of Singapore are partnering with water management faculty from TU Delft to adapt the OCW courses to their local situations. Taking the OCW video lectures and accompanying material as the basis for introducing theory, new examples from local waterways and water management needs are being incorporated to enrich the curriculum and make it relevant to different situations. These new examples allow students access to real, problem-based challenges that will broaden their understanding of the scope of water management globally. By sharing the common core of theoretical videos and materials, faculty are able to concentrate their teaching time on engaging students in problem solving and ensuring they have full understanding of concepts.[7]

Supporting Learning through OER

As the value of OER and OCW for both formal and nonformal learning became more apparent, developing support for learners was a logical next step. Several interesting models have emerged. Some, such as NIXTY (http://www.nixty.com), are built around a learning management system that functions similarly to platforms students use at many higher education institutions. Others, such as OpenStudy (http://openstudy.com), use a virtual-peer study-group model, organizing study groups around broad content areas or specific OCW courses. Learners can ask questions on the topic, either based on their own studies or on OCW materials, to which peers and volunteer mentors provide responses. Peer 2 Peer University (http://www.p2pu.org) has a learning platform based on peer support for learning, offering some courses that incorporate challenges and peer reviews as a means to build knowledge and skills. While individuals can propose courses or study groups, many universities are also using these and other platforms as a means to add value to their OCW materials for independent learners.

Learners are also organizing themselves. In China, several Internet portal companies have developed open education channels, providing OCW materials produced by Chinese universities, translating OER into Chinese, and captioning openly licensed videos with Chinese subtitles. One of the largest providers of open content in China, NetEase (http://open.163.com), has over five thousand videos available, with another nine hundred in production. Its open education channel attracts more than one million unique visitors daily. One user of NetEase's site began to microblog about the open videos she was viewing. Within six weeks, she had three thousand followers interacting on the content. They organized a series, continuously working on different videos, and she invited people to submit reflection papers based on their learning. She sent out small gifts to the authors of the papers she liked best. This spontaneous study group had no formal affiliation, was organized and run completely by the learners, and offered incentives at its own expense.[8]

Challenges

MIT first announced its OCW program in April 2001. The growth of OCW worldwide in the ten years since that announcement has been quite dramatic. While there have been many successes, there remain several important challenges. The first decade of OCW focused primarily on content creation by encouraging faculty and universities to share their educational materials with the world. A sufficient breadth and depth of materials were needed as building blocks for the improvements in teaching and learning that this sharing was expected to bring. Content creation was largely up to each contributor, with no master plan in place for soliciting contributions in particular areas.[9] Intentional creation of OCW and OER to fill in the gaps is needed, which requires a thorough inventory of existing available resources. This in turn can lead to curricular pathways for learners, such as those laid out for students in formal education programs.[10]

The movement also faces challenges in helping users find and use appropriate material. OCW and OER are not categorized under a common subject-area classification protocol; rather, each author, producer, or collection of material classifies content independently. There is no single repository for OER—it is hosted on different platforms and by different services. This makes it difficult for teachers and learners to find OCW and OER through general search engines. People searching for OCW must have at least some idea of where to start looking in order to be successful. Making OER easier to find would result in its being more usable by more people.

Another important challenge to the movement is demonstrability of its impact. Since OCW can be accessed without a login on the majority of sites, it is very difficult to know who is using it and for what purpose. The reliance on the completion of voluntary surveys does not necessarily ensure a representative sample of users. Website analytics can provide an indication of numbers of visitors, time spent on websites, and geographic origin of hits, but do not give the full picture of impact. As more learner tools are developed that require logins for meaningful implementation (such as study groups), we may gain insight into the ways OCW and OER are supporting teaching and learning, which in turn can drive improvements to both tools and content.

Future Directions

Emerging projects have exciting implications for the future of OER and OCW. Several different organizations and projects are working on video capture, rapid transcription of videos, and improvements in automatic translation programs.[11] Other projects, such as the Flexible Learning for Open Education project (http://floeproject.org), are focusing on ensuring that materials are accessible to people with disabilities and that they support learners with different learning preferences.

Awareness-raising campaigns, such as Open Education Week (http://www.openeducationweek.org), are striving to make more people aware of the resources available to help them reach their learning goals. With greater public awareness we can invite greater public participation, which will help shape the future of OCW and OER to maximize the effect that free and open sharing in education can have on supporting improvements in teaching and learning worldwide.

Notes

1. For more information on the evolution of OCW at MIT, see Cecilia d'Oliveira, Steve Carson, Kate James, and Jeff Lazarus, "MIT OpenCourseWare: Unlocking Knowledge, Empowering Minds," *Science* 329, no. 5991 (July 30, 2010): 525–26, http://www.sciencemag.org/content/329/5991/525.full.

2. OCW Consortium user survey results from April–September 2011, 512 respondents (survey results published in the OCW Consortium December 2011 newsletter and made available at http://www.ocwconsortium.org/en/community/documents/cat_view/54-ocwc-newsletters); Education-Portal.com survey conducted April–June 2011, 421 respondents (partial results from the Education-Portal.com survey were published on its blog at http://education-portal.com/articles/Understanding_OCW_A_Field_Guide_to_Free_Education.html).

3. Wen-Hao David Huang and Wendi Shen, "Who Are Using Open Courseware and How Do They Use It? An Exploratory Case Study from a Chinese-Based Open Courseware Portal in Taiwan (OOPS)," available for download at http://www.ocwconsortium.org/en/community/documents/cat_view/102-ocwoer-research.

4. For examples, see TU Delft's results at http://opencourseware.weblog.tudelft. nl/2011/09/09/tu-delft-opencourseware-user-survey, MIT's results at http://ocw.mit. edu/about/site-statistics/, and Fundação Getulio Vargas's results at http://www. slideshare.net/OCWConsortium/ocwc-fgv-onlinestavros05052011mit.

5. Response to a user survey conducted by the OCW Consortium.

6. Steve Carson, "Case_Study_112210_MIT OCW" (presentation shared with the author November 29, 2010).

7. For more information, see the presentation "New Directions in Drinking Water Engineering Education" by Jasper Verberk, Peter de Moel, and Hans van Dijk at http://www.slideshare.net/OCWConsortium/new-directions-in-drinking-water -engineering-education.

8. Presentation at the NetEase Open Education Channel international launch event, February 19, 2011. For an example of the microblog study group, see http:// open.163.com.

9. This is beginning to change with projects such as Washington State's Open Course Library, which solicited the creation and sharing of materials for the eighty-one highest-enrolled courses across the state stystem: http://www.opencourselibrary.org.

10. The Saylor Foundation (http://www.saylor.org) is providing such pathways through free and open materials related to the top ten undergraduate majors in U.S. higher education.

11. For examples, see the Opencast community (http://opencast.org), an interview with the Opencast Matterhorn Project product manager (http://videolectures.net/single_ schulte_interview/), and the website http://videolectures.net, which provides videos from the Machine Learning Summer School.

Mary Lou Forward *is the Executive Director of the OpenCourseWare Consortium. The OCW Consortium is dedicated to realizing the positive impacts of open sharing on teaching and learning globally, with membership of over 275 institutions and organizations from around the world.*

The Open University of Hong Kong: The i-Counseling System

Chun Ming Leung and Eva Tsang

Need/Rationale for Approach

ESTABLISHED BY THE HONG KONG GOVERNMENT as a self-financed tertiary institution, the Open University of Hong Kong (OUHK) offers three study modes with a total enrollment of about 19,000: distance learning for working adults; full-time, face-to-face teaching for high school leavers; and e-learning for postgraduate studies. Prospective and current students often have enquiries related to career guidance and development, study paths and methods, program or course choices, previous academic qualifications recognized by OUHK, and study plans and graduation checks. While call center systems and online FAQs can handle common enquiries, more complex academic counseling questions require campus visits and face-to-face discussions with academic staff, which are time consuming and labor intensive. To provide prompt and round-the-clock academic counseling services for prospective and current students, the OUHK has developed the i-Counseling System, an intelligent online system that uses technologies in information retrieval and the concept of ontology.[1]

Description

The i-Counseling System combines an ontology-based information-retrieval engine, a guided search methodology for sophisticated search, and a mathematical optimization model to provide relevant responses to queries on studying in the university. It uses an animated character (i-Ambassador) with multilingual and text-to-speech capabilities as a front end to offer users a better and more natural enquiry experience. The system has two modules: (a) Academic Counseling for handling general queries from prospective students about career development, program/course information, and learning modes, and (b) Academic Advisement for dealing with questions from current students on program specifics, study plans, and graduation checks. For a demonstration of the system, please see the video accessible at http://www.youtube.com/watch?v=6xDFn9Z9yC4.

Evidence of Effectiveness

The Academic Counseling module uses an ontology-based information-retrieval engine and a guided search methodology to guide prospective students step-by-step to get the information they want. It filters irrelevant results, returning only results that are relevant, thereby saving search time. It provides a one-stop integrated counseling service by integrating the Pre-enrollment Advisor, Program/Course Advisor, Administrative Services Advisor, Career/Study Advisor, and Financial Support Advisor to form a single user interface. Users no longer need to go to different places for different enquiries.

The effectiveness of the Academic Advisement module can be seen in the following examples:

- The Study Planner in the module helps students with course selection by suggesting appropriate courses and informing them of the course requirements.

- The module automates the administrative work involved in student graduation (i.e., checking whether a student is qualified to graduate in a specific program), thereby freeing staff from this very labor-intensive task. For example, it takes the module less than three hours to complete a graduation check of one thousand students in the nursing program. This task previously required three teams of academic and administrative staff working together for several weeks to complete. But most important of all, the results generated by the module are reliable and accurate.

- The module optimizes the Honor Classification for students graduating in honor-degree programs, thus eliminating human error, which may result in a downgrading of honor classification.

- Faculty members can check in real time students' outstanding courses directly via the Academic Advisement module and view the results at a glance.

Please refer to http://www.youtube.com/watch?v=bPUijlh8x0M for details on the design concept of the Academic Advisement module.

Challenges Encountered

Searching for relevant information on the university portal and the web can be a frustrating experience. Although popular search engines (e.g., Google Search API) index everything on the site, the search results are far from satisfactory. A great deal of primary data has been accumulated for many years, relevant documents and data are scattered from their sources, and some of the unstructured textual data is not easy to search. Because the portal uses HTML to present the information, mainstream search engines typically return every page containing the search words. As a result, online searches that rely only on keywords often return items that are not relevant.

In order to overcome this problem and to help students quickly locate information about career development, enrollment, programs/courses, and financial aid, the Academic Counseling module's methodology provides searching capabilities that go beyond the use of keywords common in many search engines. Unstructured information fetched from the portal and the web is first analyzed and reorganized as concepts/classes, individuals, and attributes/properties in an ontology framework. Each piece of captured information is classified and stored systematically in the ontology. The most relevant information is then extracted through information-retrieval algorithms that utilize the information captured in the ontology and then suggest related items that users may also be interested in. This helps in locating the most relevant information. For more details on the use of ontology in the design of Academic Counseling, please see the video accessible at http://www.youtube.com/watch?v=CUV5I9Vm7z0.

Ontology-based search is still an emerging discipline, with new ideas being introduced constantly. It is difficult to verify and maintain the domain ontology as new and modified classes, individuals, attributes, and relations are introduced. Constructing the required domain ontology from multiple data sources with unstructured information is a daunting task, and academic counselors generally lack the technical skills needed to develop the flows for guided searches. Also, academic counseling requires accurate answers and reliable responses to searches and queries, as an incorrect answer or misleading result can have dire consequences for students. The i-Counseling System provides functions that allow users to create the domain ontology from both internal and external sources and verify its accuracy. With domain knowledge continuing to be built up, it is likely that the system's intelligence and accuracy will further improve.

Applicability or Replicability to Other Institutions or Programs

The i-Counseling System has several innovative features: (a) a guided search methodology that analyzes the questions raised and offers step-by-step guidance to provide the most relevant answer; (b) intelligent search via an ontology-based information-retrieval engine to locate the most relevant information; (c) a smart user interface that employs a digital agent with multilingual and text-to-speech capabilities to mimic a real person handling the query process, making the system more user friendly; and (d) a mathematical optimization model to find solutions that match course-selection preference to academic-program requirements. Although the system was developed to meet the specific needs of the OUHK, the ontology framework and mathematical optimization model—with modifications—can be adopted for use at other educational institutions. Furthermore, the concepts, technologies, and tools developed for the i-Counseling System can be generalized and applied to professional knowledge-based portals (e.g., health-related services, airline and insurance industries), course-content development, and other knowledge-management-related projects.

Note

1. Chun Ming Leung, Eva Y. M. Tsang, S. S. Lam, and Dominic C. W. Pang, "Intelligent Counseling System: A 24 x 7 Academic Advisor," *EDUCAUSE Quarterly* 33, no. 4 (2010), http://www.educause.edu/EDUCAUSE+Quarterly/EDUCAUSEQuarterly MagazineVolum/IntelligentCounselingSystemA24/219101.

Chun Ming Leung *is the Vice President (Technology & Development) of OUHK, where he oversees the planning and development of technology infrastructure for the whole university. He was a physics professor in the United States before joining OUHK. His professional interest is in computational astrophysics and technology-enhanced education.* **Eva Tsang** *is the Senior Course Designer in the Educational Technology and Publishing Unit at OUHK. She is in charge of course development and various e-learning projects including the development of online learning platforms and mobile learning. She is also the Project Director of the university's Centre for Innovation.*

Central Piedmont Community College: Online Student Profile Learning System

Clint McElroy

Introduction

MORE PEOPLE THAN EVER are pursuing higher education in the United States. The increasing number of students attending community colleges reflects a broader reach into the general population as well as higher percentages of underprepared students for U.S. community colleges. For example, at Central Piedmont Community College (CPCC)—a large, urban college in Charlotte, North Carolina—more than two-thirds of incoming students need academic remediation. At the same time, colleges are tasked with providing all students the opportunity to be successful, despite multiple student risk factors, some of which are beyond the institution's control.

Since the turn of the millennium, a technology-based solution called the Online Student Profile (OSP) system has dramatically increased the success rates for at-risk students at CPCC. Developmental students at CPCC participating in the full OSP system (orientation course, developmental reading and/ or writing with an instructor trained in the system, and participation in learning style and personality assessments) are retained and are successful (A–C grades) at much higher levels than students who do not participate or do not fully participate. From 2004 to 2009, students participating in all elements of the OSP system were:

- 8.70 percent more likely to complete the courses in which they enrolled,
- 9.36 percent more likely to persist from spring to the subsequent fall term,
- 10.82 percent more likely to get A–C grades in their courses, and
- 3.45 percent more likely to earn a college degree.

These results were achieved as the result of a homegrown student success project that is still growing at CPCC and is now being adopted by six partner colleges through a grant from Next Generation Learning Challenges (NGLC, http://nextgenlearning.org).

The Evolution of CPCC

In 2002, CPCC's president, Dr. Tony Zeiss, and his cabinet charged a three-member team[1] with researching best practices in retaining at-risk students, developing a retention plan for these students, and writing a U.S. Department of Education Title III Improving Institutions grant proposal to fund implementation of the plan. The cabinet members were looking for a collaborative approach to student success, and the grant-writing team, in collaboration with a variety of faculty and staff, developed an integrated student success intervention model with three components:

1. a technology solution—the OSP—as the lynchpin to hold together a variety of student services
2. instructional and collaborative interventions
3. specific interventions targeted directly to students

One component of the grant included an assessment of students' learning styles and personality types, which informed faculty and influenced their decision to utilize various teaching methodologies; this was supported by providing faculty training. A second component was another element of the OSP—advising notes—which continues to be used to document information for advisors and instructors. Including the information technology services (ITS) department ensured that the appropriate technology was provided for student tracking, analytical reports, and comparative data. A third component was design and implementation of a one-credit student success course (ACA 111), elements of which were integrated into developmental reading and writing courses for expanded work with at-risk students taking those courses. By taking a collaborative approach with the grant, the team conveyed the fact that student success is a college-wide focus and that no single entity of the college has the sole responsibility for ensuring student success. (See Figure 1.)

The collaborative nature of the process extended to the development of the OSP system. Marcia Conston, vice president for Enrollment and Student Services, explains what she and other Cabinet members were looking for from the potential Title III project—a collaborative approach to student success: "The college's decision to establish a collaborative approach which included student

Figure 1. **Integrated Student Success Intervention Model**

Component 1: **Improve Student Services** **"Student Success Model"**	**Component 2:** **Improve Faculty Skills** **"Student Success Series"**
Develop an expanded and improved model of student services for high-risk students operating from Student Success Centers established on each of six campuses	Develop a faculty training series to increase integration of student learning styles and student success strategies into teaching
Establish two new assessment instruments to determine student learning/cognitive styles and personality types	Develop an online supplemental instruction tutoring program for developmental English and reading
Implement a comprehensive orientation course for all entering high-risk students	

Improve Academic and Student Support Services for High-Risk Students

Component 3:
Improve Technology for
Student Tracking
"Online Student Profile"

Develop and implement an Online Student Profile (OSP) system providing faculty and staff with access to demographic and performance data, student goals, and assessment results

Develop a predictive modeling/early warning program to identify students for intervention services

services, instruction, and the information technology departments was based solely on the premise of affecting student success. We recognized that success occurs both inside and outside of the classroom." A team of faculty, counselors, advisors, and midlevel administrators representing student services, instruction, and ITS worked together to develop and implement every aspect of the project. Nothing occurred in a vacuum—everyone was involved in the conversation, whether it was institutional processes, statistical analysis, how students and counselors might interact, teaching and learning, testing methodology, or how the user interfaces of the OSP should flow.

Outcomes and Developments

As a result of the collaborative work among the team members, a variety of interventions and new processes were developed and implemented during the five-year Title III grant period, including the following:

1. **Student Orientation Course:** A blended-learning course that provides incoming students with personal development skills essential to succeed in college (communication, critical thinking, teamwork, problem solving, self-advocacy).

2. **Student Assessment Tools:** An online learning–styles assessment (a CPCC product) and a personality profile (available to partners in the NGLC grant), which are essential components of the orientation course. Knowledge gained from these self-evaluations leads to students' enhanced understanding of how they learn and perceive information, strengthens their feelings of having a measure of control over their academic future, and increases their sense of self-efficacy and advocacy.

3. **Online Profile and Tracking:** An online portal that enables students, faculty, and counselors to access real-time student data that includes academic history, risk factors, demographic data, advising history, and assessment results (individual and entire-class profile). This profile facilitates enhanced delivery of instruction and advising and enables timely and effective interventions for at-risk or underperforming students.

4. **Faculty and Staff Development:** Training for faculty and counselors that outlines the effective and holistic use of all four components (learning style assessment, personality assessment, advising/counseling notes, and integrated student success course) to better understand their students, enhance learning, evaluate student risk, and provide appropriate interventions for underperforming students. Having faculty and advisors taking the course together yields integrated teaching, support, and interventions that directly impact retention and graduation rates.

Additionally, as part of the Title III project, Student Success Centers were opened on each of CPCC's six campus locations. These centers are designed to provide one-stop service to students or potential students who have questions about any program or service offered by the college. Rita Dawkins, dean of Student Success Services, explained, "It's more than an information center because you can do some up-front advising and counseling—somebody who can help from the very beginning."

The Student Success Centers are a high-touch element, in addition to the OSP, the features of which include advising notes that contain specifics of every meeting a student has with a professional advisor or faculty advisor. Date-logged, these notes allow the multiple advisors who end up working with each student to get right to work on what the student needs rather than having to re-create a student's advising history. Advisors also have access to students' learning style and personality assessments, ensuring that they are better informed. As Dawkins said of the OSP, "It shows the collaboration and the resources regarding how we have gotten to know the student and how the student has gotten to know him or herself. It is situation in which technology has pulled the best of what we can do for a student together all in one place."

Faculty also benefit from the enhanced information about their students. Class rosters show the preferred learning styles and the personality types of every student in each section faculty teach and also provide a quick, two-click intervention function for referring students for help from student services staff, including counselors, career counselors, and tutoring staff. As part of Title III funding, all full- and part-time faculty members were required to teach student success courses (including ACA 111, the one-hour student success course into which all students placing into developmental courses were referred), as well as developmental reading and writing courses. Training was developed with the students in mind, focusing on the critical first three weeks of a course and how to provide an atmosphere of success for first-year students.

Challenges Faced

In the collaborative process to develop and implement the faculty training component of the Title III grant, the team of faculty and student services staff began by asking, "What do students need in order to be successful? What can instructors do with that knowledge to leverage learning in and out of the classroom?" It was determined that students need more information about the way they learn best and that instructors can enhance their delivery methods and assess student learning daily.

Although educators would seem to be in the best position to know what students need to be successful, it became obvious that all of the partners in education must collaborate to initiate cultural change. At CPCC, teams of full- and part-time instructors and student support services initiated faculty development, incorporating techniques and strategies for content delivery and assessment to improve student success and retention. A reluctance to change is often the first hurdle that must be overcome with any cultural shift, but gradually, as instructors were given tools to improve their day-to-day interactions with students, the college learned new ways to create stimulating and interactive environments in the classroom. Those environments thrive today because of the consistent and steady reinforcement by all key stakeholders of faculty support, technology enhancement, and a systemic desire for positive change.

From a teaching and learning perspective, ACA 111 served as the starting point for all of the related instructional and student support interventions. The ACA 111 College Student Success course was originally designed to focus on three main areas:

- the student (goals, learning styles, personality type),
- CPCC (the college's resources and services), and
- college (academic planning and technology).

Students who successfully complete ACA 111 are prepared to set realistic academic goals, utilize technology to enhance coursework, use their learning style to determine their best study habits, make choices about careers and majors, prepare an academic plan for their course of study at CPCC, and access and utilize the college's resources and services.

With the expansion of the ACA 111 course to include over 3,000 students per year, one aspect of the original Title III plan had to be revisited—a required advising session for all students enrolled in the course. The number quickly overwhelmed the professional advising staff, and the college realized it had to advise more effectively and in a more efficient manner. The solution was simple: expand the advising component of ACA 111 from individuals to groups. The sessions will continue to be tweaked based on student feedback. In response to the last question of an evaluation of ACA 111 group advising sessions ("State how this session has or has not been beneficial to you"), up to 95 percent of the comments are positive. Students now encourage their friends to attend the sessions to avoid being erroneously advised by their peers or attempting to self-advise. A common student comment received regarding group advising is, "This should be mandatory for all students."

Can It Work Elsewhere?

The OSP technology and the many practices and systems that are allied with its use have changed the culture at CPCC. Usage of the OSP system has expanded beyond the parameters of the Title III project, with current OSP-based projects now beginning or operational in the areas of technical careers, continuing education (a certified nurse-assistant program), and basic skills/literacy.

Thanks to funding from NGLC, CPCC is scaling up its successful implementation of OSP and its related systems with six partner colleges: Asheville-Buncome Tech, Fayetteville Tech, and Forsyth Tech (all in North Carolina), and Lane Community College (Eugene, Oregon), Monroe Community College (Rochester, New York), and Moraine Valley Community College (Palos Hills, Illinois). The goal of the NGLC project is to ascertain whether similar student success results can be garnered at colleges that receive the OSP system and adapt its usage to their own needs, based on the system developed at CPCC. The NGLC project seeks to scale an effective innovation across multiple institutions. Most of the software built was intended for use only at CPCC—the systems are built to easily support the college's needs but not to necessarily be portable. With this project, the entire approach to development changed, forcing CPCC to think about how it could easily integrate with other colleges' systems while continuing to support its users. The college is reaping the benefit of its partners' expertise as well as its own. Through shared collaboration and technology, it was able to increase the number of innovators on a single project. This change in development style, coupled with the open-source release of the software, has proved to be a game changer in the way CPCC delivers solutions.

Is It Effective?

While assessment results from the partner colleges are not yet available, anecdotal results from the first implementation period at the partner colleges—shared at an October 2011 training and information session for teams from the partner colleges—were quite positive. With over 3,500 students from the partner colleges participating at that time, preliminary feedback from students and staff indicated that use of the OSP system and implementation of the related practices have created an on-campus energy centered on student success through collaboration. The use of technology to facilitate higher-quality human interaction has proved key to the improved success of at-risk students at CPCC, and it appears that the use of the OSP system as a catalyst for change at other colleges will lead to similar improvements.

Note

1. This team—known as the Title III Writing Team—included Emma Brown, dean of Retention Services (in the Enrollment and Student Services unit of the college), Michael Horn, director of Resource Development (the chief grants officer of the college), and this researcher (at the time the associate dean for business, international, and general studies in the instructional unit of the college).

Clint McElroy *is Dean for Retention Services at Central Piedmont Community College (CPCC) in Charlotte, NC. He earned his doctorate in Curriculum and Instruction from the University of North Carolina at Charlotte. In addition to managing CPCC's First Year Student program, TRiO Program, and Tutoring Centers, he chairs CPCC's Retention Committee and the Student Intake Steering Committee.*

The CHANCE Program in China: Transforming Students into "Global-Minded" Scientific Investigators and Citizens

Jacqueline McLaughlin

Introduction

The Risk

America's position in the world may once have been reasonably se-cure with only a few exceptionally well-trained men and women. It is no longer.

—National Commission on Excellence in Education, *A Nation at Risk*

For more than twenty-five years, U.S. educators, researchers, and policy makers have bemoaned the nation's dearth of highly qualified college graduates pursuing meaningful careers in science and technology, warning against a corresponding loss of U.S. economic, scientific, and technological supremacy in the world.[1] Numerous national reports and research findings indicate colleges need to respond, particularly in the STEM (science, technology, engineering, and mathematics) majors. By reducing science education to spontaneous, drill-and-practice paradigms centered around lectures, most college programs are sacrificing quality for the sake of "covering" quantity.[2] However, it is possible for science educators to create learning environments that foster conceptual understanding, interdisciplinary content, authentic scientific experience, and interpersonal skills that will increase the heterogeneity of students who are attracted to scientific fields and who can feel the allure of experimental science and the thrill of discovery. The end result—a scientifically literate society and a reinvigorated research enterprise—could be far-reaching. It could even be revolutionary.[3]

Recently, the National Science Foundation (NSF) and the American Association for the Advancement of Science (AAAS) implemented a national call for immediate transformation in U.S. undergraduate biology education:

> Champion more engaging and relevant biology education, both to society and to the natural world; and, foster the skills to address the challenges of the 21st century, including the ability to think like a scientist and to contribute outside disciplinary boundaries.[4]

Technology can help create learning environments in which scientific concepts, research, and real-world issues come to life—by linking students with researchers in authentic situations—to transform students into proactive, well-rounded, global-minded scientific investigators and citizens. And, when it comes to environmental education especially, environments and biomes cross national borders and must be viewed and studied from a global perspective.

CHANCE in China

The CHANCE model provides students with this much-needed environmental global perspective, by bringing students directly to the science.

CHANCE (Connecting Humans And Nature through Conservation Experiences, http://www.chance.psu.edu/) is a Penn State educational outreach and professional development program whose overarching goal is to educate undergraduates and K–12 science teachers and their students in conservation biology and global environmental sustainability by engaging students in real-world research opportunities in global environments. Besides learning essential core concepts and research skills, participants also gain the awareness, knowledge, and skills needed for a more sophisticated comprehension of the causes, connections, and consequences of global environmental destruction.[5]

For example, the reality of global urbanization and industrialization is impacting an important life-sustaining resource, water—especially in China. Through a CHANCE embedded field course (http://www2.lv.psu.edu/jxm57/explore/china2011/), both Penn State University and China's Jiangnan University students recently addressed this problem

| "China 2011 Field Course Studies and Discussions" video: http://www.youtube.com/watch?v=gHhNfioXEiE |

The course format unites Penn State undergraduate students across disciplines (science, agriculture, engineering, liberal arts, and international affairs) with their Chinese counterparts (http://www2.lv.psu.edu/jxm57/explore/china2010/photoalbum2010/index.html) to examine the impact of burgeoning

314

development upon one of China's crucial water resources, Lake Taihu. In 2007, the lake was designated a "natural disaster" when pollution (effluents such
as phosphorus and nitrogen from an estimated 1,300
nearby factories) resulted in a major algae outbreak.[6]
A two-week practicum challenged twenty-eight students and ten faculty members to examine firsthand
the effects of industrial, municipal, and urban development within the Taihu basin—one of the most industrialized regions in China—and to offer strategic solutions
for the lake's restoration.

Figure 1. **The CHANCE Logo**

The group conducted cooperative experiments on
the water quality of, and land use around, Lake Taihu to improve its awareness
of environmental problems and learn sampling and analysis methods used to
diagnose aquatic ecosystem health and stability. After the chemical, biological,
and physical characteristics were analyzed, the results were disturbing: Lake Taihu's nutrient levels continue to indicate a eutrophic state and therefore anything
coming out of the lake is unsafe for human consumption. To fully evaluate the
local, provincial, national, and international ramifications of the group's field research findings, faculty members, technical experts, government leaders, business leaders, and noted American and Chinese scientists fielded questions from
students about how to balance
the economic and environmental health of the area. Together, they also visited local algal
salvage plants, as well as industrial and wastewater treatment plants.

**"China 2011 Lake Taihu Research
and Analysis" video:**
http://www.youtube.com/watch?v=iauBCeQ2C8o

Students then delivered summative group research reports on the water
quality and sustainability of Lake Taihu, including experimental design, implementation, and data interpretation.

Figure 2. **American and Chinese Students**

The students' findings clearly indicate that more waste and industrial water-treatment facilities are warranted, as is enhanced environmental education to promote a more knowledgeable and responsible citizenry. And, restoration efforts presently in place (blue-green algae salvage ships, dredging lake bottom, factory relocation, artificial floating beds, introduction of algae-eating fish, water transferring via Yangtze River tributaries, restoration of riparian buffers) are, cumulatively, helping to lessen the eutrophication process. But, as of September 2011, algal blooms continued to threaten both the health of the lake and its water quality, deemed undrinkable.[7]

Technology as the Catalyst

Technology catalyzed every aspect of this and all other CHANCE field courses, beginning with the course planning and execution—from designing field-research activities and building an itinerary in China to e-mail blasts promoting the course to students, to online applications, Facebook, and CHANCE's own website. Travel and agenda logistics also required technological assistance—especially setting up and conducting a two-day international conference on the "Water Environment and the Ecological Restoration of Taihu Lake" that included video (Skype) participation of key researchers (see Figure 3).

And, all CHANCE field courses use the Field Course Experiential Learning Model (http://chance.psu.edu/exp-learning-model.html), which features three steps:

1. online pretrip assignments that provide essential background knowledge;

2. a field-based trip experience that includes conservation work; journal keeping; inquiry-based research on a real-world environmental issue; participation in discussion groups, lectures, panel discussions, and formal research presentations; and independent exploration; and

3. posttrip online assignments that encourage the integration and application of key concepts learned, all posted in advance through Penn State's course management system (ANGEL) and later submitted via the same from learners all over the world.[8]

Finally, we recorded video in the field and during the final student presentations and group-panel discussion forums for later use in grading student academic performance, public relations pieces, and development of future CHANCE courses.

Figure 3. **Paleoclimatologist Richard Alley, PhD, Nobel Laureate and Professor at Penn State's Earth and Mineral Institute, via Teleconference**

Evidence of Effectiveness

In addition to their final course projects, all students completed a fifteen-question course-end survey, providing details about their real-life experiences. Their trip journal and posttrip questions/reflections served as additional qualitative data. As with previous CHANCE assessments, survey results suggest these highly motivated students returned home with much more than a stamp in their passports (see Figure 4).

Working in the field also inspired students to engage in future environmental field research: 89 percent agreed or strongly agreed that the Lake Taihu

Figure 4. **Student Responses to Course-End Survey**

Student Reflections

"Reading books on the eutrophication and water pollution issues helped me learn the basics, but it was the international speakers that really made me understand how vital our research was."

Michelle O., Penn State biology major

"What was revealed beyond the data gathered was the importance of addressing global environmental concerns together."

William B., Penn State engineering major

---

project motivated them to engage in global environmental stewardship activities. "We got to do the investigation by ourselves and to get data and suggestions from the local people," one student commented. "It was real, not in our textbooks or lecture notes."

One student explained, "I want to break language barriers and understand other cultures so that I can do more research in other places like we did here in China." Another student put it this way: "If we learn from the mistakes of the past, developing nations could avoid causing future environmental problems for themselves in the future. This motivates me to work toward sustainability in my country and all over the world."

Challenges for the Future

This course exemplifies how international courses in colleges may use technology as a catalyst to create environments that foster and deliver conceptual understanding, interdisciplinary content, authentic scientific experience, and interpersonal skills in order to increase the heterogeneity of students who come to appreciate and understand science, and who use experimental science as a means to bettering society as we know it.

We need to work more efficiently and productively with academics, researchers, economists, nongovernmental and governmental officials, and businesses worldwide. We need to bring the students to the science, both virtually and physically, in order to educate them about the realities of our world.

Challenges related to funding, diplomacy, visas, and time zones are formidable, but nonetheless surmountable. It is time for colleges to not only implement NSF/AAAS's call for vision and change in biological education, but to do so by breaking out of traditional boundaries of didactic education. We need to invest institutional resources and partner with global academics to inspire globally minded students who feel empowered to define sustainable answers for life on Earth. Responding to these challenges with a "game-changer" such as detailed here may be our best CHANCE.

Acknowledgments

CHANCE thanks all its sponsors and partners—numerous academic institutions, scholarly societies, non-governmental and governmental organizations, and businesses worldwide. Together, we have created and continue to create educational environments that inspire individuals who work towards environmentally sustainable lifestyles and answers. CHANCE is also beholden to all those at The Pennsylvania State University who have been instrumental is providing oversight and direction for the CHANCE Program throughout the past years.

Notes

Epigraph: National Commission on Excellence in Education, *A Nation at Risk: The Imperative for Educational Reform* (Washington, DC: U.S. Department of Education, 1983), http://www2.ed.gov/pubs/NatAtRisk/index.html.

1. Shirley A. Jackson, *Envisioning a 21st Century Science and Engineering Workforce for the United States: Tasks for University, Industry, and Government* (Washington, DC: The National Academies Press, 2003), http://www.nap.edu/openbook. php?isbn=0309088569; Members of the 2005 "Rising above the Gathering Storm" Committee, *Rising above the Gathering Storm, Revisited: Rapidly Approaching Category 5* (Washington, DC: The National Academies Press, 2010), http://www.nap. edu/openbook.php?record_id=12999.

2. Diane F. Halpern and Milton D. Hakel, "Applying the Science of Learning to the University and Beyond: Teaching for Long-Term Retention and Transfer," *Change* 35, no. 4 (2003): 37–41, http://www.csub.edu/tlc/options/resources/handouts/ scholarship_teaching/HalpernHakel.pdf; Jo Handelsman, Diane Ebert-May, Robert Beichner, Peter Bruns, Amy Chang, Robert DeHaan, Jim Gentile, Sarah Lauffer, James Stewart, Shirley M. Tilghman, and William B. Wood, "Scientific Teaching," *Science* 304 (April 2004): 521–22, http://www.jstor.org/pss/3836701; Robert L. DeHaan, "The Impending Revolution in Undergraduate Science Education," *Journal of Science Education and Technology* 14, no. 2 (June 2005): 253–69, http:// wikifuse.pbworks.com/f/DeHaan%2B2005.pdf.

3. *Vision and Change in Undergraduate Biology Education* (2010), http://visionand change.org/finalreport.

4. "Dr. Bruce Alberts' Message to Vision and Change," http://visionandchange.org/bruce-alberts/.

5. Jacqueline McLaughlin and Kathleen Fadigan, "The CHANCE (Connecting Humans and Nature through Conservation Experiences) Program: Transitioning from Simple Inquiry-Based Learning to Professional Science Practice," in *Exemplary Science Programs: Science for Resolving Issues/Problems,* ed. Robert Yager (Arlington, VA: NSTA Press): 185–202; Jacqueline S. McLaughlin, "Reimagining Science Education and Pedagogical Tools: Blending Research with Teaching," *EDUCAUSE Quarterly* 33, no. 1 (2010), http://www.educause.edu/EDUCAUSE+Quarterly/EDUCAUSE Quarterly MagazineVolum/ReimaginingScienceEducationand/199386.

6. Joseph Kahn, "In China, a Lake's Champion Imperils Himself," *New York Times,* October 14, 2007, http://www.nytimes.com/2007/10/14/world/asia/14china.html?pagewanted=all.

7. Richard Stone, "China Aims to Turn Tide against Toxic Lake Pollution," *Science* 333, no. 6047 (September 2, 2011): 1210–11, http://www.sciencemag.org/content/333/6047/1210.summary.

8. Jacqueline S. McLaughlin and D. Kent Johnson, "Assessing the Field Course Experiential Learning Model: Transforming Collegiate Short-Term Study Abroad Experiences into Rich Learning Environments," *Frontiers: The Interdisciplinary Journal of Study Abroad* 13 (November 2006): 65–85, http://www.frontiersjournal.com/documents/McLaughlinJohnsonFrontiersXIIIFall06.pdf.

Jacqueline McLaughlin *is an Associate Professor of Biology at The Pennsylvania State University–Lehigh Valley Campus. She received her doctorate from Rutgers University and her master's degree from The Florida State University. She is an innovator in developing inquiry-based learning strategies, and she is the Founding Director of CHANCE (Connecting Humans And Nature through Conservation Experiences).*

Georgetown University: Web Conferencing—A Critical Skill for the Connected World

Pablo G. Molina

INFORMATION TECHNOLOGIES provide new ways of doing established activities, and they can create new opportunities to do things that were previously infeasible or impractical. Communications offers many examples of this dynamic, including technologies and tools such as mobile phones, text messaging, and social networking. My 11-year-old daughter spends hours chatting via Skype with her classmates, for example, and one of my former students has hired a teacher in Pakistan to teach his native Urdu language to his U.S.-born children via Skype.

In an educational setting, the communications capabilities that are enabled by information technology allow for new pedagogical models, which can have profound implications for how today's students learn and prepare themselves for a workplace that itself uses these technologies in groundbreaking ways. One example is web conferencing tools, which can be used to cultivate the skills needed to create and execute compelling academic and professional presentations online. Faculty can incorporate web conferencing into their courses, placing students into the role of instructors, which research has shown to increase comprehension and retention of material. At the same time, inviting students in traditional courses to teach online is a reversal both in role *and* medium.

Students Teaching with Web Conferencing

As an adjunct faculty member, I teach Ethics in Technology Management and Managing Diverse IT Organizations across the Globe, courses for the university's Master of Professional Studies in Technology Management program.

I regularly teach with web conferencing technologies to accommodate my professional travel schedule. While I teach online, students participate in class by speaking on their phones or computer microphones, by chatting, or by responding to instant polls.

In the summer of 2009, Georgetown University undertook a campus-wide adoption of web conferencing services as part of its planning for the possible consequences of a swine flu epidemic. Among the disruptive effects of such an outbreak for the academic community would have been an inability for many faculty, staff, and students to leave their homes. As it turned out, few in our community fell ill, but the web conferencing services proved invaluable for academic continuity during the severe blizzards of early 2010 and when many faculty and students were stranded in Europe in the spring of 2010 as a result of the Icelandic volcano eruption.

In my courses, students must work in groups to write a research paper and present it to the class. The paper process starts with an idea fair, during which each student gives an "elevator speech" about his or her proposed topic to classmates. Once the students coalesce in research groups, they present their paper proposals to the class. In the fall of 2010, I began requiring student groups to present their research-paper proposals using web conferencing technologies. Students are also required to ask questions of their classmates about their presentations, as well as answer audience questions while presenting.

I record their presentations, and student groups gain access to a recording and evaluate their performances after the online session. They also review how others presented so that they can compare their presentation with those of others. Some student comments are technical in nature (problems with the webcam, the microphones, or the multimedia materials), while others are procedural (using good lighting or posting the notes behind the webcam so students don't look down to consult them). The richest feedback, however, relates to the actual research project and the student-presentation skills. It is during the self-evaluation exchange between the students and the professor that the learning process sparks to life. Following are examples of two such moments that occurred as a result of feedback provided by two student groups in my Ethics in Technology Management graduate course in the fall of 2011. The comments illustrate that web conferencing technologies assist students in practicing and improving their teaching skills. The technologies also facilitate the solicitation of feedback from fellow students for their research projects.

> **Group One:** "In the process of preparing for and completing this assignment, we feel that we gained a solid foundation for the paper we are now writing. We feel that we did a good job putting together

a slide deck and coordinating our work. As a result, we feel that we were able to transition back and forth effectively and were prepared to reference each other's slides, which made for a more cohesive presentation. [. . .] In comparison to other teams, we also feel that we could have done better to include visual elements in our presentation. In the end, we both feel that this presentation was an extremely beneficial way to kick off our research, and it will provide us with good practice for the final paper presentation."

Group Two: "We did a really good job of keeping the listeners interested not only by what we said, but the content of the presentation. Visuals, such as the photos and the metadata, give examples of what we intend to discuss in our research paper. The examples also give an opportunity for the listener to relate or say, 'I remember when that happened,' something that we feel helps involve the listener. [. . .] With this practice run, we are now aware of these issues and can learn from them to assure [*sic*] our final presentation can go as smoothly as possible. We wanted to extend our gratitude for suggesting that we include speaking to facial recognition/social networking topics within our research paper as well. That is an interesting topic we will surely research and discuss in our paper."

Student feedback, along with formal comments from the course evaluations, supports further use of web conferencing technology in higher education. Such an approach challenges students to think critically about what they are learning and what they are trying to teach to other students. The process teaches students other beneficial activities as well, including how to

- prepare and use multimedia presentation materials, including speech, webcam video, and remote-participation tools to engage audiences online, lead discussions, and answer questions;
- collaborate with others to prepare and deliver their online presentations; and
- self-assess their online presentation skills for continuous improvement.

Learning by Teaching

In order to conduct compelling online presentations, students must research and understand their chosen topics, prepare their lectures, create and assemble supporting multimedia materials, craft participatory questions and surveys, and anticipate audience questions. Those of us who teach online and in-person recognize that teaching online often requires a preparation that differs from that associated with a traditional lecture. The instructor must cultivate a dynamic, engaged climate in an online environment to ensure fluid participation of attendees. Students teaching online are challenged to achieve higher maturity levels in their subject-matter knowledge and pedagogical skills.

In addition to developing the knowledge of the subject matter that students need, faculty strive to refine the overarching skills that can help them advance in their professional careers. These skills include critical thinking, debating, researching, writing, collaborating, and presenting. The pedagogical use of web conferencing technologies also targets the ability to make informative and convincing presentations online. For this to happen, web conferencing must be pervasively built into the curriculum. Presently, student web conferencing is only built into a few core courses (in addition to the capstone course required of students to complete their Master of Professional Studies in Technology Management degree). Beyond this program and this institution, there is great potential for extending this practice to other programs and to other educational institutions.

Additional pedagogical applications exist for web conferencing technologies, particularly regarding experiential learning. Several Jesuit universities are working together to use technology and their academic expertise to train the next generation of knowledge workers in refugee camps in Kenya, Malawi, and Syria. They have established two Internet-connected computer labs in the Kakuma refugee camp in northern Kenya, managed by Jesuit father Luis Amaral and the Jesuit Refugee Services organization. Refugee students pursue an online associate's degree in liberal studies from Regis University in Denver, Colorado.

During a site visit to the Kakuma camp in October 2011, I proposed a system of online internships to aid in improving the employment prospects of graduating students upon their relocation or repatriation. To date, three graduating refugees from the program are participating in this pilot online internship program with Georgetown University for spring 2012. In order to succeed in this program, interns will need to become proficient with web conferencing technologies, as they will need solid web conferencing skills when showcasing their work to members of the Georgetown University community remotely.

Related Resources

The following links point to case studies, videos, and podcasts about web conferencing at Georgetown University.

- http://www.cisco.com/en/US/prod/ps10352/webexcase/Georgetown.html
- http://www.cisco.com/assets/prod/webex/cases/Georgetown_Law.pdf

---

Pablo G. Molina *is Associate Vice President of IT and Campus CIO at Georgetown University. As an adjunct faculty member, he teaches Ethics and Technology Management, Information Security, and other courses. He has held similar jobs at the University of Pennsylvania, Washington University in St. Louis, and the Saint Louis Zoo.*

Blended Learning and New Education Logistics in Northern Sweden

Anders Norberg

WHEN CAMPUS-BASED EDUCATION and various forms of "distance" education converge in a more "blended" format, the phenomenon can increase educational opportunities in sparsely populated areas, creating a cloud-like combination of on-campus and distance students.

Description

In March 2010, program coordinators at Umeå University in Sweden responded to an informal survey asking for an indication of how flexible and accessible their on-campus education programs had become. The question emanated from a university-level work group addressing future strategies concerning increased educational availability in northern Sweden. The study group asked if students with time and place constraints had access to educational opportunities comparable with campus-based student opportunities. Certain programs at Umeå University had experimented with various strategies for integrating students at a distance into courses on campus, with varying results. Campus culture also recognized that more-experienced students were able to complete classes using technology-based (IT) learning strategies instead of attending lectures regularly. The work group had two overriding questions:

1. Had the increased use of IT learning tools and communication devices in campus courses created an enriched and more accessible learning environment?

2. Would the use of IT tools and devices make traditional on-campus education more accessible for "distance" students?

Many more program coordinators than expected reported that satellite regional groups existed and that individual students who had little opportunity to attend classes on campus participated in those courses using some form of technology. In some cases, "online education" had become the norm on campus, with students improvising their own learning environments; in other cases, traditional courses, enriched by instructors' use of technology, had increased access.

The majority of coordinators expressed a positive attitude toward integrating technology to increase student outreach, with many commenting that these efforts were beneficial. Only in rare instances did respondents indicate that they preferred to separate on-campus and distance students. Surprisingly, some lab-intensive education program officers believed that these innovations could increase access while maintaining or improving quality.

Looking forward, this could develop into a scenario whereby younger students would attend their courses on campus, while others work in smaller groups around learning centers, and a third group studies from home or from individual workplaces in a wider region but in the same course group.

Need/Rationale for Approach

With the emergence of IT and communication tools, "distance education" has burgeoned in Sweden as elsewhere and is frequently used to attract new groups of nontraditional students in the sparsely populated regions of the north. Umeå University (36,700 students) and Luleå University of Technology (16,000 students) have their main campuses in medium-sized cities on the coast of the Baltic Sea. Over a third of their students do not have a main campus presence, and this percentage is growing.

Asynchronous web-based distance education has shown itself to be a viable instructional format for both institutions, but it demands motivated and self-confident learners. Unfortunately, a large number of nontraditional students do not complete courses and programs in this format. Synchronous video conferencing broadcast to community learning centers has produced better results, although such arrangements are not as flexible and require minimum student cohort groups in one or two places. People in sparsely populated areas, therefore, have fewer learning opportunities, even though they have as many differentiated study preferences as other students. Further, many off-campus educational solutions have suffered from being considered lower-status and project-based, intended for disadvantaged students who cannot attend classes on campus.

During the period from 2008 to 2011, university enrollment has, in general, increased substantially in Sweden. One contributing factor for this growth has been the economic downturn and difficult workplace opportunities; another is the large numbers of college-age students. In part, this trend is being driven by younger-age cohorts entering universities directly after high school, rather than waiting a couple of years, which was previously common. Other students are remaining in universities rather than risking becoming openly unemployed. Demographic projections for the period 2012–2018, however, suggest that youth-group cohorts entering higher education will decrease by up to 40 percent. It should come as no surprise, then, that Swedish universities will try to reach more nontraditional students, especially because educational attainment is considerably diminished in parts of northern Sweden. Educational delivery options that can integrate on-campus and distance students in the same course will then be even more valuable.

Discussion

Where there is no technology at all, a teacher has to be in the same room with his or her students to build a learning environment. While those limitations no longer exist technologically, they still exist culturally. IT integration into campus courses seems to be changing that, however, and perhaps the value proposition for education at a distance, as well. Flexibility has become an added benefit, along with better access to resources and improved quality and enhanced effectiveness of learning.

This integrative strategy (on-campus and distance students together in a blended setting) enables universities to more fully subscribe their courses (if not always their classrooms) in demographic downturns. Nontraditional students in the sparsely populated inland regions get a wider variety of educational alternatives from which to choose even if they cannot come to campus on a regular basis. Even in the blended format, they can experience synchronous social interaction as a part of their studies via video or desktop conferencing.

With a diminishing number of younger-age students entering higher education, universities can reasonably expect logistical challenges when offering different distribution formats (on-campus, video conferencing, and asynchronous web-based), especially if they are kept separate with the need to enroll student-cohort groups. A consolidation of distribution formats into two forms—blended and asynchronous—can represent a viable solution to this problem. The educational environment is much more interactive and engaging if students can learn together in a blended class (at least in many courses and programs). In this arrangement, all other specialized and international educational offerings might be accomplished in an asynchronous format as an alternative to the normal/blended learning delivery format.

However, if an instructor encounters a situation where he or she is leading a learning process with students, both in the classroom and in other locations and time modes simultaneously, teaching demands increase exponentially. If the classroom is dominant as the learning metaphor, the task appears impossible. However, the process is easier to imagine if "time" and "process" replace the "place" and "transfer" perspective of higher education, with classrooms and learning centers being used as tools among others in the process. Then, blended learning becomes a conscious combination of asynchronous web-based and synchronous traditional and technology-enabled activities, rather than simply a combination of classroom activities and technology-enabled resources.

Hopefully, this game change will be a natural and generic process. When teachers and students are more accustomed to IT tools, a course becomes seamless irrespective of format. IT skills appear to develop naturally when one is teaching and studying—whether the course is at a "distance" or not. IT tools are no longer specialized distance resources for universities. They become work tools integrated into daily life. These resources enhance flexibility, options, and ease of communication.

This model demonstrates how blended learning may be viewed as the *normal* format, as well as how it offers great potential for increasing access to education. The ultimate goal of this strategy is to dramatically increase regional accessibility and turn higher education into a ubiquitous opportunity in a region, instead of being a scarce resource in designated traditional places.

Anders Norberg *is an Education Strategist for the Council of Skellefteå in Northern Sweden, working together with regional universities in the development of a young, multi-institutional campus. He has been in education development for 20 years, at Campus Skellefteå, at Umeå University, and in several European R&D projects.*

Valencia College: LifeMap and Atlas— Planning for Success

Joyce C. Romano and Bill White

Background

VALENCIA COLLEGE is a multicampus, urban community college in Orlando, Florida, that served over 70,000 students in 2010–11; 51 percent of these were underrepresented minorities, and 41 percent received Pell Grants. In the mid–1990s, we focused our strategic planning to become a more learning-centered college[1] with a focus on student success (progression and completion) and learning outcomes, which led to deep changes in systems, strategy, and engagement. During the past fifteen years, we have seen dramatic increases in the rates of student progression and completion, for which Valencia was recently recognized by the Aspen Institute as the No. 1 community college in the United States.

Description

LifeMap and Atlas are two of the projects to which we attribute this success. LifeMap is Valencia's developmental advising system that promotes student social and academic integration and education and career planning, as well as acquisition of study and life skills. It creates a normative expectation for students that they have a career and educational plan early in their enrollment at Valencia and integrates a system of tools, services, programs, and people (faculty and staff) to engage with students to document, revise, and develop those plans. LifeMap's five developmental stages, based on the ideal student progression, are as follows:

1. College Transition
2. Introduction to College

3. Progression to Degree

4. Graduation Transition

5. Lifelong Learning

(Detailed information about the LifeMap stages can be found at http://valenciacollege.edu/lifemap.) LifeMap is constantly evolving through an analysis of programs and services that align with each of LifeMap's stages, deep investment in staff and faculty development that integrates LifeMap into the college curriculum and co-curriculum, and an internal marketing campaign using engaging images and messages to connect and direct students to LifeMap resources.

Atlas is Valencia's learning portal; it is a major component of how we engage with students in LifeMap. It was designed on the principles of "connection and direction," which reflected our belief that technology could mediate our engagement with students over time and place, as well as help us reach our goal of empowering students to become increasingly self-directed in their educational journey to, through, and beyond Valencia. Atlas is built using SunGard Higher Education's Luminis portal and Banner ERP Systems. It integrates numerous applications into a single sign-on web portal that provides information and tools for students to

- explore career and educational options,
- develop concrete educational plans to graduation,
- manage course schedules and financial aid, and
- document their own learning.

Other important features include

- direct e-mail to students, faculty, and staff;
- a homepage for every course at Valencia, including an e-mail list for the classes of all faculty;
- an online syllabus and outline;
- a chat room and message board; and
- Atlas groups that anyone in the system can create and join, creating the option for limitless learning communities.

Atlas also provides students with "in the cloud" storage for files as well as free access to Microsoft Office applications from any web browser. Information sites, such as those focusing on advising, admissions, financial aid, and academic program information from Valencia's public websites, are also integrated within Atlas so that students do not leave the portal as they explore various sources of information. We have developed intentional and sequenced communication plans for various cohorts of Valencia students that prompt their "just in time" actions to keep their educational plans on track from initial enrollment through to graduation. Because Atlas requires secure sign-on, we are also able to provide online advising services through the portal.

Most college portals include the standard tools for conducting enrollment functions such as registration, progress reports, degree audits, payment records, and catalog information. To these, Atlas adds a "My LifeMap" tab that includes six important planning tools:

1. My Career Planner
2. My Educational Plan
3. My Financial Plan
4. My Job Prospects
5. My Portfolio
6. MeInTheMaking website

All of these tools started as homegrown applications developed to support LifeMap in its early years of development. Over the past several years, we have sought and found appropriate third-party applications and have now transitioned three of our LifeMap tools from our homegrown custom application to these tools while still retaining the "front face" of each Valencia LifeMap tool. MeInTheMaking (http://meinthemaking.com/) is a website that was created to support the 2010 refresh of the LifeMap marketing campaign. It provides a search function for all of Atlas and the .edu sites that link within Atlas, the stories of six peer role models and how they use LifeMap and Atlas, and categorized informational links for students to important online resources.

Valencia's IT staff also created LifeMap reporting tools that we refer to as LifeMap Analytics. For each of the LifeMap tools, we review monthly reports on usage that include detailed information on number of users, hits, and page views reported daily and in summary for the month. For the My Educational Plan (MEP) and My Portfolio we are also able to create reports that allow entry of any designated time frame and report on the number of new plans or portfolios created and on the total number of existing plans or portfolios. And, for the MEP, we can also create reports on the number of users, the average number of plans per user (students can create and save up to three plans), the highest number of plans created by program, and a list of the number of plans created for each program during the designated time period.

Additional LifeMap Analytics tools generate three reports that provide student-level information to college academic and student-services leaders on the

MEP and its correlation to other measures of student program intention and progress. The MEP Program Match report is data driven and compares the match between the MEP educational program that students have created in Atlas and their program in Banner (from their Valencia application or program-update submission to the college). The Planned vs. Enrolled Courses report is term driven and provides the percentage of courses in which students are enrolled that are included in their MEP. The MEP Graduates report is term driven and provides the percentage of graduates with an MEP and the percentage of graduates whose primary MEP is in the program in which they are graduating.

Evidence of Effectiveness

The LifeMap Analytics tools are used in a number of ways to better understand student behavior around career and educational planning, progression, and completion in order to better design student engagement with faculty and staff so that students can achieve their goals. Improvements are based on regular reviews and conversations with the faculty and staff who work with LifeMap tools. Each year the vice president of Student Affairs convenes the LifeMap Tools Group to discuss updates needed to continually improve the tools and student support. LifeMap Analytics tools are also reviewed at least annually to track the progression of their use and alignment of student intent with student behavior. Over time, we have seen increased alignment of student intent and behavior. For example, the match between student MEP and actual course taking was 43 percent in spring 2006 and increased to 60 percent in spring 2011. The LifeMap Analytics tools also provide student-level information so that we can follow up with individual students whose intent and behavior appear to be out of alignment. This work is the subject for further study, deeper understanding, and increased student engagement.

In summary, Atlas provides the technology that goes hand in glove with the intent and mission of LifeMap and complements the person-to-person interactions we have with students on our Valencia campuses. Atlas was designed to enhance, not replace, person-to-person interaction. LifeMap and Atlas are ever-evolving concepts and applications that continue to go deeper into alignment with students' purpose and goal achievement.

Note

1. R. B. Barr and J. Tagg, "A New Paradigm for Undergraduate Education," *Change* 27, no. 6 (1995): 12–25; T. O'Banion, *Learning College for the 21st Century* (Washington, DC: Oryx Press, 1994).

Joyce C. Romano *is Vice President for Student Affairs at Valencia College. Her work at Valencia has focused on the design and implementation of LifeMap, our developmental advising model and system; Atlas, our learning community portal; and an integrated student services model through which students learn the educational processes for their success.* **Bill White** *has served as the Chief Information Officer at Valencia College since 1998. In this role, White provides strategic and operational leadership for Valencia's information technology services and initiatives. Prior to joining Valencia College, he served for eleven years as the Director of the Computer Center at Rockford College in Rockford, Illinois.*

The Saylor.org Model

Jennifer Shoop

Introduction

SAYLOR.ORG IS AN OPEN-ACCESS ONLINE-LEARNING PLATFORM that provides self-paced college-level courseware to the public free of charge. The site is funded and maintained by The Saylor Foundation, a 501(c)(3) nonprofit institution.

For the past two years, we have focused on building a suite of 241 courses across twelve high-enrollment disciplines. We have recruited over two hundred instructors to design each of our areas of study and their constituent courses so that they are grounded in tried-and-true pedagogical experience; tied to clear, measurable learning outcomes; comprised of top-quality educational resources; and geared toward independent learners.

We believe that our open courseware project is game changing in its scalability: because our courses are designed to be autodidactic and self-paced and all course content is cost-free and open-access, we can serve any English-speaking learner in the world with Internet access and a desire to learn.

Rationale for Our Approach

Each year, more than 200,000 qualified U.S. students are unable to attend postsecondary institutions due to the prohibitive cost of education.[1] Access to education on a global scale is even bleaker. We believe that education should be a right rather than a privilege, and that advances in technology have given us the tools to lower and even circumvent the barriers of access and affordability that have hindered many from pursuing postsecondary education.

Guided by this vision, we have aggregated, vetted, and supplemented existing online educational content to create open-access, web-based courseware tied to learning outcomes and supported by formative and summative assignments and assessments. Our specific implementation plan was structured by several key discoveries.

The Future of Education Is Online

In the United States alone, around 4.3 million college students—over 20 percent of all college students—were engaged in distance learning in 2007,[2] and if metrics from high schools can serve as a rough proxy, it bears noting that blended education in secondary schools has doubled every year in the last three years.[3] In short, education is moving online, and we are rapidly learning to harness Web 2.0 technologies in order to administer education more widely and effectively to a variety of constituencies.

These estimates discount the substantial population of qualified students unable to afford college education who could be served by cost-free alternatives. Bolstered by the staggering traffic that open courseware sites such as MIT and Khan Academy receive, we believe that this population (and the public at large) is demanding cost-free, open-access educational resources.[4]

Looking outside the United States, we learned that more people lack access to safe drinking water than lack access to the Internet.[5] To have an impact on a global scale, we need to place open content online so that it can be accessed by anyone anywhere with an Internet connection.

A Wealth of Open Content Exists, But Is Disaggregated, Decontextualized, and Difficult to Assess in Terms of Quality

Existing content is "siloed," diffuse, and difficult to "actuate." We approached this problem in four ways:

- By training our instructors to locate and vet open content, an up-front investment that has paid off manifold in helping us avoid re-creating the wheel;
- By designing our course development process so that the framing and "stitching together" of resources is "baked into" the course structure;
- By permitting our professors to link to copyrighted content where no open content exists; and
- By dedicating staff to seek permission to host copyrighted content.

There Is Not Enough Existing Open Content to Cover the Majority of Our Elected Courses

In order to quantify and work around this problem, we made three strategic decisions:

- We begin all courseware development with highly detailed syllabi, or "course blueprints." By first identifying the learning taxonomies that a student must master, we can identify and quantify gaps in content.
- We permit our consultants to link to external sites.
- We commission the development of content only where none exists.

Overview of Our Model

Our course development process has been iteratively designed around the observations just outlined as well as best practices gleaned elsewhere.

The first step of our design process involves the recruitment and training of college instructors. Our online training module teaches professors to find, vet, and organize open content in a structured, intuitive format modeled upon the traditional college course. This module primes professors in the OER space, acquaints them with tools for finding open content, introduces them to templates and formatting guidelines, and provides basic instructional design training. Guided by this training, our professors conduct a deep search for open content. They canvass the web for openly licensed materials and, where none exist, link to open-access content. They then conceptualize a course by laying out a detailed "blueprint," or set of course-specific, outcome-aligned learning taxonomies. Finally, they pair the blueprint with the open resources discovered earlier and create new content to paper over gaps, including a standard final exam and various formative and summative assessments and assignments. The course is then subjected to extensive editorial review prior to entering a peer-review process, in which three other professors weigh in on the quality and scope of the course and its materials.

Once a course has been edited and uploaded, we have a dedicated permissions team reach out to the individuals who retain copyright to the "open-access" content to which the course points. We encourage copyright holders to adopt an open license or grant us permission to host the content locally.

Evidence of Effectiveness

Because of our open-access approach, we are hindered in the amount of data we can collect. At present, our strongest evidence is anecdotal. In two recent exchanges, we received the following unsolicited feedback:

> [Saylor.org] is so helpful and [I] wish more people knew about it. I think there should be a way to tell different professors and institutions, 'Hey, go to saylor.org and you literally have a cyber teacher.'[6]

I am a Malaysian who holds an engineering degree. I am interested in philosophy and history but couldn't study from the Internet without guidance because the information out there is simply too much. I tried to look for master courses [in which] to enroll but I don't have a huge sum of money reserved for education. Even if I [could] get a loan from the bank, most of the master courses require a relevant first degree. I am thankful that I found Saylor.org, which gave me a guideline on what to study, and open[ed] up . . . whole new channels of great sources.[7]

Challenges Encountered

We have encountered four major challenges in the process of developing our courseware and promoting its use:

Combating Link Rot

We struggle with the stability of our course materials. Because we link to a variety of external sites, we are constantly patrolling our site for link rot and requesting that our consultants find or create replacement materials. This is costly and frustrating, as entire courses can "go down" over night. We combat this issue through our permission initiative and the funding of replacement content, but it remains a challenge.

Developing Assessments

We grapple with the following assessment-related issues:

1. How do we develop sophisticated assessments to be administered in an online, unproctored setting? What sorts of "checks" do we need to put in place?

2. How do we handle assessment in courses tied to critical reading and writing skill development while maintaining our commitment to being scalable and cost-free?

3. How do we reach all interested learners, even those in low-bandwidth areas, while developing more sophisticated assessments? Adaptive assessments are costly to create and may be restricted to students with secure Internet access.

Driving Use and Adoption

We learned that in developing countries, librarians are the best contacts for disseminating open content and promoting open courseware. However, identifying and communicating with these individuals is difficult. Within the United States, we are still green in our efforts to identify and reach out to students unable to afford college.

This challenge is tied to issues of credibility: students want to know they can trust our materials and want to receive a credential to demonstrate course completion. We are cultivating partnerships with accredited institutions and have seen some traction among the founding institutions in OER University (OER-U). We plan to be early issuers within the Mozilla badges system, which could change the way in which institutions recognize and transfer credit, especially (initially) in prior learning assessment and recognition (PLAR) programs. We are still a long way, however, from securing a broad base of users.

Applicability/Replicability to Other Institutions or Programs

Our program is applicable/replicable to other institutions in three key ways.

Saylor Courseware Can Be Incorporated into Other Programs/Recognized for Transfer Credit

Our courses can be used in a variety of ways, but we see particular promise in working with organizations willing to issue transfer credit for Saylor courses. Initial talks with members of the OER University appear promising, but we also foresee that our courses could be of profound use to community colleges, which are seeing unprecedented demand while also coping with cost-cutting measures. On a smaller scale, we publish all of our content under an open license (CC BY 3.0) so that it can be adapted and remixed for use elsewhere.

The Saylor.org Platform Can Publish Courses for Institutions without a Public-Facing Learning Management System

We are pleased to publish courses from other organizations on our site. We have already adapted and published many of the Washington State Board for Community and Technical Colleges' "Open Course Library" courses, which were previously hosted in a proprietary LMS inaccessible to the public.

Our Course Development Model Can Be Useful to Other Institutions with Similar Online Courseware Plans

We have shared our development model with other programs, and several of those (including the Washington State Board for Community and Technical Colleges) have borrowed from our model and adapted various elements to suit their own needs.

Web-Based Supplement

We encourage readers to view our "Connecting the Dots" video (http://www.youtube.com/watch?v=yZzPZY5pSUg), which provides a virtual tour of our site as well as an overview of our course-development process and plans for the future.

Notes

1. Open College Textbook Act of 2009, S. 1714, 111th Cong. (2009–10) (introduced by Sen. Richard Durbin, September 24, 2009).
2. U.S. Department of Education, *The Condition of Education 2011* (NCES 2011-033), Indicator 43 (National Center for Education Statistics, 2011).
3. According to a recent iNACOL webinar, blended postsecondary education has risen from 8 percent in 2008 to 16 percent in 2009 and 30 percent in 2010.
4. Consider, for example, the tremendous popularity of the open-access Artificial Intelligence course that two Stanford professors are offering. Some reports indicate as many as 70,000 signed up to take the course.
5. The International Telecommunication Union's annual "Facts and Figures" report indicated that one-third of the world's 7 billion population (roughly 2.3 billion individuals) have access to the Internet (see International Telecommunication Union, *The World in 2011: ICT Facts and Figures* [October 25, 2011], http://www.itu.int/ITU-D/ict/facts/2011/material/ICTFactsFigures2011.pdf); meanwhile, according to the U.S. Centers for Disease Control and Prevention, 1.1 billion people still lack access to safe drinking water (see U.S. Centers for Disease Control and Prevention, *Safe Water System: A Low-Cost Technology for Safe Drinking Water* [March 2006], http://www.cdc.gov/safewater/publications_pages/fact_sheets/WW4.pdf.
6. Anonymous student, e-mail message to Saylor Foundation, November 5, 2011.
7. Anonymous student, e-mail message to Saylor Foundation, November 8, 2011.

Jennifer Shoop *is the Content Development Manager of the Saylor Foundation. She supervises course development, including all of the original content created for use in each of the Saylor.org courses. Shoop holds a B.A. in Literature and History from the University of Virginia, and an M.A. in English Literature.*

Penn State World Campus:
Ensuring Success, Not Just Access

Wayne Smutz and Craig D. Weidemann

THE PENNSYLVANIA STATE UNIVERSITY is Pennsylvania's land-grant university, a public research university whose mission is to educate students from Pennsylvania, the nation, and the world. The university provides undergraduate, graduate, professional, and continuing education through both resident instruction and online delivery from its administrative and research hub at the University Park campus and at twenty three campuses across Pennsylvania, serving more than 94,000 students.

Penn State has a rich legacy in distance learning, dating back to 1892 when courses were delivered through Rural Free Delivery. In 1998, Penn State entered the online learning market with the launch of the World Campus. Today, World Campus serves more than 10,300 students (primarily adult part-time learners), representing nearly 50,000 course enrollments, and delivers over seventy online degree and certificate programs to students in all fifty states and more than fifty countries worldwide.

Penn State prides itself on being a student-centered institution. Consistent with that goal, the World Campus takes a holistic approach to online learning characterized by a deep commitment to *student success* through rigor, quality, full integration with the academic community, outstanding student services, and a fundamental belief in innovation as a key to success. World Campus is closely integrated with the university's academic and student-support infrastructure and operates under the same policies and procedures as the rest of the university. World Campus is administered by Penn State Outreach, with oversight by a university-wide committee of academic deans and administrators that also oversees resident instruction and online learning. Integral to the World Campus's success are the academic colleges—the academic "home" of both faculty and the curricula. The collaboration between the World Campus and academic units is supported by a sophisticated revenue-sharing model that returns discretionary revenue to the colleges and that provides operational and investment funding for the World Campus infrastructure.

The World Campus provides quality administrative services that are flexible, scalable, and innovative. The services stem from an organizational culture focused on service to students, empowerment of staff, and accountability for everyone. Certain services are offered through unique partnerships and outsource agreements with external companies.

Important units in the World Campus, and their tools and services, support a game-changing experience for students.

- **Recruitment and Marketing:**
  - The marketing unit, internal to the World Campus, is critical to its success. Data-driven decisions are made about program viability. Sophisticated marketing strategies are employed to assist World Campus in meeting its goals, including increasing brand and program awareness, generating quality leads/prospective students, and promoting conversion of those prospective students into applicants and then into students. One of the critical factors in the success of World Campus has been the expertise of the marketing unit, which has been able to operate with a business mind-set within the academic environment.

  - Prospects are provided with an overview of what World Campus offers for those seeking a quality academic experience.

  - An external firm, Inside Track, provides prospective undergraduates with personal coaching from point of contact to the end of the fourth week of their first semester. Inside Track is there to provide support anytime during the critical first few weeks of a student's experience. See how online learning works at http://www.worldcampus.psu.edu/how-online-learning-works.

  - Smarter Measures, a purchased software assessment tool, helps incoming students assess their readiness for distance education. Advisors, who have access to assessment results, contact students to address the challenges identified.

  - Students are empowered by being provided with the information they need to successfully begin courses in their new field of study.

- **Instruction and Learning**—World Campus is not simply putting face-to-face learning experiences online. Learning is designed for the online environment. The Learning Design unit uses cognitive-learning theories and design theory and practice, blending the art and science of instruction to ensure student success. Integral to the mix is the recognition of what makes distance education unique—its focus on learner autonomy, learner control, and flexibility of pace, sequence, and timing. Among the products, services, and approaches available are the following:

- Archived lectures, videos, course tools, and presentations allow access whenever needed. Use of digital-learning objects facilitates learning through visualization, resulting in a more illustrative learning experience. Scalability is achieved by providing access to these digital-learning repositories for multiple students simultaneously.

- Just-in-time access to expert professional perspectives delivered through compelling video can meet the needs of various learning styles.

- Adaptive testing is a new technology that personalizes the learning process for each student. With Knewton, World Campus is pilot testing new software for helping students with remedial and developmental needs.

- World Campus students have access to Penn State's world-class research library, including digital resources, books, journals, e-journals, newspapers, microforms, databases, movies, music, and more. World Campus offers online tutorials for students who want to hone their research skills.

- World Campus faculty complete "Early Progress Reports" for all struggling students, which are then provided to the student and advisor. Advisor intervention has resulted in improved retention.

- The World Campus Faculty Development unit designs systems and services to support a competent and confident World Campus faculty. The world-class online-instruction framework focuses on excellence in online and blended pedagogy, facility with associated administrative tasks, and competence with the range of related technology. The Faculty Development unit also directs the Institute for Emerging Leaders in Online Education in partnership with the Sloan Consortium.

- **Advising and Student Engagement**—Outstanding advising and exceptional co-curricular student engagement are hallmarks of World Campus and are critical factors for students in establishing real and enduring connections with Penn State. Advising staff deliver strategic-support resources and strategies—including academic counseling, career counseling, communications and social media, student organizations and events, technical support, and undergraduate academic advising—to help adult online distance learners achieve their academic goals and build a lifelong connection to Penn State. Specific examples include the following:

- Clubs: World Campus Psychology Club and the Blue & White Society, the student contingent of the Penn State Alumni Association
- Pi Delta Chi Honors chapter for World Campus students
- Social media groups for World Campus students on Facebook, YouTube, and LinkedIn
- Blogs: microblog on Twitter and the *Corner of College and Allen* blog
- Live web streams of "Huddle with the Faculty," free lectures featuring Penn State faculty on Saturdays of home football games

Evidence of Effectiveness

In FY 2010–11, World Campus students' satisfaction with their undergraduate advisors, career counselors, and technical-support specialists averaged more than 95 percent. That same year, World Campus students joined the Penn State Alumni Association at a rate of 53 percent (almost twenty percentage points higher than other campuses), and the World Campus Blue & White Society chapter is already the second-largest chapter behind University Park. Future goals are to exceed current student-performance outcomes, maintain satisfaction and co-curricular engagement rates, increase retention to even higher levels, and enhance the quality of the total learning experience while scaling to increase course enrollments by 140 percent by FY 2020–21.

Lessons Learned

With fourteen years of experience in delivering online education, World Campus has learned a number of lessons that enable a continued focus on student success and outcome-based learning experiences:

1. Use technology where and how students expect it, where it adds value, where it can offer students options, and where it can extend student services to be available almost 24/7. For example, technology

can be used to make students feel a part of the unique Penn State community, even at a distance.

2. Use thoughtful metrics and data to determine which technology is working—and which isn't. Don't assume that it will work as intended for students. Be prepared to stop using what doesn't work.

3. The personal touch is still very important—don't try to use technology for everything. Choose wisely. For example, advisors and the Help Desk are critical links for students who need a real person to answer a question or troubleshoot a technical issue. Engage students through technology AND the old fashioned way—through human contact.

4. Experiment regularly with new approaches and technologies. For example, World Campus contracted with Inside Track to provide one-on-one coaching to prospects to map out a plan for their education and identify any barriers that would hinder their success, even before they make any long-term commitment.

5. Colleges and universities can no longer do everything themselves. Consider working with businesses that specialize in certain kinds of services, e.g., software development. Be sure to do your homework before partnering with them.

6. Student success doesn't end with the degree—career services should be offered throughout the educational experience and beyond.

7. Online learners have varying familiarity with technology. Providing excellent and timely technological support and resources is critical.

8. Invest in learning design and faculty development. The quality of the engaged learning experience is dependent upon the commitment of faculty and learning designers to exploring innovative ways of teaching and learning.

Finally, be prepared to recognize that whatever decisions are made, they will need to be revisited—probably sooner than later!

Wayne Smutz *is Executive Director of Penn State World Campus and Associate Vice President for Academic Outreach. Smutz oversees delivery of credit-based programs for adult learners through World Campus and through continuing education units at Penn State. He received his Ph.D. in Higher Education from Penn State.* **Craig D. Weidemann** *is Penn State's Vice President for Outreach, overseeing the largest unified outreach organization in American higher education, including the university's online World Campus. Weidemann received his B.S. from Illinois State University and his Ph.D. in Educational Psychology from the University of Georgia in Athens.*

Stories in Our Classrooms:
A Faculty Community of Practice
as an Agent of Change

Beverly Bickel, William Shewbridge, and Jack Suess

IN 2006, THE UMBC's (University of Maryland, Baltimore County) Division of Information Technology's (DoIT) New Media Studio (NMS) began facilitating digital storytelling workshops as a gateway opportunity for faculty to explore how student-centered assignments, creative work with course concepts, and the use of digital tools can lead students to develop digital literacies.[1] Prior to this event, UMBC had made very little progress in leveraging technology and multimedia to support scholarship and teaching in the humanities and social sciences. As faculty began to come together in support of the importance of digital storytelling in teaching and research, we realized that we were in the midst of a game-changing moment in our efforts to promote digital literacy among students.

In the first three years, the faculty workshops were funded by the NMS and led by the Center for Digital Storytelling (CDS), which was co-founded by Joe Lambert. CDS's pioneering work was a major inspiration to UMBC's early faculty adopters and inspired them to draw their colleagues into the effort. According to Kristen Drotner, this now-classic form of digital storytelling stems from Lambert's understanding that storytelling validates ordinary people's memories and experiences, serving to supplement and perhaps correct official histories.[2] While working as producers with audio and visual representations, storytellers discover how multimedia meanings are made and, in the process, are challenged to become more critical consumers of mass- and new-media messages.

Since 2006, this effort has brought together an interdisciplinary group of approximately one hundred faculty and staff representing a variety of departments that has developed into a community of practice focused on encouraging digital literacy. We call it a "community of practice"[3] because it is composed of early faculty adopters and IT staff who have worked together in the shared enterprise of digital storytelling workshops, whereby participants move fluidly between being novice learners or experts in various roles—as narrative authors and storytellers; photo, video, or sound editors; and artistic designers. In this collaborative professional context, everyone is challenged to reconsider learning and teaching as a shared social process that "differs from a mere collection of people by the strength and depth of the culture it is able to establish and which in turn supports group activity and cohesion."[4]

In the first few years, the NMS nurtured this faculty group through e-mail lists, by awarding equipment and software grants, by sponsoring research seminars and training workshops, and by helping to shine a spotlight on the innovative work of faculty and students. This "community" group has developed cohesion over the semesters and has come together in various ways to advocate for the advancement of digital literacies across the UMBC curriculum. As the importance of digital-media literacies in all disciplines and professions becomes more apparent on a national scale,[5] this group has helped jump-start campus discussions on addressing curricular changes, particularly in the humanities and social sciences. Thus, this faculty community of practice has emerged at the center of an environment that encourages collaborations across disciplinary boundaries, discussions about research, and innovation in classroom practices where new models of learning are explored.

Eventually, the annual workshops became self-sustaining as UMBC faculty and staff, who had been specially trained by CDS, assumed the role of facilitators. As this transition occurred, we knew we were on the right path to building a vibrant community of practice to support and promote digital literacies, as the peer-to-peer flavor to the workshops has enhanced faculty members' exploration of new media technologies in a collegial, interdisciplinary, and nonthreatening setting. Beyond the workshop, this spirit of collaboration and mutual support continued as participants sought opportunities to share ideas across departments. According to Jason Loviglio, director of UMBC's Media and Communication Studies (MCS) program,

> We have developed a real community of practice at UMBC based around the New Media Studio. . . . Every year we have widened the circle to the point where we had a core of people who were not only veterans of the workshop taught by Joe Lambert, but we were now the teachers of the workshop. It has been ambitious, it has felt quixotic to some of us, but it has been a really galvanizing experience where we feel like we can actually now share these ideas with our colleagues and we can watch them implement them in their classes.[6]

The community of practice has evolved from informal discussions to gatherings each semester to discuss technology-support needs, assignment ideas, grading rubrics, and stories about digital storytelling or visual assignments in over twenty courses annually. The community is supported by a website (http://www.umbc.edu/oit/newmedia/studio/digitalstories/index.html) and an active e-mail LISTSERV that boasts a membership of more than 175 faculty and staff members. The group has also served as springboard for broader discussions and has led in part to the creation of three working groups currently developing white papers on digital humanities in teaching, research, and publishing at UMBC.

With this increased interest in digital literacies came an increased demand for resources. In the absence of additional funding, faculty and staff have used the same grassroots approach that characterized the early development of the community of practice. Graduate assistants, financially supported by the NMS, began supporting faculty by providing basic technical training to students in the classroom. In addition, these assistants staffed a "genius bar" in the International Media Center's (IMC) Mac Lab, which had become the unofficial home for digital story activities. A closet in the IMC was outfitted for audio recording, and a few surplus cameras from the NMS were made available to students working on visual assignments.

In spring 2010, MCS and the NMS created a one-credit course, MCS 101L Multimedia Literacy Lab. The lab course was initially designed to accompany MCS 333 History and Theory of Mass Communication and Media Studies, a gateway course required of all MCS majors. The Multimedia Literacy Lab ensures that students develop basic multimedia skills while improving their writing abilities by creating two digital stories. Though it introduces students to a variety of production techniques, the lab stresses effective communication through the integration of written and audiovisual forms, and instructors expect all students to be able to communicate ideas effectively and creatively in multimodal work. As a result of connecting the lab to a required gateway course, the lab helps ensure that every MCS major creates at least one digital story or visual assignment early in the major. As Loviglio commented,

> The level of student engagement in digital assignments in MCS 333 has been truly astounding. Students spend more time working with course texts, researching course concepts, and collaborating with peers since we've begun to require them to answer questions about theory using digital storytelling formats. Students report greater enthusiasm both for the assignments and for the material they're covering now that some of their coursework includes digital assignments alongside traditional written assignments.[7]

Faculty members and the NMS have also explored means of using digital literacies to help connect students to communities beyond the campus. A number of unique collaborative projects have been developed in which students use digital media to give voice to first-generation female German immigrants, returning Peace Corp volunteers, youth activists, and local residents reflecting on the histories of regional communities.

One such collaboration, the Charlestown Project,[8] resulted from a partnership between the NMS and Retirement Living Television, a national network based at UMBC. Now in its fifth year, the project teams UMBC students with residents of the nearby Charlestown retirement community to create digital stories based on the residents' life experiences.[9] Based on the success of this project, a new freshman-year seminar was offered in the fall of 2011, "Creating Stories about Times of Change," in which students worked in intergenerational teams to create stories that focused on common threads and shared insights and lessons about growth. The narrative collaboration offered opportunities for empathy and a broadening of perspective about the creation of identity in times of change.

Active involvement by both UMBC and CDS in the New Media Consortium (NMC), a leader in advancing digital-media literacy and open courseware among U.S. universities, has fostered participation in a broader community of practice, resulting in collaborations with other institutions and organizations on curricula projects, joint training workshops, national and international conferences, and grant proposals. In one example, UMBC students—working directly with CDS and local community organizations—worked with members of the Somali Bantu and Bhutanese communities in telling stories of their refugee experiences.

In creating a collaborative, faculty-led environment where grassroots innovation in teaching digital literacies can thrive, UMBC has made significant progress. By taking this work into the community, members of UMBC's community of practice are also creating new opportunities for student learning and civic engagement. While sustaining momentum in the absence of new resources remains a challenge, the growing community of practice illustrates the power of committed faculty and staff in transforming a campus into a digitally literate academy.

Notes

1. To date, faculty from the following departments have attended the workshops and begun using digital assignments: Media and Communications Studies; Visual Arts;

Modern Languages and Linguistics; Intercultural Communications; Language, Literacy and Culture; History; American Studies; Psychology; Education; Gender and Women's Studies; Math; and Engineering.

2. K. Drotner, "Boundaries and Bridges: Digital Storytelling in Education Studies and Media Studies," in *Digital Storytelling, Mediatized Stories: Self-Representations in New Media*, ed. K. Lundby (New York: Peter Lang Publishing, 2008): 63

3. Jean Lave and Etienne Wenger, *Situated Learning: Legitimate Peripheral Participation* (Cambridge, England: Cambridge University Press, 1991).

4. Riel, M. & Polin, L, "Learning Communities: Common Ground and Critical Differences in Designing Technical Environments," in *Designing Virtual Communities in the Service of Learning*, ed. S. A. Barab, R. Kling and J. Gray (Cambridge, England: Cambridge University Press, 2004): 18.

5. L. Johnson, R. Smith, H. Willis, A. Levine, and K. Haywood, *The 2011 Horizon Report* (Austin, TX: The New Media Consortium, 2011).

6. Jason Loviglio, "Digital Stories in the Classroom" (profiles from UMBC's Community of Practice), accessed May 18, 2010, http://www.umbc.edu/oit/newmedia/studio/digitalstories/profiles.php.

7. Jason Loviglio, e-mail correspondence with author, November 16, 2010.

8. "Digital Stories from Charlestown," http://www.umbc.edu/oit/newmedia/studio/digitalstories/ctds.php.

9. W. Shewbridge, "Partners in Storytelling: UMBC, Retirement Living TV and the Charlestown Digital Story Project," in *Higher Education, Emerging Technologies, and Community Partnerships: Concepts, Models and Practices*, ed. M. Bowdon and R. Carpenter (Hershey, PA: IGI Global, 2011).

Beverly Bickel *is the Interim Director and Research Assistant Professor in the Language, Literacy and Culture Doctoral program at the University of Maryland, Baltimore County. Her teaching and research focus on digital storytelling and digital literacies, globalized communication in cross-cultural contexts, critical pedagogies and online pedagogies, and how the public space of the Internet supports transformational knowledge projects.* **William Shewbridge** *is founding Director of the University of Maryland, Baltimore County, New Media Studio. His work focuses on advancing media literacy and exploring new technologies for learning. He is an affiliate Assistant Professor of Modern Languages and Linguistics, teaching courses in intercultural media, television production, and digital storytelling.* **Jack Suess** *is Vice President for Information Technology and CIO at University of Maryland, Baltimore County (UMBC). He is a frequent speaker on security, identity, and cloud services and has volunteered in numerous ways with EDUCAUSE, InCommon, REN-ISAC, and Internet2. For more information, visit http://bit.ly/fSB5ID.*

Kansas State University: Creating a Virtual Faculty Consortium

Elizabeth A. Unger

Introduction

CHANGE IS RAPID and seemingly accelerating in our world. The changes often require degrees or certifications not currently provided by higher education institutions. Change in traditional institutions of higher education, including creation of new degrees and certifications, is a slow process leading to long delays in meeting the educational needs of society. From a university perspective, some of these educational needs emerge and then fade. If an institution responds and creates faculty positions to offer such a degree or certification, it may find itself with significant problems and costs to utilize the faculty hired. Even in the event the degree is viable long term, institutions may be reluctant or unable to hire the needed faculty members.

There are often one or a few faculty members at an institution who are qualified to offer the needed education, but not the critical mass needed to offer a degree or certificate. One solution is to create a virtual faculty. A virtual faculty is a faculty formed from faculty members teaching in a set of academically similar institutions. A virtual faculty allows the institutions to respond rapidly—without taking on the risks of hiring a critical mass of faculty at a single institution—to deliver the new degree via the Internet. It also solves the challenges of having faculty members whose expertise is no longer needed by the institution.

The idea for creating a "virtual faculty" arose in the mid-1990s when there was a need for new knowledge offerings in engineering, agriculture, and human sciences to include courses, certifications, and master's degrees at Kansas State University. We have established virtual faculties in all these areas, with the first in the human sciences. The university had a few qualified faculty members, but far fewer than the set of faculty members needed to offer degrees in the identified areas of gerontology and tourism. Hiring more qualified faculty in those areas was not feasible. It was recognized that a virtual faculty depended upon Internet capability sufficient to provide courses at a distance from the institution and a course or learning management system capable of allowing faculty members to provide high-quality teaching, as well as faculty members willing to experiment in this new mode of providing instruction.

By the late 1990s, the mechanisms for combining faculty members from various institutions to form a sufficient number of complementarily skilled teachers arose. The penetration of and increase in Internet capability and the introduction of learning or course management systems at a number of like institutions in the Midwest were the needed resources. Both Kansas State University and the University of Nebraska, Lincoln, for instance, were successfully delivering degrees over the Internet in the late 1990s. A logical extension was to form an agreement with a number of other similar institutions to share faculty members to form the critical mass of faculty members required. The concept of a virtual faculty was discussed with Kansas State University's IT grant writer. She worked with administrators from the College of Human Ecology to understand their views on offering the degrees in gerontology and tourism with a virtual faculty.

There was a very positive response from the dean, who had been meeting since the early 1990s with other deans of human sciences in the Midwest and had already formed an alliance—the Human Sciences Alliance—one of the purposes of which was to help stimulate and promote distance learning. The alliance was approached with the idea, and members were receptive to the concept of creating a virtual faculty. Under the leadership of a team from Kansas State University, planning funds were obtained to create the policies and procedures and to form an organizational structure. The entire planning process—informal and formal—took under two years. The formal discussions to create the organization consisted of multiday planning meetings with representatives from the institutions in the alliance. An organization to implement the policy and manage the requisite processes was created in 2002.

The facilitating organization is today called the Great Plains IDEA (Interactive Distance Education Alliance) and is physically located at Kansas State University (http://www.gpidea.org). Great Plains IDEA facilitates as a second virtual faculty providing degrees and certificates in agriculture (http://www.agidea.org), and the university participates in a third virtual faculty providing nuclear engineering education (http://www.big12engg.org).

Challenges and Solutions

Two major planning conferences for the initial human sciences effort took place involving the chief academic and financial officers; deans of human sciences, continuing education, and graduate schools; and academics from thirteen Midwestern land-grant institutions (http://www.hsidea.org/about).

Two major challenges and several minor issues arose, including which institution would count the student in its head count and which institution would grant the degree. It should be noted that it was never a consideration that Great Plains IDEA would offer the degree or certification. The institutions were all regionally accredited research institutions, and a degree from any of them was perceived as having significantly greater value than a degree from a consortium or alliance of institutions. It was decided that the earned degree would be offered by the institution providing the major professor or advisor to the student, and that institution would have to formally accept the student into the consortium program and could include the student in its head count.

The two major challenges were establishing a common tuition (credit-hour cost) for students in the programs and residency for the master's degree program. It was very important that students would pay the same tuition for every course they took, regardless of which institution was offering that course. Establishing this would mute the issue of in-state vs. out-of-state tuition, and it also eliminated a factor in the student's financial-decision process.

The traditional concept of residency for a degree was defined initially at most institutions in terms of the amount of time the student resided on the campus. The residency requirement had to be met for the degree to be granted by that institution. Later this was implemented in terms of the number of courses that had to be taken at the institution. The extension of that concept to courses taken over the Internet had been accepted at some institutions, but the concept of having a virtual faculty offer a degree went well beyond that. A virtual faculty whereby the student could, in theory, take just one course from the institution granting the degree simply did not meet the traditional meaning or impact of residency.

In 1989, the University of Phoenix established its online degree programs. One of the goals of this university from its establishment was to provide degrees that met the current needs of business and industry. During the organizational meetings of Great Plains IDEA, the deans of the graduate schools of participating institutions were aware of and supported these goals. Their discussions focused on the necessity to move past the traditional residency concept in order to meet the current educational needs of society. Residency, a concept that had been established when localized and printed knowledge was the norm, no longer seemed necessary with current communication technology. They also felt that since the institutions considering this virtual faculty concept were similar in educational mission and accreditation status, the need to ensure a student had taken the required number of courses at their institutions in order to meet residency requirements was no longer necessary. Finally, it was clear to the graduate deans that if their institutions were to be responsive to working professionals, online graduate degrees had to be a part of their offerings. The deans agreed to attempt to change residency definitions on their campuses.

Residency is in the purview of the graduate faculty of the institutions, and the process to effect change had to be initiated in each institution. Ultimately, the residency obstacle was overcome for all degrees offered by the Great Plains IDEA consortium. At many of the institutions, the concept of residency for graduate work was removed completely. Removing residency at the graduate level has had a stimulating effect on the offerings of distance-delivered degrees.

The second major challenge was the issue of offering the courses for a degree with a common tuition independent of the institution at which it is offered. Tuition in some institutions was set by a state agency, and this made it very difficult to change tuition for specified degrees. The variation in the tuition per credit hour varied significantly among the thirteen institutions. In order to allow each school to be compensated at its own tuition plus its costs, the chief financial officers had to agree on a process to establish that alliance program tuition each year. In addition, the cost of administering the program had to be recovered. Strong leadership among the chief financial officers resulted in a process to determine annually a common tuition that met all institutions' requirements.

Organizational Structure

It was determined that an organization governed by the alliance institutions would be created to facilitate administrative and academic processes such as student acceptance into each program, enrollment, and to account for the tuition and fees and redistribute them in a fashion that met the legal conditions for tuition at each institution in the consortium.

The basic principles of organizational structure were to maintain institutional control of all operational issues of the facilitating organization and faculty control of all issues related to academics (http://www.hsidea.org/PolicyProcedure/Appendices/appendix_c2.pdf). Institutions choose which programs to offer, there is a core curriculum but course names and such can vary among institutions, all courses are regular university courses, and all faculty are governed by the institutional guidelines but are given de facto faculty status in program-participating institutions. Financial accounting and program and teaching assessment are facilitated by the alliance organization.

Conclusion

The primary goals of this effort are to be more responsive to the educational needs of the nation while providing a more flexible environment in which to offer and subsequently drop degrees when no longer needed. These goals have been met. Great Plains IDEA facilitates the offering of thirteen degrees and certifications in human sciences (established 1999), with eleven of the thirteen institutions participating. AG*IDEA (established in 2007, http://www.agidea.org) offers ten degrees and certifications. And the number of degrees, certifications, and member institutions is growing. Great Plains IDEA currently encompasses institutions in seventeen states, from Texas to North Dakota and from California to Florida. Great Plains IDEA has helped other groups form alliances that facilitate virtual faculties, including in the field of nuclear engineering. The initial thirteen institutions have grown to nineteen, and there are a number of institutions wishing to join.

The concept of a virtual faculty is but one way traditional universities can respond to what is seen as their increasing responsibility to meet the rapidly changing educational requirements of the world. Collaboration with segments of industry may become commonplace, thus providing additional faculty members for the collaborative teaching of a course from qualified professionals in the specific industry. If this is to occur, additional traditional barriers may have to be broken—beginning with the professional titles of these individuals, for example. Change is in the future for higher education institutions. Institutional change must at least maintain the quality education traditional universities provide.

Elizabeth A. Unger is Professor of Computing and Information Sciences and Academic IT Research Fellow, having served 14 years as Vice Provost for Academic Services and Technology and Dean of Education. Her research is in IT security, and she has worked to move learning toward a model of individualized educational experiences, using IT as a tool.

CS50 at Harvard: "The Most Rewarding Class I Have Taken . . . Ever!"

Katie Vale

A TRAIL OF COLORFUL BALLOONS leads from Oxford Street to the Northwest Labs building. As I head downstairs, I exchange greetings with our dean. Someone hands me a tub of popcorn, a squishy ball, and a scavenger hunt list. The room is pulsing to a techno beat, and as I scan the room I can see many of my faculty and staff colleagues, including our university president, who is having an animated discussion with an undergraduate. Is this a party? A film festival? No. This is CS50.

CS50 is Harvard's introductory course in computer science for majors and nonmajors alike. In 2002, CS50 had an enrollment of about 100 students and an uneven reputation as a course that one took with caution.[1]

In 2007, a new instructor named David Malan set out to reimagine CS50 and, in the course of doing so, set forth a new path for course design. His goal was to increase excitement for the discipline of computer science through improvements in both "perception and design" of the course. While the course generally received reasonable evaluations, the consensus seemed to be—regardless of which faculty member had been teaching the course a given semester—that it was demanding and not particularly inspiring.

For the new version of the course, Malan set out to retain the demanding aspects of the course, but to amp up the inspiration factor via clear educational expectations; extensive online and human-support resources; engaging, real-world problems to solve; and an atmosphere of fun both in and out of the classroom.

Around the same time that Malan took over responsibility for CS50, Harvard College was adopting a new undergraduate curriculum in general education. "Gen Ed," as it is known, seeks to connect Harvard students to their lives outside and after college. It was in this spirit that Malan designed a new CS50 that would appeal not only to CS concentrators, but also to any students who wanted to know a little more about the technologies they use every day. Thus, CS50 counts for both the Gen Ed requirement in Empirical and Mathematical Reasoning and for the computer science concentration (the term Harvard uses in lieu of majors). Recitation sections are formed by students who self-select into tracks for the more comfortable, less comfortable, and in the middle. Indeed, the new syllabus assures students that newcomers have nothing to fear about taking the course alongside lifelong nerds:

> Know that CS50 draws quite the spectrum of students. . . . However, what ultimately matters in this course is not so much where you end up relative to your classmates but where you, in Week 12, end up relative to yourself in Week 0.[2]

The class is not graded on a curve, nor are there specific numeric cutoffs for grades. Each student's grade is determined after input from the teaching fellows (or TFs, the term Harvard uses in lieu of teaching assistants), who grow to know students well over the duration of the semester. CS50 may be taken either for a letter grade or Pass/Fail. The syllabus spells out the topics to be covered in every class session; explains assignment and quiz due dates, grading, and weight; and provides detailed information on how to seek help.

It is not surprising that a computer science course would make use of technology for teaching, but it is rare to see a face-to-face course invest as much in online resources as CS50 has done. Key to CS50's success has been its use of a spectrum of digital tools, including the course website; lecture, section, and seminar videos; virtual office hours; "anonymized" bulletin boards; TF-scribed lecture notes; tablet PCs for grading; an evening telephone-help hotline; FAQs; and curated links to helpful materials such as APIs, free software, and dozens of online tutorials.

The course website, http://www.cs50.net, serves as the hub of all this activity. Unlike the standard-course LMS page, which is updated primarily before the semester even starts, the CS50 site provides up-to-the-minute information on assignments, sections, quizzes, and seminars. CS50 employs two multimedia producers who record lectures, sections, and guest speaker seminars; teaching fellows also record their homework-help "code walkthrough" sessions. All videos are made available on the course website within 24 hours of recording, along with lecture notes, the source code shown during the presentation, the instructor's slides and demos, and even links to the music played at the beginning and end of class.

In 2006, the enrollment for CS50 was 132 students. In 2011, after four years of reinvention and refinement, the enrollment is now at 614 students.

It is the second-largest course at Harvard College and meets in the biggest auditorium on campus. Though the Computer Science Department has been thrilled with the course's expansion, Professor Malan has had to manage that growth carefully in order to preserve the "apprenticeship model"[3] that ensures every student receives sufficient individual attention and coaching. As such, CS50 has a huge support staff. While Malan lectures to the entire class twice a week, fifty-one TFs hold weekly sections of twelve students. Each TF acts as a mentor for those same twelve students throughout the semester and provides extensive comments on assignments through the use of tablet PCs for grading.[4] The TFs receive help from another forty-one student-course assistants (CAs) who do not lead sections but who provide additional support to students in help sessions, walkthroughs, and during the final project "Hackathon." Two head teaching fellows organize and lead the TFs and CAs, while a team of five graders, video producers, and systems administrators round out the course staff.

As part of his quest to make CS50 accessible to a wider range of undergraduates, Malan decided to increase the opportunities for students to obtain just-in-time help. Beyond the standard options of drop-in help sessions, scheduled office hours, e-mail and discussion forums, he also utilized a third-party application to permit students to approach TFs in real time via chat and VoIP. The application, Elluminate, also allowed TFs to view and edit the students' screens to provide remote troubleshooting as needed. Using Elluminate, students can log in and virtually "raise their hand"; the instructor or TF can see the order in which students arrived and handle the queue fairly. While only around 15 percent of CS50 students avail themselves of the virtual office hours, the consensus of those who have was that the system is convenient and works especially well for shorter questions.[5]

Malan noted that students who had grown up using iPods, e-mail, Nintendo, and texting were less than enthused by the traditional "Hello World" coding assignments. So, he set out to make the coursework more interesting and challenging for these "Digital Native"[6] students by asking students to solve real problems using a variety of programming languages.[7] For the first assignment, students use Scratch, a programming language developed at the MIT Media Lab. Scratch is a drag-and-drop, low-barrier, easy-to-learn language that allows new coders to create animations, interactive stories, and simple applications.[8] While Scratch may appear deceptively simple, it affords an opportunity for learners to begin discussing traditional beginning-computer-science topics such as variables and loops without having to worry (yet) about syntax errors.

After mastering a first Scratch assignment and gaining some confidence, the students proceed into six weeks on the fundamentals of the C programming language. Later in the semester, the class covers web programming, mobile applications, and a brief overview of compilers and assembly language.[9] Each assignment comes in a "standard edition" or "hacker edition." Students with a stronger background in computer science are invited to push themselves via the hacker-level problem sets.

These problem sets ask students to try solving problems or "reverse engineering" items that they encounter every day. These range from validation of credit card numbers to decoding forensic images of photos deleted from a flash drive, to creation of E*Trade–style financial systems to GIS mashups using Google APIs. For final projects, students are allowed to come up with their own ideas based on their particular level of comfort. To aid them, Malan provides access to as much real-world data as possible to encourage problem-based learning (PBL). He has worked with university IT staff and data providers to obtain access to resources such as dining menus, shuttle schedules, and APIs for iSites (Harvard's LMS), so that students can try their hands at writing applications that will benefit the Harvard community, such as lost-and-found applications, student organization databases, and so on. The CS50 website also has links to dozens of open APIs, data feeds, and tutorials.

To further support students working on final projects (as well as to continue their indoctrination into "geek"/CS culture), the class hosts an annual Hackathon all-nighter for students and course staff. The event begins on a Friday evening at 8 p.m.; students who choose to participate must set three goals for that evening in terms of what they want to achieve during the Hackathon. During the evening, students consult with course staff and each other in designing their final projects.

Food is served at 9 p.m. and 1 a.m., and anyone still awake at 5 a.m. is treated to a pancake breakfast at IHOP. For the past two years, the Hackathon has been generously hosted by the Microsoft New England Research Center (NERD) here in Cambridge, Massachussetts. According to one teaching fellow, the ability to spend the evening within the company's facility and chat with some of the Microsoft staff has cemented several students' decisions to continue studying computer science after CS50 is over.[10]

At the end of the semester, students are required to demonstrate their finished projects at the CS50 Fair, described at the beginning of this piece. This is not a course in which a student works on a final project alone, submits it to a lone grader, receives a score, and is done. On the contrary, the expectation for all CS50 students is that their project should be something to show to complete strangers, their friends, other professors, and even the president of Harvard. During the fair, students stand at a trade-show–style booth and give demonstrations of their project to all comers. Visitors to the fair can win door prizes if they visit a prescribed number of booths. Both students and visitors are plied with food and candy, and students have the opportunity to mingle with recruiters from technology companies including Google, Facebook, and Activision that are seeking summer interns. The CS50 Fair is now recognized as an annual "big event" and is eagerly attended by students, faculty, and staff.[11]

Student response to the reinvention of CS50 has been dramatic. Student course evaluations from 2010 gave the course a mean overall rating of 4.2/5, despite acknowledgement that the workload was heavier than in other courses.[12] Sample comments from students make note of not only what they feel they have learned, but how much their confidence in their ability to tackle new opportunities has improved.[13]

> Most well-organized course ever. So many resources on cs50.net and such a good help support system that it was sometimes overwhelming.

> It inspires and challenges like no other course.

> In just a semester, I feel that I'm able to understand all sorts of things about computer science and have the tools to explore any number of avenues in the future.

> Please take this class. Do not leave Harvard without taking it because the experience—the professor, the community, the liveliness, the pain, the triumph, the panic before Friday 7 p.m., the Fair, the Hackathon— is truly phenomenal.

Before Malan took over the course in 2007, CS50 had an enrollment of 132, 34 percent of whom were female. In the span of four years, class enrollment has soared to over 600 students, although the rough gender split of 65/35 still exists.[14] Although the male/female ratio has stayed roughly the same, huge growth has been seen in the number of students—particularly female students—choosing computer science as a primary or secondary concentration. In the class of 2006, twenty-five students chose computer science as a primary concentration, with two marking it as a secondary. Of these, only three were women. For the class of 2013, fifty-one students have chosen computer science as a primary concentration, twenty-one of them (41 percent) women. (Secondary concentration data for the class of 2012 and 2013 is not yet available, but the figure was 40 percent for the class of 2011.) As a result, the department has seen increased enrollment in CS51, the follow-up course to CS50, and has also begun developing new next steps for students who have taken CS50.[15]

The wider campus, too, has seen what we have dubbed "The CS50 Effect."

Pragmatic changes to the IT and classroom infrastructure have occurred due to the needs of the course. In Fall 2011 wireless connectivity was increased in areas that included dining halls, house (dormitory) lounges, and even Harvard Yard to accommodate the fifty-plus class sections of CS50 as well as other subjects. New initiatives in learning-space design have been launched both to support CS50 and to afford other faculty opportunities to experiment with active- and problem-based learning. A student group, HackHarvard, has begun a January-term course on extending one's CS50 project into an actual product; the group receives support from HUIT Academic Technology and the Harvard Business School Innovation Lab.

To sum up, CS50 achieved this turnaround not through the mere adding on of a particular educational technology, but through Professor Malan's careful reimagination of the course, beginning with clear pedagogical goals and a desire to include those not formerly nerds. He achieved this through

- lectures, sections, seminars, and help sessions videotaped and made available online;
- inclusion of enabling technologies for online office hours and grading via tablet PCs;
- provision of extensive online open educational resources and tutorials;
- use of problem-based learning, real-world examples, and apprenticeship models to motivate and support students of different backgrounds; and
- fostering a sense of excitement, camaraderie, and encouragement within the course through events such as the Hackathon and CS50 Fair.

At Harvard at least, it is clear that CS50 is changing the game of what a course can—indeed, *should*—be.

Notes

1. David J. Malan, "Reinventing CS50" (in proceedings of the 41st ACM Technical Symposium on Computer Science Education, Milwaukee, Wisconsin, March 10–13, 2010), Gary Lewandowski, Steven Wolfman, Thomas J. Cortina, Ellen L. Walker, and David R. Musicant, eds. (New York: Association for Computing Machinery): 152–56.
2. CS50 Syllabus, http://cdn.cs50.net/2011/fall/lectures/0/syllabus.pdf, 1.
3. David J. Malan, "Grading Qualitatively with Tablet PCs in CS 50" (paper presented at the Workshop on the Impact of Pen-Based Technology on Education, Blacksburg, Virginia, October 12–13, 2009).
4. Ibid.

5. David J. Malan, "Virtualizing Office Hours in CS50," *ACM SIGCSE Bulletin* 41, no. 3 (paper presented at the 14th Annual ACM Conference on Innovation and Technology in Computer Science Education, Paris, France, July 2009).
6. J. Palfrey and U. Gasser, *Born Digital* (New York: Basic Books, 2008).
7. S. Ahlfeldt, S. Mehta, and T. Sellnow, "Measurement and Analysis of Student Engagement in University Classes Where Varying Levels of PBL Methods of Instruction Are in Use," *Higher Education Research & Development* 24, no. 1 (February 2005): 5–20.
8. M. Resnick, J. Maloney, A. Monroy-Hernández, N. Rusk, E. Eastmond, K. Brennan, A. Millner, E. Rosenbaum, J. Silver, B. Silverman, and Y. Kafai, "Scratch: Programming for All," *Communications of the ACM*, November 2009.
9. Malan, "Reinventing CS50," 154.
10. David Kosslyn (Harvard '10), conversation with author, December 10, 2010.
11. "CS50 Fair," http://www.youtube.com/watch?v=Re_wS6xhWnk.
12. David J. Malan, Fall 2010's Q Guide Results, https://www.cs50.net/q/.
13. Ibid., https://www.cs50.net/q/?k=strengths.
14. CS50 Enrollment, https://manual.cs50.net/Enrollment.
15. Malan, "Reinventing CS50," 156.

Katie Vale *is Director of Academic Technology in the HUIT organization at Harvard University, as well as co-chair of the Harvard Teaching and Learning Consortium. Prior to her current role, she was Assistant Director in the MIT Office of Educational Innovation and Technology. She is a 2012 Frye Fellow.*

Transforming Education with Research That Makes a Difference

J. D. Walker, Charles D. Dziuban, and Patsy D. Moskal

POSITIVE CHANGE IN EDUCATION happens when faculty gain insight into the relationship between student learning and their teaching behaviors through systematic research that they conduct, present, and publish. This grounded research can improve teaching and learning and create a positive return on investment for faculty innovation and student engagement. Such research can be game changing.

Technology frequently inspires pedagogical change, encouraging faculty to rethink their approach to teaching in light of what new digital tools can do. Faculty-driven research into the effectiveness of technological innovations can positively enhance this change, supporting and guiding it in constructive ways.

First, creating new, technology-enhanced learning activities is difficult. One consistent finding from fifty years of educational research is that small details of design and implementation can significantly impact the effectiveness of teaching methods. Every instructor is familiar with the great variability in student reactions and performance across semesters that makes it difficult to assess effectiveness through unsystematic observations.

Second, changing teaching methods requires effort. Incorporating more active, student-centered methods is not easy, particularly for those instructors who are most comfortable lecturing. Without solid evidence that new pedagogical approaches benefit students, change may not be sustainable, as many faculty may revert to older methods.

In this chapter, we present a case study of five faculty from the University of Minnesota (UM) and University of Central Florida (UCF) who have used classroom-based research to investigate the impact their creative uses of technology have had on their students and their instruction. Their experiences serve as models for others in the classroom and illustrate the value in researching the impact of technology on education.

The University of Minnesota Initiative

Professor Sehoya Cotner of UM's biology program faced the first challenge just described when she created video podcasts, or "vodcasts," which combined custom animation and video segments with music and faculty voice-over, and which were designed to address topics known to be difficult for her introductory biology students. Initial reactions to the vodcasts were positive, but did they really help students learn? Dr. Cotner partnered with researchers to study their effectiveness using a comparative research design. One section of her introductory biology course received vodcasts while the other section had access to "class captures," which combined the output of the classroom's digital projector with a recording of the instructor's voice.

Dr. Cotner found that student reception of the custom vodcasts was more enthusiastic than reception of the class captures. Additionally, after controlling for potential confounding variables, including students' overall grade point average (GPA), major, gender, ethnic background, high school rank, year in college, composite ACT scores, and initial level of evolution knowledge, students who used the custom vodcasts achieved significantly higher scores on an end-of-term test of evolution knowledge than students who used the class captures.

Professor Catherine Solheim of the Department of Family Social Science utilized newly constructed "active learning classrooms" with physical layout and technological affordances designed to facilitate active, student-centered approaches to teaching and learning. Here, recent research shows that, when compared to traditional classrooms and while holding pedagogical approach constant, such new learning spaces can alter instructor and student behavior and improve student learning.[1]

So space matters. When Dr. Solheim's introductory class was first scheduled in a new learning space, she taught using her usual lecture-based pedagogy. After that experience, she participated in an eighteen-month faculty-development program designed to encourage and enable instructors to employ active learning techniques in their classes. She then used a longitudinal research design to compare the first class with a second iteration of the same course, which had been revised to feature a student-centered pedagogical approach. After controlling for all available demographic variables, she found significant improvements in student learning in the second section, demonstrating that pedagogy matters too.

The University Central Florida Initiative

Class discussions in the online learning environment can take on transformational characteristics because the nature of learning engagement can change dramatically when students are separated through time and space. Professors Kerstin Hamann, Phillip Pollock, and Bruce Wilson of the Political Science Department investigated the effectiveness of discussion groups in online classes, controlling for GPA, major, class standing, ethnicity, gender, and instructor. When they examined the frequency and quality of students' postings in the asynchronous format, they found a strong relationship to learning outcomes in political science classes. Interestingly, these findings are moderated by students' reading behavior in the classes as measured by their actual replies to peers' postings in the discussion groups. Further, they found that reading behavior in online discussion groups interacts with students' GPA. Their study led them to conclude that course modality does not dictate students' engagement levels and that the benefits of class discussion transcend class modality. Finally, they concluded that a key enabling factor in developing successful online discussions depends on the instructor providing an effective framework in which those discussions can take place.

Professors Tim Brown of UCF's Nicholson School of Communication and Amanda Groff of the Anthropology Department are conducting long-range research into the learning value brought to the instructional environment by mobile devices and social networking tools when compared to learning management systems. They acknowledge the virtual explosion of social media tools readily available to students and ask questions such as, "Can we use Facebook and Twitter as effective instructional devices?" They are examining the reasons students use varying types of communication channels and the potential effectiveness of social media as a channel for communication for academic information. The results of their research show that students prefer to get their course-related information through official channels such as e-mail and course management systems. However, students are willing to get some course information through social devices so long as they are not required to share personal information. They conclude that students compartmentalize their communication tools into social tools for social engagement and work tools for work time. Rarely do they cross boundaries, as student motivations are perceived differently with each communication tool. In this research, "the medium seems to be the message."

Professor John Shafer of the Theatre Department is conducting research into theater transformation via contemporary digital technologies. Student actors participate from three universities: UCF in Florida, Bradley University in

Illinois, and the University of Waterloo in Canada. Professor Shafer, working with George Brown at Bradley and Gerd Hauck at Waterloo, produced *Alice Experiments in Wonderland,* merging three stages, casts, and audiences into one interactive experience through an Internet2 high-speed connection. Their research has developed a new paradigm for theater, illustrating that a common venue is not necessary and that audiences do not have to be in the same location in order to experience the artistic value of a performance. Their findings reveal a favorable audience reaction and a positive experience among the actors. This particular initiative produces a completely transformed model for teaching, learning, and theatrical production enabled by the Internet. Shafer and his colleagues found that no longer is common physical space a requisite for excellent theater.

These case studies demonstrate that creating a viable culture of scholarship at the classroom level yields information that can translate into immediate improvement, thereby supporting more effective learning. We know that students become more engaged in their education when they experience a respectful and facilitative learning environment, especially when concepts and information develop in a culture of effective communication. The scholarship of teaching responds to these needs by creating an environment wherein inquiry informs effective practice that in turn generates further research to the point at which the students become the real game changers.

Note

1.   D. Christopher Brooks, "Space Matters: The Impact of Formal Learning Environments on Student Learning," *British Journal of Educational Technology* 42, no. 5 (2011): 719–26.

J.D. Walker *manages the research and evaluation team in the Office of Information Technology at the University of Minnesota. The mission of the team is to investigate the ways in which digital educational technologies are affecting the teaching and learning environment in higher education.* **Chuck Dziuban** *is Director of the Research Initiative for Teaching Effectiveness at the University of Central Florida, where he has been a faculty member since 1970. He evaluates the impact of distributed learning in higher education. Currently, he is developing data models that can help with designing effective educational environments.* **Patsy Moskal** *is Associate Director for the Research Initiative for Teaching Effectiveness at the University of Central Florida. Since 1996, she has served as the liaison for faculty research of distributed learning and teaching effectiveness. Moskal specializes in program evaluation and applied data analysis, helping faculty and organizations improve education.*

Shaping the Path to Digital:
The Indiana University eTexts Initiative
Brad Wheeler and Nik Osborne

Introduction

THE RISING COST OF COLLEGE TEXTBOOKS has long been a burden for students, often motivating them to seek creative ways to get around this expense. Though digital textbooks—with their ability to provide cheaper, easier, and better access to content—have been around for years, the use of digital textbooks for academic purposes is still not widespread.

We are now in an era of great progress for digital textbooks and digital learning experiences, collectively referred to here as e-texts. Because costs are the most salient issue, new approaches are needed that work on the root causes of textbook prices for students. Early 2012 began with three promising developments:

- First, federal and state governments—along with private philanthropy—are investing hundreds of millions of dollars in freely available open educational resources (OER). These resources are being targeted at required, high-enrollment courses where they can have broad impact for all types of institutions.

- Second, Apple and other firms are bringing forth new technologies and business models in a bid to transform the textbook industry.

- Third, some institutions are using their experiences from volume software buying to change the pricing terms for e-texts in a sustainable win-win way for students, authors, and publishers.

This case study focuses on the third approach as it went from pilot study to full implementation at Indiana University (IU) and is now in a trial phase at five peer institutions.

Attacking the Root Causes of Textbook Prices

As noted, textbook prices have been an escalating problem, causing on-going concern among students, their parents, and governmental agencies over the role of textbooks in the growing cost of college. At IU, it is estimated that textbooks may account for almost 10 percent of a student's total cost of attendance per year, while at some community colleges, the percentage is far higher—sometimes more than the cost of tuition.

Over the years, students and content creators (authors and publishers) have been engaged in a self-reinforcing, negative economic loop for textbooks. Creators only get paid for their investment and work when a new textbook is sold, and students save money by purchasing a used textbook at a lower cost. Creators price higher as fewer students buy new, and students either seek used books or older editions, go without an assigned text, or turn to digital piracy in response to higher prices.

Early signs in the shift to digital were also troubling. Shrewd students who succeeded in buying a used textbook and selling it back had a net cost of about 35 percent of the book's list price, but less than half of students generally succeeded in selling back. In 2010, e-text pricing was around 70–75 percent of a new paper book or roughly double the cost of the buy-sellback net cost for students. E-texts (naturally) had no option for sellback, and they were riddled with restrictions concerning printing, length of access, and so forth. In addition, publishers were employing a bridging strategy to kill the used-book market by combining single-use website codes with new textbooks for essential online materials. If a student bought a used book, he or she would then still need to pay retail price for a website code.

Thus, while the shift to digital provided new opportunities for students to save money and publishers to rethink their business models, the trend was heading in precisely the wrong direction for content pricing. Also, publishers, bookstores, and others were coming forward with clever new software and hardware platforms for students to read and annotate e-texts. In the absence of a university plan, it is not unreasonable to foresee that a freshman could, with five courses, have seven e-texts requiring four or five different types of software just to study! Obviously, that makes no sense.

The Early eText Pilot Program at Indiana University

These root causes of textbook prices and trends for digital texts were already becoming clear in 2009. As part of its second Information Technology

Strategic Plan, Indiana University, a research institution with 110,000 students on eight campuses, began engaging in broad conversations with publishers to assess digital content and handheld devices trends. In order to address concerns about the rising cost of textbooks, IU soon after implemented a two-year pilot project to study the use of e-texts and other digital-learning materials. IU was betting that the same successful approaches it had used in negotiating volume licensing deals with Microsoft and Adobe could be used for e-texts.

The pilot project was guided by several key objectives:

- To reduce the costs of course-related materials for students

- To provide faculty with the high-quality materials they desire

- To enable adaptive learning platforms and new tools for teaching and learning—for instance, allowing annotations in an e-text that can be shared with other users

- To develop a sustainable model that works for all stakeholders involved: faculty, students, authors, and publishers

In 2009, an initial assessment was performed at IU on twenty high-enrollment courses—including science, business, and English—to gather quantitative information about the cost of textbooks for students. The assessment looked at a student's total cost of buying a textbook (including purchase and resell) over the entire life cycle of a textbook (three to four years). Around one-third of students had a net cost of 35–40 percent of retail, while the remaining two-thirds (who weren't able to resell) had a net cost around 60–65 percent of retail. With this information, IU set out to provide faculty with an option that allowed all students to obtain e-texts at a price that was generally as favorable to students who succeeded in buying and selling back a used textbook.

Through discussions with various publishers, it became clear that content creators would drop their prices considerably *if* they could get paid for each use of their content and avoid concerns about illegal digital copies. This would require moving from a probabilistic retail-price sales model (publisher/author creates textbook, faculty assign it, some percentage of students choose to buy it) to a deterministic sales model (publisher/author creates textbook, faculty assign it, each student in a course section pays for it).

This "move the tollbooth" model could produce a sustainable win for students through vastly better pricing and terms while also fairly paying content creators. IU had long charged lab fees for consumable materials, e.g., lab fee for a chemistry class, so the university could impose a similar e-text fee for students to pay their part of licensing an e-text for a particular course section. IU subsidized the first three semesters of pilots, and students received e-texts at no cost as the program was assessed. In 2011, IU moved to charging students an e-text fee for the last two semesters of the pilot.

The pilot study culminated in the fall of 2011 when IU entered into agreements with Courseload, an e-reader software company, and five leading academic publishers to provide e-texts for the university: McGraw-Hill Higher Education; John Wiley & Sons; Bedford, Freeman & Worth Publishing Group; W. W. Norton; and Flat World Knowledge (see Table 1). The official rollout of the program began with the spring 2012 semester.

Insights in Rolling Out the IU eText Fee Model

Faculty autonomy plays a key role in textbook selection at most institutions, and that autonomy is the pillar of any successful e-text approach. IU's arrangement allows faculty to assess the price of an IU eText—to determine whether it is favorable to students—before choosing to opt in. Before implementation, the IU eText fee was socialized through many meetings with students, student leadership groups/government, faculty councils, deans, and many others across all eight campuses. Faculty were also shown the value of having a common platform for eTexts, which utilized a single sign-on and was integrated with Oncourse, IU's learning management system (Sakai), allowing students to share highlights and annotations among study partners in class.

IU also made clear from the beginning that the model does not privilege either digital or print—it is digital with print options. This was essential in avoiding the print vs. digital debate.

Beyond the cost savings, the eText pilot project resulted in the development of software tools that substantially improve content delivery while enhancing teaching and learning. The Courseload e-reader can be used to access eTexts and digital supplements, both online and offline, from all publishers. The software also gives faculty the ability to create their own digital coursepacks by uploading self-produced content, open educational resources, or content from other various sources.

Students and faculty access their eTexts and the e-reader software through Oncourse. The software gives both students and faculty the option to search, annotate, highlight, and share an eText—features that allow learning with an eText to become a more interactive, collaborative experience. For instance, an instructor can cross-link parts of a text that relate to each other, insert a comment alongside a certain passage to provide emphasis ("be prepared to discuss this in class"), or even embed a video that amplifies a specific portion of the text students are reading. This allows students to gain new insights into

Table 1. **Notable Features in the IU Agreements**

Feature	Benefits
Extended Access to eTexts	Students will be able to access their eTexts for as long as they attend the university (as opposed to having the content disappear after a set time—e.g., after three to six months).
Elimination of Print Restrictions	Students are able to print as many pages as they want from an eText and may also request a print-on-demand version of the textbook for a small fee.
Significant Cost Savings	The IU agreements focus on providing eTexts to every student at a cost similar to what students would pay if buying and selling back a used textbook—equal to about half the price of an eText available in the marketplace.
Multiple Devices	The agreements with Courseload and the publishers allow users to access the eTexts via multiple devices (laptop, tablets, smartphones, etc.) both online and offline.
Uniform Access	Through its agreement with software provider Courseload, the university has eliminated the need for students and faculty to download and learn multiple software platforms to access eTexts; instead, one platform is used to access, read, and annotate all eTexts, and one username and password are used to access the platforms (the same username and password students and faculty use to access Oncourse, IU's learning management system.

the subject and feel that the instructor is actively engaged with them in the material. Instructors also have access to analytics that show how their students are interacting with the material, which may help them determine whether students are comprehending or struggling with the material so they can intervene as needed.

Although students have the option of printing any part of an eText and can purchase a print-on-demand version for a modest fee, data from the pilot project suggested that most students prefer to consume the content digitally, thereby lowering their carbon footprint. For students with disabilities, Courseload and the university's Adaptive Technology and Accessibility Center are working together to ensure that the e-reader software and interface meet accessibility standards and continue to improve as new technologies are made available.

Students are informed at the time of registration if the course section they are considering is part of the eText program and if there will be a required eText fee associated with the class. Generally, eTexts are available to students a few weeks before classes commence (eliminating the problem of students not having their required materials), and students are able to access their eTexts as long as they are enrolled at Indiana University (eliminating the problem of students selling back or losing access to materials from previous semesters).

The university's pilot study and ongoing eText project is documented through a website (http://eTexts.iu.edu) where presentations, frequently asked questions, and articles relating to eTexts and IU's eTexts initiative in general are also collected.

The Present and Beyond

With the IU eText initiative fully under way, faculty now have the option of choosing the eText fee model for their courses with its negotiated price structure and access privileges. If faculty do not want to use an eText under IU's model, they can still choose to assign a traditional physical text or use eTexts from other publishers or sources not affiliated with the university's agreement. In cases where no electronic version of a text is available, students must use traditional methods (i.e., the bookstore or online provider) to secure their textbooks for a course.

In January 2012, 127 courses, encompassing 5,300 students, signed up for eTexts through IU's initiative. Early numbers suggest that students on average saved $25 per book or online supplement, and $100,000 collectively when compared with similar offerings. Encouraged by this initial success, officials at IU continue to educate faculty about the program, promote its use, and listen to concerns. Two task forces are addressing workflow and policy-related issues regarding the use of eTexts (e.g., how the eText fee is handled for students who drop courses or otherwise interrupt their educational careers). As the eTexts initiative continues, IU hopes that it will not only become attractive to other publishers but will also provide a scalable and sustainable model for other colleges and universities as they develop their own eTexts initiatives and chart their paths toward a digital future. (See also Table 2.)

Piloting eTexts at Five Institutions

In November of 2011, five institutions—University of California, Berkeley; Cornell University; University of Minnesota; University of Virginia; and University of Wisconsin—elected to quickly replicate eText trials on their campuses. The usual approach of each campus negotiating a separate contract for eText

Table 2. **Key Findings from IU Early eText Pilot Study**

	Of the twenty-two courses participating in the eText pilot project, data were gathered from system logs for the 1,726 students involved. A subset of twelve courses (with 1,037 students, 738 of whom responded) provided additional information through a survey.
1	More than half of the students (about 60 percent) preferred eTexts to print, with the scores ranging from 84 percent to 36 percent, depending on the course. The lowest score occurred in a class where the instructor made no use of the eTexts. The students especially preferred eTexts when the instructors actively used the text and provided annotations for the students. Students were also more likely to prefer eTexts if they had used one in a previous class.
2	Instructor annotations, sustainability, and cost were the top three reasons students gave for preferring eTexts. Students also appreciated the fact that eTexts were not as heavy as regular textbooks and liked the options for adding and sharing their own annotations (though some students remarked that reading text on a screen was hard on their eyes).
3	About 22 percent of the students reported that they read more of the eTexts than they would have if they were using a printed text; conversely, 55 percent said they read less than they would have from a printed text.
4	In general, students reported very few issues in making the transition to eTexts. Ten percent of those surveyed retained their preference for printed textbooks; however, system logs showed that 68 percent of the students printed no pages during the pilot study, and only 19 percent printed more than fifty pages. About five percent ordered full-text versions of the text.
5	Faculty participating in the study reported that using eTexts made them think more about the text they were choosing for their class and how they could use it more effectively to improve their teaching.

content with each publisher and a software platform was clearly impractical if it were to provide the option for January 2012 classes. Internet2's NET+ services quickly assembled a pilot opportunity through support from McGraw-Hill and Courseload. The pilot would allow each institution to offer eTexts to a limited number of sections as part of an overall research study.

With unprecedented speed, the five institutions, two companies, and Internet2 quickly found interested faculty, and the pilot studies went live in January 2012. Many other institutions are assessing their plans for pilot studies or options to move to full rollout for 2012–13.

Conclusion

The shift to digital course content is upon us as the rise of remarkable consumer devices, interactive content, new software platforms, and new economics pave the way. Colleges and universities have a remarkable opportunity to help determine the prices for digital material that will be with us for many years. Institutions can work directly with content and software-platform providers to vastly reduce the costs of going digital with sustainable, win-win models. The IU road to eTexts illuminates one path for that endeavor.

Brad Wheeler, *Indiana University's Vice President for Information Technology and Chief Information Officer, provides IT leadership for IU's eight campuses. He has co-founded collaborations including the Sakai Project for teaching and learning software, Kuali for financial and other administrative systems, and the HathiTrust for digital copies of scanned books as part of the Google Book Project.* **Nik Osborne,** *Chief of Staff, works closely with the Vice President and his cabinet to monitor, advise, communicate, and implement the operational and strategic agenda. Osborne led the implementation of IU's eTexts Initiative, serving as lead negotiator and contact for the university. He holds a B.S. in business and a J.D. from Indiana University.*

Index

Index